Pragmatist Aesthetics

Living Beauty, Rethinking Art

Second Edition

RICHARD SHUSTERMAN

ROWMAN & LITTLEFIELD PUBLISHERS, INC.
Lanham • Boulder • New York • Oxford

ROWMAN & LITTLEFIELD PUBLISHERS, INC.

Published in the United States of America
by Rowman & Littlefield Publishers, Inc.
4720 Boston Way, Lanham, Maryland 20706
http://www.rowmanlittlefield.com

12 Hid's Copse Road
Cumnor Hill, Oxford OX2 9JJ, England

British Library Cataloguing in Publication Information Available

Library of Congress Cataloging-in-Publication Data

Shusterman, Richard.
    Pragmatist aesthetics : living beauty, rethinking art / Richard Shusterman.—2nd ed.
        p.   cm.
    Includes bibliographical references and index.
    ISBN 0-8476-9764-9 (alk. paper) – ISBN 0-8476-9765-7 (pbk. : alk. paper)
    1. Aesthetics. 2. Pragmatism. I. Title.
    BH39.S5256 2000
    111'.85—dc21   99-056792

Printed in the United States of America

♾™ The paper used in this publication meets the minimum requirements of American
National Standard for Information Sciences—Permanence of Paper for Printed Library
Materials, ANSI/NISO Z39.48–1992.

For Three Dancing Graces

Contents

Introduction to the Second Edition

More than a welcome occasion to greet a new millennium of readers, this second edition of *Pragmatist Aesthetics* provides an opportunity to improve upon the original version published by Basil Blackwell in 1992. Favored by many translations, the book was fortunate to receive critical attention from a very wide range of cultural perspectives and from diverse disciplines outside philosophy.[1] I learned a great deal from this international, multidisciplinary critique and responded by refining, updating, and extending the book's principal arguments in a number of subsequent publications.[2]

The perfectionist temptation to cram all of these meliorative elaborations into this new edition will be resisted. By my pragmatist lights, books of philosophy should not seek to be fetishized objects of perfection, but rather useful tools for thought. The value of these tools (as even the meaning of a tool's perfection) depends on the complex circumstances that define its use. With respect to tools like philosophy books, these circumstances also include aesthetic and economic factors. In the hectic competition of today's information society, a book that is very long can become both too tedious and too expensive to function effectively for a wider-than-specialist academic audience. To make this second edition more useful for more readers, I streamlined its revisions by essentially confining them to this Introduction and adding a new concluding chapter, rather than complicating the original text with interposed comments and explications.[3] The new chapter is devoted to a topic that the book's first version frequently raised but never had a chance to develop in systematic detail: the aesthetics of the body.

This Introduction cannot rehearse all the ways in which perceptive critique and the changing realities of our cultural world have compelled me to think beyond the original edition of *Pragmatist Aesthetics*. But I should at least indicate the more important themes (and publications) in which significant refinements have been made. In exploring the contemporary aestheticization of ethics, *Pragmatist Aesthetics* did not include a detailed study of the political theories and institutions that structure this aesthetic turn. My subsequent book, *Practicing Philosophy*, therefore focused on the political implications of pragmatist aesthetics for the understanding and practice of liberal democracy. Critically engaging the political thought of Dewey, Rorty, Rawls, Putnam, Cavell, and Habermas, I tried to fill a current gap in democratic theory by developing an aesthetic justification for liberal democracy, while forging an embodied vision of aesthetic life that encourages political involvement.[4]

Deeply inspired by Dewey, *Pragmatist Aesthetics* also challenged some of his views. Since critics sometimes failed to see our differences, I formulated them more sharply in later texts that challenge Dewey's experiential definition of art and essentialist theory of aesthetic experience, question his half-hearted approach to popular art, and contest his excessive reliance on immediate experience as the foundation for all thought and the criterion for justifying aesthetic value.[5] But the core of all this critique is already found in this book's first edition.

Pragmatist Aesthetics was first written when rap music was still fairly fresh and not yet dominated by the smug commercialism and gangsta style that prevail today. Though I continue to stand by the book's positive account of rap, my newer publications contain more detailed discussion of the violence and criminality that plague rap culture, so that we can continue to distinguish and defend what is valuable in hip hop, not only as an art form but as a way of life.[6] This constructively critical direction was, however, already expressed in the meliorist project of *Pragmatist Aesthetics*: that popular art, including rap, needs melioration because it suffers from real flaws and problems, but that it richly deserves meliorative efforts because of its proven capacity for aesthetic value and progressive social praxis.

One reason for my focus on rap was its aptness for challenging a familiar argument of mass-media critics: that popular art cannot be creative or interesting since it must confine itself to the mainstream styles and established views of the general public so as to appeal to the widest audience. Rap explodes this argument by achieving its popularity precisely through defiance of mainstream tastes, thus underlining a crucial distinction between a popular-art audience and a mass audience. But rap's oppositional attitude made some readers uncomfortable about my using it as an example of popular art. Pierre Bourdieu and Richard Rorty independently objected that because rap's pose of resistance could be aligned with avant-garde traditions, it was far easier to defend aesthetically than other popular genres. They challenged me to show how pragmatist aesthetics could make a case for less oppositional forms, so I responded with a pragmatist appreciation of American country music and the popular film genre it engendered.[7] I regret there is no room to reprint that essay here.

If pragmatism's notion of fallibilism offers consolation for our errors, its doctrine of meliorism provides a spur to correct them. This book began with the bold claim that "pragmatist aesthetics began with John Dewey," since neither Peirce nor James formulated a systematic theory of art (though Peirce certainly produced a powerfully systematic semiotics). I now want to qualify my original claim by acknowledging two pragmatic thinkers who anticipated almost all of the aesthetic themes I found so inspiring in Dewey, and who could well have been deep (though unacknowledged) influences on his aesthetics: Ralph Waldo Emerson and Alain Locke.[8]

Widely recognized as a precursor of classical pragmatism, Emerson is praised by Dewey for his influence as a "philosopher of democracy." But Dewey fails to acknowledge how Emerson's essays express – with condensed intensity and poetic power, though without sustained argument – the major issues and insights of Dewey's own aesthetics: art's natural roots and service to life, its deep and comprehensive functionality, its moral import and its continuity with science, the dynamic vitality of aesthetic experience as the core of art's value, and the democratic recognition of the aesthetics of the common or popular. Almost ten years before Dewey's *Art as Experience* (1934), these crucial themes were also given a powerful (if not always systematic) formulation by Alain Locke, the African-American philosopher who got his pragmatist training at Harvard and whose theory and art criticism inspired the Harlem Renaissance. Though Dewey's publications never mention Locke, he must have known Locke's epoch-making anthology, *The New Negro* (1925). But he also could have imbibed Locke's views indirectly through the art critic Albert C. Barnes, who collaborated with Locke on *The New Negro* and whom Dewey described as the chief influence on his own aesthetics.

*   *   *

In reviewing the very varied criticisms directed at *Pragmatist Aesthetics'* first edition, I was surprised to see that they often derive from exactly the same logical error: a failure to understand the pluralism of what might be called its inclusively "disjunctive stance." As we learn in first-year logic, the notion of "either p or q" can be understood pluralistically to include either one or both alternatives (as it does in standard propositional logic and in the common occasions of everyday life where one can choose more than one thing, e.g., either wine or water or both). Of course, the "either/or" disjunctive also has an exclusive sense, where one alternative strictly excludes the other, as indeed it sometimes does in life as well as in logic. But with pragmatism's inclusive stance, we should presume that alternative values can somehow be reconciled and realized, until we are given good reasons why they are mutually exclusive. That seems the best way to maximize our goods in pursuing the multiple values of life. Unfortunately, because the exclusive sense of disjunction seems more precise and dramatic, it often gains an unconscious dominance in philosophical theory, inspiring the dualistic habit of thought in which affirming one alternative entails denying another, where one can have either wine or water but not both. This dualist distortion explains some surprising misreadings from otherwise perceptive critics of this book.[9]

Several critics, for instance, misconstrue its defense of popular culture as a condemnation of high art, mistaking my interest in rap as a conclusive mark of disdain for canonized high-brow forms, even though the book devotes a chapter to the high modernist poetry of T. S. Eliot. Only a mind enslaved by dualism would presume that appreciating popular art means condemning high art or vice versa, since so many sensible people obviously value both. In any case, I make clear how my critique of high art's ideological and institutional limitations in no way entails rejecting this art, but only serves "to reject its own exclusionary rejections" of popular forms (140). Some critics, keen to champion aesthetic merit, seem so possessed by exclusive disjunction that they misread the book's concern for art's social function as a repudiation of properly aesthetic values. Its argument, on the contrary, shows how these different goods can be deeply integrated, how aesthetic value can enhance an artwork's social function, which in turn can heighten the work's aesthetic experience.

On the other hand, sociological critiques of *Pragmatist Aesthetics* often suffer from similar fallacies of exclusive disjunction. Simply because I appreciate art's natural roots and energies, I am charged with ignoring its socio-historical constitution, even though I emphasize precisely this dimension in critiquing Dewey's essentialism of aesthetic experience. Why this confusion? Assuming an exclusionary split between the natural and social, such critics have trouble seeing how phenomena like natural languages and art clearly embrace both dimensions.

The presumption of exclusive alternatives prompts other sociological charges. Having argued that a firm distinction between high art and popular art cannot be philosophically or aesthetically justified, I am accused of concluding that no such distinction exists in the real social world and of naively thinking that demonstrations of aesthetic value in themselves confer cultural legitimacy. I plead not guilty. Likewise, in arguing that aesthetic analysis of popular art could improve its understanding and even contribute to its cultural legitimacy, I in no way imply that aesthetics should replace (or ignore) sociological studies that explore the constitution of popular art's target audiences and its modes of production, dissemination, and reception.

For pragmatism's inclusive stance, both types of inquiry are valuable and complementary, precisely because of their distinctive strengths. Therefore, in recent writings, I try to show how aesthetic criticism – through its appeal to the subject's personal experience and through the cultural prestige of its tools and practice – has certain legitimating powers that purely sociological studies of popular art cannot provide; but also that sociological research can render aesthetic criticism far more perceptive and powerful.[10]

Two further objections display the same flawed logic of exclusion: that in appreciating popular art's qualities of complexity, creativity, and form, I must be rejecting the value of the simpler or "lower" pleasures that it provides, hence not really defending popular art at all; and that by offering intellectual analyses of popular works, I dismiss the worth of more casual or physical forms of appreciation. These objections are neatly answered by other critiques that contrastingly castigate my celebration of simple, familiar, somatic delights. Fortunately, some readers understand the meaning of pluralism. As pop music maven Simon Frith rightly notes, I consistently affirm both high and low pleasures, both aesthetic and functional values. One crucial capacity of art (whether high or low) is to be appreciated in various modes and on different levels.

Sensitive to our human need for enjoyment, *Pragmatist Aesthetics* is deeply appreciative of art's pleasures. Does this entail a dangerous disregard for art's cognitive values of insight and understanding? Not in the slightest. The disjunctive stance can embrace the different values of pleasure, knowledge, and functionality, not only individually but especially when integrated together as in art. Critics who see hedonism as a know-nothing, do-nothing sensualism suffer from their own shallow understanding of the depths, varieties, and uses of pleasure. Since the time of Socrates, philosophers have repeatedly proclaimed the joys of thinking, while saints affirmed the bliss of divine truth, and psychologists have noted the pleasures of effectively executed functional action. Ever since Aristotle, art's pleasures have been recognized not as a conflicting alternative to knowledge but as products and tools of cognition. "To understand a poem," T. S. Eliot reminds us, "comes to the same thing as to enjoy it for the right reasons."[11]

But how can I promote these pleasures of *understanding*, if I advocate an aesthetics of bodily delight? Critics who suggest this incompatibility of psyche and soma in aesthetic experience, who assume that in celebrating the body I am slighting the mind, surely suffer from the most deadening and divisive dualism of them all, and the most pervasive. So in the new, concluding chapter, I try to lay this persistent prejudice to rest; but not by simply bringing old and new objections to mind/body dualism, a gambit that only tends to reinforce the problem by rehearsing its terms of debate. Instead, I ply a more constructive strategy by proposing an aesthetic discipline which pragmatically unites the somatic and the spiritual through the integrated exercise of body and mind. I call this discipline somaesthetics. Briefly introduced in *Practicing Philosophy*, it was still earlier prefigured in *Pragmatist Aesthetics'* first edition, whose closing arguments invoked the need for such a field "to cultivate the pleasures and the disciplines of the body" so as to promote "a more embodied pragmatist aesthetic." But I noted with regret that the exploration of this field would "have to wait for another book" (259, 261).

I am happy to conclude this new edition by providing, at last, a systematic outline of somaesthetics and by showing how its integration of body and mind responds to the oldest and most central aims of philosophy as an art of living. This final chapter not only extends my arguments for the body's crucial role as a site of aesthetic experience and artistic fashioning. It also enriches the book's historical perspective by returning to the theoretical work that founded modern aesthetics, Alexander Baumgarten's *Aesthetica*, in order to grasp more clearly the need for somaesthetics, while uncovering the historical roots for its philosophical neglect. Needless to say, the chapter is but a beginning in a field that eagerly calls for more research.

*   *   *

This new edition of *Pragmatist Aesthetics* would not have been possible without the many individuals who gave generous attention to its original version and translations: critics, journalists, translators, editors, publishers, colleagues, and students who tested it as a teaching text. They are too numerous to thank individually, but four acknowledgements are indispensable. Josh Michael Hayes was very helpful in proofreading and updating the Index to cover the Introduction and final chapter. A preliminary version of that chapter was published in *The Journal of Aesthetics and Art Criticism* (Summer 1999) and is redeployed here with the kind permission of its editor, Philip Alperson. I am also grateful to the book's original commissioning editor, Stephan Chambers of Blackwell, for graciously granting me the opportunity to launch a second English edition with a new publisher. Maureen MacGrogan (who edited my *Practicing Philosophy* for Routledge) again deserves my special thanks for giving *Pragmatist Aesthetics* a new home with her new house, Rowman and Littlefield.

Preface

The title of this book may raise some sceptical eyebrows. For the very notion of pragmatist aesthetics could be thought to be fundamentally paradoxical. The pragmatic, of course, is inextricably wed to the idea of the practical, precisely that idea with which the aesthetic is traditionally contrasted and even oppositionally defined as purposeless and disinterested. One of the aims of this book is to relieve this paradox by challenging the traditional practical/aesthetic opposition and enlarging our conception of the aesthetic from the narrow domain and role that philosophy's dominant ideology and cultural economy have assigned it. Aesthetics becomes much more central and significant as we come to realize that in embracing the practical, in reflecting and informing the praxis of life, it also extends to the social and political. The emancipatory enlargement of the aesthetic involves similarly reconceiving art in more liberal terms, freeing it from its exalted cloister, where it is isolated from life and contrasted to more popular forms of cultural expression. Art, life, and popular culture all suffer from these entrenched divisions and from the consequently narrow identification of art with elite fine art. My defense of the aesthetic legitimacy of popular art and my account of ethics as an art of living both aim at a more expansive and democratic reconception of art.

In rethinking art and the aesthetic, pragmatism also rethinks the role of philosophy. No longer neutrally aimed at faithfully representing the concepts it examines, philosophy instead becomes actively engaged in reshaping them to serve us better. The task of aesthetic theory, then, is not to capture the truth of our current understanding of art, but rather to reconceive art so as to enhance its role and appreciation; the ultimate goal is not knowledge but improved experience, though truth and knowledge should, of course, be indispensable to achieving this. Similarly, while it should not ignore the traditional problems of philosophy of art, pragmatist aesthetics, if it wants to make a real and positive difference, cannot confine itself to the traditional academic problems, but must address today's live aesthetic issues and new artistic forms. Thus, after considering such classic topics as aesthetic experience, organic unity, interpretation, and the definition of art, I devote two long chapters to popular culture and rap.

In seeking to bring theory closer to the experience of art so as to deepen and enhance them both, a pragmatist aesthetics should not restrict itself to the abstract arguments and generalizing style of traditional philosophical discourse. It needs to work from and through concrete works of art. These should be taken not as cursorily considered examples, but as foci of sustained aesthetic analysis, objects whose experience is enriched through close and theoretically informed critical study. I attempt this more aesthetic style of aesthetic discourse with a poem by T. S. Eliot and a rap by Stetsasonic. Though this bringing together of high modernism and hip hop within a single book might be seen as symptomatic of postmodern eclecticism (or simply of my own schizoid taste), I would rather it be taken as emblematic of a socio-cultural ideal where so-called high and low art (and their audiences) together find expression and acceptance without oppressive hierarchies, where there is difference without domination and shame.

Pragmatist aesthetics began with John Dewey – and almost ended there. He was the only one of pragmatism's founding fathers to write extensively on art and to regard aesthetics as central to philosophy. But the philosophical influence of his aesthetic theory was very short-lived. Pragmatist aesthetics was soon eclipsed and rejected by analytic aesthetics (for reasons I discuss in chapter 1); and it has not yet achieved a full recovery. This is not to deny important contributions by contemporary pragmatists to certain aesthetic issues – for example, Rorty on the ethical role of literature, and Margolis and Fish on interpretation. It is only to insist that more needs to be done. In particular, much more of the Deweyan aesthetic line should be recuperated and refashioned. Today's major pragmatists have been shy of Dewey's aesthetics, perhaps because its revolutionary spirit and emphasis on somatic experience are hard to digest within the constraints of the socio-political conservatism and "textualism" which dominate current pragmatist philosophy. To develop a more radical and embodied pragmatist aesthetic, this book looks back to Dewey for example and inspiration, but it soon strikes its own path to face issues and adversaries that perplex our present more than the Deweyan past.

Pragmatism is a distinctively American philosophy, and this book (especially with its interest in rock and rap music) may seem too American for some readers. For me personally, it represents a voyage back to American life and culture after almost twenty years of schooling and academic work abroad. Pragmatism was not taught to me in Jerusalem or Oxford; nor did I teach it in the Negev. Philosophy there meant analytic philosophy, and aesthetics analytic aesthetics. Pragmatism emerged for me as a philosophical horizon only when I returned to America in 1985 to take up an appointment at Temple University. Indeed, it was, among other things, an intellectual tool which helped me reassimilate a culture which had initially formed me but which now seemed puzzlingly yet stimulatingly new. My ultimate "conversion" to pragmatist aesthetics and the idea of this book did not take shape, however, until the Spring of 1988, when I taught an aesthetics seminar to a very mixed and lively audience of graduate students in philosophy and dance. My debt to them is greater than I can here record. I had originally intended to use Dewey primarily as a foil to what I then regarded as the far superior aesthetic theory of Adorno (which I still greatly admire). But by the end of the semester, having scrutinized the different arguments in class and tested some issues on the dance floor, I could not help but trade Adorno's austere, gloomy, and haughtily elitist Marxism for Dewey's more earthy, upbeat, and democratic pragmatism.

This sunnier pragmatist outlook was reinforced later that summer in Santa Cruz at the National Endowment for the Humanities Institute on Interpretation, directed by Hubert Dreyfus and David Hoy. My account of interpretation is deeply indebted to that institute and to the critical but caring theorists who made it a community in the full sense of the word. But three members of the staff were also particularly helpful as regards other aspects of this book. Alexander Nehamas and Stanley Cavell convinced me that philosophical aesthetics should not ignore the topic of popular art and could illuminatingly treat it through interpretive readings of individual works. And Richard Rorty was invaluable in developing my pragmatist perspective, often, as the reader will discover, by provoking intense disagreement. The fact that I spend so much effort taking issue with him should indicate how important and how close his work has been to me. But I want here to acknowledge my gratitude as well as my debt.

This book would have taken much longer to complete had I not been given time off from my normal university duties. I wish to thank Temple

University for a study leave and the National Endowment for the Humanities for a research fellowship which allowed me to devote the entire year of 1990 to research and writing.

Since my pragmatist project seemed so American, I thought I should put it in a wider perspective and test its strength and interest by seeing how well it would fare abroad. What could be better than doing this in Paris? I am most grateful to Pierre Bourdieu and L'École des Hautes Études en Sciences Sociales for inviting me there as a Directeur d'études associé and to the Collège International de Philosophie for their invitation to give a seminar in which I was able to try out the book's ideas on a foreign audience and in a foreign language. Among my Parisian colleagues, I wish to thank Françoise Gaillard, Gérard Genette, Louis Marin, Louis Pinto, Jacques Poulain, and Rainer Rochlitz for attentively reading various chapters of this book, and especially Catherine Durand and Christine Noille for helping me render some of them into palatable French. I am delighted that all this encouragement will at least be rewarded with the publication of a (somewhat abridged) French version of the book by Les Éditions de Minuit.

When I returned to Philadelphia, my Temple colleagues Joseph Margolis and Chuck Dyke were kind enough to read the completed manuscript in its entirety and offered some very useful last-minute criticisms, as did Arthur Danto. Other colleagues and friends have read parts of this book and generously offered comments. I regret not being able to list them all, but I must at least mention Houston Baker, Richard Bernstein, Jim Bohman, Noël Carroll, Reed Dasenbrook, Terry Diffey, George Downing, Edrie Ferdun, Lydia Goehr, Judith Goldstein, David Hiley, Michael Krausz, Jerry Levinson, Paul Mattick, Brian McHale, Dan O'Hara, Paul Roth, and Gianni Vattimo. Nor should I forget the word-processing efforts of Nadia Kravchenko, who managed to compose a coherent manuscript for me at Temple from the disordered texts sent from Paris. Many people and experiences outside the academic world improved my understanding of the popular music I discuss here, but I want to express special thanks to the rock critic Tom Moon for providing me with particularly helpful information and enjoyable music. I must finally thank Stephan Chambers of Basil Blackwell for his early interest in this project and for his continued encouragement of my work.

Some of the book's arguments have already appeared in print in more sketchy and tentative versions, and I wish to thank the editors and publishers of *The British Journal of Aesthetics*, *The Journal of Aesthetics* and *Art Criticism*, *New Literary History*, *Theory, Culture & Society*, *The Monist*, and *Philosophy and Literature*, as well as the University of Minnesota Press and the SUNY Press, for permission to re-use this material. Grateful acknowledgement is made to Faber and Faber and to Harcourt Brace Jovanovich for permission to reprint T. S. Eliot's "Portrait of a Lady" from his *Collected Poems, 1909–1962* and also to Tee Gee Girl Music (BMI) for permission to reprint Stetsasonic's "Talkin' All That Jazz."

Part I

Pragmatism and Traditional Theory

1

Placing Pragmatism

I

Twentieth-century Anglo–American aesthetics has displayed two characteristic forms deriving from two distinctive philosophical sources:
analytic philosophy and pragmatism, the former born in Britain, the
latter representing America's unique contribution to philosophy. Analytic
aesthetics has prospered, while pragmatist aesthetics has virtually disappeared. Yet puzzlingly, their origins suggest the opposite would have
been more likely.

Aesthetics was a very central concern of pragmatism's most active and
influential twentieth-century figure, John Dewey. But it was of only
minor philosophical importance to the major analysts: Moore, Russell,
and Wittgenstein. Russell had virtually nothing to say on aesthetic
matters; and Moore's and Wittgenstein's aesthetic discussions, though
quite significant, are rather limited in scope and detail. Moore's were
essentially confined to about a dozen sections of *Principia Ethica*; and
Wittgenstein's aesthetic views, though enormously influential, were
nevertheless very schematic, loosely organized, and essentially based on
posthumously published transcriptions from lectures.[1] In short, there is
nothing in aesthetics by any of the analytic patriarchs that can compare
with the comprehensive scope, detailed argument, and passionate power
of Dewey's *Art as Experience* (1934).[2] Yet, though this book initially
aroused considerable interest,[3] it is hardly studied today, let alone
regarded as a promising source for future aesthetic theory. Already by
the late fifties, pragmatist aesthetics had been almost totally eclipsed by
analytic philosophy of art, which has ever since constituted the only
mainstream tradition in Anglo–American aesthetics.

But there are signs of change. The analytic hegemony in Anglo-American aesthetics is being severely challenged by continentally-inspired theory based on hermeneutic, poststructuralist, and Marxian philosophies. In contrast to traditional analytic philosophy but in accord with pragmatism, these philosophies oppose foundationalist distinctions and ahistorical positive essences, emphasizing instead the mutability, contextuality, and socio-historical praxical constitution of thought and its objects. Moreover, recent analytic work of Quine, Goodman, and Davidson can be seen as converging with some of these continental themes by undermining many of analysis's foundational assumptions and distinctions (e.g. atomistic verification and the analytic/synthetic, scheme/content, and world/world-description distinctions). It is not surprising that in response both to analysis's unflinching self-criticism and to the appeal of continental theory, pragmatism is experiencing a sort of renaissance in American philosophy, though it has not yet clearly expressed itself in a new aesthetic.

As a propaedeutic to elaborating one, it is necessary to place pragmatist aesthetics in its philosophical context and amongst its rivals. To do this and to explain why it was stifled by analytic philosophy, this chapter will explore the major contrasts between traditional pragmatist aesthetics (as represented by Dewey) and analytic aesthetics. Through these contrasts we can also see how some of the enriching themes of contemporary continental theory which make analytic aesthetics seem poor by comparison are powerfully present in Dewey, where they often find clearer and more encouraging expression. Placed between analytic and continental aesthetics, combining the latter's insights and wider concerns with the former's empirical spirit and down-to-earth sense, pragmatism is very well placed to help us redirect and reinvigorate contemporary philosophy of art. This view of pragmatism as a more promising middle way and mediator between the analytic and continental traditions is launched in this chapter with respect to Dewey's aesthetics, but it motivates much of my book.

There are many reasons why Dewey's aesthetics had a rather limited and short-lived appeal for Anglo-American philosophers. One obvious reason was the general dominance of analytic philosophy over pragmatism, and here is surely not the place to attempt a full explanation of that. On the broadest, most fanciful level of speculation, and adapting Oscar Wilde's *aperçu* on art, one might suggest that conquests in philosophy are the product of either a strong new personality or a new medium. In the domineering personalities of Moore and Russell, together with the latter's new symbolic logic, analysis amply meets both conditions. Pragmatism, for all its talk of being a method, never presented any special method or medium anywhere near as impressively scientific as the logic of *Principia Mathematica*. Moreover, while all pragmatists praised science and its methods, and though Peirce and James were clearly men of science, pragmatism did not see scientific philosophy as all that philosophy could or should be. In an age of professionalism where science was the king and model of university disciplines, it is not surprising that pragmatism lost out to the more single-mindedly scientific program of analytic philosophy.

Nor could pragmatist aesthetics be easily incorporated into analytic philosophy. For though sympathetic to pragmatism's empirical and tough-minded spirit, analysis was always deeply opposed to its most central doctrines on truth, knowledge, and experience. Part of this opposition is surely traceable to analytic philosophy's hostility to Hegelian themes of holism and historicist anti-foundationalism which are central to pragmatism and particularly to Dewey. Analysis, we must remember, established itself by vigorously attacking and disenfranching the neo-Hegelianism of Bradley, Bosanquet, and McTaggart which was the dominant orthodoxy of the day. Essential to Moore and Russell's attack on Hegelianism was a critique of the holistic doctrine of internal relations and organic unity, the idea that no element or concept had an independent identity or essence but rather is entirely a function of its interrelations with all the other elements and concepts of the whole to which it belongs. The analytic program was launched under the aegis of logical atomism, the idea that there are at least some logically independent facts or things in the world (even if these be only sense-data) which constitute an immutable foundation for reality, truth, and reference, and which are somehow represented to us in experience through our conceptual scheme. In a basically Kantian division of labor, philosophy was distinguished from science by the special task of analyzing the concepts through which these facts, and indeed all empirical facts, are represented and known; it was to provide not just another brand of empirical truth but rather issue in conceptual truths which, being non-empirical, could be known apodictically and could thus serve as the foundation for all claims of knowledge.

Richard Rorty indeed suggests that the epistemological and metaphysical conflict between analysis and pragmatism reflects a more ancient quarrel between Kant and Hegel; and I think this can be roughly extended to aesthetics.[4] Dewey's aesthetics was distinctly Hegelian in its holism, historicism, and organicism, indeed, even too Hegelian for some of his pragmatist followers.[5] Moreover, it was likened to Croce's aesthetic, which was associated with Hegelian idealism and which formed the focus of the analytic critique of "Idealist Aesthetics."[6] As we shall see, some of the Hegelian aspects of Dewey's aesthetics were so contrary to the frequently Kantian assumptions, methods, and concerns of analytic philosophy of art as to make Dewey's theories irredeemably unpalatable to succeeding generations of Anglo-American aestheticians working within the style, if no longer within the original program, of analytic philosophy.

However, my purpose here is not to vindicate the Kant/Hegel – analysis/pragmatist parallel, but to contrast pragmatist and analytic aesthetics, so that we can understand why analysts typically dismissed Dewey's *Art as Experience* as "a hodgepodge of conflicting methods and undisciplined speculations."[7] To make the contrast manageably clear and illuminating, I shall be characterizing analytic aesthetics in the rather bold and simplifying strokes of a Weberian "ideal type," though one firmly based on the movement's actual history.

II

(1) One of the most central features of Dewey's aesthetics is its somatic naturalism. The first chapter of *Art as Experience* is entitled "The Live Creature"; and like all the subsequent chapters, it is dedicated to rooting aesthetics in the natural needs, constitution, and activities of the human organism. Dewey aims at "recovering the continuity of esthetic experience with normal processes of living" (*AE* 16). Aesthetic understanding must start with and never forget that the roots of art and beauty lie in the "basic vital functions," "the biological commonplaces" man shares with "bird and beast" (*AE* 19–20). For Dewey all art is the product of interaction between the living organism and its environment, an undergoing and a doing which involves a reorganization of energies, actions, and materials. Though the fine arts have become increasingly more spiritualized, "the organic substratum remains as the quickening and deep foundation," the sustaining source of the emotional energies of art which make it so enhancive to life (*AE* 30–1). This essential physiological stratum is not confined to the artist. The perceiver, too, must engage her natural feelings and energies as well as her physiological sensorimotor responses in order to appreciate art, which for Dewey

amounts to reconstituting something as art in aesthetic experience. Thus the preparatory training of such channels of response "is a large part of esthetic education. To know what to look for and how to see it is an affair of readiness on the part of motor equipment," though it also requires a store of funded "meanings and values extracted from prior experiences" (*AE* 103–4).

What standardly characterizes aesthetic experience and artistic objects is the presence of form. But form, even in painting and sculpture, is not static spatial relations but the dynamic interaction of elements displaying the kind of "cumulation, tension, conservation, anticipation, and fulfill-ment" which, together with emotional intensity, are defining features of an aesthetic experience. Such "formal conditions...are rooted deep in the world itself," in our own biological rhythms and the larger rhythms of nature, which gradually get reflected and elaborated into the rhythms of myth and art and the rhythmic "laws" of science (*AE* 152). Dewey thus claims: "Underneath the rhythm of every art and of every work of art, there lies...the basic pattern of relations of the live creature to his environment"; so that "naturalism in the broadest and deepest sense of nature is a necessity of all great art" (*AE* 155–6). For art's role is not to deny the natural and organic roots and wants of man so as to achieve some pure ethereal experience, but instead to give a satisfyingly integrated expression to both our bodily and intellectual dimensions, which Dewey thinks we have been painfully wrong to separate. Art's aim "is to serve the whole creature in his unified vitality" (*AE* 122).

The major thrust of analytic aesthetics is sharply opposed to naturalizing art and aesthetic value. G. E. Moore, though hardly the most typical analytic aesthetician, provided the dominant analytic strategy on this matter with his doctrine of the naturalistic fallacy, a fallacy which "has been quite as commonly committed with regard to beauty as with regard to good."[8] We simply cannot identify beauty with any natural quality, since we can always meaningfully ask whether any given object having that quality is in fact beautiful; and if beauty were identical to that natural quality, such a question would be entirely senseless. Even when the appeal of this "open-question" argument had greatly waned, analytic aestheticians refused to identify aesthetic qualities with natural ones, or even regard them as logically entailed by natural perceptual properties. This is why Margaret Macdonald held that "works of art are esoteric objects"; and it is precisely the point of Frank Sibley's seminal paper "Aesthetic Concepts," which argued that such concepts could not be correctly applied on the basis of natural sensory perception and intelligence, but required a special faculty of taste. Such taste, it seems with Sibley, is neither rule-governed nor common to all as a universal gift of human nature.[9]

Though the notion of a non-rule-governed faculty of taste is a clear throwback to Kant, one might regard Kant's aesthetics of taste as instead resolutely naturalistic, in insisting that the standard of taste be based "in human nature..., in fact in that which we may expect everyone to possess and may require of him."[10] But Kant's aesthetic naturalism is largely an illusion. Not only does his account of aesthetic judgement presuppose special cultural conditioning and class privilege,[11] but the human nature to which Kant ultimately appeals in order to ground that judgement's validity is something beyond the realm of nature as we can understand it: "the supersensible substrate of all the Subject's faculties (unattainable by any concept of understanding)" which is posited as a metaphysical article of faith. This flight to the supersensible signals the fact that Kant's aesthetic naturalism represents a very ethereal and impoverished notion of human nature. In contrast to Dewey's regard for the whole live creature, Kantian aesthetic judgement concentrates narrowly on intellectualized properties of form. Only the pleasure from "the quickening of...cognitive powers," "not what gratifies in sensation but merely what pleases by its form" is properly aesthetic. The natural gratifications deriving from emotion and sensual pleasure are refused on the grounds that they imply interest and desire. Hence, for Kant, "a taint is always present where charm or emotion have a share in the judgement by which something is to be described as beautiful"; and taste which advocates such gratifications "has not yet emerged from barbarism."

(2) The Kantian notion of disinterestedness finds expression in much analytic philosophy of art and presents a second contrast to pragmatist aesthetics. It is not only the Moorean point that beauty, like good, is a purely intrinsic value, a non-instrumental end in itself, which can only be misconceived or misapplied as a means. There is the further characterization of art as something which is defined by its non-instrumentality and gratuitousness. Strawson explains the impossibility of any general rules for art by defining our interest in art as totally devoid of any "interest in anything it can or should do, or that we can do with it, not even an interest in specific responses (say, excitement or stupefaction) which it will produce in us." Stuart Hampshire likewise tells us that "a work of art is gratuitous," something "made or done gratuitously, and not in response to a problem posed."[12] The underlying motive for such

attempts to purify art from any functionality was not to denigrate it as worthlessly useless, but to place its worth apart from and above the realm of instrumental value. This strategy, a carry-over of "art for art's sake," was to protect the autonomy of art from unfair competition with ruthlessly dominant utilitarian thinking, for fear that art could not adequately compete in terms of instrumental value. The hope was to protect some realm of human spirituality from the crassly calculative means–end rationality which had not only disenchanted the world but ravaged it with the festers of functionalized industrialization. The aesthetic would represent a separate realm of freedom; art would be free from function, use, and problem solving; and this freedom from use would be its defining and ennobling feature.

All this is alien to the pragmatist aesthetic of Dewey. Though he was no less devoted to defending the aesthetic and to proving its infungible value, Dewey did so by insisting on art's great but global instrumental worth.[13] For anything to have human value, it must in some way serve the needs and enhance the life and development of the human organism in coping with her environing world. The mistake of the Kantian tradition was to assume that since art had no specific, identifiable function which it could perform better than anything else, it could only be defended as being beyond use and function altogether, as having pure intrinsic value. This error was often compounded by the idea that instrumentality was somehow opposed to intrinsic value, because of an assumed means–ends dichotomy and the association of instrumentality with "some narrow, if not base, office of efficacy" (*AE* 144).

Dewey's corrective was not simply to reject the opposition (though not the difference) between instrumental and intrinsic value by reinterpreting the means–end distinction (*AE* 143–6, 201–4). It was, more importantly, to argue that art's special function and value lie not in any *specialized*, particular end but in satisfying the live creature in a more global way, by serving a variety of ends, and above all by enhancing our immediate experience which invigorates and vitalizes us, thus aiding our achievement of whatever further ends we pursue. Art is thus at once instrumentally valuable and a satisfying end in itself (*AE* 144). "That which is merely a utility satisfies...a particular and limited end. The work of esthetic art satisfies many ends...It serves life rather than prescribing a defined and limited mode of living" (*AE* 140). "We are carried to a refreshed attitude toward the circumstances and exigencies of ordinary experience." Nor does art's instrumentality "cease when the direct act of perception stops. It continues to operate in indirect channels" (*AE* 144).

The work-song sung in the harvest fields not only provides the harvesters with a satisfying aesthetic experience, but its zest carries over into their work, invigorating and enhancing it and instilling a spirit of solidarity that lingers long after the song and work are finished. The same wide-ranging instrumentality can be found in works of high art. They are not simply a refined set of instruments for generating a specialized aesthetic experience. They work to modify and sharpen perception and communication; they energize and inspire because aesthetic experience is always spilling over and getting integrated into our other activities, enhancing and deepening them (*AE* 101, 110, 138, 248–9, 335, 348–9).

Art thus "keeps alive the power to experience the common world in its fullness" (*AE* 138) and renders the world and our presence in it more meaningful and tolerable through the introduction of some "satisfying sense of unity" in its experience (*AE* 199). This deep role of art as justifying existence by giving it a pleasing sense of form and wholeness aligns Dewey's aesthetic with the Nietzschean view "that this world can be justified only as an esthetic phenomenon," a view which reemerges in Foucault's Greek ideal of an "aesthetics of existence." Moreover, in advocating a fully embodied aesthetic and rejecting Kantian disinterestedness, Dewey is right in tune with Nietzsche's recognition of "the 'physiology' of esthetics" and its "excitement...of 'interest'."[14] He shares these somatic Nietzschean themes with Foucault and Bataille, whose radical accent on deviance, socio-cultural distortion, and excess makes Dewey seem either encouragingly wholesome or naively unsophisticated. For better or for worse, his upbeat aesthetic of natural energies is more likely to inspire hopeful "New Age" explorers than disenchanted European intellectuals, including those born and bred in America. But in any case, it captures the aesthetically essential theme of the body which was lacking in analytic aesthetics but increasingly important and alluring in continental theory. Dewey's somatic standpoint resonates perhaps more closely with Merleau-Ponty's grounding focus on the lived body. The latter's claim that "it is the expressive operation of the body, begun by the smallest perception, which is amplified into painting and art" could have been taken right out of *Art as Experience*, though it surely wasn't.[15]

(3) Dewey's recognition of the global functionality of art links up with another view where he differs sharply from most analytic philosophers – the cultural primacy and philosophical centrality of art and the aesthetic. Since aesthetic experience is the "experience in which the whole creature

is alive," and "most alive," Dewey argues, "To esthetic experience, then, the philosopher must go to understand what experience is." A philosophy's ability to grasp aesthetic experience is, for Dewey, a test of its capacity "to grasp the nature of experience itself...There is no test that so surely reveals the one-sidedness of a philosophy as its treatment of art and esthetic experience" (*AE* 24–5, 33, 278). Dewey further insisted that "the final measure of the quality of...culture is the arts which flourish" (*AE* 347), while for analytic philosophers the ideal and paradigm of human achievement was, instead, science.

Since analytic philosophy modeled itself as scientific philosophy, art and aesthetics were accorded marginal status and often intentionally skirted as hopelessly beyond the scope of scientific understanding. Analytic aesthetics, at least initially, was largely an attempt to apply the logically rigorous and precise methods of scientific philosophy to the wayward and woolly realm of art, to clarify its murky concepts and the confused methods of interpretation and evaluation through which it is understood and appreciated. Dewey, though intensely appreciative of science and its gifts to civilization, could not help but regard scientific experience as thinner than art. For art engages more of the human organism in a more meaningful and immediately satisfying way (*AE* 90–1, 126, 278), an engagement which includes the higher complexities of thinking: "the production of a work of genuine art probably demands more intelligence than does most of the so-called thinking that goes on among those who pride themselves on being 'intellectuals'" (*AE* 52). Dewey therefore held "that art – the mode of activity that is charged with meanings capable of immediately enjoyed possession – is the complete culmination of nature, and that 'science' is properly a handmaiden that conducts natural events to this happy issue."[16]

I see no clear way of proving this rather extravagant claim or the claim that aesthetic experience is the necessary key to understanding philosophically "the nature of experience itself" (*AE* 278). Nor am I even sure how much aesthetic experience should be analyzed in philosophical terms, though in studying and applying Dewey I shall be discussing it at length. Two things, however, are clear. Dewey's privileging of art over science on a fundamentally naturalist and empiricist philosophical base was both a brave and a therapeutic gesture in an increasingly technological world whose dominant cultural hero was the scientist. Secondly, aesthetic inquiry would seem best served by a philosophy which treats not only art but its theory as having the highest philosophical importance and recompense for our cultural self-understanding. Here again, Dewey's pragmatism, along with continental philosophy, enjoys an advantage over analytic aesthetics.

(4) In insisting that hard thinking was as important to art as to science, Dewey was quick to compensate by recognizing that science itself was more than pure thought devoid of feeling and imagination, and that "esthetic quality...may inhere in scientific work" (*AE* 202). For scientific inquiry can occasionally provide that "satisfying emotional quality... [emerging from] internal integration and fulfillment reached through ordered and organized movement" involving all our human faculties, which is the Deweyan hallmark of art and the aesthetic (*AE* 45). Indeed, he was eager to underline the deep similarities of art and science as forms of ordering and coping with experience, noting that they are hardly distinguished in ancient and primitive cultures (*AE* 153–4). Dewey went so far as to declare that "science itself is but a central art auxiliary to the generation and utilization of other arts," and that both science and philosophy can afford their practitioners aesthetic experience (*AE* 125–6).

All these connections and assimilations of different disciplines signal one of Dewey's most crucial themes in aesthetics and elsewhere – the continuity thesis, as it is often called. In contrast to analytic philosophy (and perhaps again reflecting the Kant/Hegel opposition), Dewey was intent on making connections rather than distinctions. He was keen to connect aspects of human experience and activity which had been divided by specialist, compartmentalizing thought and then more brutally sundered by specialist, compartmentalizing institutions in which such fragmented disciplinary thinking is reinscribed and reinforced. He thus in some ways anticipates Foucault's more elaborate analysis of disciplinary power and Adorno's more embittered critique of the social and personal disintegration wrought by our administrative society, which dominates by dividing and then homogenizing under its bureaucratic forms. Lamenting the painful fragmentation of experience that distinction-reification had promoted, Dewey cried out against the unbearable social divisions and cultural contradictions that were both its typical source and abiding consequence. Always alive to the social and historical conditioning of thought and experience, Dewey recognized that

> *theories* which isolate art and its appreciation by placing them in a realm of their own, disconnected from other modes of experiencing, are not inherent in their subject-matter but arise because of specifiable extraneous conditions. Embedded as they are in institutions and in habits of life, these

conditions operate effectively because they work so unconsciously. Then the theorist assumes they are embedded in the nature of things. Nevertheless, the influence of these conditions is not confined to theory..., it deeply affects the practice of living, driving away esthetic perceptions that are necessary ingredients of happiness, or reducing them to the level of compensating transient pleasurable excitations. (*AE* 16)

The institutional life of mankind is marked by disorganization. This disorder is often disguised by the fact that it takes the form of static division into classes, and this static separation is accepted as the very essence of order as long as it is so fixed and so accepted as not to generate open conflict. Life is compartmentalized and the institutionalized compartments are classified as high and as low; their values as profane and spiritual, as material and ideal. Interests are related to one another externally and mechanically... Since religion, morals, politics, business has each its own compartment, within which it is fitting each should remain, art, too, must have its peculiar and private realm... Those who write the anatomy of experience then suppose that these divisions inhere in the very constitution of human nature....[Though for] much of our experience as it is actually lived under present economic and legal institutional conditions, it is only too true that these separations hold. (*AE* 26–7)

Dewey's aesthetic naturalism, aimed at "recovering the continuity of esthetic experience with normal processes of living," is part of his attempt to break the stifling hold of "the compartmental conception of fine art," that old and institutionally entrenched philosophical ideology of the aesthetic which sharply distinguishes art from real life and remits it "to a separate realm" – the museum, theater, and concert hall (*AE* 9, 14, 16).

But Dewey's aesthetics of continuity connects more than art and life; it insists on the fundamental continuity of a host of traditional binary notions whose long assumed oppositional contrast has structured so much of philosophical aesthetics: the fine versus the applied or practical arts (*AE* 11–12, 33–4, 87), the high versus the popular arts (*AE* 191), the spatial versus the temporal arts (*AE* 187), the aesthetic in contrast both to the cognitive (*AE* 45, 52, 80, 202) and to the practical (*AE* 45–7, 265–7),[17] and artists versus the "ordinary" people who constitute their audience (*AE* 54, 60, 80). Indeed, to secure such continuity in aesthetics, Dewey extends his assault on dichotomous thinking to undermine more basic dualisms which underly and reinforce the sequestration and fragmentation of our experience of art. Foremost among these are the dichotomies of body and mind, material and ideal, thought and feeling, form and substance, man and nature, self and world, subject and object, and means and ends.

This is not the place to address Dewey's critique of all these dualisms.[18] But it is crucial to note how radically his emphasis on continuity contrasts with the analytic approach, whose very name connotes division into parts and which prides itself on the clarity and rigor of its distinctions. Analytic aesthetics first made its mark by attacking the woolly and empty generalizations which seemed to result from approaching the arts and the aesthetic as one continuous whole about which one could profitably generalize. Its chief critical target was not Dewey but Croce, who, in defining art as freely creative intuition-expression, denied the validity of all genre distinctions, denied any essential distinction between artist and audience, between so-called art and other expression, and in fact explicitly conflated the aesthetic with the linguistic. The analysts' prime argument was that commitment to aesthetic continuity yielded global theories that would either be so vague and accommodatingly ambiguous as to be virtually empty or, if more definite, would distort the special character of certain arts in order to make them fit the general theory. The remedy they advocated for the woolly "dreariness" and distortions of general aesthetics was instead "a ruthlessness in making distinctions" and a more specialized disciplinary approach. It was even suggested "that there is no aesthetics and yet there are principles of literary criticism, musical criticism, etc.," and that general aesthetics be repudiated and abandoned for "an intensive special study of the separate arts."[19]

This compartmental focusing of aesthetic inquiry into close analyses of the different arts and their criticism was in some ways very fruitful. Nor was it the only valuable effort of analytic aesthetics, which contributed significantly to the general understanding of symbolization and representation. But three points need mentioning. First, the compartmentally specialized study of the separate arts was largely a product of the sudden burgeoning of specialized academic criticism of these arts, institutionally based in the separate departments and disciplinary journals of the universities. Pressures of professional legitimation made the advocacy of specialization irresistible. Secondly, even if these separate studies were mostly carried out under the vague notion that the arts – despite their manifest and highlighted differences – were somehow (at the very least, historically) connected, the abiding effects of such disciplinary specialization cannot have been so satisfying. For we are now witnessing a countersurge advocating the interdisciplinary study of the arts. The growing number of new journals and departments of cultural studies gives welcome institutional expression and support to this promising turn toward holistic integration.

Third, the analysts' strongest argument for the necessity of making distinctions – that without distinctions to structure discourse no productive inquiry is possible – is perfectly acceptable to Dewey. For he willingly accepted distinctions and definitions as flexible and provisional tools which marked tendencies and provided insight. He only rejected them as inviolable principles of classification or evaluation, as marking necessary and unbridgeable gaps between things that are (or could be) deeply and fruitfully connected in concrete experience. Dewey himself distinguished aesthetic experience from other experience (*AE* 61), aesthetic emotion from ordinary emotion (*AE* 85), and he distinguished the different arts through their different media (*AE* 111, 231). But in contrast to the typical analytic approach which looked for a single, special property or experience to define art or the aesthetic, "a single *fundamentum divisionis*,"[20] Dewey's distinctions were in terms of prominent or "significant *tendencies*" in complex constellations of connected features (*AE* 221, 227, 287). Aesthetic experience is differentiated not by its unique possession of a particular element but by its more consummate and zestful integration of all the elements of ordinary experience, "making a whole out of them in all their variety" and giving the experiencer a still larger feeling of wholeness and order in the world (*AE* 199, 278). "The experience is marked by a greater inclusiveness of all psychological factors than occurs in ordinary experiences, not by reduction of them to a single response" (*AE* 259).

For Dewey's holism, it is an analytic error to try to define the aesthetic by isolating "one strand in the total experience" of an object (be that strand sensory, emotional, formal, or whatever), when that so-called aesthetic strand is only "what it is because of the entire pattern to which it contributes and in which it is absorbed" (*AE* 295). Similarly, the distinctions between the arts and between their media are not rigidly sharp. Apart from obvious works of mixed media, we find metaphors and other literary features in painting, sculpture, and dance; and there is aesthetically shaped graphic visuality in the text of printed poems.[21] Hence for Dewey "such words as poetic, architectural, dramatic, sculptural, pictorial, literary…designate *tendencies* that belong in some degree to every art, because they qualify any complete experience, while, however, a particular medium is best adapted to making that strain emphatic" (*AE* 233). Distinctions (such as between form and matter or between different genres) are context-dependent; their value and "real office is as instruments of approach to the changing play of concrete material, not to tie that material down to rigid immobility" (*AE* 137, 229). The danger of distinctions is that we end up fetishizing them, "erecting them into compartmental divisions" (*AE* 257).

Dewey's actual arguments against classificational distinctions in aesthetics are very sketchy and hardly decisive. One seems to be that by separating and separately studying what in experience is a salient whole, we tend to distort and impoverish our understanding of that experienced whole as a whole. For by the principle of organic unity to which Dewey subscribes, any aesthetic whole is more than the sum of the properties of its parts as isolated parts. Indeed, the parts themselves would not even appear as they do, were it not for their integration into the whole from which compartmentalization separates them out (*AE* 43–4, 140–1, 166, 196).

A related argument seems to be that seeing things as unified rather than divided is simply more enriching and satisfying. And this can perhaps be explained by the idea that in dividing human faculties, interests, and objects in any rigid way, we are dividing the human crea-ture against herself, forcing her to choose between capacities (emotional, intellectual, sensory) which are naturally at work together, thus creating inner conflict and a sense of self-alienation from part of oneself (*AE* 26–8, 34, 252–3). Moreover, as Dewey brings out long before deconstruc-tion, distinctions tend to take on evaluative coloring, and in privileging one term over the other they obscure or degrade the real value of the dominated term which deeper reflection shows to be essential to the value of the "superior." The terms and their generated "institutionalized compartments are classified as high and as low; their values as profane and spiritual, material and ideal," sensory and intellectual. "Under such conditions, sense and flesh get a bad name," and we ignore their irreplaceable contribution to the fullness of life, even in its moral and intellectual dimensions (*AE* 26–7).

Perhaps Dewey's most important argument against classificatory dis-tinctions is that they harden thinking and perception into fixed routines, standardized automatic channels with predetermined paths and familiar limits. This inhibits the range and richness of perception, impedes creativity, and constrains that openness to experience which Dewey sees as essential to discovery and the enhancement of life. The fixity of aesthetic genre "classification sets limits to perception...[and] restricts creative work....There are obstructions enough in any case in the way of genuine expression. The rules that attend classification add one more handicap" (*AE* 229–230).

In contrast to Dewey's holism, analytic aesthetics has for the most part concentrated on projects of distinction, devoting enormous efforts to clearly distinguishing the aesthetic from the non-aesthetic, art from non-art, and (most notably in the work of Nelson Goodman) the particular work of art from other objects (like forgeries and unfaithful texts and performances) which falsely presume to represent it. But at least one influential analyst, Morris Weitz, comes very close to Dewey in questioning the value of classificational definitions of the arts. For he asserts not only that it is logically impossible to provide real definitions (in terms of essences or necessary and sufficient conditions) for these logically open concepts. He further argues that no good would come from trying to close them to make them definable. Such definitional closure would only constrain or "foreclose...on the very conditions of creativity in the arts."[22]

On the other hand, Weitz is responsible for drawing one very influential distinction that has predictably hardened into a limiting dichotomy which has impoverished analytic aesthetics. His view that "art" has two distinct uses, as a classificatory description and as a term of praise, was erected by George Dickie into a compartmentalization of two different "senses" of the concept of art: the purely descriptive or classificatory versus the evaluative. And the former, as devoid of evaluative content, hence controversy, was held to be amenable to objective definition and became the focus for the value-neutral institutional definition of art. The rigorous search to distinguish and demarcate art in an uncontested "objective" manner led to defining it in an empty formal way apart from its value. A work of art is simply any artifact conferred the status of art by an institution dubbed "the artworld", whether or not that artifact is worthy of being so treated.

(5) We shall return to Weitz, Dickie, and the definition of art in the next chapter. But here we should note that this separation of descriptive and evaluative senses of art and the consequent preoccupation with the former are symptomatic of analytic aesthetics' general tendency to shirk the question of evaluation, a tendency which derives from its desire to be scientific philosophy and its conception of the scientific as value-neutral truth.[23] Analytic aesthetics' dominant self-conception as metacriticism makes this tendency clear. The aim was to analyze and clarify the

concepts and practices of established criticism, not to revise them in any substantial sense. It was to give a true account of our concept of art, not to change it. In vivid contrast, Deweyan aesthetics is interested not in truth for truth's sake but in achieving richer and more satisfying experience, in experiencing that value without which art would have no meaning or point, without which it cannot as a global phenomenon exist or be understood, let alone be defined. In Dewey's pragmatism, experience rather than truth is the final standard; even "the value of ideals lies in the experiences to which they lead" (*AE* 325). His instrumental theory of knowledge sees the ultimate aim of all inquiry, scientific or aesthetic, not as mere truth or knowledge itself but as better experience or experienced value. The value of knowledge is in being "instrumental to the enrichment of immediate experience through the control over action that it exercises" (*AE* 294); and for Dewey nothing can match the enriched immediacy of aesthetic experience.

From this radically experiential standard of value, it follows that science is subordinate to art. Yet it also follows that aesthetic values can never be permanently fixed by art theory or criticism but must be continually tested in experience and may be overturned by the tribunal of changing aesthetic perceptions. "The conception that objects have fixed and unalterable values is precisely the prejudice from which art emancipates us," since with "the work of art the proof of the pudding is decidedly in the eating" rather than in any "a priori rule" or critical principle (*AE* 100–1).

(6) But there is a further and far more radical consequence of this experiential standard: namely, that our aesthetic concepts, including the concept of art itself, are but instruments which need to be challenged and revised when they fail to provide the best experience. This can account for Dewey's obvious attempt to direct his aesthetic theory at radically reforming our concepts of art and the aesthetic, an attempt which was alien to the essentially accepting, clarificatory spirit of the analytic project. While analytic aesthetics followed the romantic and modernist tradition of defending art's value and autonomy by identifying the concept of art with the concept (and associated sublimity and genius) of "high" fine art, Dewey deplores this elitist tradition, which he attacks under the labels of "the museum conception of art" and "the esoteric idea of fine art" (*AE* 12, 90).

Dewey's opposition to the spiritualized sequestration of art was earlier noted in connection with his naturalism. But the dominant motive of his attack stemmed not from ontological considerations of naturalistic continuity and emergence. It was the instrumental aim of improving our immediate experience through socio-cultural transformation where art would be richer and more satisfying to more people, because it would be closer to their most vital interests and better integrated into their lives. The compartmentalization and spiritualization of art as an elevated "separate realm" set "upon a far-off pedestal," divorced from the materials and aims of other human effort, has removed art from the lives of most of us, and thus has impoverished the aesthetic quality of our lives (*AE* 9–15). It is effectively quarantined to the museum, concert hall, classroom, and theater, kept apart from free and casual daily access. Not only does the elitist equation of art with high art alienate and intimidate many people from seeking satisfaction in the fine arts; it denies them recognition of the artistic legitimacy and potential of the so-called "low" arts or entertainment they do enjoy – "the movie, jazzed music, the comic strip." They are thus driven to despair cultivating artistic sensibility and instead seek satisfaction in things increasingly "cheap and... vulgar" (*AE* 11–12). Identification of art with the high tradition of fine art can thus serve an oppressive socio-cultural elite seeking to assert and bolster its class superiority by making sure that art (at least in its canonized modes of appreciation) will remain beyond the taste and reach of the common man, at once marking and reinforcing his general sense of inferiority.

Moreover, for Dewey, even the experience of the cultural elite is ultimately impoverished and constrained by the spiritualized, esoteric concept of fine art. Since they too, to survive and prosper, must be more than aesthetes but active individuals engaged in life, their appreciation of art can be richer and more satisfying when it more closely relates to and enhances life's experience. Even the artist is thwarted by the concept of art as distinct from and above life. Professionally isolated "from the main streams of active interest," "less integrated than formerly in the normal flow of social services," cut off from so much of the people who could constitute their audience, artists are more narrowly constrained in the experiential materials and sources which can serve them in artistic creation. They are also forced (by a logic of spiraling specialization and originality, impelling them to assert their sharp distinction from other professions and even other artists) to develop a peculiarly acute individualism, which makes their works increasingly difficult to fathom and to appreciate with deep satisfaction (*AE* 15).

But more than art suffers from its spiritualized sequestration; nor was this compartmentalization established simply by and for aesthetes to secure and purify their pleasures. The idea of art and the aesthetic as a separate realm distinguished by its freedom, imagination, and pleasure has as its underlying correlative the dismal assumption that ordinary life is necessarily one of joyless, unimaginative coercion. This provides an excuse for the powers and institutions that structure our everyday life to be brutally indifferent to natural human needs for the pleasures of beauty and imaginative freedom. These are not to be sought in real life, but in art, whose contrast and escape from the real gives us human sufferers temporary solace and relief. By thus compartmentalizing art and the aesthetic as something to be enjoyed when we take a break from reality, the most hideous and oppressive institutions and practices of our civilization get legitimated and more deeply entrenched as inevitably real; they are erected as necessities to which art and beauty, by the reality principle, must be subordinated. Still worse, those rigid and cruelly divisive institutional realities then further justify and glorify themselves through the high art our civilization produces in trying to transcend and escape them. Art becomes, in Dewey's mordant phrase, "the beauty parlor of civilization," covering with an opulent aesthetic surface its ugly horrors and brutalities. These, for Dewey, include class snobbery, imperialism, and capitalism's profit-seeking oppression, social disintegration, and alienation of labor (*AE* 14–16, 345–7).

Here again, we find Dewey anticipating currently influential themes imported from the Frankfurt school. The plaint of Benjamin and Adorno that the flip side of our highest culture is the basest of barbarism already rings in Dewey's view of art as "the beauty parlor of civilization," where "civilization is not civil" (*AE* 339, 346). Adorno, who praised Dewey as "a truly emancipated thinker" in aesthetics, laments the same brutal social reality, where "luxurious" bourgeois art is the response to an "ascetic" life, "deprived...of real gratification in the sphere of immediate sense experience."[24] But while Adorno cautiously insists that art keep itself resolutely apart from life, maintaining its sacralized yet socially culpable autonomy and narrow identification with high culture so as to avoid contamination by a corrupt world and thereby sustain a purer criticism of that hideous reality, Dewey's pragmatism seems closer to Marx in its ambitiously positive thinking. Art's role (like philosophy's) is not to criticize reality but to change it; and little change can be effected if art remains a cloistered domain. Dewey therefore urges that, despite the risk of corruptive misappropriation by an unaesthetic world, art should be removed from its sacralized compartmentalization and introduced into the realm of everyday living where it may more effectively function as a guide, model, and impetus for constructive reform, rather than merely an imported adornment or a wishfully imaginary alternative to the real.[25] More in the spirit of Benjamin than Adorno, he is willing to exchange high art's autocratic aura of transcendental authority for a more down-to-earth and democratic glow of enhanced living and enriched community of understanding. In short, for Dewey, our concept of art needs to be reformed as part and parcel of the reform of our society, whose dominating institutions, hierarchical distinctions, and class divisions have significantly shaped this concept and have been, to some extent, reciprocally reinforced by it.[26]

(7) The divergence here between Deweyan and analytic aesthetics lies not only in his attack on elitist aesthetic compartmentalization and his concern with reform rather than clarification, with theory that will change practice rather than explain, ground, or justify it. It lies also in the historical and socio-cultural thickness of Dewey's theory, his insistence that art and the aesthetic cannot be understood without full appreciation of their socio-historical dimensions, an emphasis which reflects his Hegelian historicist holism and which aligns his thought with the Marxian tradition in continental aesthetics. Until fairly recently, most analytic aesthetics simply ignored these background dimensions as irrelevant, probably because aesthetic experience was traditionally conceived as pertaining to immediacy, not only because of its immediate satisfactions but because of its assimilation to direct perception rather than inferential thinking. In any case, Moore recommended for all aesthetic appreciation a "method of absolute isolation," the intuitive assessment of different aesthetic objects as "if they existed *by themselves*, in absolute isolation." Clive Bell, a seminal art theorist for the analytic tradition, expresses the same characteristically dismissive attitude to historical context. "I am not a historian of art or of anything else. I care very little when things were made or why they were made; I care about their emotional significance to us. To the historian everything is a means to some other means; to me everything that matters is a direct means to emotion." This dehistoricizing tendency was further supported through Monroe Beardsley's theories of the affective and genetic (including the intentional) fallacies, which are clearly meant to isolate the aesthetic object from larger historical contexts of production and reception.[27]

It was probably Arthur Danto who first made analytic aesthetics pay attention to the ineliminable socio-historical dimension of our appreciation of art. In response to works like Duchamp's *Fountain* and Warhol's *Brillo Box*, he wrote in 1964: "To see something as art requires something the eye cannot descry – an atmosphere of artistic theory, a knowledge of art history: an artworld."[28] Danto's notion of the artworld was transformed into Dickie's institutional definition of art, while Danto, Wollheim, and other analysts have stressed the crucial role of art history in constituting our concept of art and the aesthetic. But such analytic attempts at a social and historical understanding of art are very narrow, internalistic, and rarified compared to Dewey's. For him the artworld was not an abstract, autonomously aesthetic notion, but something materially enmeshed in the real world and significantly structured by its socio-economic and political factors. He saw art history as similarly conditioned by such factors, not as the essentially autonomous "internal development" portrayed by Danto and his analytic cohorts.[29] Most significantly, Dewey realized that not only the concepts of art and aesthetic about which we theorize, but also our very concepts of theory and philosophy are themselves structured and conditioned by the social practices and institutions which inform our lives and thought, and thus by the contingencies and struggles of history which in some way shape those structuring practices and institutions.

To advocate the integration of art and life, Dewey must argue that their accepted opposition is not the product of some necessary incompatibility; yet he does this not by hair-splitting conceptual analysis but through historico-political and socio-economic genealogy. The rift between the practical and the aesthetic is not a necessary evil but a historic catastrophe. Dewey thus begins his theorizing by invoking the more aesthetically integrated society of ancient Greece, where good acts were also described as beautiful (*kalon-agathon*; *AE* 46) and where the arts were such "an integral part of the ethos and institutions of the community [that the]...idea of 'art for art's sake' would not have been even understood" (*AE* 13–14). He then goes on to suggest, in very brief and general terms, some of the "historic reasons for the rise of the compartmental conception of fine art" in order to undermine it through the taints of its genesis.

Our present museums and galleries to which works of fine art are removed and stored illustrate some of the causes that have operated to segregate art instead of finding it an attendant of temple, forum, and other forms of associated life....I may point to a few outstanding facts. Most European museums are, among other things, memorials of the rise of nationalism and imperialism. Every capital must have its own museum of painting, sculpture, etc., devoted in part to exhibiting the greatness of its artistic past, and in other part, to exhibiting the loot gathered by its monarchs in conquest of other nations; for instance, the accumulations of the spoils of Napoleon that are in the Louvre. They testify to the connection between the modern segregation of art and nationalism and militarism. (*AE* 14)

The socio-historical factors which helped engender and entrench the museum conception of art were economic as well as political.

The growth of capitalism has been a powerful influence in the develop-ment of the museum as the proper home for works of art, and in the promotion of the idea that they are apart from the common life. The *nouveaux riches*, who are an important by-product of the capitalist system, have felt especially bound to surround themselves with works of fine art, which, being rare, are also costly. Generally speaking, the typical collector is the typical capitalist. For evidence of good standing in the realm of higher culture, he amasses paintings, statuary, and artistic *bijoux*...Not merely individuals, but communities and nations, put their cultural good taste in evidence by building opera houses, galleries, and museums. These show that a community is not wholly absorbed in material wealth, because it is willing to spend its gains in patronage of art....These things reflect and establish superior cultural status, while their segregation from the common life reflects the fact that they are not part of a native and spon-taneous culture.
...[Fine art can then reflect] a holier-than-thou attitude...toward the interests and occupations that absorb most of the community's time and energy. (*AE* 14–15)

Dewey goes on to argue how international capitalism and industrial-ization have helped change art's production and reception so as to make art a cloistered world of its own.

The mobility of trade and of populations, due to the economic system, has weakened or destroyed the connection between works of art and the *genius loci* of which they were once the natural expression. As works of art have lost their indigenous status, they have acquired a new one – that of being specimens of fine art and nothing else...[which] are now produced, like other articles, for sale in the market. (*AE* 15)

In contrast to past economic patronage from individuals known to the artist or from community based institutions like the Church, artistic production is abandoned to "the impersonality of a world market" and deprived of "intimate social connection" with (or even knowledge of) its public. Hence the artist is increasingly marginalized and isolated from "the normal flow" of society and driven to call attention to her work by emphasizing its unique particularity. Moreover, since our society is dominated by mercenary profit, she may well regard social isolation as essential for her art and necessarily expressed in it. Art thus becomes still more compartmentally specialized, remote, and "esoteric" (*AE* 15).

Combining all these factors, along with the general social conditions which so divide between free enjoyment and "externally enforced" labor, between imaginative emotional satisfaction and mechanical joyless production, and more "generally between producer and consumer in modern society", and we have the unthought background which structures the reigning philosophical theories of art and the aesthetic. We have the "chasm between ordinary and esthetic experience," the gulf between life actively practiced in the real world and art to be contemplated by escaping from that world into the museum, theater, or concert hall (*AE* 15–16, 285).

Dewey cautions that his brief genealogy is not meant to endorse a full-blown economic determinism of the arts; and indeed, as Pierre Bourdieu's work makes clear, the relations between wealth and social class and between economic capital and cultural status are far more complex than Dewey suggests.[30] Cultural status and class snobbery obtain not only through the possession and admiration of art's sacralized objects, but as much through the specialized valorized modes of their appropriation. These can also be placed on a pedestal and one which can be constantly shifted through changing critical fashion to keep them in remote, privileged isolation from ordinary experience and experiencers. What Dewey's genealogy, however, successfully aims to show is that the standard "*theories* which isolate art and its appreciation by placing them in a realm of their own, disconnected from other modes of experiencing," are themselves not the unchallengeable findings of pure reason seeing the true and necessary nature of things, but instead the result of "specifiable extraneous conditions," socially embedded "in institutions and in habits of life" (*AE* 16). As historically and contingently constituted, such theories and their concepts cannot claim the status of privileged truth immune to the sort of reformatory reconstitution at which Deweyan aesthetic theory aims.

Moreover, for Dewey, the socio-historical constitution of theory is not confined to aesthetics. The rigid distinction in ethical theory between means and ends and the "sharp psychological distinctions" of traditional philosophy of mind are largely the product of "formulations of differences found among the portions and classes of society" in ancient Greece (*AE* 252, *EN* 298–9). This Hegelian-pragmatist view of philosophy not as timeless conceptual truth but as a historically shaped expression of "its own time apprehended in thoughts,"[31] coupled with a criticism of such thoughts to create better times as well as better thinking, is quite alien to analytic philosophy. So, of course, is the outspoken anti-capitalist fervor which pervades Dewey's aesthetic theory and informs the socialist direction of his intended theoretical and social reforms. Such a combination of Hegel and Marx would hardly make his theory of art an attractive option for American philosophy in the McCarthy era of the 1950s when analytic aesthetics suddenly burgeoned, though I doubt whether this alone can explain the extent to which his aesthetics was eclipsed and neglected.

(8) I shall conclude my introductory sketch of Dewey by considering another issue where his opposition to the dominant assumptions of analytic aesthetics promisingly converges with powerful currents in contemporary continental philosophy. It is perhaps Dewey's most important aesthetic theme: the privileging of dynamic aesthetic experience over the fixed material object which our conventional thinking identifies – and then commodifies and fetishizes – as the work of art. For Dewey, the essence and value of art are not in the mere artifacts we typically regard as art, but in the dynamic and developing experiential activity through which they are created and perceived. He therefore begins by distinguishing between "the art product" – an object like a painting, sculpture, or printed text that, once created, can exist, "externally and physically," "apart from human experience" – and "the actual work of art [which] is what the product does with and in experience" (*AE* 9, 167). With this privileging of aesthetic process over product, art gets defined as "a quality of experience" rather than a collection of objects or a substantive essence shared only by such objects, and aesthetic experience thus becomes the cornerstone of the philosophy of art.[32]

Dewey does not deny the importance of art's material objects. He insists, like Adorno, on the unavoidable "need for objectification," for something reasonably fixed and qualitatively conducive to guide and structure the creation of aesthetic experience.[33] For Dewey, "there can be no esthetic experience apart from an *object*, and...for an object to be the content of esthetic appreciation it must satisfy those *objective* conditions without which...[the necessary conditions of aesthetic experience] are impossible" (*AE* 151). Just as "an esthetic product results only when ideas cease to float and are embodied in an object," so the work of art as aesthetic experience results only when one's "images and emotions are also tied to the object, and...fused with the matter of the *object*" (*AE* 280). But notwithstanding the necessity of art's fixed objects, Dewey privileges what Adorno later describes as "the processual essence of aesthetic experience and of the art work," the fact that "works of art exist only in *actu*," in lived dynamic experience.[34]

Dewey's prime purpose in defining art as aesthetic experience was to break the stifling domination of the museum concept of art, whose power is reinforced by our excessive preoccupation with fine art's sacralized objects. For aesthetic experience clearly exceeds the limits of fine art and its objects. But Dewey's experiential turn claims to offer an enhanced appreciation of fine art as well, and in some ways the claim seems credible. First, understanding fine art in terms of vivid experience rather than static objects does better justice to the dynamic power and moving spirit which makes art so captivatingly alive and enlivening (*AE* 181, 197). For aesthetic experience, even of the contemplation of so–called static arts, is always a temporally moving process of doing and undergoing where experience is developed cumulatively and brought to fulfillment; and where the perceiver, like the creative artist, is captured and pushed forward to that fulfillment through his own engaged, contributing energies which find satisfaction and increased vitality through being so engaged and absorbed (*AE* 57–62, 70–1, 142–3, 165–6, 178–81). Secondly, the claim to art's intrinsic and immediate value is much more convincing and much less socially repugnant when art is construed as aesthetic experience rather than the commodified objects of capitalist speculation. Thirdly, the shift from compartmentally isolated and independent objects to their role and their history in experience provides a better base for accommodating the complex socio-historical contextuality of art. Since the work cannot be logically severed either from its original generation in the experienced world of its creator or from its varied and changing reception in the experience of others, both its original socio-historical conditioning and the subsequent mutations of its interpretation and evaluation become pertinent to its meaning and value. Thus the work's meaning and value can indeed change with the changing realities and practices that condition our experience of it (*AE* 113, 325–7, 334). As Adorno concurs, "Works of art are not fixed once and for all, but are in flux...have a historical existence owing to their processual quality...

[and] change in accord with the historically changing attitudes of people," though such changes need not be so great as to prevent us from talking meaningfully of the same work of art.[35]

The aims, merits, and problems of Dewey's experiential definition of art will be pursued at length in the next chapter, which concentrates on the issue of art's definition and the role of theory, and which sketches the ways my pragmatist project differs from its Deweyan source. Here, however, I should explore why analytic philosophy contrastingly privileged art's objects over its aesthetic experience, and why indeed the very notion of aesthetic experience was often shunned and sometimes savaged by analytic philosophers of art.

One reason was the traditional analytic fear of psychologism, the worry that any concept of experience must be so completely tainted with the private subjectivity of the experiencing subject that to think of art in terms of aesthetic experience is necessarily to render it solipsistically private and thus deprive it of any real communicability or collaborative criticism. Dewey's effective response is that such fear stems from identifying experience with but one narrow philosophical conception of it: as essentially subjective, atomistic sensation or feeling. This conception, whose roots he traces to empiricism and the romanticist advocacy of the inner life, is not only historically parochial and philosophically narrow, but empirically false.[36] "To the Greeks, experience was the outcome of accumulation of practical acts, sufferings, and perception gradually built up into...skill....There was nothing merely personal or subjective about it" (*EN* 189). This older notion still survives today, and indeed forms the heart of perhaps our most common conception of experience outside of technical philosophy. When we speak of an experienced person or ask whether someone has the requisite experience for a certain job, we are not concerned with that person's having enough private sensations or the right "raw feels."

But what constitutes the core of Dewey's aesthetic experience is another common sense of "experience" – that which refers to a memorable and ultimately satisfying episode of living, one that stands out from the humdrum flow of life as "*an* experience" by its "internal integration and fulfillment" reached through a developing organization of meanings and energies which affords "a satisfyingly emotional quality" of some sort. Distinctively aesthetic experience, for Dewey, is simply when the satisfying factors and qualities of "*an* experience are lifted high above the threshold of perception" and appreciated "for their own sake" (*AE* 42, 45, 63).[37] But the introduction of emotional satisfaction does not render an experience necessarily private or entirely subjective. For no one but the philosophical sceptic in his professional capacity doubts for a moment that we can ever share such memorable experiences, even if they are always somewhat differently inflected through our different personalities and histories. Indeed, such heightened experiences are frequently remembered not only *as* shared but *because* they are shared. It is only philosophy's rigid quest for certainty which, seeing the troubling recurrence and perpetual possibility of personal misunderstanding, constructs this into a prison of privacy which bars shared emotional experience.

Dewey further insists that even so-called private mental experience is always more than psychologistic privacy. For experience is always the "interaction of an organism [itself always more than a mental subject] with its environment, an environment that is human as well as physical, that includes the materials of tradition and institutions as well as local surroundings" (*AE* 251). Our most private thoughts are always in a language that is shared and public, just as our sensory experience is to some extent shared since it rests on a physiological but linguistically and culturally inflected "constitution [more or less] common to all normal individuals" in the culture (*AE* 250).

A second reason why analytic philosophy recoiled from the Deweyan emphasis on aesthetic experience was that such experience seemed as evanescent and discursively elusive as it was allegedly important. In contrast to art's objects, which sturdily endure as discrete, itemizable things and which satisfy what Austin called philosophy's existential bias for "middle-sized dry goods," aesthetic experience did not stand still as a stable substance or clearly definable phenomenon for analysis and demarcation. It also seemed hopelessly difficult to isolate from experiences not ordinarily classified as aesthetic or artistic, things like the pleasures of sport, conversation, or fine dining. Conversely, aesthetic experience could not be trusted to present itself without fail before art's masterpieces. But if not as an experience common and peculiar to all that is aesthetic, how can we say that a distinctively aesthetic experience exists? Since it seemed both intrinsically resistant to analytic definition and unserviceably out of line with our entrenched habits of distinguishing the aesthetic from the non-aesthetic and art from non-art, aesthetic experience was condemned as a useless and confused metaphysical "phantom."[38] Though the analytic critique was in part a justifiable reaction to certain misguided ways of defining and applying such experience, the indefinability of aesthetic experience and its overflow into the traditionally non-aesthetic do not constitute an argument against its existence and importance for the philosophy of art. Indeed, the power of aesthetic experience to flout definitional limitations and so break the bonds of encrusted conventional divisions is precisely what makes it so important for a reformatory aesthetic such as Dewey's.

A third reason for privileging art's objects over aesthetic experience (and for more generally privileging the notion of art over the aesthetic) was the standard conception of aesthetic experience as something dominated by a trivial concern with pleasure, sensuality, and emotion; as something which belied art's essential cognitive and spiritual power as well as its practico-political potential. For our traditional notion of "aesthetic," as Danto complains, represents philosophy's "effort to trivialize art by treating it as fit only for pleasure," as essentially confined to the formal and the trivial.[39] Dewey would not gainsay this charge in the least. But he would instead insist that art's wide-ranging value is better established not by shunning the notion of the aesthetic but rather by reconstructively reinterpreting it in richer terms which recognize the cognitive and practical import of aesthetic experience and, more generally, the continuity of art and the aesthetic with the everyday world of thought and action. Yet Dewey would also insist that mere pleasure is far from a trivial thing, for we humans (philosophers included) live primarily not for truth but for sensual and emotional satisfaction.[40] So even if the pleasure of aesthetic experience is inseparable from perception and cognition, its on-the-pulse affective value cannot be discounted in assessing the value of aesthetic experience, which thus cannot be reduced to cognitive merit (as Nelson Goodman suggests) or to practical utility.[41]

In contrast to the Deweyan goal of pleasurable aesthetic experience, analytic philosophy aimed at objective truth, which it too narrowly construed as the truth about mind-independent objects. There is no doubt that analytic aesthetics was exceedingly preoccupied with art's objects. Enormous efforts were spent trying to determine the ontological status of the art object in the different arts and to fix the precise criteria for identifying the same artwork in its various manifestations (in authentic copies, prints, performances, etc.) so as to individuate it from other works and distinguish it from false manifestations. The socio-cultural pressures for this are pretty obvious. The demise of religious faith made works of high art the closest thing we had to sacred texts and holy relics; and fetishized as such, they had to be preserved in their purity and protected from impostors. But perhaps even more influential in transfiguring the artistic text from a vehicle for experience into a fetishized "verbal icon" (as the critic Wimsatt approvingly dubbed it[42]) were the professional pressures of the academy.

Criticism in the university had to profess objective knowledge rather than enhanced experience. Objective knowledge was assumed to require a well-defined object; and analytic aesthetics as metacriticism saw this as its goal. Even Beardsley, whose first book made aesthetic experience central to his metacritical philosophy of art, later gave uncontested privilege to the object as the necessary guarantor of objective criticism. "The first thing required to make criticism possible is an object to be criticized – something...with its own properties against which interpretations and judgments can be checked." He therefore posited the reifying principles of "Independence" and "Autonomy": "that literary works exist as individuals" and "are self-sufficient entities" whose properties and meaning are independent of their contexts of genesis and reception in experience.[43] In Nelson Goodman's influential *Languages of Art*, the metacritical desire for precise definition of the art object approaches paradoxical extremes. In order to define the artwork in a theoretically precise way so as to preserve it from distortion, Goodman treats the work's identity and the authenticity of its manifestations as independent of its "aesthetically important properties." The defining "constitutive properties of a work...cannot be identified with the aesthetic properties" it has, for such aesthetic properties admit of too much ambiguity and variation for definitional precision. Since, for Goodman, musical work-identity and performance authenticity are defined by "complete compliance with the score," "the most miserable performance without actual mistakes" counts as a fully authentic instance of the work, "while the most brilliant performance with one wrong note does not." Similar paradoxes arise with his notational definitions of literary and dramatic works of art.[44] But what, Dewey would ask, is the purpose of defining and preserving works so rigidly if not to employ them for structuring aesthetic experience? And what then is the point of so defining them that the "aesthetically important properties" need not be preserved for experience, while the aesthetically miserable is legitimated if notationally correct?

Poststructuralism appeals to us by protesting the analytically endorsed notion of the artwork as a fully fixed, self-sufficient, and inviolable object, a fetishized unity of closure. Its insistence that a text's meaning is not a permanent given but the changeable product of (changeable) practices of writing and reading resembles pragmatism's ontological insistence on an open, plastic universe to be shaped by human effort, as in Dewey's notion of the world as "material for change."[45] In fact, the move from closed work to open, developing textual practice, from criticism as discovery of prior truth to criticism as the creation of enjoyed meaning, is explicitly prefigured in Dewey's aesthetics. Just as poststructuralism argues that a text's meaning is constantly changing because it is the product of the ever changing context of language, of the interactive play of linguistic relations between it and other texts (including the embodied textual formations and practices we identify as our reading and writing selves); so Dewey argues that the work's meaning is constantly changing. For it is the product of the ever changing context of experience, which always involves the interactive play between the relatively stable art product and the organism and its environing factors, which are both in continual flux. While "a piece of parchment, of marble, of canvas...remains (subject to the ravages of time) self-identical throughout the ages," since "a work of art only...lives in some individualized experience," it must be somewhat differently "recreated every time it is esthetically experienced" (*AE* 113). For "experience is a matter of the interaction of the artistic product with the self. It is not therefore twice alike for different persons...It changes with the same person at different times as he brings something different to a work" (*AE* 334). Even the artist "himself would find different meanings in it at different days and hours and at different stages of his own development. If he could be articulate, he would say 'I meant just *that*, and *that* means whatever you or anyone can honestly, that is in virtue of your own vital experience [and close attention to the art product], get out of it.' Any other idea makes the boasted 'universality' of the work of art a synonym for monotonous identity" (*AE* 113–14).[46]

But Dewey can be less extreme than poststructuralism in his rejection of the identity, structural closure, and organic unity associated with artistic objecthood (and also with the experiencing self). For once these notions are pragmatically interpreted as flexible and functional rather than foundational, there is no reason not to employ them. Moreover, his appreciation of change and difference is tempered by the realization that stability, consensus, and unity can come in various and flexible forms and that they represent values too essential for good living and effective socio-political action to be demonized as necessarily equivalent with stagnating rigidity, monotonous uniformity, and oppressive totalization. Since Dewey's notion of aesthetic experience is a celebration of unity (*AE* 43–9), it must face at least one more objection – this time from the poststructuralist perspective. The charge is that it renders aesthetic experience too neat and ordered, too smugly closed in the complacent satisfaction of its achieved unity, to do justice to the often jarring effect which makes art a positively disturbing and motivating force. Experience, as its etymology suggests, is a continuing passage through peril and risk; and aesthetic experience, so it might be argued, is no different.[47]

However correct this charge might be against the organicism of classicist aesthetics and the New Criticism, it simply misses the mark with respect to Dewey, who repeatedly insists that the unity of aesthetic experience is not a closed and permanent haven in which we can rest at length in satisfied contemplation. It is rather a moving, fragile, and vanishing event, briefly savored in an experiential flux rife with energies of tension and disorder which it momentarily masters. It is a developing process which, in culmination, deconstructively dissolves into the flow of consequent experience, pushing us forward into the unknown and toward the challenge of fashioning new aesthetic experience, a new moving and momentary unity from the debris and resistance of past experiences and present environing factors.

Moreover, for Dewey, the permanence of experienced unity is not only impossible, it is aesthetically undesirable; for art requires the challenge of tension and disruptive novelty and the rhythmic struggle of achievement and breakdown of order. "Since the artist cares in a peculiar way for the phase of experience in which union is achieved, he does not shun moments of resistance and tension. He rather cultivates them, not for their own sake, but for their potentialities" for transformation into a unified experience (*AE* 21). Thus, for Dewey, "There are two sorts of possible worlds in which esthetic experience would not occur." In "a world of mere flux" no unity, stability, or sense of culmination would be possible. But, on the other hand, "a world that is finished, ended, would have no traits of suspense and crisis, and would offer no opportunity for resolution. Where everything is already complete, there is no fulfillment. We envisage with pleasure Nirvana and a uniform heavenly bliss only because they are projected on a background of our present world of stress and conflict." Their actual experience, like that of a permanently enduring aesthetic unity of experience, would be deathly boring. We need disturbance and disorder, since "the moment of passage from disturbance to harmony is that of intensest life" and most gratifying experience (*AE* 22–3). Nor can we linger in such harmony; aesthetic experience is but a temporary savored culmination, a rhythmic interval of rest, which, sharing in life's demand for variety, cannot be satisfied with order and so "pushes us out into the unknown" (*AE* 173). It is as much a stimulating disturbance toward the new as an achieved ordering of the old. Dewey is very clear on this point.

> In the process of living, attainment of a period of equilibrium is at the same time the initiation of a new relation to the environment, one that brings with it potency of new adjustments to be made through struggle. The time of consummation is also one of beginning anew. Any attempt to perpetuate beyond its term the enjoyment attending the time of fulfillment and harmony constitutes withdrawal from the world. Hence it marks the lowering and loss of vitality. (*AE* 23)

What Dewey earlier says about organic life applies also to the developing, decomposing, and hence provoking unity of aesthetic experience which he sees as emerging from the rhythms of organic life: "To overpass the limits that are set is destruction and death, out of which, however, new rhythms are built up" (*AE* 22). Aesthetic experience shines as living beauty, not only because it is surrounded by the death of disorder and monotonous routine, but because its own sparkling career projects the process of its dying as it lives.

2

Art and Theory between Experience and Practice

I

The question of what is art has long exercised aesthetic theory, but none of the many definitions thus far offered has proved philosophically satisfactory or enjoys uncontested acceptance. Dewey's pragmatist definition of art as experience is no exception and can be subjected to numerous philosophical criticisms. Most obviously, it seems far too vague and general. Since its defining notion of aesthetic experience covers countless things not ordinarily regarded as artistic (e.g. the tidying of a room, the activity of sport), it clearly fails to reflect the precise content and scope of our concept of art.

Art's definition has proved so resistant to theoretical resolution that several philosophers have suggested abandoning the project as altogether futile. And some contemporary pragmatists, rightfully respectful of the primacy of practice, have gone so far as to deny the value or possibility of theory altogether. The pragmatist theorist is in a bind. Sceptical of the traditional claims and success of theory, he is reluctant to propose one more definition of art for philosophical examination and eventual relegation to the dustbin of aesthetic history. But, he is equally aware that the question "What is art?" is too central to dodge. Theory at once seems unachievable and unavoidable.

The only way I see to resolve this historical bad fit between art and its theory is to suggest that the aims of theory and definition have been misconceived and could be profitably altered to serve art better. But this does not leave art immune from criticism and reconception. For by being in large part a product of misguided theory, our concept of art may itself be misguided and in need of reorientation.

To help clarify and justify these points, I shall be arguing the paradox that Dewey was right to define art as experience even though, by traditional philosophical standards, it is clearly an inadequate and inaccurate definition. Of course, more argument than this is needed to suggest the reconception of theory and art. If theory's aims and orientations have been misguided, if art has been misconceived, we need to see why and how by looking at the history of art's definition. Moreover, if Dewey's experiential definition is somehow right, we need to see why it is better than today's most powerful theory which defines art as a practice and thus seems as eminently pragmatist as Dewey's. Let us begin with art's definitional history.

II

Defining art has been a perennial problem for philosophy, even long before aesthetics emerged as a distinct philosophical discipline at the end of the eighteenth century. Indeed, art's definition was crucial to philosophy's own generation and self-formation.[1] For philosophy arose in ancient Athenian culture by aggressively defining itself in contrast to art as the source of superior wisdom, as the highest pursuit, which could afford not only the best guidance but the noblest and most intense joys of contemplation. With Socrates and Plato, philosophy was born of a struggle for intellectual supremacy fought against the rhetoricians or sophists on the one hand and the artists on the other (poetry being the prime artistic enemy, since it best captured the sacred wisdom of tradition and lacked the banausic character of plastic art).

Just as it employed the argumentative strategies of rhetoric, so philosophy seemed to take some of its epistemological and metaphysical orientation from art. The ideal of knowledge as *theoria*, the model of knowing as detached contemplation of reality rather than active interaction and reconstruction of it, reflects the attitude of a spectator at a drama or an appreciative observer of a finely finished work of plastic art. Similarly, the idea that reality ultimately consists of well-defined and stable *forms* that are rationally and harmoniously ordered and whose contemplation affords sublime pleasure suggests a preoccupation with fine works of art, an envious fixation on their clear shapes and distinct contours, their enduring and intelligible harmonies, which set them above the confusing flux of ordinary experience and make them seem more vivid, permanent, compelling – in a sense more *real* – than ordinary empirical reality. Since the poets were highly esteemed not only as creators of beauty but as purveyors of wisdom, philosophy had to establish its autonomy and privilege by defining art in more negative terms. With keen dialectical ingenuity, it transformed its epistemological and metaphysical imitation of art into a depreciative definition of art as imitation, or *mimesis*.

For Plato, not only was art (as imitation of mere appearance) twice removed from the true forms of reality, not only did it deceive and appeal to the lowest part of the soul, but it could not even compete with philosophy in terms of beauty and the pleasures of desire. While art might provide a view of beautiful objects, philosophy could offer the rapt contemplation of the more perfect transcendental forms which make art's imitative objects (and indeed all objects) beautiful, providing a program of visionary delectation culminating in the ultimate beauty of the very form of Beauty. The philosopher is therefore described (in the *Symposium*) as "the master of erotics" and not merely portrayed as the high priest of truth.

Plato thus defined art not to promote its practice or enhance its appreciative understanding, but rather to deprecate, confine, and control it – even, as we see in the *Republic*, to the extent of censorship and banishment. And in defining art, he also defined philosophy of art, which, like the rest of philosophy, can be seen as reactive footnotes to Plato. Initially conceived and directed by such negative and questionable motives, aesthetic theory could be expected to be misguided. Moreover, given the formative platonic imprint on the field, even when philosophers felt increasingly free of Plato's condemnatory agenda, they remained enslaved by the misdirections it initially engendered. We see this already in Aristotle's defense of art. Seeking to rescue art from the platonic charge of mimetic preoccupation with sensuous particularities, Aristotle asserted that tragedy imitates the universal and thus presents a higher "more philosophic" truth than history. But this only reinforced the imitation theory and the hegemony of philosophy. Moreover, as his doctrine of catharsis implies, Aristotle continued the platonic attitude of treating art as a distinct realm of objects essentially apart from ordinary life and action. In short, while Plato's definition of art as *mimesis* categorized art both in the sense of delimiting compartmentalization (so as to nullify its influential connection with life) and in the original Greek sense of "categorization" as accusation, subsequent theory dropped the accusation but persisted in the habit of compartmentalizing definition.

When *mimesis* eventually lost its appeal and authority, other theories were proposed, the most dominant being the theories of expression, form, play, and symbol. None of them, however, satisfied philosophy's traditional demand to define art as a special category of things and reflect its singular essence. All failed to provide an essence which is both common and peculiar to all works of art, to provide the conditions that are both necessary and sufficient for something to be a work of art rather than an ordinary thing. Such definitions, which concentrated on saliently exhibited properties of artworks, failed by being too wide or too narrow. Like imitation, the features of expression, play, form, and symbol were clearly not features peculiar to art; nor did they singly or collectively account for all of art's important traits. As for the narrower Bell–Fry theory of Significant Form, not only did it rely circularly on a mysterious aesthetic emotion itself identified only through significant form; it also clearly could not cover those arts where representational content was undeniably crucial.

Surveying the long history of failed attempts at essentialist definitions of art and clearly aware of art's own recent history of repetitive revolution, Morris Weitz, in 1955, proposed a radical remedy.[2] The quest for a real definition of art (i.e. one in terms of essence or of necessary and sufficient properties) must be abandoned as logically impossible, because art has no common essence to be defined. To the argument that such an essence was necessary for the shared meaning and intelligible usage of the general term "art," Weitz countered, *à la* Wittgenstein, that the complex networks of similarities and family resemblances through which artworks were related supplied all the commonality that was necessary or available for effectively employing and teaching this general concept. On the basis of this background of known artworks and their networks of similarities, we can also apply the term "art" to new and unfamiliar objects. Weitz's argument is not merely that art lacks an essence, a set of necessary and sufficient properties which is and must be exhibited by any work properly called art. It is rather that the very logic of the concept prohibits its having such an essence. Art is an intrinsically open and mutable concept, a field which prides itself on originality, novelty, and innovation. Thus, even if we could discover a set of defining conditions that captured all existing artworks, there would be no guarantee that future art would conform to its limits; indeed, there is every reason to think that art would do its damnedest to violate them. In short, "the very expansive, adventurous character of art" makes its definition "logically impossible."

Philosophers were therefore urged to forsake the bootless project of definition and instead devote their efforts to analyzing the logic of the concept of art, whose analysis showed it to be not only open but also complex and essentially contested. For Weitz, it was complex in having two distinct uses, classificatory and evaluative. Not everything that we label "a work of art" do we praise by such terms. It is the evaluative use which makes the concept so contested, the conflicting past definitions of art being disguised attempts to recommend what we should value in art. These traditional theories, Weitz insisted, have been valuable as evaluative proposals of "certain criteria of excellence in art" or as reasoned recommendations "to attend in certain ways to certain features of art." But they are misguided as philosophical theory, whose job is not evaluation or recommendation but logical description and conceptual elucidation.[3]

To overcome Weitz's arguments, a new style of definition was provided. If the evaluative issue made any definition irremediably contestable, then definition should be confined to the classificatory sense of art. If works of art seemed to exhibit no set of common and peculiar properties, perhaps the defining essence of art is not in their exhibited properties but in their generative process. Mere similarities, it was argued against Weitz, cannot explain the unity of the concept of art. For similarities can be found between any two things, while the alternative notion of family resemblance already implies a common generative core or shared history. These arguments form the fulcrum for George Dickie's institutional theory of art, which defines an artwork as "an artifact... upon which some person or persons acting on behalf of a certain social institution (the artworld) has conferred the status of candidate for appreciation."[4]

This theory is worth discussing not only because of its considerable impact on analytic aesthetics, but because it vividly displays both the skillful ingenuity and the underlying perversity of reflective, compartmentalizing definition. Though it defines "work of art" in terms of necessary and sufficient conditions, it is purely formal or procedural and thus would neither foreclose on aesthetic innovation nor prejudice with respect to evaluative criteria. (Such foreclosures and prejudices are conveniently left to the artworld, as are all other substantive matters). The theory moreover has the advantage of highlighting the social context through which art is generated and provided with properties that are not directly exhibited to the senses. This compensates for art's lack of an exhibited shared essence and gives art both an unlimited horizon and a defining ground, one which will not be shaken by anything that any artwork will present or not present, even if it presents nothing.

In its formalistic reliance on procedural conferral of status and in its exclusion of evaluative and substantive content, Dickie's definition of art is an analogue of legal positivism's definition of law, and it is subject to the same sorts of criticism.[5] The institutional act of conferring status seems neither necessary nor sufficient. Some works, arguably most, arise in a context where art status need not be explicitly conferred but is assumed automatically; and a given act of conferral could hardly secure art status were it not taken up in the proper way by the artworld. Similarly problematic is the definition's narrow concentration on a purely classificatory sense of art. For apart from recognizing the artworld and its generative power, what substantive illumination or purpose can this definition possibly have? Even Dickie admits that the strictly classificatory judgement "This is art" has virtually no use in aesthetic discourse. As for the substantive aesthetic issue which traditionally gave point to the definitional quest – the issue of whether and how we should appreciate a particular artifact as a work of art – this is merely deferred to the artworld and its evaluational decisions and criteria.

Finally, though Dickie is right to insist that being a work of art must not entail being a good one or being valuable, he is wrong to assume that "work of art" can be defined in a sense exclusive of value. Indeed, in Dickie's own definition, the very notion of candidate for appreciation presupposes a background where art is appreciated, just as the very concept of "artworld" presupposes a world where art is valued as a cultural practice and achievement. Holistically, art and value cannot be separated, which means that essentialistically defining art in a purely classificatory sense perversely eliminates what is essential to art, even though it be absent from many of the objects so classified.

If Dickie's theory provides no substantive insight which would explain why art is valued and which would enrich our appreciative experience and understanding of it, this is not because he doesn't have such knowledge. It is rather that he is driven by a model of reflective, compartmentalizing definition whose essential aim is more to capture the current understanding of art than to deepen or improve it. Given the presumption that art is a distinct domain of objects which must be clearly individuated from other domains, the exercise of definition is to find a verbal formula that will fit all and only those objects which would be called works of art according to the accepted understanding of that domain. We challenge the proposed definition by bringing counterexamples which its verbal formula would either wrongly cover or fail to cover and so would either wrongly include or exclude from art's domain.

The definition is thus shown to be either too wide or too narrow; its motivating ideal is perfect coverage, and it might well be called the "wrapper" model of theory.

Like the better food wraps, such theories of art transparently present, contain, and conserve their object – our understanding of art. They do not significantly transform that understanding; nor, except incidentally, do they enhance or modify our experience and practice of art. If they win our admiring assent, it is because of their philosophical agility and imaginative ingenuity in the game of "covering" and argumentation, or because of the sensitive and insightful discussions of art that are offered in their support. Dickie's wrapper theory, with its contentless transparency of the artworld, was especially attractive to philosophers because of its tremendous elasticity; it could cover anything the institutional artworld demanded. Ironically, it was also rejected largely because its institutional picture of the artworld was not elastic enough.

Institutions (like those of state, religion, or education) typically involve an articulate network of roles, structures, and practices that are clearly codified and strictly administered. The artworld is obviously much more vague and elastic than this. One is not formally registered, baptized, or matriculated into the artworld (or exiled, excommunicated, or expelled from it). There are no specified conditions one must meet to act on its behalf; nor are there any formulated rules to regulate such action. To respond by pleading that the artworld's rules and regulations are informal and implicit is simply to admit that art is not strictly an institution but more a cultural tradition or social practice. This idea, with its more flexible and historically informed vision of the artworld, represents what is probably today's most powerful "wrapper" theory of art.

III

Arthur Danto, one of today's more imaginative and artistically sensitive aestheticians, has increasingly come to define art in terms of its history. Though it was his "discovery" of the artworld which inspired Dickie's definition, and though he continued to insist that "without the artworld there is no art," Danto rejected the institutional theory largely because of its lack of historical depth.[6] Ignoring Wölfflin's famous insight that not everything is possible at every time, it left everything magically to the omnipotent and arbitrary power of artworld agents without considering

the historical constraints which structured the artworld and thus informed and limited its agents' actions. Thus, even if it could explain
how Andy Warhol's Brillo boxes (the avowed inspiration of Danto's
theorizing) could be proposed for art status, it could hardly account for
why this work should be so accepted but an indistinguishable one
rejected or why it itself would not have been accepted had Warhol
produced it in *fin-de-siècle* Paris or quattrocento Florence.

The explanation, Danto argues, depends on the history of art and art's
theory. The status of artwork must involve more than just being conferred appreciative candidacy by an artworld agent. A museum guard
might offer us a beautiful flower on behalf of the curator without that
making it a work of art, even if it is visually indistinguishable from an
artwork of a real flower (entitled *Living Beauty*) currently exhibited there.
For Danto, any object successfully claiming to be art must bear an
interpretation as a particular artwork (the artwork flower, for example,
as an artistic comment on the moribund character of still life and of
museum art in general). As "nothing is an artwork without an interpretation that constitutes it as such," so for the requisite interpretation to
be possible, certain structures and contexts in art history and art theory
must obtain.[7] Thus, the Brillo box as work of art required an interpretation to that effect, both creatively by Warhol and responsively by his
audience; and the artworld "required a certain historical development" to
make that interpretation possible. Objects are artworks if they are so
interpreted (i.e. constitutively interpreted) in the artworld; and since the
artworld is but an abstraction from the artistic, critical, historiographical,
and theoretical practices which constitute art's history, art is essentially a
complex historical *practice* or *tradition* (though Danto uses neither term)
which must be defined historically.

Danto's theory of art is, of course, too rich and ramified to capture
in such summary form. But though its substantive content and historical
depth set it apart from Dickie's theory, it is governed by the same wrapper model of definition with its metaphor of perfect coverage, expressed
in his motivating concern that "any definition of art must compass the
Brillo boxes" of Warhol but not cover their indistinguishable ordinary
counterparts.[8] Indeed, Danto's astonishingly acute preoccupation with
this particular icon of "art in a box" may well be the expression of
his definitional compulsion for art's compartmentalized containment.
Sharing "the philosophical aspiration of the ages, a definition which will
not be threatened by historical overthrow," Danto ingeniously seeks that
definition in history itself by essentially defining art in terms of its history

and, further, by depicting art's recent history as a development toward the "understanding of its own historical essence."[9]

This tale, for Danto, has the ironic twist that, having brought us to the understanding of its historical essence, art has fulfilled its historical mission and thus, in a sense, has finished its history (though it still survives in the dazed gropings of its postmodernist posthistory). But this does not refute art's definition as a historically extended cultural practice; for what has allegedly ended is only its history in the sense of linear progression toward a conceived goal, not its history as a cultural tradition developing from past achievements and evolving in response to them by continuation, elaboration, and reactive rejection. History, then, is the ultimate container for defining art, since all and only those objects taken as artworks by art's history will necessarily be contained by such historical definition.

Danto is not alone in treating art as a complex and temporally developing socio-cultural tradition essentially defined by its history. Richard Wollheim basically says the same thing in asserting that "art is, in Wittgenstein's sense, a form of life" with autonomous procedures and institutions, and that "art is essentially historical."[10] Adorno, from his very different Marxian perspective, concurs that art cannot be defined by any "invariable principle" since "it is a historically changing constellation of moments" whose content and constitutive unity is best defined by "looking backward" to its "concrete development" as a distinct practice, at once socially embedded and resistantly autonomous.[11]

More recently, a number of aestheticians have preferred to express the same fundamentally historicist view by defining art as a social or cultural *practice*, where the notion of practice is to be understood briefly as follows.[12] A practice is a complex of interconnected activities which require learned skills and knowledge and which aim at achieving certain goods internal to the practice (e.g. the capturing of a likeness in portraiture), even though external goods (like profit and fame) may also be desired as by-products. As practices are directed at internal goods, so are they governed by internal reasons and standards of achievement which are not so much explicitly formulated as embodied in the history of the practice, in its traditional achievements or masterpieces. Since these internal reasons, standards, and goods are not rigidly defined, a practice involves a temporally extended debate over their interpretation and relative validity. This can result in a variety of competing achievements and in the expansion or revision of the practice's internal goods, reasons, and standards. But despite such variety, and though it shares no common essence, it still hangs together as a distinct unity, a given practice, through a common history.

Art, it is argued, is best defined as such a complex practice, composed of the different arts and their different genres, which themselves are also practices of varying complexity. The traditional definitional function of identifying artworks from other objects no longer depends on finding art's essence but is left to the internal reasons and standards of the complex practice of art and perhaps ultimately to its various subpractices (the practice of music identifying its artworks, while poetry identifies its own). Moreover, as Wolterstorff and Carroll remark, the definitional coverage of art as a practice extends beyond artworks. For, since the notion of practice highlights human agency as well as recognizing its products of achievement, defining art as a complex practice helpfully comprehends not only art's objects but also its subjects who sustain the practice, the makers and receivers of works of art.

As a complex practice of practices developing and changing through history, art should be defined not by a fixed essence but in terms of a complexly coherent historical narrative which at once explains and helps sustain its unity and integrity. The precise form of art's defining narrative must be open and revisable, not only to allow for future works but because the task of narration is itself an open and contested practice, the practice of art history and criticism. But the impossibility of narrative completion and hence definitional closure is not seen as a vitiating flaw. For the openness of narrative definition is necessary to capture the openness of art. Besides, if Carroll is right, we could always give, at least in principle, a full narrative up to the present which would define "the practice of art as we know it," pending future changes and future narratives which could be complete for future presents.[13]

There is much truth in the view of art as practice. Indeed, in terms of theory's traditional aims, the definition of art as a historically defined socio-cultural practice is probably as good as we can get. Because of its scope, flexibility, and potential art-historical substance, it seems the culmination of philosophy's attempt to theorize art by fully capturing the content of this concept and differentiating it from other things. In faithfully representing how art's objects and activities are identified, related, and collectively distinguished, it best realizes the dual definitional goals of accurate reflection and compartmental differentiation. However, in doing so, it also betrays how futile and wrongheaded such theoretical purposes may be.

First, even assuming with Carroll that a full, unifying narrative definition is possible in principle (a questionable assumption since the essentially contested nature of art and its history can elicit contradictory and probably incommensurable narratives), such definition, as Carroll himself admits, is neither feasible nor indeed desirable in practice. For the overwhelming mass of details and of insignificant, uninnovative artworks would make a full narration both practically impossible and impossibly tedious. Indeed, insistence on all the repetitive details could well obscure the developmental narrative structure through which art is defined and unified.

Moreover, even if we ignore such difficulties and assume we can find a manageable narrative which gives only what is necessary for fully and faithfully representing our concept of art, what is the value of such a definition? What does it do for us? In defining art as a practice defined by art-historical narrative, all substantive decisions as to what counts *as* art or *in* art are left to the internal decisions of the practice as recorded by art history. Philosophy of art simply collapses into art history, and the live and momentous issue of what is art gets reduced to a backward-looking account of what art has been up to the present. Art theory realizes its aim when it faithfully represents "the practice of art as we know it." But if it merely reflects how art is already understood, philosophy of art condemns itself to the same reductive definition with which it condemned art. It is essentially an imitation of an imitation: the representation of art history's representation of art. What purpose does such representation serve apart from appeasing the old philosophical habit for theory as mirroring reflection of the real? And while this epistemological habit is deeply entrenched, it seems just as deeply misguided, having outlived the transcendental metaphysics which gave it meaning.

The theoretical ideal of reflection originally had a point when reality was conceived in terms of fixed or necessary essences lying beyond ordinary empirical understanding. For in that case, once we achieved an adequate representation of the real, it would always remain valid and effective as a criterion for assessing ordinary understanding. However, once our realities are the empirical and changing contingencies of art's career, the reflective model becomes pointless. For here, theory's representation neither penetrates beyond changing phenomena nor can sustain their changes. Instead, it must run a hopeless race of perpetual narrative revision, holding the mirror of reflective theory up to art's changing nature by representing its history.

But art's mutable history need not merely be represented; it can also be made. And it can be made not only by the works of artists and the narratives of historians, but also by the interventions of theorists, whose views have traditionally been central to the creative and critical context in which artists, critics, and art historians function. Consider, for example, how Aristotle's poetics dominated centuries of dramatists and critics, or how Kantian ideas of aesthetic imagination and judgement helped shape romantic poetry and justify modernist formalism. In today's postmodern crisis, where art seems to have so lost direction that not only its end but its death is envisaged, there is both need and opportunity for theoretical intervention, for revisionary reorientation rather than quiescent reflection.

Pragmatist aesthetics recommends such an activist role in rethinking and reshaping art; and Dewey originally tried to do this by defining art as experience. But does not such theoretical activism mean abandoning philosophy by forsaking its traditional project and self-image as the wholly disinterested pursuit of truth? To this objection there are two rejoinders.

First, as Dewey insists, philosophy's major achievements were never really governed by this goal. Its theories and chosen problems were rather an intellectual response to the socio-cultural conditions and perplexities of the day.[14] Certainly Plato's theory cannot be seen as disinterestedly representing the nature of art. It was clearly a politically motivated response to the pressing problem of whose intellectual leadership (art's ancient wisdom or philosophy's new rationality) should guide Athenian society at a time of troubled change, when its traditions, stability, and power had been severely challenged not only by internal dissension and revolution but by the humiliation of military defeat. Though Plato's aims of denigration and limitation were the very opposite of Dewey's, the engaged and activist role of philosophy was the same.

Secondly, the very idea that any momentary gains of intervention will be outweighed by philosophy's loss of its neutrally reflective ideal, that philosophy must keep itself pure even at the price of tolerating corruption elsewhere, is itself an impure bias. This rigid posture of lofty disinterestedness reflects the interest of a narrow and professionalized philosophical conservatism which is either happy to reinforce the status quo by representing it in philosophical definition, or is simply too timid and effete to risk dirtying its hands in the messy struggle over the shaping of art and culture. More dangerously, the fetishism of disinterested neutrality obscures the fact that philosophy's ultimate aim is to benefit human life, rather than serving pure truth for its own sake. Since art is a crucial instance and cherished resource of human flourishing, philosophy betrays its mission if it merely looks on with abandoning neutrality at art's evolving history without joining the struggle to improve its future.

IV

We can better appreciate Dewey's reconstructive definition of art as experience by further criticizing art's definition as practice. Conceived on the wrapper model, that definition has the twofold goal of art's representational coverage and compartmental differentiation. Our criticism so far has concentrated on the former goal, its practical futility and the empty quietism of its reflective collapse into art history. But there are also problems of narrowing compartmentalization when art is equated with the specific historically defined practice honored by that name; and these problems seem best overcome through a Deweyan insistence on art as experience.

(1) The first concerns what and who determine art's value. With art's compartmental definition as a distinct historical practice, the whole question of value is shunted to the interior of this practice, fragmenting into narrow questions over particular internal goods whose value is to be determined by the standards and procedures internal to the practice. This total interiorization of value does not explain the source of the practice's value as a whole, nor does it really account for the goodness of its internal goods and standards. For to say they are good because the practice so defines them seems transparently circular. Moreover, confining all question of value to the inner arbitration of the artworld's practice effectively removes that practice from critique through a wider normative perspective which could guide the reconstruction of that practice should it become misdirected and increasingly alien to the lives and joys of most people.[15] Such is the danger of art's autonomy when art is identified as a specific historically defined practice, a danger which seems all the more sinisterly real when that practice has long been shaped under lamentable historical conditions of socio-political injustice.

But still more unacceptable is the contrary idea that art's value must be justified by something altogether external to it. To view art's value as *merely* instrumental to some other end, be it cognition, morality, psychic balance, or cultural stature, is to reenact the same castrating logic which first disenfranchised art and subjected it to other cultural practices like philosophy. Nor is this externally instrumentalist view very convincing. For there seems, after all, to be something autonomous about art's value, something about its own goods for which we pursue them as ends in themselves rather than means to other goods in other practices. That something is surely aesthetic experience. For the immediate, absorbing satisfaction of such experience makes it uncontestably an end in itself. And this experienced value, directly impressed on our senses and imagination with an often overwhelming power, supplies art with an irrefutable (albeit unformulable) normative vindication.[16] Although the intrinsic ends of art are sometimes identified with its material end products (the carved or painted objects, acoustic events, etc., we call works of art), these products have no artistic value divorced from their (actual and potential) use-value in aesthetic experience.[17] Without an experiencing subject, they are dead and meaningless; and to treat them as independently valuable encourages the distortions of reification, commodification, and fetishization which plague the contemporary art scene.

If aesthetic experience constitutes an intrinsic end and value, then there may be good reason to define art in its terms, even though many works of art fail to produce it. Such definition (one of evaluative rather than logical essence) aims not at compartmentally covering all art as historically understood, but rather at highlighting what most matters in art, so as to increase art's appreciation, even if that means also recognizing art outside its traditionally chartered domain. For aesthetic experience is not constrained to the narrow confines of the historically defined practice of art and is consequently not subject to the exclusive control of those who dominate this practice and determine its internal goods. It thus can serve as a somewhat independent, yet not wholly external, touchstone by which to criticize and improve art's practice, particularly when the aim is to redirect the practice so as to afford more full and frequent aesthetic experience for more members of society.

That aesthetic experience extends beyond the historically established practice of art should be obvious. It exists, first of all, in the appreciation of nature, not least that part of nature which is the animate human body. But we also find it in ritual and sport, in parades, fireworks, and the media of popular culture, in bodily and domestic ornamentation, from primitive tattoos and cave drawings to contemporary cosmetics and interior decorating, and indeed in the countless colorful scenes and moving events which fill our cities and enrich our ordinary lives. Against such independent aesthetic experience two related arguments are sometimes advanced. The first is that since all meaningful and consummatory experience requires a background practice, no aesthetic experience is possible apart from the practice of art. Though it may appear spontaneous in its immediacy, aesthetic experience (as Dewey himself insists) always depends on a background of prior perceptions, prestructuring orientations, and funded meanings which themselves entail background practices. But all that follows from this point is that *some* background practice is required, not necessarily the particular background practice of art as historically and compartmentally defined.

The second argument builds on the fact that the term "aesthetic" (despite its Greek root) was coined only in the eighteenth century, as part of the same process of differentiating cultural spheres (into the scientific, the practico-moral, and the artistic) which also gave birth to our modern concept of art as the narrower practice of fine art. If the very concept of "aesthetic" never existed before art was established in modernity as a compartmentally distinct practice, then aesthetic experience could never have existed without it and remains dependent on it. Thus, even when focused on nature, aesthetic experience derives its particular attitude and quality from appreciative habits learned from modernity's practice of art, and hence remains essentially contained by it.[18]

This argument is extremely problematic. For first, even granting that aesthetic experience's emergence was historically dependent on the modern evolution of the concept and practice of art, this in no way entails that it remains wholly circumscribed by that practice today. Such an inference would be a rather crude commission of the genetic fallacy, especially when we consider how variously and sometimes antithetically the practice of art and the notion of the aesthetic have since evolved. Secondly, to argue that there could be no aesthetic experience before we had the term "aesthetic" seems to be taking a blind linguistic turn. By the same kind of logic, we would have to argue (as did Collingwood) that so-called Greek arts were not really art because they were described as *technē* and *poïesis*, the modern conception and practice of art (nor even its Latin root) not yet having been shaped. But this is like arguing that no one suffered from appendicitis before the malady was so diagnosed and labeled. Experiences of beauty and sublimity undoubtedly predate the eighteenth-century birth of the aesthetic, but they cannot therefore be reasonably excluded from the domain of aesthetic experience. Indeed, the term "aesthetic" was introduced to account for and structure these prior experiences which were too various in quality to be subsumed under the terms "beauty" and "sublimity," too rich in meaning to be described as mere taste, and obviously too extensive to be circumscribed by the practice of art.[19]

Of course, the formative theorists of the aesthetic did not merely give a new name to familiar experiences which had existed without variation since the dawn of humankind. For aesthetic experiences do not constitute an ontological class or natural kind with some unchanging substantive essence. In characterizing the experiences of beauty, sublimity, and the like as "aesthetic" and in defining the sense of that characterization, aesthetic theorists also tried to develop and reshape these experiences in certain favored directions. Not surprisingly, most philosophers were keen to direct aesthetic experience toward increasing rationality and spirituality; and one way to promote this was by coaxing it away from the robust materiality of natural beauty and consigning its future to the practice of fine art, whose rationally purposive crafting of objects could not be questioned and whose spiritualizing potential had been proved by centuries of religious art. This drive toward aesthetic disembodiment and denaturalization became quite obvious with Hegel, who not only privileged art's beauty over nature's but also ranked the arts according to their freedom from matter, poetry being highest since the most ideal; and the same drive motivates the view that aesthetic experience is circumscribed by and dependent on the historically defined practice of art.

(2) Consigning aesthetic experience to the practice of art is not only limiting; it is arguably progressively so, since this practice almost paradoxically seems to grow by getting narrower and more specialized. The constricting and exclusionary tendencies implicit in art as a historically defined practice represent another danger in defining it as such a practice. If the notion of art once included a vast variety of skill, learning, craft, and technology, it is today reserved for the practice of fine art as compartmentally constituted by modernity. This narrowing construal of art may perhaps be defended as simply an anodyne and clarificatory precision of the concept. But, as Dewey would argue, the shrinking separation of art into fine art both reflects and reinforces a vicious division in modern society between practical labor (deemed to be intrinsically disagreeable) and aesthetic experience (held to be enjoyable but functionless), a division which too often manifests itself in painfully unaesthetic industry and uselessly irrelevant fine art.[20]

The sharp division of fine art from productive crafts rests on a fundamental opposition between the practical and the aesthetic which needs to be questioned. For there is no doubt that practical labors can be undertaken and enjoyed aesthetically (think of the hobbies of carpentry, pottery, or fishing), just as aesthetic efforts can clearly serve practical ends (of romantic love, religious worship, social celebration, and so on). If it is not simply residual prejudice based on past class distinction (between a working class too overburdened with dolorous toil to savor

second is its definition as a practice of external making whose ends are conceived as independent objects divorced from their effects on their creating human agents. If Plato's mimetic theory inaugurated the first, Aristotle's classification of art as *poiēsis* (making) in contrast to *praxis* (action or practice) effectively established the second. Both these theoretical moves served, of course, to disenfranchise art vis-à-vis other domains like philosophy, ethics, and politics, which were held to involve reality and action rather than merely imitating them in artificially fabricated objects. If both maneuvers have limited art's role and appreciation, some of the difficulties they engender seem best redressed by emphasizing art as experience.

(a) The gap Plato maliciously posited between art and reality has become an unquestioned dogma that has even been thematized and reinforced by many works of art. But, in an obvious way, the idea of this gap is quite simply false. Art is undeniably real; it exists concretely and vividly in our world and in our lives, for many of us as a cherished and irreplaceable part of what we would call good living. Of course, we can always distinguish between a real object and its artistic representation, but this does not entail that the representation is either unreal or intrinsically deceptive.

Art's alleged separation from reality served not only to brand it as cognitively worthless but also to isolate its practice from practical life and socio-political action by dismissing it as intrinsically impractical through its fictionality. Thus, though art came to be highly valued by modern aestheticians, its proper role and appreciation remained exiled from the cognitive and practico-ethical realms; art was instead quarantined in an aesthetic domain essentially defined, after Kant, by its utter disinterestedness, by "complete indifference" to "the real existence" of things.[24] This view not only belies the efforts of artists who sought to change the world by transforming our attitudes. It also encourages the practice and reception of art as something essentially purposeless and gratuitous. Ignoring art's wide-ranging cognitive and social potential, it has inspired the perversions of the artist as isolated dreamer and social renegade, and of the true aesthete as frivolous dandy and wastrel.

Finally, the historical separation of art from life has issued in the impoverishing evisceration of aesthetic experience by repudiating its connection to bodily energies and appetites, by defining its delight in contrast to the sensual pleasures of living. From Kant's determination that aesthetic pleasure is wholly "independent of charm and emotion" and must have "no empirical satisfaction...mingled with its determining ground," philosophical aesthetics has put the experience of art on a path of disembodied spiritualization, where full-blooded and widely shared appreciative enjoyment is refined away into anemic and distanced connoisseurship by the few. If the legitimated pleasures of high art have become too ghostly and ascetic for most people, the expressive forms which do provide us the most potent pleasure are typically declassed as mere entertainment.

Viewing art as experience responds to all these problems of the presumed gap between life and art. As experience, art is obviously part of our lives, a particularly vivid form of our experienced reality, rather than a mere fictional imitation of it. Secondly, since experience must combine the different motives and environing materials involved in our behavioral context and since we approach any context as purposive perceivers, art's experience should be expected to admit of cognitive and practical elements without losing its legitimacy as artistic or aesthetic experience. Dewey is quite explicit on this point. "Esthetic experience is always more than esthetic." Its different materials, not in themselves intrinsically aesthetic, "become esthetic as they enter into an ordered rhythmic movement toward consummation. The material is widely human" (including "the practical, the social, and the educative"), and art's function is to shape it into a satisfyingly integrated whole.[25] While art as a collection of sacralized objects may be locked up in museums, segregated from the rest of life, the same cannot be said for art's experience, whose effects flow into and enhance our other pursuits. Lastly, Dewey's emphasis on the experience of art as fully embodied enjoyment, engaging "the whole creature in his unified vitality" and rich in sensual and emotional satisfactions, challenges the spiritualizing reduction of aesthetic pleasure into a purely intellectual delight.

(b) Plato condemned art as deceptively unreal partly because he feared its power to penetrate and contaminate the human soul and thereby corrupt proper action. Artistic creation and appreciation were both conceived as a form of irrationality, artist and audience being linked in a chain of divine possession whose source was the Muse. Aristotle's reactive defense was to separate art from character and action by conceiving art as a rational activity of external fabrication, as *poiēsis*. Poetic activity, as the making of a distinct object through some productive skill, was, however, sharply contrasted with the superior activity of practical action (or *praxis*), which both derives from the agent's inner character and reciprocally helps shape it. While art's making has its end outside itself and its maker (its end and value being in the object made), action has its end both in itself and in its agent, who is affected by how he acts, though allegedly not by what he makes (*Nichomachean Ethics*, book VI, 1140a1–1140b25).

Since Aristotle, the practice of art has been governed by this model of making, and its distortive one-sidedness demands rethinking art as experience so as to redress the balance. Preoccupation with the productive model has led to the fetishization of art's objects with little regard for their actual use in appreciative experience; enormous sums are devoted to the acquisition and protection of artworks, while next to nothing is spent on aesthetic education so that these works could be put to better work in enriching the lives of more people. Moreover, equating art with the production of definite objects altogether independent of the artists who make them, not only neglects forms of artistic expression where it is hard to speak of such a definite, independent work (as in improvisational dance), but more importantly ignores the undeniable effects that art has on its creators as well as its audience. Rethinking art as experience rather than external making, we are reminded that artistic creation is itself a powerful experience which shapes the artist as well as the work.

Finally, the fabricational model of art tends to suggest an essential division between artist and audience, between the active maker or author and the contemplative receiver or reader. One way to bridge this troubling gap is to reconceive appreciation as creative production where the reader actively reconstructs the aesthetic object; and Dewey insists on this (*AE* 261, 285). But the model of art as external making, when coupled with academic criticism's institutional and professional pressures, has recently engendered the more radical view that legitimate appreciation be exclusively identified with the production of new texts, so that the only valued form of reading is revisionary rewriting, making the text say what we want by producing a text of transformative interpretation. This reduction of appreciation to self-assertive critical production denies us the enrichment and pleasure gained from submitting ourselves to art's alterity and seductive power. Its ideal of dominative fabrication reflects the model of the artist as a maker knowing exactly what he wants to make and in full control of the productive process. And while that "macho" model of making was a helpful response to Plato's condemnatory view of art as passive and irrational possession, it remains no less falsely partial and is eloquently refuted by the testimony of artists, who recognize elements of inspirational surrender and loss of control in the creative process.[26]

Rethinking art as experience overcomes the conflictual stand-off and one-sidedness of these two views by combining their contrary (gender-linked) principles as necessary and complementary moments of experience. For experience, as Dewey insists, involves both receptive undergoing and productive doing, both absorbing and responsively reconstructing what is experienced, where the experiencing subject both shapes and is shaped. The notion of experience does better justice to the fullness of art and links artist and audience in the same twofold process. Art, in its creation and appreciation, is both directed making and open receiving, controlled construction and captivated absorption.

V

We have seen some good reasons for redefining art in terms of aesthetic experience. But there are obviously difficulties as well, and these go beyond the objections to aesthetic experience already addressed in the previous chapter: its subjectivity, self-satisfied unity, trivializing goal of pleasure, and failure to demarcate art's accepted limits.

(1) One problem is that aesthetic experience seems too slippery to have much explanatory power. Though it undeniably exists, it does not exist as something we can clearly isolate and define; hence in defining art as aesthetic experience, we are defining the comparatively clear and definite by something obscurely elusive and indefinable.

Dewey is unhelpfully inconsistent on this matter. On the one hand, he provides a long and detailed discussion of aesthetic experience in terms of its characteristic features, implying that it *can* be adequately defined. Thus, aesthetic experience involves the whole vital creature and sustains integretative unity in variety, both in itself and in connection with the rest of experience (*AE* 42–9, 61–3, 166); it is comparatively intense or heightened, having a special pervasive quality which binds its parts together as a distinctive whole (*AE* 22–4, 33, 196–9); it is active and dynamic, with rhythmic processual progress that involves moments of comparative rest (*AE* 57–60, 159–62, 177); it is shaped through obstacles and resistance which enable it to be aesthetically expressive rather than simply emotive (*AE* 67–70); it is an experience of satisfying form, where means and ends, subject and object, doing and undergoing, are integrated into a unity (*AE* 53–5, 142–4, 201–4, 253–5); above all, it is an "immediate experience," whose value is "directly fulfilling" and not deferred for some other end or experience (*AE* 87, 91, 120–6). Dewey even defines "cumulation, tension, conservation, anticipation, and fulfillment as formal characteristics of an esthetic experience" (*AE* 149).

On the other hand, he also seems clearly committed to the indefinability (and indeed discursive unknowability) of aesthetic experience. For, while claiming "the immediacy of esthetic experience" as "an esthetic necessity," he also insists that all such qualitative "immediacy of existence is ineffable...and may be pointed to by words, but not described or defined" (*AE* 123, *EN* 73). In fact, when Dewey later talks about the particular quality which pervasively unifies and thus constitutes an experience as aesthetic, he says "it can only be felt, that is, immediately experienced...[and] cannot be described nor even be *specifically* pointed at − since whatever is specified in a work of art is one of *its* differentiations" (*AE* 196).

If aesthetic experience is essentially indefinable, to explain art in terms of it will not take us very far.[27] Still worse, such definition can inspire confusions in aesthetics similar to those of the "myth of the given" in epistemology, where the certainty of experience's testimony depends on its utter muteness. In defining art as aesthetic experience, we may think we have gained an effective criterion for classifying experienced objects and events into art and non-art in terms of their experiential effects and potential. Moreover, in defining aesthetic experience as the source of art's value, we are tempted to erect experience as a standard for evaluating and ranking works of art. Even a careful philosopher like Monroe Beardsley succumbed to this temptation. Perhaps the sole major analytic aesthetician to appreciate Dewey's experiential theory, Beardsley argued that we could ultimately explain our evaluative judgements and rankings of works in terms of their capacity to produce aesthetic experience of "a fairly great magnitude"; the greater the magnitude, the better the work.[28]

But, given the unformulability of its rich yet fleeting immediacy, aesthetic experience is inadequate as a justificational standard for critical judgement. How are we supposed to measure (let alone communicate) magnitudes of an experience which cannot even properly be defined or marked off for measurement? There is no way the critic can prove his verdict to others by mere appeal to his immediate experience, which in its qualitative immediacy and tremulous transiency is not discursively demonstrable or preservable as evidence. Of course, he can try to justify his verdict by descriptions of the work which aim to induce a similar experience in his reader, but that already involves much more than mere appeal to immediate experience.

This is not to deny, as we noted earlier, that the satisfactions enjoyed in aesthetic experience provide a kind of direct "on-the-pulse" demonstration of art's value, which is extremely important both for understanding and for adjusting our orientation to art. But in recognizing this, we must also recognize that such non-propositional evidence cannot do the serious, detailed epistemological work of critical justification; and translating it into propositional terms amounts to little more than saying that art (or a given work thereof) is valuable because it is so experienced, which is not really saying much at all.[29] So, given the explanatory poverty of aesthetic experience, why should we define art in its terms?

Dewey's answer depends on reconceiving philosophical definition and theory in distinctly pragmatist fashion, as aimed not primarily at the resolution of abstract philosophical puzzles but at bringing us closer to achieving more and better concrete goods in experience (though intellectual satisfaction in philosophical abstractions is not excluded from such experiential goods). Dewey was not seeking a traditional wrapper theory of art which would issue in a formal definition giving art's necessary and sufficient conditions or some algorithm for classifying and evaluating its works, for he felt such "formal definitions leave us cold" (*AE* 155).[30] Instead, he thought "a definition is good when it…points the direction in which we can move expeditiously toward having an experience" (*AE* 220). So a good definition of art should effectively direct us toward more and better aesthetic experience.

Defining art as experience expeditiously directs us toward this goal in at least two ways. First, it primes us to look for and cultivate aesthetic experience in our transactions with art by reminding us that *experience* (rather than collecting or criticism) is ultimately what art is about. Secondly, it helps us to recognize and valorize those expressive forms which provide us aesthetic experience but which could provide us far more and far better, if they could be appreciated and cultivated as legitimate art. Rethinking art as experience thus motivates my efforts to defend the artistic legitimacy of popular culture (in chapters 7 and 8), and it also underlies the ethical ideal of living beauty through fashioning life as art (sketched in chapter 9). In short, redefining art as experience liberates it from the narrowing stranglehold of the institutionally cloistered practice of fine art. No longer limited to certain traditionally privileged forms and media (authorized and dominated by historical art's past practice), art, as the purposeful production of aesthetic experience, becomes more rewardingly open to future experimentation through the vast variety of life's experienced materials, which it aesthetically shapes and transfigures.

(2) At this point, another problem with Dewey's definition must be faced: that its attempt to make theory practical is itself hopelessly impractical, since its revisionary aims are too quixotically ambitious. Philosophical theory is just far too puny to come anywhere near achieving Dewey's goal of redefining art. Our classificatory conceptual scheme with respect to art is just too deeply entrenched to be successfully overhauled in Dewey's wholesale fashion. There is simply no way we can reclassify accounting as art, no matter how imaginatively we limn our assets to the tax form. Nothing – except perhaps muddle – results from trying to redraw art's conceptual limits by redefining it in terms of aesthetic experience.

To this argument there are two responses. The first is that Dewey's *prime* aim (and certainly mine) is not to effect a global reclassification of art but to promote greater aesthetic experience. Defining art as experience can do this without changing our habits of classification; it functions simply as a persuasive rhetorical tool to get us to focus on the experiential dimension of art and to appreciate the aesthetic value of what is not so classified but could be, if we could group things together by their satisfyingly consummatory experience. Secondly, while the wholesale revision of art's conceptual borders may be futile, there are boundary cases where classificational changes *can* be made. One important and contested boundary concerns the expressive forms of mass-media culture, which are standardly relegated to the status of mere entertainment. Here, rethinking art as experience might help effect the artistic legitimation of a form like rock music, which affords such frequent and intensely gratifying aesthetic experience to so many people from so many nations, cultures, and classes.

It is in this narrower focus that my project differs most from Dewey's. While he valiantly struggled to achieve the global redefinition of art as aesthetic experience by describing the formative features of that indescribable experience, I am not interested in defining the indefinable or establishing it as a general philosophical definition of art. If Dewey's definition is valuable, its value lies not in achieving a wholesale conceptual revolution and satisfying our traditional impulse for general definition, but in its directive gesture towards remedying certain painful limitations in art's institutional practice. To attempt to heal all these ills by a globally reconstructive definition of art as experience was a heroic effort. But such heroism, I think, is better admired and applied than strictly imitated. So rather than pursuing Dewey's totalizing definitional quest, I instead aim, in the spirit of piecemeal pragmatist labor, to make a more specific case for widening art's borders to forms of popular culture and to the ethical art of fashioning one's life.

(3) But even my limited aims are called into question by a more radical argument asserting the futility of any attempt to revise art's established concept or practice by theoretical intervention. This argument, which arises most troublingly from the pragmatist's own camp, insists (in the words of Stanley Fish) that "theory has no consequences" for practice, since it is "an impossible project."[31] It is impossible in its old foundational sense as something pure and detachable from practice, governing it from above with transcendental cognitive privilege and lack of practical interest. For, as pragmatism rightly insists, theory, like all human thinking, always occurs within a particular situation and is motivated by purposes which help define that situation. And the situation in which we turn to theory is one that practice has shaped and led us to, most typically a problem or conflict in the practice which we look to theory to resolve. Theory, then, is not only shot through with practical motives, it is founded on practice and itself constitutes a practice.

But if theory is impossible as the transcendental and contextless revelation of eternal truths for governing practice, what formative consequential role can it have? To reconceive theory as a generalized, faithfully mirroring account of actual contingent practice makes it eminently more reasonable, but robs it of transformatory power; so that art theory, as we saw, gets reduced to a quiescent second-order representation of the history of art's practice. Thus, if not impossibly detached from practice, theory simply collapses into practice and so cannot constitute a force for redirecting it.

Apart from ignoring theory's palpable and abiding effects on the actual history of practice, this argument neglects the possibility of an intermediate pragmatist position, one which situates theory between transcendental cognitive privilege and servile impotence, one which recognizes the primacy of practice but also the power of theoretical intervention. Theory is here understood as critical, imaginative reflection on practice, emerging from practice and the second-order problems that practice always generates: justificatory problems of how to determine what constitutes proper practice, and problems of projection regarding how the practice should be continued or modified. Not only rooted in background practice, theory is also judged pragmatically by its fruits for that practice, which it helps to develop and improve. Its assertions and transformatory recommendations thus enjoy no privileged epistemological status intrinsically superior to practice; and they change practice not by transcendental fiat or apodictic demonstration but by persuasion, which is always contestable, and by the experimental success in practice of the changes they propose.[32]

The arguments denying a role for such non-foundational pragmatist theory are all problematic. To insist that we confine ourselves solely to first-order questions of practice neglects the point that the very distinction between first- and second-order questions is itself already a second-order product of theoretical reflection.[33] To claim, with Stanley Fish, that all controversial questions of practice which putatively call for deliberative theoretical reflection are readily resolved in a way "immediately obvious," issuing " 'naturally' – without further reflection – from one's position as a deeply situated agent" who has "thoroughly internalized" the practice,[34] is to ignore the obvious fact that the effortless resolution of these issues has not been achieved. For the debate over practice rages on, and it does so because the internalized practice is always already marked by conflict and points in different directions. Theory's job is to critically assess these different directions and through such criticism to promote the conception and pursuit of better ones.

Fish, of course, is right that theory's conscious-heightening critical reflection does "not necessarily" issue in any change of practice and that such heightened consciousness and change can be produced by other means.[35] But this does not in any way refute theory's power of intervention; it only denies the irresistibility and exclusivity of that power. As for the argument that theory cannot guide or affect practice because "it is itself a form a practice," this simply involves a confusion of logical scope by totalizing the notions of theory and practice and thereby homogenizing all the differences between varieties of practice (which include practices of theory).[36] The fact that art *theory* is itself a *practice* does not imply it is (or is fully reducible to) the very practice it theorizes, which is not to deny that it should be based on and in some sense be continuous with the practice of art.

There remains one more pragmatist argument for the radical impotence of theory. Since theory is structured and even assessed in relation to existing practice, its imagination and critical perspective must be wholly imprisoned by the horizon of that practice and so be devoid of any real capacity to transform it. Fish therefore concludes: "No theory can compel a change that has not in some sense already occurred" within the practice.[37] Practices, he further insists, can change only by their own internal mechanisms, since whatever lies outside the belief system of the practice cannot be understood as relevant, hence acceptable, and since no change can be effected in the practice unless that change be understood and accepted. But this argument has two problems. First, the reasonable assumption that nothing new can be understood without relating it to an already existing structure of belief and practice is falsely conflated with the dubious view that everything understood must already have an *accepted* place within that structure. Secondly, the argument neglects not only the deep vagueness of our practices but also their intersecting, imbricated, and often conflictual variety, which allows theory to criticize its object-practice by means of understandings and perspectives gained through another.

Thus, though our theoretical imagination is always largely constrained by established practice, it is not confined to slavish conformity and reactive repetition. For changing circumstances and encounters with other practices can provide new nourishment and alternative orientations. Since no practice is defined for all possible situations, there will always be a need for imaginative projections and creative decisions as to which of the possible projections should be actually pursued, decisions which are apt to be contested and which again raise second-order problems of how to justify these decisions. Since no practice exists in utter isolation, unaffected by others, there remains the need to relate, coordinate, or arbitrate between different practices. As long as our practices present us with such problems and admit of improvement, theory will not only be possible but necessary.

Conceived in this pragmatist fashion, which recognizes the primacy but also the problems of practice, theory is not exterminated but revitalized by the loss of its traditional status of transcendental cognitive privilege. For, once we give up the foundationalist view of theory as revealing the invariably necessary principles for practice, and further relinquish its hope of apodictic, incontestably final justification; once we instead see our practices (and our theories) as contingent products whose encounter with changing situations has necessitated continual adjustment, clarification, justification, and improvement; then theory's abiding role as critical reflection on practice is secure and seemingly ineliminable. Philosophy remains perennial, but in a new sense.

3

Organic Unity: Analysis and Deconstruction

I

Pragmatist aesthetics, as I conceive it after Dewey, aims at rethinking art in wider and more democratic terms. But aesthetics involves more than the concept of art. Other aesthetic concepts demand critical analysis, as do the practices of art criticism; and a pragmatist aesthetic should be capable of treating such topics. Since most of this book will be devoted to the reformatory project of rethinking art, I want at least to consider how pragmatism can help treat other issues traditionally central to aesthetic theory. I choose as specimen issues organic unity and interpretation. In both, pragmatism reveals itself as a promising middle road between foundational analytic philosophy and deconstruction, not only in aesthetics but on deeper questions of ontology, language, and epistemology, on which these two "aesthetic" issues turn. Indeed, as we shall see, the issues of organic unity and interpretation go well beyond the traditional domain of aesthetics.

Dating back to the Greeks (and even implicit in their very idea of the cosmos), the notion of organic unity has found significant application in a host of other philosophical enterprises: ethics and political theory, philosophy of mind, cosmology, and, of course, the philosophy of biology, with whose central concept of organism it is clearly and etymologically connected. Moreover, just as organic unity provides one of the two classical goals of art (the other being *mimesis*), so it furnishes one of the two most fundamental models of truth and knowledge – that of a systematic unity or coherence of belief. Here again, the other major epistemological model is that of representational correspondence to the real. It is intriguing that, for all their apparent differences, aesthetics and epistemology share the same basic alternative strategies: representation or unity.

Since mimetic theories of art have long been discredited by twentieth-century art and criticism, it would be nice to find reassurance in organic unity. Certainly, most contemporary Anglo-American aesthetics has sought its ultimate principles in such a notion, whether it located that unity in the external art object or its asethetic experience.[1] But organic unity has itself been radically challenged by recent developments in postmodern art and aesthetics, and not without reason. For this notion can become fetishized and frozen into a repressively rigid ideal which stifles creativity and formal experiment, and can induce in us an overly facile and complacent sense of harmony in the world. Coupled with postmodern art's emphasis on fragmentation and decentering, there has been an intense theoretical attack on the whole idea of unity, where not merely its value but its grounding and even its coherence are questioned. Foucault, of course, provides a wide-ranging challenge to presumed structures of unity and continuity in our thinking, including the unities of the genre, the book, and the author's *oeuvre*. Pierre Macherey, from his Marxist perspective, similarly lashes out against the traditional presumption of unity in aesthetics: "The postulated unity of the work which, more or less explicitly, has always haunted the enterprise of criticism, must now be denounced....Rather than that *sufficiency*, that ideal consistency, we must stress that determinate insufficiency, that incompleteness which actually shapes the work."[2] But probably the most radical and rigorous attempts to discredit and overthrow the notion of organic unity in aesthetic theory come from deconstruction.

One of Derrida's central aims is to challenge and dismantle the traditional idea of structure as a centered and complete organic whole, limiting the field of "freeplay." This field, through the inescapable medium of language, must always be "a field of infinite substitutions"; and through its infinite play of substitutions "excludes totalization" and overruns all putatively fixed limits of structural closure.[3] Such a vision of decentered, unlimitable freedom and substitution clearly conflicts with our most familiar (originally Aristotelian) understanding of organic unity as a complete whole having a definite "beginning, a middle, and an end" and having parts so integrally connected "that if any one of them is displaced or removed, the whole will be disjointed and disturbed."[4]

In Paul de Man (and after him in Culler and Norris), the deconstructionist attack on organic unity is aimed more directly at Anglo-American aesthetics as represented by the New Criticism, whose celebration of semantic richness in the unity of a text is said to end up by revealing "a plurality of significations that can be radically opposed to each other."

But this, according to de Man, "explodes" the very idea of any organic unity in poetry, of any unity analogous to "the coherence of the natural world." "This unitarian criticism finally becomes a criticism of ambiguity, an ironic reflection on the absence of the unity it had postulated."[5]

De Man's argument begs two very crucial and dubious premises (which for him are perhaps ultimately the same): namely, that organic unity can never embrace any radical oppositions and that the unities or coherences of "the natural world" (which de Man equates with "the organic world") involve no similar oppositions or conflicting forces. Yet a whole skein of thinkers stretching back to Heraclitus insist on the possibility that such unity not only contains but is sustained and enhanced by the tension of the opposites it embraces;[6] and modern science seems to reveal that radical opposition inhabits the unities of nature right down to the positive and negative charges of the atom. De Man's unwarranted and unconvincing assumptions are never argued for. They appeal to a univocal, monolithic concept of organic unity which is never articulated, and their problematic character points to the need for a more careful and rigorous treatment of this concept to see what, if anything, can be redeemed from it for contemporary thought.

I shall undertake this here by pitting deconstruction against analytic philosophy. For deconstruction not only provides the most penetrating indictment of this notion in aesthetics, but also the most powerful challenge and alternative to the analytic philosophy of language on which much of the Anglo-American aesthetics of unity rests. Indeed, organic unity provides a peculiarly fruitful focus for mapping the oppositional relations in which deconstruction and analysis are most deeply interlocked.[7] For though deconstruction opposes organic unity in aesthetics, we shall find that beneath this aesthetic surface, at a much deeper logical level, it is itself fundamentally committed and inextricably wedded to one central (originally Hegelian) sense of organic unity. Moreover, its attack on aesthetic unity relies precisely and essentially on this organic principle. Conversely, analytic philosophy, while advocating some form of organic unity as an aesthetic principle, vigorously denies the more radical logical principle of organic unity which forms the crucial foundation of deconstruction's assault not only on aesthetic unity but on the very possibility of reference and individuation – the foundational core of the analytic project. From the agonistic deadlock between these rival philosophies, pragmatism will emerge as the most likely option for recuperating the advantages of each.

To chart these oppositional reversals and the pragmatist alternative, we need first to distinguish the various senses of organic unity; and the best place to begin is with its tripartite analysis by G. E. Moore, who, together with Russell, established analytic philosophy at the beginning of this century through their common revolt against the then prevailing Hegelian idealism.

II

Moore's treatment of organic unity is complex because complexly motivated. This notion plays a central role in his two major philosophical projects of defending realism and the objectivity of intrinsic value. In the former it is a demon of idealist thinking which must be exorcised, while in the latter it plays a very positive role in explaining how the intrinsic value of something can be dependent on its parts (themselves of possibly negligible value) but still not be reducible to the sum of the values of its parts. This organic principle by which wholes can have intrinsic value even if their necessary constitutive parts have none greatly widens the range of possible intrinsic goods and hence the opportunities for realizing the good life. It is thus crucial to Moore's ethics. Moore sought to resolve the conflicting valencies that organic unity had for his ontological and ethical projects by clearly distinguishing different senses of the notion to which the conflicting valencies could then be allocated. He thus moves from a virulent blanket rejection of organic unity in "The Refutation of Idealism" to a more careful and balanced tripartite analysis in *Principia Ethica*.[8]

For Moore's realism, organic unity is an inimical principle to be savaged, since it supplies his idealist opponents with a weapon for denying the force of the distinction between "a sensation or idea and...its object," a distinction crucial to Moore's argument that there is some real object beyond or distinct from what is perceived. According to Moore, though idealists would in some sense grant that green and the sensation of green can be distinguished, they would counter that "the things distinguished form an 'organic unity'...[such that] each would not be what it is *apart from its relation to the other*." Hence to consider them as "separable" or independent from each other is an "illegitimate abstraction," and thus any apparent distinction between them cannot be used to argue for the reality of green or green objects outside our ideational experiencing of green. Moore describes the principle of organic unity as asserting "that whenever you try to assert *anything whatever* of that which is a *part* of an organic whole, what you assert can only be true of the whole"; and he roundly condemns it as absurdly implying (given the premise of true universal substitutivity entailing identity) that the whole is absolutely identical with the part while at the same time presuming them somehow distinct by contrasting them (*RI* 14–15). This summary rejection of organic unity is accompanied by a derisive denunciation of its Hegelian source.

> The principle of organic unities...is mainly used to defend the practice of holding both of two contradictory propositions, wherever this may seem convenient. In this, as in other matters, Hegel's main service to philosophy has consisted in giving a name to and erecting into a principle, a type of fallacy to which experience had shown philosophers, along with the rest of mankind to be addicted. No wonder that he has followers and admirers. (*RI* 16)

The critique of Hegelian organic unity gains detail and rigor in *Principia Ethica*, where Moore distinguishes between three senses of "organic unity" or "organic whole," two of which he endorses. The first is where the parts of a whole are so related "that the continued existence of...one [part] is a necessary condition for the continued existence of the other [parts]; while the continued existence of...[the] latter is also a necessary condition for the continued existence of the former" (*PE* 31). This conception is more than the mere assertion that an organic whole could not exist precisely as it does if its parts were not precisely what they were. For that will hold for any whole rather than mark a specifically organic one. It seems a trivial logical truth that any change of a whole's parts must change to some extent that whole, which then, *ex hypothesi*, would have different parts and thus be a different whole.[9]

What Moore's first sense of organic unity instead asserts is that not simply the whole, but its constituent parts could not survive the destruction of other parts. In such an organic whole the constituent parts (or at least some of them) have "a relation of mutual causal dependence on one another" (*PE* 32), the sort of relation once thought (before recent advances in medical technology) to exist between the various vital organs of the body. One's heart would not simply stop being a part of the same body if one's lungs and liver were removed; it would soon stop existing altogether. But, as Moore implies (*PE* 32), such reciprocal dependence of parts can exist also in non-living structures.

Though Moore accepts this first, "causal" sense of organic unity, it is not the sense he finds so indispensably useful to his ethics and aesthetics. The crucial organic phenomenon is rather that a whole can have emergent properties which are not reducible or even proportionate to the properties of its constituent parts. Moore typically expresses this principle of holistic organicist emergence in terms of value: that an organic whole "has an intrinsic value different in amount from the sum of the values of its parts"; indeed "that *the value of such a whole bears no regular proportion to the sum of the values of its parts*" (*PE* 27, 36). But since he clearly recognizes that there is no difference in value without difference in properties (*PE* 35), this sense of organic unity can be more generally regarded as a unity where the properties of the whole are different from the sum of the properties of its individual parts and not reducible to them.

This sense differs from the first by allowing no inference from the existence of one part to the existence of the others without which that part could not exist. Here the organic relation is not a matter of the parts' reciprocal dependence for their existence but of the whole's dependence on the parts for its qualities and value. Of course, this second organic unity applies to living organisms, where the bodily system as a whole has special properties and value absent from its specific parts. Yet such unity is considered especially characteristic of works of art (which are not ordinarily organic in the first sense), and Moore thus illustrates it aesthetically: "All the parts of a picture do not have that relation of mutual causal dependence, which certain parts of the body have, and yet the existence of those which do not have it may be absolutely essential to the value of the whole" (*PE* 33). But again, such unity can easily be found outside the living and the (standardly) aesthetic, as any salad- or sandwich-maker knows.

These two notions of organic unity are then contrasted with the Hegelian one condemned in "The Refutation of Idealism." That suspect unity claims to be one where "just as the whole would not be what it is but for the existence of its parts, so the parts would not be what they are but for the existence of the whole." Therefore, "any particular part could not exist unless the others existed too" (*PE* 33). However, this is not the mere causal dependence of the first sense. It is rather a logical dependence, where the very essence or identity of the part involves the whole to which it is related, so that without the whole it would not strictly be the same part. The idea is that when a thing forms a part of such a whole, it possesses properties it would otherwise not possess – not merely the property of being part of the whole, but also more substantial emergent properties acquired through its participation in the whole. A hand when part of an organically whole human being has powers and properties different from that hand as a detached member. Things with different properties cannot be identical, so the hand as an organic part must be essentially different from that same hand cut off from the whole. Its different identity clearly seems due to or constituted by the whole to which it belongs. Since the whole allegedly forms part of its part's identity, that part cannot be what it is and loses its very "meaning or significance apart from its whole." Hence such "parts are inconceivable except as parts of that whole" (*PE* 34, 36).

Moore repudiates this form of organic unity as both confused and self-contradictory. It confuses emergent properties belonging properly only to the whole with intrinsic defining properties of the part itself. Secondly, it asserts, in effect, that any part of such a whole necessarily has that whole as part of that part itself; but this is inconsistent with the part's being a distinguishable part of that whole. The first point is that for a part to display an emergent property or value in conjunction with the whole's other parts but not to display it by itself in isolation means that it itself (i.e. the part) does not really have this property as part of its identity. For to display a property *only* as part of a whole, only together with other parts, is not to have the property at all, but rather to be part of that (i.e. the whole) which does have it. This idea that emergent properties and values belong only to the organic wholes as *wholes* and not properly to the parts whose conjunction in the whole produce them is the crucial point for Moore, and one he shrewdly employs in questions of ethical valuation. But it is easy enough to apply in aesthetics. We may, for example, point to a part of an artistic whole (say, a line in the picture of a face) and assert that this part is a silly or sly smile but wouldn't be one if not for the arrangement of the other lines of the face. But the silliness or slyness of the smile is, strictly speaking, a property of the whole face, not just of the single line; even though we may just point to that line, a single part of the whole, in order to focus perception so that this emergent expressive property of the whole is better grasped. Moore makes this point non-aesthetically in arguing against investing the human arm with the emergent properties it displays when connected with the living body.

we may easily come to say that *as* a part of the body, it [the arm] has great value, whereas *by itself* it would have none; and thus its whole 'meaning' lies in its relation to the body. But in fact the value in question does not belong to *it* at all. To have value merely as a part is equivalent to having no value at all, but merely being part of that which has it. Owing, however, to neglect of this distinction, the assertion that a part has value, *as a part*, which it would not otherwise have, easily leads to the assumption that it is also different, *as a part*, from what it would otherwise be; for it is, in fact, true that two things which have a different value must also differ in other respects. (*PE* 35)

There remains the further charge of self-contradiction. At the same time that this organic principle asserts that there is a part (*P*), which helps to form a whole (*W*) and is therefore logically distinguishable from *W*, it denies that *P* has any such independent or distinguishable nature of its own, but rather that its very identity involves the whole (*W*) and its system of interrelations of which it is a part. Thus, while *P* is originally identified as being distinct from *W*, as being a mere part of *W*, it is then contradictorily taken as analytically including *W* as part of itself, since it itself is constituted by the whole set of *W*'s interrelations of parts. In other words, the radical notion of organic unity requires that any individual part we distinguish as contributing to form the whole cannot be so distinguished. It cannot be the same part in itself and as part of the whole, because as part of the whole it has different essential or constitutive properties (viz. those of its emergent interrelations and value with the other parts in the whole). Thus we are led to the contradiction that *P* is and is not part of the whole, *W*; or alternatively that *P* is not *P* (since it is not the same thing when it is part of the whole and when it is isolated). As Moore sums it up, "the assumption that one and the same thing, because it is a part of a more valuable whole at one time than at another, therefore has more intrinsic value at one time than at another, has encouraged the self-contradictory belief that one and the same thing may be two different things, and that only in one of its forms is it truly what it is" (*PE* 35).

III

Moore's critique of organic unity derives its power from such deeply entrenched principles as the laws of identity and contradiction and the reality of self-identical particulars or logically independent individuals.

But it is not immune to criticism. In the first place, his tripartite analysis does not exhaust the senses of organic unity that have been influential in intellectual history. What is most clearly lacking in Moore is any awareness of the temporal, vitalistic, developmental sense of organic unity, which was very important in romantic aesthetics[10] and, of course, in Dewey's. For Dewey and the romantics, an organic whole was a dynamic unity whose parts evolve and unfold into the whole they form by some process of natural growth or ordered development.

There is good reason why Moore's account of organic unity ignores temporality and vitalistic development. For to admit such fluidity to his account might suggest that what his commonsense understanding grasps firmly as the particular, logically independent, and stable parts of a whole are not fixedly given in the nature of things. And if what counts as a part can change with time, if parts can simply be differently constituted by different temporal interpretations of an array into parts and wholes, then the whole idea of the logically durable self-identity of parts becomes more problematic, while the Moorean commonsense argument from contradiction which relies on it becomes much less compelling. From a Hegelian perspective, one might say that in ignoring the temporal aspect and the formative play of the mind in its shifting interpretive constitution of what the parts and whole are, Moore locks himself into the secure but philosophically jejune level of commonsense understanding. This level naively thinks that the objects, parts, and wholes with which we deal are fixed, autonomous realities, while the Hegelian and deconstructionist will instead regard them as but the flexible abstractions and constructed products of the activity of mind or of language's play of differences.[11] Pragmatism also regards them as products of human practices and purposes; but it insists that our commonsense objects, parts, and wholes can still be quite firm and reliable, given the adamant durability of some of our practices.

Not only does deconstruction challenge Moore's analytic commitment to the fixed self-identity of parts, but it attacks the analytically endorsed *aesthetics* of organic unity by relying precisely on the radical logical sense of this notion which Moore put in question. The best way to show this is by showing how deconstruction's critique of aesthetic unity relies on the notion of *différance* and by showing how *différance* is essentially a version or corollary or application of the older notion of radical organic unity. Let us start from the second point.

Derrida's concept of *différance* is based on the Saussurian structuralist idea that in the linguistic system "there are only differences, *without posi-*

tive terms."[12] For example, the identity of any particular phoneme is not constituted by any positive essence, any real distinctive acoustic sound (for it is realizable in a multitude of qualitatively different sounds), but instead by its differential relations with other phonemes in the system. Building on Saussure and recognizing further that all the objects and concepts of our world are linguistically mediated, Derrida asserts that all the objects, elements, or categories of discourse are also differentially constituted and do not rest on foundationally real, positive essences beyond the differential network of language. They "do not have as their cause a subject or substance, a thing in general, or a being that is somewhere present and itself escapes the play of difference"; and he warns against the metaphysical response to supply such positive elements, "to respond with a definition of essence, of quiddity, to reconstitute a system of essential predicates."[13]

Différance, then, is "a structure and a movement...of...the systematic play of differences, of traces of differences, of the *spacing* by which elements are related to each other...without which the 'full' terms would not signify, would not function" (*Pos* 27). In other words, since any thing or element depends for its individuation and meaning on its differential interrelations with other elements, it follows that what any thing is, is essentially a function of what it is not. Since it is thus constituted by its differential relations with elements which, as different, are neither simply present *in* it nor necessarily simultaneously or contiguously present *with* it (and here the deferring sense of *différance* is displayed), any thing or element is never fully present in itself or constituted simply by (or for) itself.

> The play of differences supposes...syntheses and referrals which forbid at any moment, or in any sense, that a simple element be *present* in and of itself, referring only to itself..., no element can function...without referring to another element which itself is not simply present. This interweaving results in each "element"...being constituted on the basis of the trace within it of the other elements of the chain or system....Nothing, neither among the elements nor within the system, is anywhere ever simply present or absent. There are only, everywhere, differences and traces of traces. (*Pos* 26)

The essential sameness of *différance* and the radical concept of organic unity should now appear obvious, especially if we take the notion of whole as representing the (perhaps not fully totalizable) system or structure of linguistic differences. For, as we saw, radical organicism asserts that any part or element "can have no meaning or significance apart from its whole," that no individual part can be a self-identical, self-sufficient "distinct object of thought," since all "the parts would not be what they are but for the existence of the whole," "are inconceivable except as parts of that whole," for each part derives its meaning from its relations to the whole's other parts (*PE* 33, 34, 36). Now since any object that we ordinarily conceive as a whole can itself be seen as part of a larger whole, structure, or system (at the very least in the minimal, vague sense that it is part of the world), we can apply this principle of organic, differential identity to any object. From this logical principle of organic unity or *différance*, it then follows that what any object is, is essentially a function of what it is not; it is essentially constituted by its differential relations with other objects from which it is distinguished but without whose associative, relational distinctions it could not be, or be distinguished as, what it is.

As Moore recognized, this idea can be traced back to Hegel, that philosopher of the whole most repudiated by analytic thinkers: "Everything that exists stands in correlation, and this correlation is the veritable nature of every existence. The existent thing in this way has no being of its own, but only in something else."[14] But the same idea is also salient in Nietzsche (another Teutonic protodeconstructor and analytic anathema), where it forms the logical core of his central doctrines of the will to power and the eternal recurrence. "'Things that have a constitution in themselves' – a dogmatic idea with which one must break absolutely," exhorts Nietzsche. "In the actual world...everything is bound to and conditioned by everything else." Thus "no things remain but only dynamic quanta, in a relation of tension to all other dynamic quanta: their essence lies in their relation to all other quanta."[15]

IV

How is this organicistic logic of *différance* deployed in deconstructing organic unity as an aesthetic notion? It provides the structuring logical foundation for the two major arguments aimed at undermining the very coherence of the notion of a work of art's unity. As is characteristic of deconstructive arguments, both start with assumptions of aesthetic unity, but then work through them to reveal aporia or internal contradictions within the very idea of such unity and necessarily violating it.

The first argument concerns the sense of wholeness and integrity contained in the idea of a work's organic unity. We regard the work as a distinct integral whole, composed of the parts belonging to it and complete in itself as constituted by those and only those parts. But such unity, it is argued, is constituted only on the basis of distinguishing and excluding something outside it, elements not part of or constitutive of the unified whole. If we hold with Aristotle that an organically unified work must have a beginning, middle, and end (or even just a beginning and end), we must recognize that it can't have them without having something before the beginning and beyond its end in order to mark them and shape or frame the work they try to enclose. Thus, what is alleged to be outside, apart from, or irrelevant to the self-sufficient work as a whole, becomes essential to it and constitutive of it. What seems to lie outside the work and beyond it is as much a part of what makes the work as the constitutive parts inside the work. The whole distinction between inside and outside the work, on which the notion of integral unity rests, becomes problematized when what lies outside the work becomes essential to its inside. The very possibility of the work as a distinct organic unity composed only of its parts is voided when the work is seen to be equally constituted by what are not its parts but rather that which frames them. Its unity of parts, constituted by what is foreign and contrastively opposed to this unity, is thus fundamentally and ineluctably self-divided rather than unified.

Culler employs this line of argument, asserting "that the 'organic unity' of works of art is the product of framing," which relies on "the distinction between inside and outside [that] evades precise formulation," a distinction between an external background or supplementary frame and the unified totality of the work this frames. But then "this marginal supplement" or outside is therefore "essential, constituting, enshrining"; for "framing is what creates the aesthetic object." Though outside the work's intrinsic structure, "the frame is what gives us an object that can have an intrinsic content or structure." So for Culler, the external or marginal to the work "becomes central by virtue of its very marginality" (*OD* 195–9).

Culler's dialectical argument of the frame (elaborated both in terms of criticism as a framing discourse of literature and in terms of the framing metalinguistic devices in the literary work itself) is taken from Derrida's analysis of the frame as *parergon*. Their formulations may seem somewhat more complex than the organicistic argument I outlined above. But this is only because the frame itself, as they see it, is not clearly identified with the outside of the work. Rather, in Derrida's words, "it is a *parergon*, a composite of inside and outside, but a composite which is not an amalgam or half-and-half but an outside which is called inside the inside to constitute it as inside."[16] Nonetheless, we have here the same essential argument. For it is the frame's being outside which makes it be summoned and drawn into the inside to make the inside an inside, just as it is the excluded external non-parts in the logical principle of organic unity which are ineluctably reinscribed as essential and constitutive of the internal parts.

The second argument against the work of art as a unified whole concerns not the work's distinction from what is outside it, but rather distinction within the work itself. To constitute the work as a unity of parts, we need to distinguish some coherent structure of parts in the whole, a structure which is in some sense privileging or hierarchical. We therefore typically speak of what is central as opposed to marginal in a work; and analytic aestheticians often distinguish the work's "hard core of essential features" from "the surrounding penumbra of inessential ones," or in Goodman's terms its "constitutive" from its "contingent" properties.[17] We are all familiar with the conventions of literary competence by which we disregard some features of the text as ancillary, inessential, or accidental in order to concentrate on what really counts in the text. Apparently insignificant words or punctuation, the text's visual shape and color[18], the homonymic meanings or alternative uses of its words, distant associations that they might raise in other fields but which are plainly out of place in the given literary context – all these we standardly dismiss as being beside the point and as obstructing, if we focus on them, the real meaning and unity of the work.

However, the deconstructors ask, if these irrelevant aspects belong to the text, what justification is there for branding them irrelevant or inessential vis-à-vis some contrasting essence of the text? For by the logical principle of organicism, the essential properties or meanings could neither be nor be distinguished as essential if not for the so-called irrelevant and inessential ones which frame them. And if the inessential is thus revealed as essential to the essential, this would undermine the privileging structure of parts and meanings which constitutes the work as a unity. It would moreover suggest that the inessential (as essential) deserves our attention as critics and appreciators; but such attention would seem to disrupt the psychologically experienced unity of the work. Unity is thus undone both objectively and subjectively.

This argument, saliently reflected in Derrida's logic of marginality or supplementarity and in deconstruction's interpretive practice of focusing on textual "irrelevancies," is set out most clearly in Culler. "Interpretation generally relies on distinctions between the central and the marginal, the essential and the inessential: to interpret is to discover what is central to a text or group of texts." But since marginality is not something ontologically given but a product of interpretational framing, "what has been relegated to the margins or set aside by previous interpreters may be important for precisely those reasons." Yet the fact that we can "reverse a hierarchy to show that...[the] marginal is in fact central" does not lead "to the identification of a new center..., but to a subversion of the distinctions between essential and inessential, inside and outside. What is a center if the marginal can become central" (*OD*, 140)? Moreover, building on de Man's suggested reversal of the traditional "ethos of explication" by attempting "a reading that would no longer blindly submit to the teleology of controlled meaning,"[19] Culler repudiates "our inclination to use notions of unity and thematic coherence to exclude possibilities" of meaning that would pose a problem for a coherent interpretation of the text "because they would disrupt the focus or continuity" of such a reading (*OD* 246–7).

This further twist of the argument is important, since a defender of unity might concede the point that the marginal or inessential is logically essential for framing but then go on to argue that we must not confuse such essentiality with aesthetic centrality or worthiness for aesthetic attention. In rejoinder, Culler would first point out that our standard for judging what in a text is central or appropriate for aesthetic appreciation is the criterion of its fit or contribution to the postulated unity of the text. But this, he would then insist, is precisely to beg the question that the text is unified. We cannot appeal to the text's disputed organic unity to prove that unity. Nor do we have the right to posit as a metaphysical axiom that literary works are organic unities by virtue of some special ontological status, irrespective of the intentional acts of authors and interpreters. De Man's critique of New Criticism for reifying the literary work into an autonomously organic form is compellingly correct here. The postulated unity of a text (like the text's meaning) is at most an intentional structure, hermeneutically and contextually constructed; it is not a foundational and unchanging given.

But before we deconstructively scrap the idea of unity, pragmatism intervenes to recover it. For without foundational unity, there remains pragmatic justification for postulating unity in the work as a strategy of reading and an interpretive criterion of relevance and centrality. For rich unity and the satisfactions it affords are what we primarily seek in reading literary texts. Culler is quick to reject this aim as reflecting a narrowly formalist hedonism, as falsely relegating literary works to the realm of play and pleasure, devoid of the cognitive rigor and seriousness which close reading involves. Defensively reacting to alleged hedonistic excesses of some older deconstructors like Barthes and Hartman, he and Christopher Norris eschew the interpretive aim of "enriching elucidations" and "refuse to make aesthetic richness an end." Instead they posit deconstruction's "demonstrable rigour" and the "feelings of mastery" achieved through its decentering readings as the privileged, overriding aim of criticism.[20] But if the pleasure of aesthetic richness provides its own immediate justification, Norris and Culler's indictment of it lacks any similarly compelling power. Their attitude rather reflects not only a perverse puritanism (directed at the dismembering of "seductively" pleasurable verbal icons) but also the presumption of a false dichotomy between reading for pleasure and reading for empowerment.

If our human need to perceive and experience satisfying unities in the disordered flux of experience is what motivates our interest in art, this need should not be rejected. What we should reject is the repressive limitation of art to the expression of only such unity, the prohibition of jarring fragmentation and incoherencies which can have their own stimulating aesthetic (and cognitive) effect, and which can result in more complex forms of coherence. Similarly, we should reject the fetishizing of art's objects as if they were independently valuable unities in themselves, apart from their work in experience. Finally, as we stressed in chapter 1, even the unity of aesthetic experience must not be fetishistically embalmed into something static, permanent, and isolated from the flow of life. Pragmatism's insistence on these provisos does not deny, however, its firm recognition of the value of unity.

Culler might dismiss our presumptive bias for unity as merely a cultural "convention" of literary competence, and therefore arbitrary and dispensable. But such a move falsely assumes that all our cultural conventions are indeed superficially arbitrary, an assumption based on an uncritical acceptance of the natural/conventional distinction. As I have elsewhere argued, there is no sharp line to be drawn between natural and culturally informed or "conventional" human interests and practices. Many of our so-called conventions are so deeply entrenched that we naturally employ them and take them as basic to our form of life. Doing without them, if indeed feasible, would be doing most poorly, alienating ourselves from what constitutes our very forms of thinking, action, and experience.[21] With respect to our conventional aesthetic prejudice toward unity, Culler is honest enough to admit that "the critical writings that most vigorously proclaim their celebration of heterogeneity are likely to reveal, under exegetical scrutiny, their reliance on notions of organic unity which are not easy to banish" (*OD* 200). This indeed is precisely what we have seen in Derrida and Culler's own celebration of the philosophical heterogeneity of *différance*.

There is another pragmatic justification for the interpretive presumption of a work's unity. It is the Heideggerian-Gadamerian idea that interpretive understanding is the working-out of a partial fore-understanding based on "the fore-conception of completion," the presumption "that only what really constitutes a unity of meaning is intelligible." The very same pragmatic linkage of unity with intelligibility underlies Dewey's definition of inquiry as the transformation of a confusing problem-situation "into a unified whole." We always expect a text (or action) to issue in some coherent whole when it is worked out and understood. Thus, when it seems incoherent, either in itself or in its relation to our views on what it concerns, we need to interpret it so that some "unified meaning can be realized."[22] We typically do this either by interpreting the text as more coherent with itself and with our beliefs or by interpreting its incoherencies within a coherent explanatory account (e.g. its author's different cultural or psychological context or his desire to express incoherence so as to shock us); in other words, understanding incoherence and disunity within a larger coherent totality of meaning. Even de Man, while criticizing organic unity as a naturalistic reification, still recognized its hermeneutic reality: the undeniable "intent at totality of the interpretative process," "the necessary presence of a totalizing principle as the guiding impulse of the critical process."[23]

However, this principle of interpretive holism, the idea that intelligibility somehow relies on some idea of unity, has been denounced by Derrida as the pervasive error of "the axiomatic structure of metaphysics, insofar as *metaphysics itself* desires, or dreams, or imagines its own unity." "Since Aristotle, and at least up until Bergson, 'it' (metaphysics) has constantly repeated and assumed that to think and to say must mean to think and to say something that would be a *one*, one *matter*."[24] Analytic philosophy has expressed this assumption in the view that all intelligible thought and language rely on "individuating reference" and that anything we can refer to (hence speak about) must be self-identical. As the once popular dictum put it, "no entity without identity." But to what extent is this assumption of unity and identity really necessary, valid, or even possible? Are there "ones" that we can really refer to and distinguish as independent from others? Must we at least presume that there are, and in what way must these "ones" be unified?[25] We are thus led back to organic unity at its most fundamental and challenging level – as a principle of logic, metaphysics, and philosophy of language, a principle which perhaps most sharply divides analysis and deconstruction, yet binds them in an unavoidable and perhaps interminable agon of confrontation.

V

We should recall that Moore attacks organic unity first for mistaking the emergent relational properties of the whole for defining properties of a given part, and second for self-contradictorily holding that a part is both logically distinct from the whole (and other parts in the whole) and yet essentially includes them all as part of its own nature. The force of both these criticisms clearly depends on the assumption that we can really talk about a part and its intrinsic nature. Yet it is precisely this assumption that radical organic unity is challenging when it asserts that everything (hence any part) lacks intrinsic features of its own but is constituted solely through its interrelations with and differences from everything else – relations which (as Nietzsche and Hegel would urge) are not foundationally fixed but the product of (possibly changing) interpretation. Any identification of a part depends on what other parts it is interpreted as being related to and distinguished from; there are no parts, like no facts, without interpretation.[26] But if there is no identity apart from interpretation, we can dismiss the charge that the part's identity is misdescribed or self-contradictorily construed. Parts simply become different parts by being differently interpreted in terms of different interrelations. Moore's logic-chopping argument has lost its blade.

To this differential, interpretive account of identity the analyst might respond in two related ways. He could argue that the whole notion of differences or interrelations presupposes that there are entities differentiated or interrelated and that we cannot speak of an entity without identity. Difference relies conceptually on identity as much as identity seems to presuppose the idea of difference. The inseparability of these notions seems to be James's pragmatist point in listing "the same or different" as *one* of our most important commonsense concepts.[27] But the deconstructor and pragmatist could cogently reply that this need not entail foundational self-identical substances, since sufficient identity for differentiation is provided in the idea of "identity according to a particular interpretation." Similarly, the analytic argument that real particulars are required as the individual referents necessary for thought and discourse can be answered by allowing that such referents could simply be individuals according to some interpretation.

The analyst might then press further by questioning more specifically the basic differential terms or Nietzschean "dynamic quanta" that deconstruction sees as entering into the interrelational interpretations which constitute all objects. What are these interpretational elements? If they are basic atoms, then some things which enter into the interpretive constitution of objects are not themselves so constituted. If, instead, these basic elements are themselves the product of interpreting still more basic elements in *their* interrelations, then we can and should ask the same question about those. Recursively applying this analytic strategy (the essential strategy of logical atomism), we must either end in atomic elements of some sort or instead "never end" in an infinite regress or circle of interpretations where ultimately there is nothing beyond interpretations to interpret. This is not simply a question of the independent world collapsing into the texts which represent it. Here the very idea of text itself dissolves into interpretations without any independent "interpretation-free" text or object which they are interpretations of.[28]

Derrida would hardly flinch at such consequences, and he would certainly repudiate the analytic argument (with its reductive quest for original foundations) as a paradigm symptom of that onto-theological metaphysics which has so long enthralled our thought. In responding to Searle, he warned that the analytic "enterprise of returning 'strategically', ideally, to an origin or to a 'priority' held to be simple, intact, normal, pure, standard, self-identical...is not just *one* metaphysical gesture among others; it is *the* metaphysical exigency."[29] Pragmatism would similarly reject the metaphysical strategy of infinite regress, insisting that in actual life and thinking there is always a point where it is pointless or even meaningless to go back further in regressive analysis or explanation.

The metaphysical roots of traditional analysis are surely clear.[30] What is far from clear, however, is whether deconstruction, in its very critique of analysis, is not itself ensnared by a metaphysics which it desperately seeks to avoid. For the notion of organic unity which underlies its critique seems to reflect a potent and pervasive metaphysical gesture of its own. The deconstructive idea that everything is a product of its interrelations and differences from other things, that nothing has an independent or intrinsic nature, rests at bottom on the idea that all things are indeed ineluctably interconnected. This idea of the world as an organic totality or system of terms, whose relationality undermines the existence of independent substances, is explicit in Hegel and Nietzsche, where it saliently looms as a metaphysical thesis. To recall, in Hegel: "Everything that exists stands in correlation, and this correlation is the veritable nature of every existence. The existent thing in this way has no being of its own, but only in something else." Similarly with Nietzsche, who is probably closest to Derrida: "In the actual world...everything is bound to and conditioned by everything else." There is nothing "but dynamic quanta, in a relation of tension to all other dynamic quanta: their essence lies in their relation to all other quanta." "Every atom affects the whole of being."[31]

This view of the world as a totality of interrelated and reciprocally defined elements, a world whose apparently independent individual objects are simply interpretive constructs of such internal systemic relations – is this not a metaphysical view? And why should we accept it as a true one? Derrida himself has condemned the idea of "a totality of beings" as a dangerous metaphysical idea, one from which he would like to extricate Nietzsche (and ultimately, if unknowingly, himself).[32] Perhaps the best way to effect this escape would be to regard Nietzschean cosmological organicism not as a foundational metaphysical view but simply as one more interpretive perspective on the world. The problem, then, is that mere perspectival status seems to rob organic unity of its power to refute the "atomist" or ordinary perspective which sees the world as having things with definite properties or constitutions of their own. As merely another perspective on the world, what does radical organicism have to offer? It surely does not provide a view either congenial to or practical for our entrenched logocentric ways of speaking, thinking, and acting; and its advocates quite openly and happily admit this. Is it then offered on more aesthetic than pragmatic grounds? There is, we should stress, nothing wrong with assessing ontological perspectives aesthetically; and perhaps nothing ultimately divides their aesthetic and pragmatic justification. Certainly Quine's ontological minimalism was simultaneously linked both to pragmatism and to "a taste for desert landscapes."[33]

Though primarily employed to undermine the aesthetic satisfaction of the alleged unities of artworks, the ontological perspective implied by deconstructive organic unity or *différance* may seem to offer some other sort of aesthetic satisfaction: a peculiarly metaphysical aesthetic gratification. For it presents the chaotic and unfathomable congeries of our world as ultimately (or, at least, best construable as) an organic whole of essentially interrelated elements which have no life or meaning apart from their interconnections and which can be differently arranged, shaped, and manipulated by intervening interpretation. We can therefore look through the shattered and disjointed fragments of our postmodern wasteland and see them all as one vast sum and unity of essentially interrelated objects. Moreover, besides the satisfying, reassuring consolation of this comprehensive unity, there is the comforting promise that any disturbing fact or object in the world can simply be transfigured or deconstructed by reinterpretation of the differential elements into more pleasing interpretive constructions.

This unity will strike many (the analyst, the pragmatist, and the layman) as too remote and metaphysical to be of much real comfort. It seems an unsatisfying substitute for the loss of the traditionally entrenched unities we are accustomed to regard as the individual objects or beautiful artworks of our ordinary world, things which deconstructive organic unity asks us to question or abandon. But if our faith in those unities has already been lost – if, as marginalized intellectuals in the humanities, we have become disenchanted with both the ideology of facts and the facts themselves and even with the works of art through which we hoped to escape the facts – then the principle of organic unity offers some solace of unification. For not only is everything essentially connected, but all facts dissolve into interpretations.

Pragmatism, to my mind the best mediator and option between analysis and deconstruction, can also see things as being in some sense (or having been at some time) interpretations, but interpretations so inextricably entrenched in our actual thinking that they take the status of fact or reality. However, it need not rush from the unavailability of foundational facts to hermeneutics' and deconstruction's totalizing conclusion that all understanding is interpretation (or misinterpretation), that in the free and fluid play of intelligible experience there is nothing to distinguish them, no priority or hierarchy. For this would be giving up a frequently useful distinction between understanding and interpretation, between what we grasp without requiring further elucidation and what needs to be interpreted for us to handle it satisfactorily.[34] Because reality for the pragmatist is basically what has "coerciveness, in the long run, over thought," while truth is roughly "whatever proves itself to be good in the way of belief" and "expedient in the way of our thinking," "in the long run and on the whole," pragmatism will be closer than deconstruction to the world view of common sense, with its particular objects and independent things having properties of their own.[35] But it will not want to proceed from this way of taking the world to a fundamental metaphysical inference regarding what ultimately there is. It will want to leave that ontological question open or, perhaps better yet, simply leave it as futile and empty.

Derrida would no doubt deny that his version of organic unity or *différance* is caught up with the metaphysics of totality. For does he not explicitly repudiate the idea of totality? But it is hard to see how we can make sense of the systematic differential production of meaning without presupposing the idea of at least a provisional (and possibly ever expanding) totality of interrelated terms. Derrida himself, while maintaining that language excludes totalization, characterizes its differential field as "a field of infinite substitutions in *the closure of a finite ensemble.*"[36] Moreover, even forgoing the question of totality, the very presumption that *all* the elements or objects of our world are essentially differentially interconnected and reciprocally constitutive of each other (however untotaled or untotalizable they may be) clearly seems in itself to constitute a metaphysical perspective predisposed to cosmic unity and coherence.

Confronting traditional analytic philosophy with deconstruction on the deepest ontological level, we are confronted with a choice: Russell and Wittgenstein's atomistic metaphysics of foundationally independent and self-identical entities which form the structure of facts through their external relations, versus the Nietzschean deconstructive picture in which there are no such separate individual entities or unities, but only because there is a much vaster differential unity of all there is, an all-embracing unity whose internal differential relations are what constitute that which the analyst takes as individual things. What the pragmatist sees on this ontological level (where she is reluctant to tread) is neither: neither a world of autonomous atoms nor one solely of integrated interrelations and their essentially connected, reciprocally constituted terms. What she instead sees (on an ontological level where she feels more comfortable) is rather "a world imperfectly unified still," largely "the common-sense world, in which we find things partly joined and partly disjoined," things which are self-identical but whose individuation depends on our practices and purposes.[37]

And what does the pragmatist want with respect to organic unity? James provides a handy declaration which suggests an answer while it weaves some themes and catchwords of analysis and deconstruction. "Provided you grant *some* separation among things, some tremor of independence, some free play of parts on one another, some real novelty and chance, however minute, she is amply satisfied, and will allow you any amount, however great, of real union."[38] Though deeply appreciative of unity, pragmatism should equally respect difference; and this respect goes beyond ontology and aesthetics – to ethics, politics, and race and gender issues. Organic unity, at least in those versions where the different parts enjoy some relative autonomy, can perhaps provide a model for non-repressive unity or harmony in difference.

Finally, where should pragmatism stand on the question of essence? Clearly, it must reject the foundationalist idea of immutable essences which permanently define the different identities of our objects and concepts. Like deconstruction, pragmatism recognizes that such identities are the product of perspectival grasping and revisable linguistic practices, and thus are always subject to reinterpretation. This insight may incite a radical anti-essentialism which insists not only on the ubiquity of interpretation but on the absolute contingency and arbitrary particularity of everything. Such a pragmatism, strongly advocated by Richard Rorty, seems, however, to turn into an inverted essentialism of anti-essentialism which asserts "the universality and necessity of the individual and contingent."[39]

Of course, in the sense of logical necessity, everything may be contingent. But some things are clearly more contingent than others, and failure to distinguish between these differing sorts of contingencies simply reflects our bad philosophical habit of absolutist thinking. If there are no logical necessities in our world, there remain probabilities that constitute practical certainty; if there are no foundational essences, there remain historical norms (alterable and contestable as they are) which structure and regulate our linguistic and other social practices, thus serving, so to speak, as relative historicized essences.

A post-Rortyan pragmatism needs to recognize this more moderate yet more liberated option. For once we really break free of foundationalist metaphysics, the notion of essential properties (and the distinction between essential and inessential) can be pragmatically reinterpreted and redeemed for use. Similarly, a true break with foundationalist epistemology allows the pragmatist to reinterpret the nature and role of interpretation itself. To this issue we now turn.

4

Pragmatism and Interpretation

I

There are at least three rather different and influential theories of interpretation which claim to be pragmatist. Knapp and Michaels' theory is rigidly intentionalistic and author-bound, while Richard Rorty's contrastingly emphasizes the production of non-authorial readings. The third, advanced by Stanley Fish, submits (and dissolves) both author and reader to the notion of the interpretive community as the authority determining the proper meaning of a text. In this chapter I shall investigate these rival theories, examining them in the light of more general pragmatist principles. The purpose of this exercise is not to award the birthright for the most authentically pragmatist theory, but to reach a better understanding of interpretation and its variety, and this might not be formulable in a single global theory of interpretation.[1]

Before examining these pragmatist theories, we should place them in the context of the analytic and deconstructive theorizing with which they must contend. Both analysis and deconstruction have been largely concerned with interpretation's locus of authority and cognitive status after the interpretive authority of the author had been challenged both by Wimsatt and Beardsley's doctrine of the intentional fallacy and by Barthes' declaration of the "death of the author."[2] Authorial intention long thrived as interpretation's alleged aim and criterion, for it provides (in theory) a determinate unchanging standard for judging the legitimacy of different interpretations. But since this unique and fixed meaning is guaranteed *only* in theory, it also allows a continuing diversity of interpretive efforts and approaches.

In short, the elusive notion of authorial intention paradoxically offers the security of objective truth and convergence in literary interpretation (something that academic criticism requires for its legitimation as a scientific enterprise), while at the same time providing the security that this objective truth or meaning cannot be conclusively demonstrated once and for all, thereby ensuring the continued demand for interpretation.[3] This demand may be even more crucial than truth to the critical profession, where the production of ever new interpretations and critical perspectives is necessary for its own reproduction and advancement (as it is for the personal careers of its participants). Such pressures can explain why recent academic criticism has so enthusiastically embraced, first, the banishment of the author (already in New Criticism) and then, the further banishment of the circumscribed, determinate work so as to exult in the productive freedom of pluralistic textuality advocated by Barthes and deconstruction. Anglo-American theorists who oppose this freewheeling interpretive productivity express the fear that it will destroy the coherence of criticism as a scholarly cognitive discipline converging on the truth.[4] Much of the debate between analytic and deconstructive interpretive theory can be seen as a debate over the primacy of truth versus creative productivity.

Even when it abandoned authorial intention, analytic theory typically assumed that interpretive intentions were (or should be) essentially uniform in being motivated by some determinate truth. In arguing for the difference between a text's meaning and what its author intended it to mean, Beardsley recognizes that this difference permits at least two different interpretive projects, "to discover the textual meaning...and to discover the authorial meaning." While he recommends the choice of textual meaning because of its greater availability and richer aesthetic rewards, he insists that the interpreter's aim is not aesthetic richness *per se* but truth or correctness, where interpretations "must be *in principle* capable of being shown to be true or false." The "*general* and *essential task*" of interpretation is thus discovery of the text's own meaning, a meaning determined by public linguistic rules and determinate enough not to permit contradictory interpretive statements to be correct.[5]

The theorists whom Beardsley attacks nevertheless share his assumption that legitimate interpretation essentially aims at descriptive truth or some relativized cognitive analogue. Hirsch is committed to the goal of "knowledge in interpretation," believing that literary study must be a form of "humanistic knowledge," where qualified interpreters, "working together or in competition, can add to the knowledge" of literature through "empirical inquiry."[6] Indeed, he advocates authorial intention as the criterion of textual meaning expressly to secure the goal of objective interpretive knowledge, the argument being that only a text's determinacy of meaning will allow such knowledge and that only authorial intention can provide such determinacy. Thus, though aware that "authorial intention is not the only possible norm of interpretation," Hirsch holds that "it is the only practical norm for a cognitive discipline of interpretation."[7] Without it, he claims, there is simply too much freedom, indeterminacy, and instability in the public linguistic conventions governing meaning to secure convergence on a single interpretation with which the work may be identified, thereby constituting a stable object for study and criticism.

Joseph Margolis, Beardsley's other major target, might seem an exception to the cognitive monism of Anglo-American interpretive theory, since he advocates a "robust relativism" which frees interpretive validity not only from authorial intention but also from strict determinacy of meaning, thereby allowing the possible validity of conflicting interpretations.[8] Yet, although he liberally accepts the plurality and non-convergence of interpretive approaches and conclusions, Margolis remains confined to a "cognitive conception of interpretation." Critical interpretation (in contrast to interpretive performance, to which it is in many ways quite similar) is essentially aimed at generating true or "truth-like" propositions; and the notions of plausibility and implausibility are introduced to supply such relativized " 'truth-values' other than true and false." Moreover, any plausible interpretation of a work must be based on descriptions of the work that are strictly true, rather than merely relativistically plausible: "interpretative claims must be compatible with what is (minimally) descriptively true of a given work.... No plausible account may be incompatible with an admittedly true statement." It is what Margolis calls "description," as distinguished from interpretation but as the necessary substratum for it, which provides the true statements on which any plausible interpretation must be based. Descriptions, unlike interpretations, are simply true or false of the artwork independent of relativizing critical context. They display the intolerance of incompatibles which Beardsley and Hirsch also ascribe to interpretations: either "an object...*has* or *has not* the properties... described." In contrast, " 'interpreting'...suggests a touch of virtuosity, an element of performance,...with emphasis...on some inventive use of the materials present, on the added contribution of the interpreter, and on a certain openness toward possible alternative interpretations."

Margolis here cleverly tries to satisfy the conflicting demands of determinate truth and continued productivity, which is also what Beardsley and Hirsch seek in their own, implicit manner. If for Hirsch the author's intention satisfies the claim of truth, its elusiveness promises continuing interpretation. If for Beardsley truth can be secured through public conventions of meaning, continued productivity of interpretation is assured through the fact that these conventions are continually changing. For Margolis, truth is given in description's account of the work of art's hard and undeniable properties, while interpretation's creative contribution toward extending the work beyond those core descriptive properties not only allows but encourages a continued, never ending interpretive productivity, based and constrained by truth but not confined to it. This strategy of distinguishing the moments of description and interpretation would be an ideal solution were it not for the fact that the distinction cannot be maintained in a firm, principled, more than pragmatic way.

Any idea of a firm and definite distinction between descriptive truth (presenting the work's core of incontrovertible properties) and interpretive elaboration is undermined by the fact that what is taken as descriptively true will often depend on which interpretation of the work we come to adopt.[9] For example, Hamlet's love for his father (which he both declares and expresses in mourning, melancholy behavior) has been taken as a descriptive "hard fact" of the play. But if we come to adopt the plausible Freudian interpretation of Hamlet's mood, delay, and behavior towards his mother, this apparent firm fact evaporates into Hamlet's self-deluding rationalization. More generally, we can be led from what we originally see as simple facts about the work to reach an interpretation of the work which dislodges or recasts the facts by showing the work in such a way that the original descriptions no longer ring true or adequate. Indeed, narrative art and our enjoyable surprises in reading are often based on this sort of phenomenon.

In other words, it is not that we all agree on how to describe the facts and differ only in what interpretations we elaborate from them. It is rather that the descriptive facts are simply whatever we all and strongly agree upon, while interpretations are simply what command less consensus and display (or tolerate) wider divergence. But if there is no fixed core of determinate descriptive properties which constitute the work and the incontrovertible factual base for any valid interpretation, then theories which presuppose it are undermined. Deconstruction exploits this perceived lack of permanent descriptive essence to argue that interpretation must always involve distortive change, that "all readings are misreadings".

II

Harold Bloom provides an excellent example of this monism of mis-reading and of the professionalist parochialism and productive pressures which foster it. In preaching "the defensive necessity of 'misprision' or strong 'misreading'," he insists that we "read to usurp, just as the poet writes to usurp"; and the essential thing that all seek to usurp is power or influence, which requires a certain freedom from past influence.[10] Bloom makes the common error of conflating reader with professional critic or interpreter, and thus equating the act of reading with the critical performance of formulating or presenting a critical interpretation. Such an interpretation, in order to make its professional way, must make some claim to originality so as to distinguish itself. Only thus can it emerge from the domination of prior interpretations which influenced it and be singled out for study among the many critical interpretations which the given work has already received (themselves often the product of professional pressures to provide published interpretations or "readings.") There is something more to the professional reader-interpreter than the simple desire to understand and enjoy. He must make his mark by creating his own interpretation which will influence others. When Bloom earlier says that "Reading...is a belated and all-but-impossible act, and if strong is always a misreading," he comes close to recognizing that there are other readers, malignly implicated as weak, who are free enough from literary ambition as to perhaps submit themselves sufficiently to a text and thus manage to read it. But Bloom immediately goes on to dismiss the importance of such reading, since it is only "the strong reader... whose readings will matter to others as well as to himself."[11] Only the critic who *writes* a novel interpretation, rather than a mere reader who simply performs a reading, will make his mark on the professional map, will enjoy the power (and avoid the anxiety) of influence which so preoccupies Bloom as professional critic.

If we find Bloom's argument for "the necessity of misreading" unconvincingly based on an unjustified dismissal of amateur, "weak readers," his fellow deconstructors are quick to bring heavier epistemological reasons to show that even the most submissive non-professional is compelled to misread. The fundamental line of argument is that all linguistic meaning and hence textual meaning is essentially context-dependent; and since contexts inexorably change, the meaning of a text cannot be exactly reproduced or recovered in a faithful reading. Building on Saussure, Derrida and his disciples see linguistic meaning not as based and anchored on a prior extra-linguistic reality to which language refers and from which it gets its meanings. Linguistic meaning is rather a product of the differential relations (paradigmatic and syntagmatic) between the various elements of the language system, which is ever open to new elements and continually transforming itself, and thus does not really constitute a structuralist *system* in the normal, closed, completely regulated sense. Language, with its root of *différance*, is instead a changing "systematic play of differences" which "is incompatible with the static, synchronic, taxonomic, ahistoric motives in the concept of *structure*" and displays "an irreducible and *generative* multiplicity."[12] This protean vision of language is then coupled with a naively pre-Wittgensteinian picture of understanding as the recapturing or reproduction of a particular intentional content or meaning-object so as to render true reading and understanding an altogether hopeless pursuit.

Thus Culler maintains that the notions of "reading and understanding [claim to] preserve or reproduce a content or meaning, maintain its identity, while misunderstanding and misreading distort it; they produce or introduce difference."[13] Yet he goes on to argue that this claim is groundless, since language (and hence its understanding) is always changing with context and thus always involves some difference, thereby making absolute identity, preservation, or replication of meaning an impossibility. As Culler pithily puts it, "meaning is context-bound but context is boundless;" "new contextual features...alter illocutionary force". Since meaning can never be completely circumscribed contextually so as to permit its perfect replication, then true reading or interpretation is rendered impossible, and "all readings are misreadings." While Bloom holds that all good readers purposely misread to usurp, even if they are not aware of this intention, Culler levels all readerly intentions by contending that with respect to the particular issue of misreading they do not really matter. For whatever the intentions of the reading subject (whose status as a fully autonomous agent is anyway challenged), he or she cannot help but misread since linguistic meaning necessarily can never repeat itself.

But Culler's argument is not compelling, for one of its two central premises is dangerously false. We should not deny deconstruction's tenet that language is to some extent in perpetual change and development, though we need to remember that much of this change is hardly significant and occurs on a dominant background of continuity. But the second premise – which construes reading, understanding, and interpretation as the recovery or reproduction of an identical semantic object, "a content or meaning" – purveys a perverse but pervasive philosophical picture which has long misguided interpretive theory. Meaning is hypostatized as a separate and autonomous object rather than recognized as something whose existence is essentially relational and inextricable from human socio-linguistic practices, a point that deconstruction, in its better moments, does well to emphasize.

As Wittgenstein labored to teach us, meaning is not a separate object or content, but merely the correlate of understanding. And understanding something is not the mirror-like capturing or replication of some fixed and determinate intentional object or semantic content. It is fundamentally an ability to handle or respond to that thing in certain accepted ways which are consensually shared, sanctioned, and inculcated by the community but which are nonetheless flexible and open to (divergent) interpretation and emendation. What counts as the proper response of true understanding not only depends on the normative practices of the given society but also varies with respect to different contexts within that society and its subcultures. We should expect, for example, different responses of understanding to figure in the ordinary, the literary, and the psychoanalytic understandings of an utterance. Wittgenstein himself recognized that understanding is contextual and not governed by a single universal criterion. He insisted that two general criteria for understanding the meaning of a word are the ability to use it correctly and the ability to explain its meaning; yet he also contends that one general criterion for understanding a poem would be to read it with suitable expression or cadence.[14]

III

Why, despite Wittgenstein's critique, is there such a persistent presumption that meaning is an object of determinate content (whether for true description or misreading)? Part of the reason is that such "meaning realism" provides a clear model of interpretive knowledge. For how, Hirsch argues, can there be any truth or knowledge of a text's meaning, if there is no meaning-object to be true to, to serve as the "object of knowledge"?[15] Underlying this justification for reifying meaning is a correspondence theory of truth and knowledge which is extremely problematic and now very much in retreat.[16] The bare idea of truth as correspondence to reality is simply too vague to be helpful; and to speak more specifically (in the idiom of the early logical atomists) of correspondence to facts or states of affairs immediately raises the sort of problems which frustrated the atomist project. For example, since we can't seem to individuate or refer to these facts apart from the true propositions which express them, how can we meaningfully differentiate between such propositions and the facts which make them true, so as to allow for any comparison or correspondence? And how are we to understand negative truths without having to swallow the indigestibly bizarre notion of negative facts?

Correspondence to independent objects is no less problematic, because, like facts, they cannot be isolated from our discursive practices so as to function as a standard for their correct, knowledge-yielding correspondence. For objects can only be referred to in terms of some linguistic characterization of them, and there are various ways in which language constitutes a domain into different objects. There is no single description of the world and no transcendental, non-linguistic God's-eye perspective of its objects that would be available for us to appeal to, that would even be intelligible to us as language-users. Thus, given that the objects we refer to are always linguistically mediated, there can be no workable notion of an unmediated object "as in itself it really is" for correspondence theories to employ epistemologically.[17] Particularly when the object or reality in question is the meaning of a text, it is hard to avoid Rorty's pragmatist conclusion that the notion of truth as correspondence is "an uncashable and outworn metaphor."[18]

Given such difficulties, why not abandon the whole idea of interpretive truth as correspondence to the work's meaning? Perhaps the fear is that to abandon it would be to abandon all claims to interpretive knowledge. But this fear is unfounded, and not because of alternative (coherence and pragmatist) theories of truth which might legitimate such claims. For even if such alternatives and indeed all theories of truth are unsuccessful or misguided, there remains the crucial point that truth does not exhaust knowledge. There is also what Ryle called "knowing how." Knowing how to dance or swim, to behave respectfully or insultingly, to express oneself in gestures or in English, is not simply reducible to knowledge of any set of articulable truths. Such knowledge is instead constituted by an ability, a dispositional capacity to perform in certain ways in general conformity (rather than slavishly rigid adherence) to certain socially endorsed practices, criteria, and models, which may be largely unarticulated and may admit of contesting alternative interpretations. Having such dispositional practical knowledge requires, in Wittgenstein's phrase, "knowing how to go on," how to make reasonable, fruitful, or at least defensible projections of the relevant practices beyond the range of past applications and criteria. Rather than passive mirroring contemplation, such knowledge, as Dewey affirms, "is a mode of interaction" between an active responsive agent and a structuring but flexible environment, an interaction through which both can be changed.[19]

Interpretive knowledge may also be seen in this fashion as a performed ability to respond to the work in ways conforming to the range of culturally appropriate response, ways already accepted or ways capable of winning acceptance. On this account, our aims in interpretation are not to dig out and describe the objectified meaning already carefully buried in the text by its author, but rather to develop and transmit a richly meaningful response to the text. The project is not to describe the work's given and definitive sense, but rather to *make sense* of the work. Though our sense-making activity is not enslaved to mirroring or capturing a fixed antecedent meaning, it is neither totally free nor condemned to arbitrary, deviant "misreading." For not only are we initially constrained by our cultural training to interpret literary works in certain ways which highlight their coherence, depth, and reflection on life's problems, but we are powerfully impelled to continue this practice by the fear that so much beauty will be lost by interpreting them differently. Our most established and respected practices of literary interpretation seem informed by a twofold principle that could be called "coherent comprehensiveness of understanding."[20] For it aims at connectively constituting a greater wealth of meaningful features into a more coherent whole, a coherent understanding which exceeds the limits of the work itself and which can indeed be constructed on the inconsistencies of the work and its interpretive aporia by explaining and placing them in a larger context.

However, from this general hermeneutic direction no strict uniformity of interpretive aims is implied, since there is a vast variety of socially entrenched, aesthetically proven, yet mutually competing interpretive strategies for making sense of texts, for rendering them coherent (even in their incoherence) to our understanding. The interpretation sought by the textual critic piously reconstructing a text is hardly that of the poststructuralist playfully deconstructing it. Contemporary criticism is largely divided between reading with and reading against the text; and even within a single sense-making strategy (like authorial intention), the precise aims and consequent standards of interpretive validity will vary with context, which always determines the whole in which understanding takes place. What is adequate for the Sunday paper may not do for the lecture hall or for academic journals, whose standards again are hardly uniform.

Two other points contribute to the fundamental variety of textual sense-making. First, not all interpretive responses are dominated by cognitive purposes; the goal of enhanced aesthetic experience (as in creative interpretive performance) can override the aim of trying to be "true" in some non-aesthetic sense. Knowledge, we philosophers need reminding, is not the only worthy reason for reading and interpreting. Secondly, sense-making is not always a matter of constructing some articulate verbal response to represent the work's content or form. Indeed, some ways of sense-making can be so direct, immediate, and unthinking that they are better described as simply reading or understanding rather than interpretation.

The pragmatist account of interpretation as sense-making must face one last argument for objectified meanings as the target or goal of reading and interpretation: Without some fixed meaning-object with which to identify the work, there would be no adequate way to individuate or refer to it as a common object of response or understanding, and thus there would be no possibility of fruitful critical dialogue concerning how it should be understood. Surely, to understand a literary work (or anything else) must be to understand something; but without an objectified meaning there would be no common meaningful object for readers and critics to understand.

We obviously cannot identify a literary work merely with any one (or the sum total) of its physically inscribed or orally performed texts. For, as Hirsch suggests, without the assumption of meaning, these texts are simply marks on paper or noises in the air, and without the assumption of some shared meaning binding them together (as tokens of the same type), they would be unrelated objects and events. But if the text's identity as something meaningful is only a product of efforts to make sense, then, as its readers make sense of it differently, how can we continue to identify it as the same work? It rather seems to disintegrate into as many works as there are different meanings given by different readers. There would then be no common work for different readers to react to or interpret differently, no common object for critical discussion. However, since we do seem able to discuss a given work, it is argued that there must be some common intentional object which we are discussing, whether we identify it with the author's intention (Hirsch) or with the objective meaning of the text itself (Beardsley).

Persuasive as this argument appears, it should not compel us to posit a fixed independent meaning as the work's identity in order to guarantee identity of reference for its critical discussion. The key is to distinguish the logical issue of referential identification from the substantive issue of the nature, properties, or meaning of what has been identified. Certainly, however much we allow our interpretations of a work to differ, we must allow for the reidentification of the same work among this difference in order to talk about "the" work (and indeed "its" different reception) at all. The ordinary referential and predicative functions of discourse simply require this bare logico–grammatical identity of individuation. But such identity does not entail that what is identified on different occasions is completely or even substantially the same.[21] For practical purposes of discourse, we can agree that we are talking about the same thing while differing radically as to what the substantive nature of that thing is, whether it's a bird, a plane, or indeed Superman. Agreement about referential identity can be secured by agreeing on a certain minimum number of identifying descriptions, or it can be (and most often is) simply assumed by our deeply entrenched cultural habits of individuation. In distinguishing between referential and substantive identity, we can similarly distinguish between change *in* the object interpreted and change *of* the object interpreted, where the former need not (but can, if sufficiently extreme) involve the latter. A novel interpretation or authorial revision can make a poem new without making it an altogether different poem in the referential sense of individuation.

For Dewey, interpretation and knowledge are always rendering changes in the objects they appropriate. But if there are sufficient background continuities through these changes, we continue to identify and refer to them as the same objects. Such objects are not fixed but "relatively constant" or stable; and the degree and nature of the desired stabilities depend on our (changing) purposes of individuation.[22] Artworks or texts are cultural entities that are constituted and reconstituted as individual objects by the social and linguistic practices and traditions of the culture they serve. Their individuation and identity rest on nothing beyond such practices and are thus as open to change as these practices are. Recognizing this, we can easily explain how a work's substantive identity of properties and meaning can change significantly over time, even though the work has already been written or "completed" by its author and even though we continue to identify it as the same work. Nor would we need to continue agonizing over the question of whether or not, given such change, it *really* is the same work, assuming that the question must have a definite answer, as indeed it should if we assume that the work must exist as an antecedently determinate and independent object of reified meaning.

Instead, on the pragmatist account I have been sketching, an artwork turns out to be a continuous and contested construction of the efforts to determine its understanding and interpretation – that is, of efforts to determine how and what the work will be taken to be, which amounts, pragmatically speaking, to how and what it actually is. Though such efforts to determine understanding can perhaps be said to begin with the author (if we forget the memorable fact that artistic and linguistic traditions are already determining her determining efforts), the intentions which continue to guide and shape understanding extend far beyond her authorial control.

IV

The problematic of identity and interpretation and the dialectic of truth versus productivity are both central to the three currently dominant pragmatist theories of interpretation. Knapp and Michaels' theory of interpretation is paradoxically advanced in a polemic "Against Theory," where "theory" is narrowly defined as "the attempt to govern interpretations of particular texts by appealing to an account of interpretation in general."[23] The gist of Knapp and Michaels' strategy is to argue that the whole project of theorizing about interpretation rests on the mistake that there is something to theorize about, a question of what in general a text means and how it should be interpreted. Only on the assumption that there exist alternative possibilities of what textual meaning and interpretation could be, "the illusion of a choice between alternative methods of interpreting," could theory situate itself in the space of this question and take for itself the function of assessing and deciding between these possibilities (*AT* 18).

Since most interpretive theorizing has centered on the question of whether a text's meaning should be identified with the intention of its author, Knapp and Michaels challenge the very validity of this question by insisting that it is logically impossible for textual meaning to be anything but authorial intention. And if there is no possible alternative or choice, there is simply no place for theory to argue whether literary interpretation should be intentionalist. In this way they distinguish their position from more traditional intentionalist theories (like Hirsch's) and claim not to be theorizing at all but simply to be reporting on a conceptual necessity about textual meaning and interpretation: namely, that "what a text means and what its author intends it to mean are identical,"

and hence that interpretation must necessarily be "faithful to the historical author's intention" (*AT* 19, 103).

But in both ordinary and critical discourse, "meaning" and "authorial
intention" are not conceptually identical. We know this not only because
the issue of intentionalism is hotly debated, but by the mere fact that we
can meaningfully ask whether a given text really conveys the author's
intention. Yet Knapp and Michaels ignore such homespun empirical
facts and argue transcendentally that the conceptual identity of textual
meaning and authorial intention follows logically and necessarily from the
very nature of language.

They ground their argument on a now widely held view (developed
from Austin by Grice and Searle) which insists that linguistic meaning
must be understood in terms of intentions and the speech acts which
embody them. Though analytic philosophy often eschewed intentionalism for relying on entities that seem too spectrally private and because
intentional contexts resist standard truth-functional accounts of meaning,
it shows growing recognition that sentence and utterance meaning cannot
be fully explained in purely extensional terms, and thus that language
must be in some sense intentional (even if our intentions are in turn
viewed as essentially dependent on language). We need not resolve this
general issue here. For even if we agree with Knapp and Michaels that
"meanings are always intentional," this still does not entail their conclusion that "what a text means and what its author intends it to mean
are identical" and that "the necessary object of interpretation," indeed
"of all reading," "is always the historical author's intention" (*AT* 24,
101, 103). We must be careful not to confuse the view that all textual
meaning is in some sense intentional with the very challengeable assertion
that the meaning of a text is identical with the *historical author's* intention
or intended meaning.

But this is precisely Knapp and Michaels' mistake. By conflating
"meaning" with "authorially intended meaning" they thereby preclude
the possibility of someone's speech or writing failing to mean what it was
intended to mean, a possibility which is indeed a very frequent actuality.
Rejecting this conflation, one could still grant the basic intentionality of
language, which Knapp and Michaels rightly emphasize. One could grant
this first in the holistic sense that there could be no linguistic meaning
without a background of human intentionality, no "possibility of language prior to and independent of intention" (*AT* 19). But one might
plausibly hold further that every individual linguistic text requires some
particular intention for its meaning. A string of letters accidentally

produced by a computer or by waves on the sand (as in Knapp and Michaels' example) would still depend for its meaning on an intentional act – here the intention of the reader to see and use the marks as a meaningful text, as language rather than mere marks.

However, even if we follow Knapp and Michaels in denying that "there can be...intentionless meanings" and in asserting that (in some sense) "what is intended and what is meant are identical," this still does not entail that "the meaning of a text is simply identical to the author's intended meaning" (*AT* 12, 15, 17). All that follows is that the meaning of the text is inseparable from *some* intention (or group of intentions) or another. But the necessary meaning-securing intentions could belong to readers of the text (or collectively to an interpretive community) rather than to its original "historical author" with whose intention Knapp and Michaels identify the text's meaning.[24]

The only way for them to secure this identification would be to count any of a text's readers as its meaning-giving author. But such a drastic remedy undermines the whole idea of intentionalist, author-oriented interpretation by dismantling the very notion of author. Knapp and Michaels understandably reject this move, confining "the author" to "the historical author" and confining her meaning-giving intention still more narrowly to that of the "particular occasion" when she produced the text (*AT* 103, 141). For them there can be no issue of choosing whose meaning-given intention is more fruitful for our purposes or which intentional context is more useful to employ in dealing with the work (though these are pragmatist considerations *par excellence*). There is only "the empirical difficulty of deciding what its [historical] author intended" (*AT* 142).

Knapp and Michaels are, of course, aware that the literary interpreter often claims and seems to be concerned with meanings other than the historical author's. To counter this recalcitrant empirical evidence, they do not argue that such non-authorial interpretation is ultimately counterproductive for criticism – a legitimate and characteristically pragmatist argument of cost-accounting. Instead, they take the road of high theory and transcendental argument which they pretend to eschew. They simply relegate the finding or making of other meanings to a realm altogether outside the activities of reading and interpretation by treating this as the *writing* of another work: "*replacing* the authorial intention with some other intention...[is] rewriting and is no longer interpretation at all" (*AT* 103).

To justify this relegation, Knapp and Michaels claim that the same text cannot logically bear two different intentions or interpretations. To interpret an intention other than the defining one of its author is thus to interpret or write a different text. What we ordinarily take as a text's different possible meanings or expressed intentions should be construed as the meanings of different texts. A text simply cannot have different meanings, they argue, because sameness of text requires sameness of meaning, which itself is defined as sameness of intention. Thus their case for outlawing plurality of interpretation and for identifying textual with authorial meaning ultimately rests on a theoretical argument concerning the issue of textual identity. Only by strictly identifying its meaning with its historical author's particular intention can the text be adequately individuated; only the intention of "a particular author on a particular occasion...[can be] what gives a text its identity as a text" (*AT* 141). But, conflating referential and substantive identity, they offer no real argument for this being the only workable criterion of individuation; and once again, in stark opposition to their theory, the plain fact is that texts are not so individuated as to preclude divergent intentions or interpretations.[25]

Finally, even if we agree to individuate the text in terms of a particular authorial intention, this still will not exclude a plurality of interpretations or possible meanings. For, first, intentions themselves share much of the indeterminacy of the language in which they are typically formulated, and thus they themselves can be differently interpreted. Knapp and Michaels simply assume that intention will ground the meaning and the identity of a text in something fixed and transparent which itself neither needs interpretation nor allows divergent ones. But we have no reason to believe that such a transparent, language-neutral, self-interpreting and unambiguous idiolect of intentionality does or even could exist. And since intention itself is indeterminate and variously interpretable, it cannot guarantee the disambiguation and univocal interpretation of a text. Secondly, the individuating intention might in fact be the generation of textual polysemy and multiple interpretation whose specific varieties are not all foreseen and foredetermined. Certainly the intentional production of an ambiguous open text is characteristic of contemporary art and aesthetic interpretation, and in part distinguishes them from more practical discourse where univocity of intention and interpretation is more important. It is therefore not surprising that Knapp and Michaels unquestioningly assimilate literary texts into more ordinary speech-act situations, just as they take issue with the practice of interpretive theory that helps nourish the notion of the open, polysemic text.

Though problematic and unconvincing, Knapp and Michaels' intentionalist theory is nonetheless instructive for pragmatist hermeneutics, for it seems to go most wrong where it goes against the spirit of pragmatism, which it purports to represent. First, their position denies the possibility of any choice of what interpretation could be; it allegedly "describes the way interpretation *always* works" and must necessarily work irrespective of the intentions and activities of literary critics and institutions (*AT* 105). And in denying any choice of the ways we can interpret, Knapp and Michaels similarly disallow any change or development of what interpretation could be so as to render it more serviceable and satisfying to our (changing) needs. This rigid interpretive monism runs counter to the pragmatist tradition, which challenges the putative necessities of thought and the fixities of a static universe and instead aims to emphasize and enlarge the realm of choice in cognition and action.

The pragmatist attitude, says James, is pluralistic and open, "looking away from...*supposed necessities*" and instead recognizing and furthering the role of choice and the range of possibilities in carving out the objects of our world "to suit our human purposes."[26] Pragmatism is also a forward-looking philosophy, which emphasizes future consequences and the importance of change.[27] Its insistence "not upon antecedent phenomena but upon consequent phenomena, not upon the precedents but upon the possibilities of action" is what (in Dewey's words) distinguishes pragmatism from "historical empiricism."[28] Knapp and Michaels reveal themselves more as old-fashioned empiricists not only in their backward-looking and static account of meaning, but in their attempt to prove its necessity by appeal to the alleged conceptual truth that textual meaning necessarily means authorial intention. For this appeal involves Quine's first dogma of empiricism, the belief in unchallengeable analytic truths of meaning.

In sharp contrast to pragmatism's meliorism, Knapp and Michaels' necessitarianism proudly eschews any aim of improving interpretive practice. For, like the project of theory it opposes, their "anti-theory" can have "no consequences for the practice of literary criticism" except for the practice of theory itself which it seeks to arrest (*AT* 99). But if interpretation is always necessarily the same enterprise of discovering authorial intention, and interpretive theory can therefore have "no practical consequences" (*AT* 25), why all the fuss? The mere fact that theory sometimes distracts us from practice simply cannot justify the vehemence of Knapp and Michaels' will to extirpate theory and to establish the conceptual identity of textual meaning and authorial intention. Their vehemence rather betrays the fearful recognition of both theory's power to transform interpretive practices and its past success in generating different interpretive modes free from authorial intention. Their anxiety is that such interpretive pluralism and instability of meaning will undermine the convergence necessary for conceiving literary criticism as a cognitively respectable discipline. To shore up such interpretive convergence, Knapp and Michaels seek at once to homogenize and to outlaw interpretive difference by maintaining that such difference is only apparent while prohibiting it as logically illegitimate. By relegating non-authorial interpretation to the category of "rewriting" and by denying the very possibility of interpretive change, they seek to fix and limit the scope of interpretation and thus constrain what a text can mean or be. That "the object of all reading is always the historical author's intention" assures in principle a fixed and common interpretive aim and object (*AT* 103).[29]

Recognizing that critical discourse would be incoherent without the possibility of individuating and reidentifying texts, theorists typically assume that such identity can only be understood and sustained by fixing it in some permanent substantive stratum, some unchanging essence of the text that lies outside changing interpretive practices. Knapp and Michaels, like the more traditional intentionalists, anchor it in the author's intention, whereas textualists like Beardsley and Goodman locate it in the text itself.[30] Both parties are guilty of confusing the need for individuation and referential continuity with the demand for fixed substantive identity. In challenging the assumption that we need some substantive fixity beyond discursive practice to allow coherent individuation and fruitful inquiry, Deweyan pragmatism opens the literary work to change, entrusting its identity and meaning to the changing practices and purposes of its community of interpreters. Rorty and Fish follow this flexible, future-looking, and practice-dependent direction. Contemporary pragmatism should therefore welcome their recognition of interpretive change and difference; but it must also carefully consider the limits and price of their endorsement of variety and change.

V

In many ways, Rorty presents the most striking contrast to Knapp and Michaels' necessitarian and authorially backward-looking theory.[31] While they regard textual meaning as something permanently defined by the past intention of the historical author, Rorty regards it as something to be continually redefined by the future, by the intentions and practice of future readers. While Knapp and Michaels think that interpretation has one necessary object and purpose, Rorty insists that the objects and ends of interpretation are always "a matter of choice" (*PP* 134), always the product of a recontextualizing redescription aimed to "get us what we want" by reweaving our web of beliefs and desires (*CP* 150). For Rorty, what we want from literature and its criticism are variety and novelty: new meanings, new vocabularies, "new ways of speaking" (*CP* 150), whereas Knapp and Michaels seek conformity and fixity to past meaning in the name of critical truth. Though they require a fixed substantive identity without which talk about the text would make no sense, Rorty rejects this need to "postulate an object," "an enduring substrate of changing descriptions," as the only and necessary base for critical communication. Instead, he dissolves the objecthood of texts into "nodes within transitory webs of relationships," foci of "possibilities for use" (*TL* 12; *CP* 153).

But if not as an enduring substantive object, how is a text to be identified for purposes of critical discourse? Employing the pragmatist strategy sketched above, Rorty argues that discursive practice itself provides sufficient individuation for critical communication to be fruitful. To establish identity of reference so that our different interpretations and changing descriptions can be directed at and illuminate the same text, we need not assume some substantive and permanent identity or essence of the text – "the very text itself, or the true meaning of the text," which provides the permanent reference for predication and the permanent criterion of interpretive adequacy. "All that is required is that agreement be obtainable about what we are talking about – and this just means agreement on a reasonable number of propositions using the relevant term" (*TL* 12). This agreement between interpreters, an agreement (not necessarily explicit) on a requisite number of discursive applications of the text's name (or pronominal substitutions thereof), can provide us with the required individuating focus or logical referent on which to structure our further discussion about what we have thus identified. Rather than a static substantive identity, the work becomes an organizing focus and field for the production of discourse. Yet it is only constituted as a focus by agreement in ways of talking or reacting which pragmatically identify it as the same work while allowing its descriptions and interpretations (but never simultaneously all of them) to change without necessarily implying that we have changed the object of discourse.

This pragmatist dereification of the objects of interpretation may initially seem strange and perhaps even viciously circular. Yet there is nothing here but the familiar linguistic turn: namely, that individuation of linguistic items like texts depends on further linguistic practices, and that there is simply no way outside of language to talk about any individuals at all, a view which need not entail reducing all the world and its experience to language. But though the strategy of common individuation through discursive agreement seems perfectly acceptable in itself, it is arguably incoherent when combined with Rorty's one-sided emphasis on discursive "diversification and novelty" and his radical privileging of the autonomously private over the shared (*CIS* xiv, 77).

Rorty repeatedly insists that what should be paramount in our use of language is neither the realist goal of discovering the truth nor even the Habermasian goal of cooperative problem solving to promote consensus of belief, but rather the goal of private perfection through original creation. The primary aim is "to make things new," "to make something that never had been dreamed of before," to achieve autonomy over oneself and one's world "by inventing a new language" which redescribes these things in one's "own terms," so as to escape from the oppression of shared "inherited descriptions" which involve a Bloomian anxiety of influence, "the horror of finding oneself to be only a copy or replica" (*CIS* 13, 27–9).

This linguistic strategy, Rorty believes, is particularly right for literary works and criticism, since what we "want [of] both these works and the criticism of them [are] *new* terminologies" (*CP* 142). And to insure that there are no constraints on proliferating new vocabularies to stimulate "the intellectual's private imagination," Rorty maintains that we need "no common language in which critics can argue" (*CP* 158). But in denying such common language, Rorty seems to deny the very conditions of propositional agreement which, by his own account, allow him to talk about texts (or indeed any objects) at all. To have objects of interpretation that we can talk about, no matter how transient they be and no matter how differently they are interpreted, there must be some agreement as to propositions and thus some common language or discursive practice to provide it. To deny any common language is to deny any effective referential individuation, hence any effective discourse. This is just an aspect of the Wittgensteinian case against private language which Rorty in fact endorses.

There are two ways for Rorty to meet this objection. One is by adapting Davidson's account of metaphoric meaning and his "passing theory of language"[32] to argue that we need no common set of linguistic norms to reach provisional agreement on propositions and hence on object-individuation, since we can do this through intuitive predictions of meaning based on context and on our previous habits of linguistic understanding which are essentially stable and conservative. But the rejoinder is that those habits would be undermined and unprojectible if language were as radically innovative, protean, and privatized as Rorty urges it to be.

Another way for Rorty to outflank this inflection of the private-language argument is to distinguish a public use and a private use of language. The former is shared and serves the basic needs of linguistic community (including individuation of objects). The latter need not and should not be shared if we aim to maximize diversity, novelty, and autonomy, but it can be sufficiently anchored or related to shared public language so as to escape the force of the private-language argument. Rorty's recent advocacy of an ethics of individualist self-creation and self-perfection within a liberal *polis* rests on such a distinction between public and private language, one which privileges the private use or personal dialect as more valuable and significant to our lives, but nonetheless recognizes its dependence on public language to keep the whole linguistic and societal project afloat.[33] In the same way, with respect to our question of textual identity, Rorty could hold that the shared public language provides sufficient agreement for identification of the text while leaving critics completely free to spin their own private vocabularies and webs of significance in filling out the meaning or content of what has been publicly identified, without fear of dissolving this identified focus. This strategy would reflect the actual practice of criticism, where we typically have no problem in agreeing which text we are discussing but endless problems in agreeing what it precisely means.

However, any strategy which so heavily relies on "a firm distinction between the private and the public" (*CIS* 83) cannot help but be as problematic as the firmness of that shifty distinction. What Rorty calls the critics' private vocabularies and ways of reading are always more than private, and not merely because they are always largely prestructured by the public language and interpretations they inherit. They are also public in the important sense of being typically published and essentially designed for publication. The new vocabularies and readings Rorty valorizes are from the outset thoroughly motivated by the aim of making themselves not only public but publicly accepted and influential. The autonomous private reader whom Rorty praises is explicitly identified with Harold Bloom's "strong misreader" (*CP* 151–8), one whose novel transformative interpretations aim to escape the domination of already influential readings by becoming influential themselves. The strong misreader, we recall, is one "whose readings will matter to others as well as to himself."

Hence, for all their initial divergence from the public's shared interpretations (which allows Rorty to distinguish them as "private"), these readings and the vocabularies in which they are formulated cannot be regarded as merely private. Rorty cannot therefore argue that their private status renders them incapable of disrupting "public" ways of reading or threatening the shared public discourse used for the very individuation of texts to be read. The undeniable fact is that such innovative "private readings" (whose intrinsic public status is standardly highlighted by their authors' publishing and institutional affiliation) *do* impose themselves on the reading public, and they challenge (both for better and for worse) its familiar, shared, and perhaps cherished understandings of literature. Since our individuation of textual objects depends on our literary interests and values, radically changing our understanding and experience of texts can result in changing their individuation. We may no longer find them worth individuating in the same way, no longer care about distinguishing their authentic copies from drastically abridged or bowdlerized versions. In other words, though we can and must distinguish individuation of the work from the particular meanings and content interpretively ascribed to it, the latter can sometimes reciprocally modify our determining of the former. Applying this lesson to Rorty's strategy, we realize that although widely variant private readings *can* swing free of each other and remain focused on a shared "publicly" individuated text, if such interpretive swinging is long and violent enough, the initial organizing focus can become unhinged.

Rorty's so-called private readings exceed and violate the private in a more general way. Collectively, they create a field which structures and constrains the range of acceptable public response to texts, valorizing some as currently informed and up to date, while deprecating others as naive and old-fashioned. This structuring works not only within the critical profession, but in fact marks off (so as to dismiss) the large and valuable range of more truly "private" reader response which lies outside its regulated borders, at once classifying and declassing such response as "unprofessional." What facilitates this dismissive exclusion of unprofessional reading and interpretation is a twofold confusion common to contemporary theory. The conflation of reading with interpretation is coupled with an implicit identification of all legitimate forms of literary interpretation with the interpretive forms legitimated by the literary critical profession. The upshot is that all reading worthy of the name must conform to the conventions and aims of professionalized interpretation. Since such interpretation is supposed to make a novel contribution to our understanding of the text, and since it is always explicitly articulated (hence is as much a matter of writing as of reading), any interpretive effort which fails to issue in an innovative interpreting text should not qualify as interpretation.

The deplorable drift of such totalizing professionalism and preoccupation with novelty is that all legitimate reading must also be writing, and that interpretation must be professionally original to have any value. This attitude brutally constrains the possibilities of value in reading and interpretation. First, it suggests that these activities can be properly practiced only by a professionalized elite. Secondly, it denies crucial values even to members of that elite. For these professionals are always both more and less than professionals. As concrete individuals they are always more; and since they can hardly be specialists with respect to all literatures and authors, they are inevitably also mere lay readers as well. Surely, outside their specific area of scholarship (but I suspect also in it), professional critics can find value in familiar shared readings, and indeed in the very fact that they are so shared. Community of response is one of the irreducibly social goods that art can foster, though art can also generate divisiveness when its appreciation becomes too far removed from the common sphere of experience and is instead posited in the hands of an institutionalized priestly class of professional appreciators.

By Rorty's own pragmatist standards, the case for interpretive innovation must be made in terms of evaluative cost-accounting rather than by appeal to transcendental conceptual necessity. His argument for hermeneutic novelty seems to be that it provides greater pleasure and autonomy. Both points can be challenged. Though I'm not clear how reading pleasure should be measured, my (professional and non-professional) experience suggests that trying to crank out academic papers with novel interpretations is not always more satisfying than simply reading a literary work as an amateur focused on its more common understanding. Certainly, this should be the case for non-professional readers, whose claims, if not existence, seem neglected here. More important, even if the pleasures of "strong misreading-writing" are indeed superior, we must not let the best become the enemy of the good by rejecting the value of ordinary readings because of the greater thrill of extraordinary ones. Here, as elsewhere, what mars Rorty's interpretive theory is not the advocacy of innovative individualist reading, but its one-sided, virtually exclusive valorization which neglects and demeans the common. Pragmatists should be pluralists.

The argument that novelty is the best or only expression of autonomy seems similarly suspect. True autonomy, one would think, should allow us the choice of whether we wish to seek novel interpretations or whether we prefer just to have a good read, experiencing the work without producing a significantly innovative interpretation or even a formulated one at all. Though Rorty equates it with autonomy, the demand for novelty of interpretation betrays an obvious obeisance to the pressures of academic publication and professional advancement, compounded by an abiding and unquestioning bondage to the late romantic and modernist aesthetic which only has eyes and praise for the radically new.[34] Moreover, both the professional and the aesthetic demands for rapid and relentless innovation can themselves be seen as obeying a greater master, as dependent cultural reflections of capitalism's increasing demand for new commodities to produce continued profits.

VI

If Rorty's one-sided insistence on innovative private interpretation can neither be justified by its privileged consequences for reading experience nor sustained by his doctrine of the public/private split, we must finally turn to Fish's theory. For here the idea of interpretive novelty as programmatically generated and institutionally controlled by the literary critical profession is more explicitly and systematically defended. Fish in some ways represents a middle ground between the theories of Rorty and of Knapp and Michaels. While Rorty advocates the reader's interpretive autonomy and the latter fix the locus of textual meaning and interpretive authority in the historical author, Fish aims to subsume both reader and author under the master concept of interpretive community, which governs them both in the production of textual meaning and constitutes the source of interpretive authority. His whole theory of interpretation rests on this concept. Like Knapp and Michaels, Fish confuses the issues of logical individuation and substantive identity, and thus mistakenly conflates identity of text with identity of interpretation. Regarding texts as constituted by interpretation, he thinks that identification of "the same text" depends on interpretive agreement. To give a significantly different interpretation means that "the resulting text would be different"; "the same 'stretch of language'...[can be] no longer the same, since each [interpretation] would be characterizing it differently." From this conflation of textual individuation and substantive identity and from the view he shares with Rorty that interpretations should always be new, Fish concludes there can be no "distinction between explaining a text and changing it."[35]

Like Knapp and Michaels, Fish identifies the text's true meaning and interpretation with "the intention of its author." But rather than take their realist line of presuming that there exists an immutable fact of the matter concerning the author's intention, an empirical fact which interpretation simply has to discover but cannot change, Fish more pragmatically treats that authorial fact as itself constantly up for grabs and transformation through ongoing interpretation. "Intention like anything else is an interpretive fact" which is never fixed or given but always "must be construed" (*WC* 213); and interpretive construing, for Fish, ultimately means construction. Thus, the "fact" of authorial intention and textual meaning not only *can* change with interpretation; it *should* change if criticism is to be a healthy enterprise.

This advocacy of interpretive change and novelty, with its insistence on the plasticity of textual meaning resulting from the changing interpretive strategies of its readers, is what aligns Fish with the future-looking Rortian view of interpretation and against Knapp and Michaels' backward-looking interpretive rigidity. For Fish as much as for Rorty, interpretation is not the uncovering of meanings and properties already given, but rather their production; it is never just reading, but always writing. All "interpretive strategies [are] not for reading but for writing texts, for constituting their properties." "Interpretation is not the art of construing but the art of constructing. Interpreters do not decode poems; they make them" (*ITT* 14, 327). And for Fish, even more than for Rorty, they must make them new. Novel interpretation is not (as with Rorty) just the only good or "strong" choice; it is not a choice at all, but an institutional necessity. Working on a background of established interpretations, the interpreting critic "is obliged by the conventions of the institution to dislodge them...[with] something different" (*ITT* 350).

In therapeutic contrast to Rorty's fantasy of the autonomous interpreter who is free to pursue and publish personal readings which just happen to be new and can remain essentially private, Fish recognizes that the "private" self is always already public, "a social construct" which "does not exist apart from the communal or conventional categories of

thought that enable its operations...and...have their source in the interpretive community" (*ITT* 335).[36] He more correctly locates the cause of
interpretive novelty not in individual freedom but in the professional
constraints of the interpretive community, which is essentially "an engine
of change" whose main job is to expand its scope and professional
opportunities by constantly introducing new views and topics (*C* 433). As
Fish frankly puts it: "in this profession you earn the right to say something because it has not been said by anyone else, or because it is a reversal of what is usually said...You do not offer something as the report of a
communion between the individual critical sensibility and a work or its
author; and if you did,...your articles...would not be given a hearing"
(*NB* 739).

Fish thus recognizes that besides the particular intentions of authors
and readers, there are also general institutional intentions which indeed
prestructure the former; and he is refreshingly candid in recognizing the
economic and political agenda of increased growth and power which
motivates the profession's insistent intention for novelty and change. The
more new interpretations are introduced, the more they can in turn be
challenged by the writing of more articles, and the more members of the
profession can be advanced in terms of such interpretive and reinter-
pretive work. And through that work and their advancement, the more
the profession can grow. It is the business of the critical profession "first
to create the work and second to make sure that it will never get done,"
so that there will always be room for more interpretive commodities to
be marketed so as to foster professional advancement and expansion
(*NB* 743).

The interpretive community functions to promote change but also
(just as importantly) to regulate it, since radically indiscriminate and
uncontrolled change could threaten the community's coherence and
consequently that of its (constituted) objects or texts. Fish therefore
insists that change must be "orderly – constrained by [the community's]
evidentiary procedures and tacit understandings." Indeed, he denies the
very possibility of change that is not under such control by further arguing (on very shaky epistemological grounds[37]) that all change must be
generated from inside the community and that it is in fact controlled and
"set in motion by certain persons" of "authority" in that community
(*C* 429, 440). Thus, though denying the idea of individual "free agents"
by dissolving the self into a construct of the community, Fish still wants
to find room for authoritative individuals whose agency transforms the
community through influential readings; and he obviously wants to see

himself as one of those more than private individuals who nonetheless serves his private interest by directing and speaking for the interpretive community. The "pure of heart" may be troubled by such an emphasis on community which seems more self-serving than unselfishly communitarian. But to be fair to Fish by presuming no such purity, I shall waive this ethico-political issue between neo-conservative liberalism and its communitarian critics. Instead, I shall consider some logical difficulties with his notion of interpretive community, whose nature, scope, and individuation are neither clearly nor consistently characterized.

First, its status ambiguously wavers between theoretical abstraction and effective concrete entity. On the one hand, it is portrayed as the former, not a concrete historical community of real people but a set of interpretive strategies and conventions, "not so much a group of individuals who shared a point of view, but a point of view" with "distinctions, categories of understanding, and stipulations of relevance" that "shared individuals" (*C* 423–4). On the other hand, the interpretive community is often identified with the academic profession of literary criticism, a very concrete but extremely problematic identification which I shall soon criticize.

A second problem concerns individuation and agreement. Fish first seems to define the interpretive community in terms of full agreement in interpretive practice. "Interpretive communities are made up of those who share interpretive strategies," so that "members of the same community will necessarily agree" in their interpretations and only by such agreement constitute the same text (*ITT* 14, 15). But, as Fish later recognizes, disagreement forms part of the critical enterprise, indeed a necessary part if there is to be novelty and change; so the interpretive community must be allowed to contain interpretive disagreement and cannot be monolithic. The problem, then, is that given such disagreement and given his conflation of interpretive identity with textual individuation, Fish should be unable to maintain that the community of differing interpreters are still constituting and hence debating the same text.

His only attempt to negotiate this difficulty is by describing the community as "at once homogeneous with respect to some general purpose and purview, and heterogeneous with respect to the variety of practices it can accommodate" (*C* 432). But this maneuver of appealing to a vague unarticulated "general purpose" in interpretation, one which unites all differing interpreters in the same community and lets them constitute the same text, seems a rather empty dodge that is inadequate to the work of individuation that Fish wants the notion of interpretive community to perform. For even if we could unify all interpretive difference under some vague general purpose like "seeking the meaning of the text," such a unifying formula is clearly not precise or concrete enough to individuate interpretive communities in such a way that will adequately sort an array of different interpretations into interpretations of the same text and interpretations of different texts. But the constitutive individuation of the text is precisely what Fish's notion of interpretive community is supposed to do. Members of the same interpretive community "constitute... the same text, although the sameness would not be attributable to the self-identity of the text, but to the communal nature of the interpretive act. Of course, if the same act were performed by members of another community...the resulting text would be different" (*C* 424).

Yet another problem of individuation is how we can even recognize interpretive communities different from our own so as to individuate them. Fish regards all understanding as necessarily internal to the interpretive community, since understanding is limited by the community's horizons, categories, and belief structures. This does not mean we must always be confined to the same set of community assumptions, for these can and should change. But such change in the community can only be "self-transformation" by "mechanisms that are themselves internal" to it. The community remains logically closed to change from without, since what is genuinely outside the interpretive scope of its belief structures "would not have been noticed at all" or understood enough to initiate a change (*C* 429–32). But if things and practices outside our interpretive community are indeed incomprehensible, how can we understand them enough to recognize them as belonging to a different interpretive community, let alone individuating them into, say, three different interpretive communities? In other words, the self-enclosed nature of Fish's interpretive communities does not merely close the door to communicating their differences but even to allowing the intelligibility of their being different (hence individualizable) at all.

Fish occasionally speaks of different "subcommunities" of the same interpretive community (*ITT* 343). And given his "internalist" epistemological constraints, the only way he could account for intelligible difference between different interpretive groups would be to treat all allegedly different interpretive communities as simply subcommunities of the same global one, whose differences are intelligible only on a background of sameness. This strategy would be analogous to Gadamer's attempt to insure the possibility of understanding different hermeneutic horizons by presuming that one essential horizon of tradition underlies them all.[38]

Fish, however, does not appeal to such a vastly totalizing idea of tradition as the global interpretive community which embraces all intelligible interpretive practices. But he does make an equally dubious totalizing move which is still more dangerous, substituting *profession* for *tradition* as the all-subsuming notion. He implicitly but pervasively identifies the global interpretive community of literary understanding with the institutional profession of academic literary criticism, thus effectively excluding non-professionals from membership and denying them their inalienable right to read and interpret. The way he assimilates one to the other is extremely subtle and persuasive, largely because it works less by explicit argument than by rhetorical suggestion (where the terms "community," "institution," and "profession" are freely associated and interchanged) and also by the narcissistic self-deception of its audience. It relies on our own professional preoccupation with academic criticism and our self-seeking presumption of its privilege and unlimited dominion.

The skeleton of the argument is this: The interpretation and appreciation of literature, which the literary interpretive community as a whole must engage in and which we can summarily call "literary criticism," is a cultural practice and therefore depends on the existence of cultural conventions or institutions which constitute it as a practice. If literary criticism is essentially institutional, it should be identified with its most institutionalized form, which is professional academic criticism. If literary criticism means professional academic criticism, then the global literary interpretive community is, in essence, simply the academic critical profession. In short, since "the notion of extra-institutional activity is incoherent," the activity of literary understanding has "no...choice between professionalism and some extra-institutional form" and no possibility of "operating independently of the profession" (*PD* 357, 362).

Openly stated, the argument is clearly flawed. It relies on a confusion between *extra-institutional* and *extra-professional*, or, more deeply, between two distinct senses of "institution": the first being "any established custom or conventional practice," the other "an organization devoted to promoting such a practice." Moreover, it falsely presumes that we can identify a practice only with its most advanced and specialized form. Yet in reading Fish's suasive rhetoric, the conflation may seem plausible, partly because he subtly runs the ideas of interpretive and professional community together in his arguments (defending professionalism through his idea of interpretive community and clarifying the latter in terms of the former). But the main reason why it seems convincing is that we professional academics are trained to think of literary criticism only in terms of institutionalized academic criticism. So when Fish claims that "the literary community teaches its members...[that] literary criticism is a profession – ...not something anyone can do" (*NB* 744), the statement seems plausible because he and we are already implicitly identifying the literary community as a whole with its narrow professional sector.

Fish's conflation of the literary interpretive community with the profession of academic criticism may be an honest mistake deriving from his own professional preoccupations and a worthy desire to give some concrete reality or exemplification to the very vague and theoretical notion of interpretive community. But however innocent the motive, the conflation is as wrong as it is elitist and oppressively constraining. First, we must recognize that there is more to the profession of literary criticism than academic criticism. There is a large and powerful domain of journalistic criticism, which thrives independently of the institutional conventions of academic publishing that Fish regards as essential. More important, we simply have no good reason to limit literary criticism to professional criticism at all. What makes the identification seem plausible is only the presumption that literary criticism can involve nothing less than the writing of articles for publication. Since the organs of publication are under professional control, the critic has to "earn the right to say something" by showing mastery of the profession's conventions of publishable work. Thus "the very writing of an article only makes sense within an institutional framework" that "provides both the questions and acceptable ways of answering them." If you ignore them and just report your "experience" of the work without contributing something new, "your articles...would not be given a hearing" (*NB*, 739–40, 743).

Limiting legitimate critical discourse to the writing of innovative articles easily leads Fish to regard interpretation as a matter not of reading but of writing and changing texts. Moreover, by maintaining that "interpretation is the only game in town" (*ITT* 355, 356) and that it can be played only within the professional league of writer-interpreters, the possibility of simply reading and understanding a text is necessarily excluded as illegitimate and even incoherent. But why presume that literary criticism must take the form of published articles? Why can't an oral report or a casual discussion of a work constitute an act of literary criticism? Why can't such discussion at least demonstrate interpretive competence and membership in the literary interpretive community at large? Fish asserts that "acts of criticism" cannot be performed "free of the profession's norms and constraints" (*NB* 747). But he gives no argument to support this, except to point out that professional critiques of professionalism (like the one you are now reading) inevitably subscribe to the profession's norms and therefore testify to the impossibility of criticism outside the profession. However, refutation of this impossibility is not hard to find if we look outside professional publications and lectures. Indeed, everyday, at coffee breaks and on subway trains, it is constantly proved false by non-professional interpretive and evaluative judgements, judgements which are rendered neither senseless nor useless by their lack of professional legitimation.

Ordinary non-professionals regularly engage in such informal literary criticism; and if they could not — if they were excluded from the interpretive literary community and thus unable to read (or constitute) the same texts — then the profession of literary criticism could not flourish as it does. For it would lose the support in audience, finance, and recruits from the larger literary community. Fish correctly insists through his notion of interpretive community that no man is a self-sufficient interpretive island, but he must also realize that professional criticism cannot be one either. The academic literary profession is but a (relatively recent) strand of the larger literary interpretive community, and the latter in turn is interwoven into the still larger matrix of more global interpretive communities and traditions which support and inform our literary activities and institutions, professional and non-professional.

Thus, despite its advocacy of openness to change, Fish's professionalist pragmatism betrays a deep desire for narrow institutional control of literary meaning which involves an unnecessary limitation of literary experience. The only understanding and experience of literature that is legitimate is confined to what appears in professional discourse. This exclusionary professionalism seems foreign to pragmatism's pluralistic openness and represents the critical counterpart of the compartmentalization of art that Dewey so vehemently indicted. The same sort of parochial professionalism and its pressures underlie the truth-seeking intentionalism of Knapp and Michaels and even motivate Rorty's one-sided demand for interpretive novelty. The profession of academic criticism can underwrite these conflicting theories, since it paradoxically legitimates itself by the goal of interpretive truth, yet sustains and expands itself through continuous novelty which cannot allow the final finding of such truth. Knapp and Michaels appeal to the former goal, while Rorty goes for the latter. And Fish tries to combine them by equating truth with whatever new interpretation temporarily gains professional credence (*ITT* 16).

All these three leading pragmatist theories, in contrast to Dewey's, impoverish the domain of aesthetic experience by failing to recognize the value of non-professional responses which seek neither interpretive truth nor publishable novelty but simply enriched experience, experience which may perhaps be communicated in writing but does not need to be to count as legitimate and meaningful. Perhaps Dewey had a wider vision because he wrote at a time when academic modes of reading literary art were less cut off from those of non-professionals in the wider literary community, when the literary academy was neither so dominant nor yet so dominated by such intense professional pressures of cognitive legitimacy and innovative productivity in publication.

We cannot turn back the clock on academic criticism, nor should we want to. There is no doubt that professionalism has increased our knowledge and appreciation of literature, and thus has enhanced the aesthetic experience and lives of many men and women. But however pleased we are with professional practice, we must, as philosophers, see (and see the value of) what lies outside it. When we theorize how literature is read, we need to remember that the range of our legitimate and fruitful intentions in interpretation includes more than professional ones.[39] I think we should also realize that our intentions and activities in reading go beyond – or at least beneath – what can be usefully called interpretation; that, in other words, reading (and, more generally, understanding) is not always interpreting. But to defend this latter claim against the arguments of universal hermeneutics requires a fresh start and a chapter in itself.

5

Beneath Interpretation

I

Kohelet, that ancient postmodern who already remarked that all is vanity and that there is nothing new under the sun, also insisted that there is a time for everything: a time to be born and a time to die, a time to break down and a time to build up, a time to embrace and a time to refrain from embracing. There is no mention of a time for interpretation, but surely there is one; and just as surely that time is now. Our age is even more hermeneutic than it is postmodern, and the only meaningful question to be raised at this stage is whether there is ever a time when we refrain from interpreting. A host of global hermeneuts answer this firmly in the negative, maintaining that simply to perceive, read, understand, or behave at all intelligently is already, and must always be, to interpret. They hold that whenever we experience anything with meaning, such meaningful experience must always be a case and product of interpretation.

This position of hermeneutic universalism[1] dominates most current interpretive theory. Loss of faith in foundationalist and realist objectivity has made it the current dogma. Having abandoned the ideal of reaching a naked, rock-bottom, unmediated God's-eye view of reality, we seem impelled to embrace the opposite position – that we see everything through an interpretive veil or angle. Indeed, one might further argue that since the terms "veil" and "angle" inappropriately suggest that we can make sense of the idea of a naked, perspectiveless reality, we do not merely *see* everything through interpretation but everything *is* in fact constituted by interpretation. In other words, there is nothing real (and certainly nothing real for us) that is not interpreted. This theory can, of course, be traced back to Nietzsche's famous remark that "facts are precisely what there is not, only interpretations"[2]; and it is not surprising that today's hermeneutic universalists have resurrected Nietzsche as a major philosopher and as a precursor of the postmodern. Alexander Nehamas's fine book on Nietzsche is in large part a contemporary defense of Nietzschean perspectivism and universal hermeneutics.[3] Nehamas in fact identifies the two positions by defining Nietzsche's perspectivism as "the thesis that every view is an interpretation," and he goes on to assert that not only all views but "all practices are interpretive," since "all our activity is partial and perspectival" (*N* 66, 70, 72).

Pragmatists, like Nietzcheans, insist on rejecting the very idea of any permanently fixed reality which could be grasped or even sensibly thought of without the mediation of human structuring. Such structuring or shaping of perception is today typically considered to be interpretation, and so we find contemporary pragmatists like Stanley Fish repeatedly insisting that interpretation comprises all our meaningful and intelligent human activity, that "interpretation is the only game in town."[4] All perception and understanding must be interpretation, since "information only comes in an interpreted form." Even in our most primitive and initial seeing of an object, "interpretation has already done its work."[5] Moreover, quite apart from such radical Nietzschean and pragmatist perspectives, we find hermeneutic universalism firmly endorsed by a traditionalist like Gadamer who baldly asserts that "all understanding is interpretation."[6]

In short, the various camps of the ever growing anti-foundationalist front seem united by the belief that interpretation subsumes all meaningful experience and reality, that there is nothing beneath interpretation which serves as the object of interpretation, since anything alleged to be such is itself an interpretive product. Though I share their rejection of foundationalism and their commitment to interpretation's pervasive and irreplaceable role, I think its role is better understood by more modest pretensions than hermeneutic universalism. Interpretation is better served by letting it leave room for something else (beneath or before it), by slimming it down from an over-bloated state which courts coronary arrest, by saving it from an ultimately self-destructive imperialist expansion.

In this chapter, I shall challenge hermeneutic universalism by critically examining what appear to be its best arguments. Having shown that those arguments need not compel belief in hermeneutic universalism, I go on to suggest why such a belief is more dangerous and unprofitable than the contrary idea that our intelligent and meaningful intercourse with the world includes non-interpretational experience, activity, and understanding, so that we should not think interpretation is the only game in town. Finally, I shall try to determine what distinguishes interpretation from those uninterpreted understandings and experiences which hermeneutic universalists insist on fully subsuming under the concept of interpretation. In drawing this distinction, I am not claiming it is a rigid ontological one, where interpretation and understanding are different natural kinds that can never share the same objects. But I hope to show that some functional distinction between them is pragmatically helpful and illuminating, and can itself be helpfully illuminated.

II

Before undertaking these tasks, however, I need to distance my challenge of interpretation from an earlier and influential critique advanced by Susan Sontag in "Against Interpretation."[7] Sontag's attack is directed not at interpretation *per se* but at the global claims of interpretation over *art*. Indeed, she explicitly endorses hermeneutic universalism's notion of "interpretation in the broadest sense, the sense in which Nietzsche (rightly) says, 'There are no facts, only interpretations'" (*AI* 5). But what *are* the claims of interpretation's dominion over art? Danto and others have argued that a work of art is ontologically constituted by interpretation. Since physically identical things can be different works if they have different interpretations, "interpretations are what constitute works, there are no works without them"; without them, works would be the "mere things" of their material substance.[8] This view that the art object is not a physical or foundational fact but must itself be constituted by an interpretive perspective is essentially an application of the Nietzschean view of objects which Danto here confines to the domain of art, elsewhere remaining a realist. Such *constitutive* interpretation of art, as Danto notes, should not be the target of Sontag's attack, though its alleged necessity – that art cannot be meaningfully experienced without being interpreted – will be a target of mine.

The interpretation she instead impugns is the deliberate act of explaining, disclosing, or decoding the content or meaning of the object (interpretively) constituted. Such interpretation of content is indicted as a corruptive act "of translation.... The interpreter, without actually erasing or rewriting the text, *is* altering it," making it "into something else," distracting us from "experiencing the luminousness of the thing in itself" by putting us on a false quest for its meaning (*AI* 5, 6, 8, 13). Rather than opening us up to the powerful sensuous experience of art's surface form, which is the essence of art's liberational challenge to the primacy of the cognitive and discursive, interpretation "poisons our sensibilities" and represents "the revenge of the intellect upon art" at the expense of our "sensual capability" (*AI* 7). Sontag therefore urges, "In place of a hermeneutics we need an erotics of art," and she conceives this erotics in terms of a criticism that gives "more attention to form in art," "that dissolves considerations of content into those of form," and that "would supply a really accurate, sharp, loving description of the appearance of a work of art," "to show *how it is what it is*" (*AI* 12–14).

Though I support Sontag's protest against hermeneutics' imperialist conquest of all artistic understanding and share her insistence on greater recognition of sensuous immediacy in aesthetic experience, I cannot accept her critique of interpretation. This is not because its repudiation of content for pure form and eros seems to reflect and legitimate what is arguably the worst of American culture – meaningless sex, empty formalism, and contempt of intellect. Such ideological complaints we can leave to students of Adorno and to our own moments of alienated discontent. What I wish to show is that whatever our verdict on its ideological stance, Sontag's critique is severely crippled by deep confusions and unwarranted assumptions.

First, in claiming that all interpretation "sustains the fancy that there really is such a thing as the content of a work of art" and in subsequently demanding that criticism instead confine itself to form, which is contrastingly real, Sontag relies on a naively rigid content/form distinction which suggests that form itself has no content and which she herself later wishes to deny (*AI* 5, 11–12). Secondly, Sontag betrays a naive realism about the work of art's identity and form which is not only unconvincing but totally at odds with the Nietzschean interpretive position she claims to endorse. Her attack on interpretation for necessarily "altering" or "translating" the work "into something else" rather than describing the work as "just what it is," "the thing in itself," presumes, first, that there is some foundational identity of the work "just as it is" apart from our constitutive and perspectival grasping of it and, secondly, that we can transparently grasp that identity (*AI* 6, 8, 11, 13). "Transparence," which Sontag claims as the highest value in art and criticism, "means experiencing the luminousness of the thing in itself" (*AI* 13). But the Nietzschean notion of constitutive identity not only rejects such non-perspectival transparency; it repudiates the very idea of the uninterpreted "thing in itself" as a dogmatic notion.[9]

Sontag's third confusion is her presumption that while interpretive content represents "the revenge of the intellect on art" by taming art's sensuous liberational power into something "manageable, conformable" (*AI* 8), form, on the other hand, is neither intellectual nor constraining but simply liberationally erotic. This is obviously false, as the very morphology of the word "conformable" makes clear. Indeed, since the time of Plato and Aristotle, who essentially framed our notion of form, we regard form as something paradigmatically intellectual and constraining. Moreover, as has been emphasized since Kant, the formalistic appreciation of aesthetic objects demands much more intellectual power and repressive austerity than appreciation based on content, which can simply rely on our ordinary feelings associated with and immediately evoked by the content. Formalists like Kant and Clive Bell condemn the more natural, less intellectualized appreciation of content as philistine barbarism.[10] Sontag similarly condemns interpretation of content as philistinism, and privileges the appreciation of form. But she mistakenly confuses formal analysis with unintellectual "sensuous immediacy" (*AI* 9), when it instead requires no less (and usually much more) intellectual mediation than the interpretation of content.

This leads to the fourth crucial error in Sontag's position – her failure to recognize that she is not really sustaining a global rejection of interpretation; for the formalistic analysis she advocates is itself a recognized form of interpretation. It is simply a mistake to think that all interpretation is governed by the depth metaphor of uncovering hidden layers or kernels of meaning. Interpretation is also practiced and theorized in terms of formal structure, with the aim not so much of exposing hidden meanings but of connecting unconcealed features and surfaces so as to see and present the work as a well-related whole. Recognition of this formalist interpretive mode which aims "to grasp the whole design" of the work is what swayed an earlier rejector of interpretation, T. S. Eliot, from his view that "the work of art cannot be interpreted" to an acceptance of interpretation's ineliminable role and value.[11]

Sontag should similarly recognize that her apparent critique of all interpretation is but a privileging legitimation of one interpretive form above and against all others. She provides no argument that we ever should or could do without interpretation altogether or that in fact we ever do do without it in at least its Nietzschean constitutive sense. She does not even consider hermeneutic universalism's arguments for holding that interpretation is necessarily present in any meaningful experience of art, or of anything else. In short, Sontag's critique is simply that we should not interpret for content. What I instead contest is the view that, logically and necessarily, we are always interpreting whenever we meaningfully experience or understand something, the view expressed in Gadamer's dictum that "all understanding is interpretation." I must therefore address the powerful arguments for this view.

III

Since our current hermeneutic turn derives in large part from the rejection of foundationalism, it is not surprising that the central arguments for hermeneutic universalism turn on rejecting foundationalist ideas of transparent fact, absolute and univocal truth, and mind-independent objectivity. For such ideas underwrite the possibility of attaining some perfect God's-eye grasp of things as they really are, independent of how we differently perceive them, a seeing or understanding that is free from the corrigibility and perspectival pluralities and prejudices that we willingly recognize as intrinsic to all interpretation.

I think the universalists are right to reject such foundational understanding, but wrong to conclude from this that all understanding is interpretation. Their mistake, a grave but simple one, is to equate the non-foundational with the interpretive. In other words, what the universalists are successfully arguing is that all understanding is non-foundational; that it is always corrigible, perspectival, and somehow prejudiced or prestructured; that no meaningful experience is passively neutral and disinterestedly non-selective. But since, in the traditional foundationalist framework, interpretation is contrasted and designated as *the* form of non-foundational understanding, the inferior foster home of all corrigible, perspectival perception, it is easy to confuse the view that no understanding is foundational with the view that all understanding is interpretive. Yet this confusion of hermeneutic universalism betrays an unseemly residual bond to the foundationalist framework, in the assumption that what is not foundational must be interpretive. It thus prevents the holists from adopting a more liberating pragmatist perspective which (I shall argue) can profitably distinguish between understanding and interpretation without thereby endorsing foundationalism. Such pragmatism more radically recognizes uninterpreted realities, experiences, and understandings as already perspectival, prejudiced, and corrigible – in short, as non-foundationally given.

So much for a general overview of the universalist arguments. I now want to itemize and consider six of them in detail. Though there is some overlap, we can roughly divide them into three groups, respectively based on three ineliminable features of all understanding: (a) corrigibility, (b) perspectival plurality and prejudice, and (c) mental activity and process.

(1) What we understand, what we grasp as truth or fact, frequently turns out to be wrong, to require correction, revision, and replacement by a different understanding. Moreover, this new understanding is typically achieved by reinterpreting the former understanding and can itself be replaced and shown to be not fact but "mere interpretation" by a subsequent understanding reached through interpretive thought. Since any putative fact or true understanding can be revised or replaced by interpretation, it cannot enjoy an epistemological status higher than interpretation; and interpretation is paradigmatically corrigible and inexhaustive. This is sometimes what is meant by the claim that there are no facts or truths but only interpretations.

The inference, then, is that since understanding is epistemologically no better than interpretation, it is altogether no different from interpretation (as if all meaningful differences had to be differences of apodicticness!). The conclusion is reinforced by the further inference that since all interpretation is corrigible and all understanding is corrigible, then all understanding is interpretation. Once formulated, the inferences are obviously (indeed pathetically) fallacious. But we tend to accept their conclusion, since we assimilate all corrigible and partial understanding to interpretation, as if genuine understanding itself could never be revised or enlarged, as if understanding had to be interpretive to be corrigible. But why make this rigidly demanding assumption? Traditionally, the reason was that understanding (like its cognates truth and fact) was itself defined in contrast to "mere interpretation" as that which *is* incorrigible. But if we abandon foundationalism by denying that any understanding is incorrigible, the idea of corrigible understanding becomes possible and indeed necessary; and once we recognize this idea, there is no need to infer that all understanding must be interpretation simply because it is corrigible. When hermeneutic universalists make this inference, they show an unintended and unbecoming reliance on the foundationalist linkage of uninterpreted understanding with incorrigible, foundational truth.

(2) The second argument for hermeneutic universalism derives from understanding's ineliminable perspectival character and the plurality of perspectives. We already noted how Nehamas builds his argument that all understanding is interpretive on the premise that all understanding, indeed "all our activity is partial and perspectival." I think the premise is perfectly acceptable and can be established by an argument which Nehamas does not supply. All understanding must be perspectival or aspectual, since all thought and perception exhibit intentionality (in the phenomenological sense of being about something) and all intentionality is aspectual, i.e., grasping its object in a certain way. But the very idea of perspective or aspect implies that there are other possible perspectives or aspects which lie (in Gadamer's words) outside "the horizon" of a particular perspectival standpoint and thus outside its "range of vision" (*TM* 269). Thus there can be no univocal and exclusive understanding of any thing, but rather many partial or perspectival ways of seeing it, none of which provides total and exclusive truth.

So much for the premise; but how does it follow that all understanding is interpretive? Again, in the traditional foundationalist framework, interpretation marks the realm of partial, perspectival, and plural ways of human understanding in essential contrast to some ideal understanding that grasps things as they really are univocally, exhaustively, and absolutely. Rejecting the very possibility and intelligibility of such univocal and complete understanding (as Nehamas and Gadamer rightly do), the universalists infer that all understanding is thereby reduced to interpretation – the foundationalist category for understanding which is not necessarily false or illegitimate (not a *mis*understanding) but which cannot represent true understanding since it is perspectivally plural and not necessarily and wholly true. However, again we should realize that once we are free of foundationalism's doctrines, there is no need to accept its categorizations. There is thus no need to deny that true understanding can itself be perspectivally partial and plural, and consequently no reason to conclude that since all understanding must be perspectival, it must also be interpretation.[12]

(3) In speaking of understanding as perspectival and hence partial, we have so far meant that it cannot exclude different perspectives and can in principle always be supplemented. But partiality also has the central sense of bias and prejudice. The third argument why understanding must always be interpretation is that it is always prejudiced and never neutrally

transparent. This is a key point in the Nietzschean, Gadamerian, and even pragmatist attacks on foundationalist understanding. Any understanding involves the human element which prestructures understanding in terms (and in service) of our interests, drives, and needs, which significantly overlap but also frequently diverge among different societies and individuals. Moreover, for Nietzsche, Gadamer, and the pragmatists, the fact that understanding is always motivated and prejudiced by our needs and values is a very good thing; it is what allows us to thrive and survive so that we can understand anything at all.

From the premise that "all understanding inevitably involves some prejudice" (*TM* 239), "that every view depends on and manifests specific values" and "antecedent commitments" (*N* 67–8), it is but a short step to the view that all understanding and perception is interpretation. But it is a step where the more canny pragmatist fears to tread, and where she parts company from grand continental hermeneuts like Nietzsche and Gadamer. In rejecting the foundationalist idea and ideal of transparent mirroring perception, she recognizes that understanding is always motivated and prejudiced, just like interpretation. But she wonders why this makes understanding always interpretive. It just does not follow, unless we presume that *only* interpretation could be prejudiced, while (preinterpretive) understanding or experience simply could not be. But to her, this inference is as strange and offensive as a sexist argument that all humans are really women because they all are influenced by emotions, while presumably real men are not.

(4) The fourth argument for hermeneutic universalism inhabits the overlap between understanding's perspectival partiality and its active process. The argument is basically that since all understanding is selective – focused on some things and features but not on others – all understanding must therefore be interpretive. The fact that understanding is perspectivally partial (in both senses of incompleteness and purposive bias) implies that it is always selective. It always grasps some things rather than others, and what it grasps depends in part on its antecedent purposes.

This much seems uncontestable. What I challenge is the inference that since understanding (or indeed any intelligent activity) is always selective, it is therefore always interpretive. Such a conclusion needs the further premise that all purposive selection must be the product of interpretive thinking and decision. But this premise is false, an instance of the philosophical fallacy Dewey dubbed "intellectualism."[13] For most of the selection involved in our ordinary acts of perception and understanding is done automatically and unconsciously (yet still intelligently and not mechanically) on the basis of intelligent habits, without any reflection or deliberation at all.[14] Interpretation, in its standard ordinary usage, certainly implies conscious thought and deliberate reflection; but not all intelligent and purposive selection is conscious or deliberate. Walking down the stairs requires selecting how and where to place one's feet and body; but such selection involves interpreting only in cases of abnormal conditions when descent of the staircase presents a problem (as with an unusually dark or narrow winding staircase, a sprained ankle, or a fit of vertigo).

Just as it is wrong to confuse all purposive intelligent choice with interpretive decisions requiring ratiocination, so we can distinguish perceptions and understandings that are immediately given to us (albeit only corrigibly and based on prior experience) from understandings reached only by interpretive deliberation on the meaning of what is immediately given. When I awake on the beach at Santa Cruz with my eyes pierced by sunlight, I immediately perceive or understand it is daytime; only when I instead awake to a darkish gloom do I need to interpret that it is no longer night but merely another dreary morning in Philadelphia.

In short, I am arguing that although all understanding is selective, not all selective understanding is interpretive. If understanding's selection is neither conscious nor deliberate but prereflective and immediate, we have no reason to regard that selection or the resultant understanding as interpretation, since interpretation standardly implies some deliberate or at least conscious thinking, whereas understanding does not.[15] We can understand something without thinking about it at all; but to interpret something we need to think about it. This distinction may recall a conclusion from Wittgenstein's famous discussion of seeing-as, where he distinguishes seeing from interpreting: "To interpret is to think, to do something; seeing is a state."[16]

(5) Though insightful, Wittgenstein's remark is also problematic. For it suspiciously suggests that we could see or understand without doing anything; and this suspicion suggests the fifth argument for hermeneutic universalism. Understanding or perceiving, as Nietzscheans, pragmatists, and even Gadamerians insist, is active. It is not a passive mirroring, but an active structuring of what is encountered. To hear or see anything,

before we even attempt to interpret it, involves the activity of our bodies, certain motor responses and tensions in the muscles and nerves of our organs of sensation. To characterize seeing or understanding in sharp contrast to interpretation as an achieved "state" rather than as "doing something" suggests that understanding is static rather than active; and if passively static, then it should be neutral rather than selective and structuring. The fifth argument for hermeneutic universalism therefore rejects this distinction between understanding as passively neutral and interpretation as actively structuring, and then infers that since all understanding is active, all understanding must be interpretive.

My response to this argument should already be clear. As a pragmatist, I fully accept the premise that all perception and understanding involve doing something; but I deny this entails that they always involve interpretation. The inference relies on an implicit premise that all "doings" that are cognitively valuable or significant for thought are themselves already cases of thinking. Hence any active selection and structuring of perception must already be a thoughtful, deliberate selection, one involving an interpretive decision. This is the premise I contest, the assimilating conflation of all active, selective, and structuring intelligence with the active, selective structuring of the interpreting intellect. Understanding can actively structure and select without engaging in interpretation, just as action can be intelligent without engaging thought or the intellect. When, on my way to the beach, I am told that the surf is up, I immediately understand what is said, prereflectively selecting and structuring the sounds and meanings I respond to. I do not need to interpret what is said or meant. Only if I were unfamiliar with idiomatic English, or unable to hear the words, or in a situation where the utterance seemed out of place, would I have to interpret it. Only if there were some problem in understanding, some puzzle or doubt or incongruity, would I have to thematize the utterance as something that needed interpretation, something to think about and clarify or resolve.

(6) But this assertion is precisely what is challenged by the sixth argument for universal hermeneutics, an argument which highlights the intimate link between the hermeneutic turn and the linguistic turn in both continental and Anglo-American philosophy. Briefly and roughly, the argument goes as follows. All understanding is linguistic, because all understanding (as indeed all experience) involves concepts that require language. But linguistic understanding is essentially a matter of decoding or interpreting signs which are arbitrary rather than natural and whose

translation into meaningful propositions thus requires interpretation. To understand the meaning of a sentence, we need, on the Quinean-Davidsonian model, to supply a translation or interpretation of it in terms already familiar to us (whether those terms be in the interpreted language itself or in another more familiar "home" language). So Davidson boldly asserts that "All understanding of the speech of another involves radical interpretation", and firmly equates "the power of thought" with "speaking a language."[17] And from the continental tradition, Gadamer concurs by basing the universal scope of hermeneutics on "the essential linguisticality of all human experience of the world" and on a view of language as "itself the game of interpretation that we are all engaged in every day."[18] Hence, not only all understanding but all experience is interpretive, since both are ineliminably linguistic – a conclusion endorsed by Rorty, Derrida, and a legion of hermeneutic universalists.

Though the consensus for this position is powerful, the argument strikes me as less than persuasive. It warrants challenging on two points at least. First, we can question the idea that linguistic understanding is always the decoding, translation, or interpretation of arbitrary signs through rules of meaning and syntax. This is, I think, an overly formalistic and intellectualized picture of linguistic understanding. Certainly it is not apparent that we always (or ever) interpret, decode, or translate the uncoded and unproblematic utterances we hear in our native tongue simply in order to understand them. That is precisely why ordinary language distinguishes such direct and simple understandings from decodings, translations, and interpretations.

The hermeneutic universalists will object that we must be interpreting here, even if we don't realize it, since no other model can account for our understanding. But an alternative model *is* available in Wittgenstein, where linguistic understanding is a matter of being able to make the right responses or moves in the relevant language-game, and where such ability or language-acquisition is first gained by brute training or drill.[19] Language mastery is (at least in part) the mastery of intelligent habits of gesture and response for engaging effectively in a form of life, rather than the mastery of a system of semiotic rules for interpreting signs.

So I think a case can be made for some distinction between understanding and interpreting language, between an unreflective but intelligent trained habit of response and a thoughtful decision about how to understand or respond. I have to interpret or translate most utterances I hear in German in order to understand them, but I understand most sentences I hear in English without interpreting them; I interpret only those that seem unclear or insufficiently understood. To defend the conflation of understanding with interpretation by arguing that in simply understanding those alleged uninterpreted utterances, I am in fact already interpreting sounds as words – or, perhaps further, that my nervous system is busy interpreting vibrations into sounds – is not only to stretch the meaning of "interpretation" for no productive purpose; it is also to misrepresent our actual experience. Certainly we can make a distinction between the words and the sounds, and between the sounds and the vibrations that cause them. But this does not mean they are really distinct or distinguishable in experience and that I must therefore interpret the sounds in order to understand them as words. On the contrary, when I hear a language I understand, I typically don't hear the sounds at all but only the understood words or message. If any interpretive effort is needed, it is to hear the words as sounds or vibrations, not vice versa.

Secondly, even if we grant that linguistic understanding is always and necessarily interpretation, it still would not follow that all understanding is interpretive. For that requires the further premise that all understanding and meaningful experience is indeed linguistic. And such a premise, though it be the deepest dogma of the linguistic turn in both analytic and continental philosophy, is neither self-evident nor immune to challenge. Certainly there seem to be forms of bodily awareness or understanding that are not linguistic in nature and that in fact defy adequate linguistic characterization, though they can be somehow referred to through language. As dancers, we understand the sense and rightness of a movement or posture proprioceptively, by feeling it in our spine and muscles, without translating it into conceptual linguistic terms. We can neither learn nor properly understand the movement simply by being talked through it.

Moreover, apart from the non-linguistic understandings and experiences of which we are aware, there are more basic experiences or understandings of which we are not even conscious, but whose successful transaction provides the necessary background selection and organization of our field which enable consciousness to have a focus and emerge as a foreground. We typically experience our verticality and direction of gaze without being aware of them; but without our experiencing them, we could not be conscious of or focused on what we are in fact aware of, and our perceptual field would be very different. As Dewey insisted, there is a difference between not knowing an experience and not having it. "Consciousness...is only a very small and shifting portion of experience" and relies on "a context which is non-cognitive," a "universe of non-reflectional experience."[20]

To all such talk of non-linguistic experience or understanding, the hermeneutic universalists have a ready and seemingly irresistible response. How can I claim that any experience is non-linguistic, when in that very claim I have had to talk about it, refer to it by language? Any attempt to characterize something as non-linguistic or describe it as linguistically inexpressible self-refutingly renders it linguistic and linguistically expressed. Therefore whatever can be said to exist, or even is explicitly thought to exist (since explicit thinking can be seen as conceptual and language-dependent), is and must be linguistic. Hence Gadamer, for example, concludes "Being that can be understood is language" (*TM* 432), and the likes of Derrida and Rorty similarly deny any "*hors-texte*."

This argument has, I admit, considerable suasive power, and it has long swayed me. But recently it has come to seem more like a sophistic paradox about talking without language than a deep truth about human experience and the world. Surely, once we have to talk about something, even merely to affirm or deny its existence, we must bring it into the game of language, give it a linguistic visa or some conceptual-textual identity, even if the visa be one of alien or inferior linguistic status, like "inexpressible tingle" or "non-discursive image." But this only means that we can never talk (or explicitly think) about things existing without their being somehow linguistically mediated; it does not mean that we can never experience them non-linguistically or that they cannot exist for us meaningfully but not in language.

We philosophers fail to see this because, disembodied talking-heads that we are, the only form of experience we recognize and legitimate is linguistic: thinking, talking, writing. But neither we nor the language which admittedly helps shape us could survive without the unarticulated background of prereflective, non-linguistic experience and understanding.[21] Hermeneutic universalism thus fails in its argument that interpretation is the only game in town because language is the only game in town. For there is both uninterpreted linguistic understanding and meaningful experience that is non-linguistic. They reside in those unmanageably illiterate and darkly somatic neighborhoods of town that we philosophers and literary theorists are occupationally accustomed to avoid and ignore, but on which we rely for our non-professional sustenance and satisfactions.[22] After the conference papers are over, we go slumming in their bars.

IV

Thus far I have resisted the universalists' arguments that understanding and interpretation cannot possibly be distinguished since all understanding is and must be interpretation. What remains, for the final sections of this chapter, is to show why the distinction is worth making and how it should be made and understood. There are three reasons why I think it important to preserve some distinction between understanding and interpretation.

First and most simply, it provides interpretation with a "contrast-class" to help delimit and thus shape its meaning. Without an activity to contrast with interpretation, what can interpretation really mean? The possibility of alternatives is a necessary condition of meaningfulness. This principle of choice, endorsed not only in structuralist semantics but in analytic information theory, recognizes that the meaning of a term or proposition is a function of those terms or propositions it opposes or excludes.[23] Notions of unlimited extension, like tautologies that are universally true, tend to evaporate into semantic emptiness. If everything we do or experience is always and must always be interpretation, the notion of interpretation becomes synonymous with all human life and activity, and thus loses any real meaning or specific role of its own. Uninterpreted understandings and experiences provide a relevant contrast-class for interpretations, enabling interpretation to be distinguishable as having some definite meaning of its own, since its meaning is in some way defined and limited by what falls outside it and is contrasted to it.

Secondly, understanding provides interpretation not only with a meaning-giving contrast, but also with a meaning-giving ground. It supplies something on which to base and guide our interpretations and represents something by which we can distinguish between different levels or sequential acts of interpretation. How does understanding ground and guide interpretation? We can find the makings of an answer in Heidegger and Wittgenstein, two revered progenitors of hermeneutic universalism who I think wisely resisted that doctrine. The complexly reciprocal and stratified relationship between understanding and interpretation is suggested in the second dimension of the hermeneutic circle, which Heidegger calls to our attention in his famous remark that "any interpretation which is to contribute understanding must already have understood what is to be interpreted."[24]

Elucidating this idea with respect to a literary text, we can say that before and while we try to interpret its meaning, we must be struck and directed by some sense of what it is we are trying to interpret. At the very least, we need some primitive understanding of what we are individuating as the textual object of interpretation, simply to identify it as such. Moreover, it is our initial understanding or experience of the text as something meaningful and perhaps worth understanding more fully that generates our desire to interpret it. We do not interpret every text we encounter. But our attempt to interpret the given text is not only motivated but also guided by this prior understanding, though it be inchoate, vague, and corrigible. For we form our interpretive hypotheses about the text (and accept or reject alternative interpretations) on the basis of what we already understand as properly belonging to the text rather than falsely foisted onto it.

But how do we determine whether our initial guiding understanding is valid and not a misunderstanding? We cannot appeal to the apodicticness or incorrigibility of understanding, because we have rejected all foundationalist accounts of understanding. Nor can we simply test the validity of our initial understanding by measuring it against the meaning of the text. For, since the text's meaning is not self-evidently given but is precisely what is in question, we would first have to determine more clearly what this meaning is. Yet to do this, we must interpret, and thus we can only test our prior understanding by subsequent interpretation. In other words, though interpretation of the text must be based on some prior understanding of it, this understanding itself requires interpretation of the text for its own clarification and justification, if indeed we wish to pursue this. But that clarificatory and justificatory interpretation depends again on the very understanding it has to sharpen or validate. And so the hermeneutic circle revolves in a cycle of understanding and interpretation.

Considerations of this sort have led Gadamer and other hermeneutic universalists to the radical claim that "all understanding is interpretation" (*TM* 350). But this claim, I have argued, is not only uncompelling but actually misleading in suggesting that we can never understand anything without interpreting it. For in many cases we are simply satisfied with our initial understanding and don't go on to interpret; there are always other – and usually better – things to do.

Moreover, if we could never understand anything without interpreting it, how could we ever understand the interpretation itself? It too would have to be interpreted, and so would its interpretation, and so on *ad infinitum*. As Wittgenstein notes, "any interpretation still hangs in the air along with what it interprets." Interpretation must ultimately depend on some prior understanding, some "way of grasping...which is *not* an *interpretation*."[25] This is just a point of philosophical grammar about how these notions are related: understanding grounds and guides interpretation, while interpretation enlarges, validates, or corrects understanding. We must remember that the distinction is functional or relational, not ontological.[26] The prior and grounding understanding "which is not an interpretation" may have been the product of prior interpretations, though now it is immediately grasped. Moreover, it need not be an explicitly formulated or conscious understanding, and the ground it provides is not an *incorrigible* ground.[27]

Though the universalists are wrong to deny that any valid and helpful distinction can be drawn between simply understanding something and interpreting that which was understood, their attempts to deny it have not been unhelpful. For they showed that there is no rigid or absolute dichotomy, but rather an essential continuity and degree of interdependence between understanding and interpretation. What is now immediately understood may once have been the product of a labored interpretation and may form the basis for further interpretation. Words of a French song I once labored to interpret are now immediately understood, and this understanding affords me the ground for an interpretation of their deeper poetic meaning. Though frequently what we encounter neither demands nor receives interpretation, many things are felt to be insufficiently understood until they are interpreted by us or for us. We seek an interpretation because we are not satisfied with the understanding we already have – feeling it partial, obscure, shallow, fragmented, or simply dull – and we want to make it fuller or more adequate. Yet the superior interpretation sought must be guided by that prior inadequate understanding. We no longer feel the need to interpret further when the new, fuller understanding that interpretation has supplied is felt to be satisfactory. Criteria of what is satisfactory will obviously vary with context and will depend on the sort of understanding sought. Wittgenstein aptly puts this pragmatic point: "What happens is not that this symbol cannot be further interpreted, but: I do no interpreting. I do not interpret, because I feel at home in the present picture."[28]

The third reason why I think it worth distinguishing between understanding and interpretation is to defend the ordinary: not only ordinary usage, which itself draws and endorses the distinction, but also ordinary experiences of understanding, whose legitimacy and value tend to get discredited by universal hermeneutics' assimilation of all experience to interpretation. In commonplace discourse, not all understanding is interpretation. There are countless contexts where one might justifiably reply to a query of how one interpreted something by denying that one actually interpreted it at all: "I didn't bother interpreting what he said; I just took it at face value." "I didn't pause to interpret her command (question); I immediately complied with it (ignored it)."

Even if these direct or immediate understandings are always based on habits and capacities resulting from prior interpretation, there is still a difference between such effortless, unthinking understanding and acts of interpretation, which call for deliberate, focused thought. In marking a difference between interpretation and the more direct experiences or understandings on which it is based, ordinary language respects the role of the unformulable, prereflective, and non-discursive background from which the foreground of conscious thinking emerges and without which it could never arise. In rejecting this distinction by asserting that all experience is interpretation, hermeneutic universalists deny this very ordinary but very crucial *unthinking* dimension of our lives and indeed of our thinking.

We saw a variation of this discrediting denial of the ordinary and unreflective in Stanley Fish's account of reading. As hermeneutic universalist, he asserts that all our activity is essentially interpretive. We cannot simply read or even recognize a text without interpreting it, since the text can only be constituted by an act of interpretation. Now since interpretation implies active thinking and discourse, it must in some way supplement, shape, or reconstruct the text. Hence all our apparent practices of reading are really "not for reading but for writing texts." And having conflated reading with interpretation, Fish further conflates interpretation with the institutionalized interpretation of professional academic criticism, where an interpretation must not only be discursively formulated but must provide "something different" or significantly new in order to be legitimate and "be given a hearing." Hence any proper reading of a text involves "changing it" in some professionally meaningful way.[29] The result is that ordinary, unreflective, non-professional modes of reading are discredited and dismissed as foundationalist myth. Yet precisely these unreflective unoriginal readings, which anticipate the attempt to interpret, are what in fact provides the basis for professional transformative interpretations by supplying some shared background of meaning which enables us to identify what we agree to call "the same text" so that we can then proceed to interpret it differently.

Here, as elsewhere, universal hermeneutics' dismissal of the preinterpretive reflects an intellectualist blindness to the unreflective, non-discursive dimension of ordinary experience, a bias at once haughtily elitist and parochially uncritical. To defend this ordinary, unassuming, and typically silent dimension, we need to preserve something distinct from interpretive activity, even if it cannot and should not be immune from interpretation and may indeed rest on what was once interpretation.

V

I have argued that we can eschew foundationalism without maintaining that all experience and understanding must be interpretation. We can do so by insisting that understanding should itself be understood non-foundationally – that is, as corrigible, perspectival, pluralistic, prejudiced, and engaged in active process. I have further argued that there are at least a few good reasons for admitting some meaningful human activity or experience other than interpretation and thus for allowing, or indeed drawing, some distinction between interpretation and understanding. What remains is to suggest how this distinction might best be drawn or understood, largely by recollecting and recasting some of the central points already made here.

First, the distinction between understanding and interpretation is not a rigid ontological one, where the two notions cannot share the same objects. Second, they cannot be distinguished by epistemological reliability, where understanding implies univocal truth while interpretation connotes pluralistic error. Nonetheless, understanding and interpretation are epistemologically different in terms of their functional relations: understanding initially grounds and guides interpretation, while the latter explores, validates, or modifies that initial ground of meaning.

Other differences to be drawn between understanding and interpretation are probably more debatable. While understanding – even highly intelligent understanding – is often unreflective, unthinking, indeed unconscious (even if always purposive), interpretation proper involves conscious, deliberate thought: the clarification of something obscure or ambiguous, the deciphering of a symbol, the unraveling of a paradox, the articulation of previously unstated formal or semantic relations between elements. While understanding is frequently a matter of smoothly co-ordinated, unproblematic handling of what we encounter,[30] interpretation characteristically involves a problem-situation. We stop to interpret only in order to resolve a problem – some obscurity, ambiguity, contradiction, or, more recently, the professional academic problem of *generating* an interpretive problem. The intrinsic problem-solving character of interpretation explains why it involves conscious, deliberate inquiry. Solving a problem demands thinking; seeing the obvious does not.

On this question of consciousness, our ordinary linguistic usage (to which I earlier appealed) does not give unchallengeable support. Although it sounds strange to speak of someone unconsciously interpreting some remark or event, it is ˙not a blatant contradiction or solecism. But that is simply because language aims more at loose flexibility than at precision, and because hermeneutic universalism has accustomed us to think loosely of interpretation as subsuming all construals, understandings, or meaningful experiences, some of which are obviously unconscious. If our ordinary speech does not always draw a distinction between interpreting and understanding, it makes it more often than not and never implies that it is not worth making.

The conscious and problem-solving character of interpretation suggests yet another feature that might help distinguish it from understanding. Though both are inevitably perspectival, interpretive activity seems intrinsically aware that alternative interpretations may be or indeed have been given to resolve the problem, while understanding can be unreflectively blind to the existence or possibility of alternative understandings, since it can be unaware of any problem of understanding which might present alternative solutions.

I conclude with one last suggestion for distinguishing interpretation from more primitive or basic understandings and experiences, one which reaffirms the link I established between hermeneutic universalism and the linguistic turn. Interpretation is characteristically aimed at linguistic formulation, at translating one meaningful expression into another one. A criterion for having an interpretation of some utterance or event would be an ability to express in some explicit, articulated form what that interpretation is. To interpret a text would be to produce (at least mentally) a text.[31] Understanding, on the other hand, does not require linguistic articulation; a proper reaction, a shudder or a tingle, may be enough to indicate that one has understood. Some of the things we experience and understand are never captured by language, not only because their particular feel defies adequate linguistic expression but because we are not even aware of them as "things" to describe.[32] They are the felt background we presuppose when we start to articulate or to interpret.

"There are, indeed, things that cannot be put into words. They *show* themselves. They are the mystical."[33] So said the greatest twentieth-century philosopher of language in his first philosophical masterpiece. What Wittgenstein fails to emphasize here is that the ineffable but manifest is as much ordinary as mystical, and it is only mystifying to those disembodied philosophical minds who recognize no understanding other than interpretation, and no form of meaning and experience beyond or beneath the web of language.

Part II
Rethinking Art

6

Aesthetic Ideology, Aesthetic Education, and Art's Value in Critique

I

Beauty, whatever it may be, is clearly so powerfully appealing to human-kind as to be its own excuse and require no apologists. Art is not so fortunate. Since its initial attack by Plato and through its emergence as an autonomous field, art has been hard put to justify itself. Though often conducted under the more limited titles of "An Apologie for Poetry" (Sidney) or "The Defence of Poetry" (Shelley), the justification of art has always been, since Aristotle's first reply to Plato, a central aim of aesthetics. One reason for its enduring importance is that art's defense (like art's definition) has never received a decisively satisfactory solution that would silence further questioning. It seems as if each age needs to struggle anew to determine and affirm both art's nature and its value, and to determine and affirm them differently in terms of the different needs (and dominant art forms and styles) of the age and in response to the different charges being leveled at art.

Some of these charges (e.g. art's blaspheming "graven image," frivol-ous inutility, and propagation of illusion) are stubbornly persistent through-out history, while others (e.g. that art is complicitous with oppressive socio-political hierarchies) are obviously of more recent vintage. The future, if art has one, is bound to bring new indictments. We cannot therefore expect a permanent and final justification that would quell all radical critique of the phenomenon or institution of art. Nor should we want one. For art builds on and grows from its critique; and the end of vigorous criticism in the smug complacency of art's unquestionable value might well spell the end of art, the arrest of its evolution.

Much of my argument in chapters 1 and 2 was directed against the conception of art that has long dominated our aesthetic thought and experience, hardening and narrowing the institution of art and impoverishing its practice. This dominant aesthetic ideology identifies art with the institution of high fine art. In dubbing this view "the museum conception of art," Dewey aptly conveyed its dual dimensions of compartmental institutionalization and elitism, its separation from life and praxis, its distance from ordinary people and their experience. The following chapters will continue to criticize this narrow conception of art for its monopolistic exclusion of popular art as aesthetically illegitimate, an exclusion which helps sustain forms of socio-cultural oppression (which is not to deny that popular art has also been exploited as a tool of such oppression).

My extended critique could give the false impression that high art should be altogether repudiated, its institutions dismantled, and its works abandoned as inevitably life-repressing and socially pernicious. But rejecting the narrowness of our dominant conception of art is to reject its own exclusionary rejections, not to reject the art this conception in fact comprises. Moreover, the fact that our entrenched institution of art has long been elitist and oppressive does not mean that it must remain such, that art is necessarily, by its very nature, "an enemy of the people" which we therefore "should resist."[1]

The pragmatist project in aesthetics is not to abolish the institution of art but to transform it. The aim, to adapt Dewey's museum metaphor, is not to close or destroy art's museums but to open and enlarge them. The pragmatist defense against the charge that art is necessarily a conservative force of social oppression and class privilege involves a twofold opening. First, it involves an opening of the concept of art to include popular arts whose support and satisfactions spread far beyond the socio-cultural elite. But we also need a greater openness to the ways high art can further a progressive ethical and socio-political agenda through greater critical attention to the ethical and social dimensions of its works, many of which embody their own potent critique of high art's ethical limitations and socio-cultural dangers. This second point is perhaps best made through the concrete criticism of specific works, and I shall undertake this here with respect to T. S. Eliot's poem "Portrait of a Lady."

But since philosophical readers, even in aesthetics, are typically more fond of argumentation than interpretation, it seems prudent to preface my study of the poem by considering some of the powerful arguments likely to be raised against high art from the socio-ethical standpoint. It is just as prudent to insist that my counterarguments in defense of high art are not at all aimed at exonerating it as perfectly innocent, but more at redeeming its socio-ethical value in terms of mitigating compensations and promising potential.

II

(1) One way that the tradition of high art serves established and oppressive social orders is in its promotion of pious respect for the past, an adulatory nostalgia achieved through the mystifying beauty of past works of art. Their entrancing genius tends to inspire an attitude of humble admiration before the individuals, age, and order that could produce them, implying (in Eliot's words) that today "the only wisdom we can hope to acquire is the wisdom of humility" before such past achievement.[2] But such humility is both an effective deterrent to new thinking and a preemptive criticism of any new ideas claiming to be better than the inherited ideology of the past. Art thus provides an oppressive conservative establishment with a most powerful weapon to sustain existing privilege and domination, to affirm the status quo and the past which engendered it, despite all the misery and injustice they contain. Bewitched by the glorious art of Greece, we forget its slavery and barbarism, and our own. For such reasons, the continued existence of high art may be seen as a menace to radically new cultural creation and social liberation; and the "Proletkult" cultural movement in post-revolutionary Russia therefore wished to eliminate it altogether: "In the name of our future we are burning Raphael, destroying the museums, and trampling on the flowers of art."[3]

But must high art always foster an uncritical quiescent humility toward our ideological tradition and inherited social order, thus inducing an entranced blindness and impotence regarding their entrenched but potentially alterable evils? There are at least three reasons to doubt this. Most simply, it is historically false that works of high art have never functioned as instruments of social criticism, protest, and transformation. There are novels, poems, plays, and even paintings of biting social satire; and art's social critique and protest need not be in the radically political manner of Brecht in order to be persuasive. Secondly, apart from concern with explicit social criticism, past art's inviting vision of alien social worlds and ways of life can help us realize that our own socially entrenched practices are neither necessary nor ideal, thereby opening the way for change. The charge that high art's masterpieces cannot help but implicitly endorse or reinforce the status quo rests on two false assumptions. The first presumes that there is essential community between the established social order, ethos, and values of today and those of past generations and cultures. But there simply is not, and discovering this is one of the crucial benefits of appreciating past art. In their alterity (not least the very alterity of their pastness), they show up the smug parochialism of the present, a present obsessed with its own changing moment and the worship of the superficially new. Past art, like history, shows how things can be (since have been) otherwise and that such differences may in some ways be better. It thus demonstrates that what currently seems a natural social necessity is a historically generated and hence alterable contingency. In short, it can effectively provide the raising of consciousness necessary for more explicit social critique and change.

Moreover, apart from their critical contrast to the present, past works and the visions of life they portray are not in themselves mutually consistent and reinforcing. And it is only the (second) false presumption of such convergence which makes it plausible to argue that in admiring past art, we are enslaving ourselves to an oppressively narrow ideology of the establishment. Our tradition is intrinsically pluralistic, contestatory, and open-ended; it develops as much by continuing debate as by consensus; and the artworks which help constitute it share in this debate, representing rival ideologies which cross and criticize each other. Taken holistically as the structurally related field of competing artworks, high art can generate its own immanent critique by stimulating a more refined and critical consciousness in its audience, which is faced with the task of digesting, comparing, and mediating art's variant visions and values in the very act of appropriating art's works and determining their import.

This introduces a third reason not to condemn high art as necessarily promoting a repressive conservatism by inducing, through the auratic beauty of its masterpieces, an admiring affirmation of the past. Such an indictment unfairly lays all the blame on the artwork, rather than criticizing our own devotional and aesthetically constrained modes of receiving it. For all its power to speak, art is dumb without a dialogical intelligence for it to speak to. It cannot therefore be judged on its own, apart from its manner of appropriation. The upshot is that artworks are less guilty of malevolent power than of impotence in determining their own significance and use. "That is why," Adorno says, "criticism is an essential and necessary complement of art works."[4] Art's social import depends on how it is appropriated and deployed, and we should be able to appropriate works of high art to promote progressive socio-ethical aims. Indeed, given the ingenious hermeneutic strategies currently available – like reading against the text to see what it tries to conceal or smooth over – even a work expressly slanted toward conservatism can be eristically appropriated to advance opposing positions.

But this line of argument raises a counter-objection which also challenges the two previous points of defense. For the standard mode of appropriating and criticizing artworks in our institution of art is rather narrowly "aesthetic," in precisely that sense where the aesthetic is principally defined through its sharp separation from the praxis of life. Thus, whatever explicit social critique we find in specific works and whatever heightened critical consciousness of social difference we achieve through the juxtaposition of their different visions, all this is claimed to be neutralized by belonging to the institution of art, whose ideology effectively circumscribes art's reception within its own autonomous realm of imaginative aesthetic contemplation, removed from the real material world of praxis. Much of high art's socio-political protest has indeed been aestheticized and neutralized in this way.

However, there is no compelling reason to accept the narrowly aesthetic limits imposed by the established ideology of autonomous art (or indeed its traditional definition of the aesthetic as utterly disengaged from life's practical and material interests). Nor does challenging the established form of artistic autonomy mean rejecting the whole idea of a relatively autonomous institution of art. For such autonomy need not be construed in terms of a sharp separation from the praxis of life, but merely in terms of art's having a distinctive productive and distributive framework for its works and its own characteristic modes for their reception, which can nonetheless overlap and intersect with non-artistic institutions and discourse.

The idea of art's radical autonomy as totally divorced from socio-ethical praxis was aesthetically valuable and socially emancipatory in freeing art from its traditional role of serving the ideology of Church and court. But its rigid isolation from the praxis of life to preserve its purity is no longer so profitable or even credible. One of the great contributions of recent Marxist and feminist criticism has been to show how art and the aesthetic are deeply political and hence require criticism from a socio-ethical point of view. Such criticism works to expose the injustices and antagonisms of social life, which are always somehow reflected in art, by its very nature as a mediated social product, even when art seeks to transcend them in its quest to create satisfying harmonies and unities. These traces of social conflict may be found in the form as well as the content of artworks. But the socio-ethical criticism of high art should go not only through, but beyond, individual works to criticize the institutional framework of art which structures their reception, and still further to the general ideological structures and non-artistic institutions which help shape the institution and role of art in our society.

(2) A second argument for condemning high art as an oppressive social evil is that it provides a devastating strategy by which the socio-cultural elite can at once disguise and assert its proud claim to intrinsic superiority through privileged association with high art's illustrious tradition. For our high-art tradition (which includes not only its canonized works but its canonized modes of appreciation) is unfamiliar and insufficiently accessible to the culturally underprivileged, who are and remain such largely through socio-economic and political domination. But their relative and socially determined incapacity to appreciate high art is instead projected as a sign of a more intrinsic inferiority, a lack of taste or sensitivity, terms which suggest natural and not socio-economic disability.[5] In devastating contrast, the elitists' apparently humble respect for the cultural supremacy of the high-art tradition expresses in fact a powerful assertion of their own inherent supremacy as its only true guardians and interpreters. Thus, art serves to naturalize and legitimate social difference and entrenched class hierarchies, not only through its physical possession but through its very mode or possibility of appreciation.

We should be suspicious of the typical humanist response to this argument, the dream that even the underclasses will acquire the requisite appreciation of high art if only they receive a bit more time and education for the arts, if only more Shakespeare were taught in school and more opera broadcast on PBS. For the dominant logic of high art and its aesthetic has long been one of relentless differentiation and distance from commonly accepted modes of understanding and experience. Such differentiation is expressed not only through the appreciation of radically new styles or works incomprehensible to all but the *cognoscenti*, but also through new modes of appropriating what is already appreciated by the general public (as in deconstructionist readings of literary classics).

High art's persistent elitism and removal from ordinary life are powerfully confirmed by the failure of its own avant-garde efforts to challenge the bourgeois cultural establishment by negating the autonomous and sacral quality of high art.[6] Duchamp's satiric conferral of artistic status on mass-produced functional objects like urinals and bottle racks which clearly belong to ordinary experience, Tzara's work of instructions for making a Dada poem, and Breton's for writing automatic texts, all these were attempts to defy and change the idea of art as an elite realm of individual genius and refined taste set apart from ordinary life and ordinary people. Recent performance art has sometimes been motivated by similar aims of radical protest and change. Yet while such attempts are, with little difficulty, "aesthetically" disarmed and reappropriated by the institution of high art, they totally shock and mystify the culturally dominated population, whose incomprehension serves only to reinforce its sense of inferiority and the apparent justice of its domination and exclusion from high culture. Thus, even in its most liberational moments, high art seems an oppressive obstacle to socio-cultural emancipation.

The avant-garde's failure to liberate our concept of art by negating the institution of high art and breaking free of its elitist ideology could suggest a significant conclusion. Art's liberation and reintegration into the praxis of ordinary life cannot be achieved only through the agency of high art's own attempts at radical reform. The institution of high art is too strong, its powers of accommodating and reappropriating its products of protest much too supple and effective, for it alone to overcome its entrenched ideology and stranglehold on artistic legitimacy. It would be nice to think that art criticism and aesthetic theory could provide the needed leverage to break the exclusionary dominance of high art and transform our conception of art. But they themselves, so long enthralled by high art's institutional ideology, need some alternative cultural base from which to argue and nourish their critique. Popular art could provide this and so could be a promising force for transforming our concept and institutions of art towards greater freedom and closer integration into the praxis of life. The popular arts of mass-media culture (movies, TV dramas and comedies, pop music, videos) are enjoyed by all classes in our society; and recognizing their status as aesthetically legitimate cultural products would help reduce the socially oppressive identification of art and aesthetic taste with the socio-cultural elite of high art. Moreover, as even its critics affirm,[7] the aesthetic direction of popular art is largely toward reintegrating art and life.

Of course, as we shall see in the next chapter, the issue of popular art is far from simple: the very distinction between high and popular art is problematic, and their socio-cultural positioning and emancipatory functioning or malfunctioning are complex and equivocal. Indeed, just as it is wrong to see popular art as appealing exclusively to the socio-

culturally impoverished, so it is inaccurate to see the creators and prime
initiates of high art as comprising the most dominant class in contemporary society. This ruling class or class-fragment is comprised not of elite
artists and their audience of intellectuals, but rather of big business,
banking, and industry. Nor is high art its major cultural instrument of
domination. Instead, under the sly guise of democratic populism, it
exploits the arts of popular culture and the manipulative art of advertising to promote a docile conformism and worship of the new which keeps
the dominated consumer in a confused frenzy of changing fashion and
consequent insecurity about his tastes. In contrast, high art (along with
education) represents, at least for the moment, the only serious rival to
material capital and conspicuous consumption as a source of social status
and legitimation, even if we regret that much of its legitimating potential
comes from its traditional class markings. Its symbolic "cultural capital,"
as Bourdieu calls it,[8] constitutes the artist's and intellectual's prime
weapon against the total hegemony of the dollar; and it is the dollar, not
the opera, which sustains and motivates the inequitable society that so
many of us deplore.

(3) High art must also face the charge that it implicitly supports a
wretched and iniquitous social reality by providing a substitute imaginary
realm where our frustrated desires for a happier life and our just
demands for a better society are displaced, sublimated, and gratified –
but in imagination only. Progressive praxis is thus paralyzed through the
hallucinatory bliss of what Marcuse calls art's "real illusion."[9] Enchant-
ment with art's glorious products gives the lie to the miserable and sinful
material conditions in which they are generated and admired. We are
seductively lulled by art's satisfying beauty and perfection into assuming
that its creators – humankind and society – have likewise approached
perfection and satisfaction, at the very least in the spiritual world of art,
which is deemed superior to crass, prosaic material existence. Such
escapist illusions allow us to tolerate and so perpetuate real conditions
which are no less deplorable when deplorably ignored, concealed by an
enthralling aesthetic surface. This is why Dewey denounced our institution of high art as "the beauty parlor of civilization."[10] And Marcuse
makes the same point in criticizing what he calls "the affirmative character of culture." Not only through its satisfying image of a better order
of "unity" and "freedom," but through its demand to be universally
appreciated as superior to material reality, high art serves as "the
justification of the established form of existence" (*N* 96, 98).

Its decisive characteristic is the assertion of a universally obligatory, eternally better and more valuable world that must be unconditionally affirmed: a world essentially different from the factual world of the daily struggle for existence, yet realizable by every individual for himself "from within", without any transformation of the state of fact. (*N* 95)

Moreover, this concentration on personal cultivation and appreciation of the higher world of art provides a dangerous escape into interiority and individualist isolation, which not only reinforces (as it reflects) the lonely fragmentation of society but inhibits solidarity in praxis. Indeed, even when art portrays and protests against social misery and loneliness, such protest is aesthetically reappropriated and satisfyingly discharged in the individual's imaginative experience as part of his enjoyment of the work, rather than generating real critique and desire to change the world. Thus, Marcuse concludes, even "the rebellious idea becomes an accessory in justification" (*N* 121).

We can recognize the considerable force of this line of argument without drawing the conclusion that high art's seductive works must be altogether shunned like the fatal Sirens. We simply need to insist that our criticism of art be more ethically acute and socio-politically engaged, that it lead from the aesthetic appreciation of individual works to the critique of our socio-cultural reality, including our institution of art. We need, moreover, to recognize that many works impel us toward such critique by pointing out the social and ethical limitations of high art and its purist aesthetic ideology. Thus, as Adorno reminds us, even if all artworks are in some sense "socially culpable," "the worthy ones among them try to atone for their guilt" (*AT* 333). We can find such atonement through socio-ethical self-criticism even in the poetry of a staunch political and cultural conservative like T. S. Eliot, to whom I now turn.

III

Though sometimes condemned as a formalist aesthete,[11] Eliot insisted on art's social essence and function. But he also took pains to insist (against the likes of Shelley, Arnold, and Richards) that art itself can neither save the world nor provide personal salvation. In mordant debunking of the poet's putative status as world legislator, prophet, and savior, Eliot says he would be pleased to secure for the poet "a part to play in society as worthy as that of the music-hall comedian."[12] And though the difficulty of his verse suggests elitism, Eliot's poetic ideal was to reach the largest possible audience. This is evident in his praise of Dante and Shakespeare, but even more so in his advocacy of the poetic drama and in his own struggle to achieve a wider audience by turning to the theater. "I believe that the poet naturally prefers to write for as large and miscellaneous an audience as possible...I myself should like an audience which could neither read nor write...The ideal medium for poetry, to my mind,...[therefore] is the theatre."[13]

While deeply committed to the tradition and canon of high art, Eliot was also critical of its pretensions and its effects of social division and isolation. Moreover, while insisting on art's power to educate and edify, he equally warned against its power to deceive and corrupt. Hence we find his admittedly benighted condemnations of Hardy and Lawrence as heretical writers.[14] Eliot in fact thought that art was most dangerous and distortive when appreciated simply as aesthetic fare – when, for example, literature is read "purely for pleasure." He therefore criticized the idea of pure literary appreciation as a dangerous "abstraction" and insisted that the criticism of literature go beyond the narrowly literary to include ideological critique – for example, "criticism from a definite ethical and theological standpoint."[15] Eliot, like Adorno, consequently advocated a two-stage theory of art appreciation, the first stage involving a sympathetic, tentative acceptance of the work and its world-view, the second a conscious ideological critique of that world.[16] There is, then, no one answer to the question of art's socio-ethical or cognitive value. Depending on how successfully both stages are performed, art can be an educating liberator or an enthralling deceiver. In what follows, I shall apply this idea to Eliot's own verse to show how art calls for critical appropriation to reveal both its socio-ethical shortcomings and its potential. Let us turn to his early poem "Portrait of a Lady," written between 1910 and 1911.

PORTRAIT OF A LADY

> *Thou hast committed –*
> *Fornication: but that was in another country,*
> *And besides, the wench is dead.*
> The Jew of Malta.

I

Among the smoke and fog of a December afternoon
You have the scene arrange itself – as it will seem to do –
With 'I have saved this afternoon for you';

And four wax candles in the darkened room,
Four rings of light upon the ceiling overhead,
An atmosphere of Juliet's tomb
Prepared for all the things to be said, or left unsaid.
We have been, let us say, to hear the latest Pole
Transmit the Preludes, through his hair and fingertips.
'So intimate, this Chopin, that I think his soul
Should be resurrected only among friends
Some two or three, who will not touch the bloom
That is rubbed and questioned in the concert room.'
– And so the conversation slips
Among velleities and carefully caught regrets
Through attenuated tones of violins
Mingled with remote cornets
And begins.
'You do not know how much they mean to me, my friends,
And how, how rare and strange it is, to find
In a life composed so much, so much of odds and ends,
(For indeed I do not love it...you knew? you are not blind!
How keen you are!)
To find a friend who has these qualities,
Who has, and gives
Those qualities upon which friendship lives.
How much it means that I say this to you –
Without these friendships – life, what *cauchemar!*'

Among the windings of the violins
And the ariettes
Of cracked cornets
Inside my brain a dull tom-tom begins
Absurdly hammering a prelude of its own,
Capricious monotone
That is at least one definite 'false note.'
– Let us take the air, in a tobacco trance,
Admire the monuments,
Discuss the late events,
Correct our watches by the public clocks.
Then sit for half an hour and drink our bocks.

II

Now that lilacs are in bloom
She has a bowl of lilacs in her room

And twists one in her fingers while she talks.
'Ah, my friend, you do not know, you do not know
What life is, you who hold it in your hands';
(Slowly twisting the lilac stalks)
'You let it flow from you, you let it flow,
And youth is cruel, and has no remorse
And smiles at situations which it cannot see.'
I smile, of course,
And go on drinking tea.
'Yet with these April sunsets, that somehow recall
My buried life, and Paris in the Spring,
I feel immeasurably at peace, and find the world
To be wonderful and youthful, after all.'

The voice returns like the insistent out-of-tune
Of a broken violin on an August afternoon:
'I am always sure that you understand
My feelings, always sure that you feel,
Sure that across the gulf you reach your hand.

You are invulnerable, you have no Achilles' heel.
You will go on, and when you have prevailed
You can say: at this point many a one has failed.
But what have I, but what have I, my friend,
To give you, what can you receive from me?
Only the friendship and the sympathy
Of one about to reach her journey's end.

I shall sit here, serving tea to friends....'

I take my hat: how can I make a cowardly amends
For what she has said to me?
You will see me any morning in the park
Reading the comics and the sporting page.
Particularly I remark
An English countess goes upon the stage.
A Greek was murdered at a Polish dance,
Another bank defaulter has confessed.
I keep my countenance,
I remain self-possessed
Except when a street-piano, mechanical and tired
Reiterates some worn-out common song
With the smell of hyacinths across the garden

Recalling things that other people have desired.
Are these ideas right or wrong?

III

The October night comes down; returning as before
Except for a slight sensation of being ill at ease
I mount the stairs and turn the handle of the door
And feel as if I had mounted on my hands and knees.
'And so you are going abroad; and when do you return?
But that's a useless question.
You hardly know when you are coming back,
You will find so much to learn.'
My smile falls heavily among the bric-à-brac.

'Perhaps you can write to me.'
My self-possession flares up for a second;
This is as I had reckoned.
'I have been wondering frequently of late
(But our beginnings never know our ends!)
Why we have not developed into friends.'
I feel like one who smiles, and turning shall remark
Suddenly, his expression in a glass.
My self-possession gutters; we are really in the dark.

'For everybody said so, all our friends,
They all were sure our feelings would relate
So closely! I myself can hardly understand.
We must leave it now to fate.
You will write, at any rate.
Perhaps it is not too late.
I shall sit here, serving tea to friends.'

And I must borrow every changing shape
To find expression... dance, dance
Like a dancing bear,
Cry like a parrot, chatter like an ape.
Let us take the air, in a tobacco trance –
Well! and what if she should die some afternoon,
Afternoon grey and smoky, evening yellow and rose;
Should die and leave me sitting pen in hand
With the smoke coming down above the housetops;

Doubtful, for a while
Not knowing what to feel or if I understand
Or whether wise or foolish, tardy or too soon...
Would she not have the advantage, after all?
This music is successful with a 'dying fall'
Now that we talk of dying –
And should I have the right to smile?

This poem charts the awkward relationship between a sentimental older woman, whose love of art and whose aesthetic manner bordei on affectation, and a young man, who is both painfully aware of this aesthetic artificiality and agonizingly afraid of her very genuine emotion which underlies it. The relationship is portrayed in three visits the young man (the poem's narrator) makes to her home over a period from December to October. Though younger than Eliot's Prufrock, the narrator shares Prufrock's irony, his pained self-consciousness in confronting women (which in both poems is associated with the difficulty of negotiating stairs), and also shares his frightened incapacity for direct communication of emotion. The young narrator is revealed in the last stanza as the writer of the poem "sitting pen in hand," recalling and describing the relationship.[17] He seems unencumbered by ordinary work, since we can find him "any morning in the park"; and, as the lady recognizes, he is both promising and ambitious: "You are invulnerable, you have no Achilles' heel. / You will go on, and when you have prevailed / You can say: at this point many a one has failed." Indeed, their last meeting is on the occasion of his going abroad where he "will find so much to learn."

The rich irony of this poem is at least two-levelled. We appreciate the narrator's Laforguian deflation of the woman's overdone romanticism, but we also see that what he presents as his legitimate concern for individual integrity and "self-possession" is but a guise for callow, self-protecting selfishness and fear of candor. Certainly, as Hugh Kenner and Stephen Spender suggest, the themes of self-protecting "self-sufficiency" and "failure of communication" are central to the poem. So is the unsatisfying tension between "decadent romanticism" and ironic but "dull realism" which A. D. Moody hails as the poem's theme.[18] What I take to be no less central and what will be the motivating theme of my reading is the tension between two views on art's socio-ethical worth: the romantic idea of art as a moral educator which awakens and deepens our human sympathies and concern for others versus the contrary doctrine that art morally corrupts by breeding affectation, misdirected feeling, and elitism. Through the course of the poem, Eliot struggles and vacillates between these two views and ultimately emerges with what seems to be a very qualified vindication of art which matches that given in his prose theorizing. The idea is that art is morally valuable only through criticism of its moral limitations and dangers. And this idea is ingeniously demonstrated and expressed only through our critical reflection on those limitations in the poem itself as written by the young narrator-poet. But before examining how the poem portrays and works out the controversy over art's socio-ethical worth, we should get better acquainted with the two contestant views.

The seminal and paradigm text for the romantic doctrine of art as moral educator is Schiller's *On the Aesthetic Education of Man* (1795).[19] Writing amidst the general upheaval of the French Revolution, Schiller argues that we can achieve a good political society and high-quality intellectual thought only through "the ennobling of character." But how can this last be achieved without circularly relying on good society and good thinking? His answer and "instrument is Fine Art," which provides exemplars of beauty and perfection that can inspire and elevate our character (*AEM* 55–7). Art, which is primarily concerned with semblance and guided by imagination, is not confined to the political and intellectual conditions of its age. Aesthetic imagination can perceive the ennobling beauty and truth of past art produced in more harmonious times. "Humanity has lost its dignity; but art has rescued it and preserved it in significant stone. Truth lives on in the illusion of Art, and it is from this copy, or after-image, that the original image will once again be restored" (*AEM* 57). Art's imagination can also look forward to envisage as yet unrealized beauteous forms existing in its realm of Semblance (*AEM* 57–61). It is vain, says Schiller, to try to refine character and sentiment by inculcating moral rules upon the coarse and merely "sensuous man", "we must first alter his very nature" to and through the aesthetic (*AEM* 163). "Banish from their pleasures caprice, frivolity, and coarseness, and imperceptibly you will banish these from their actions and, eventually, from their inclinations too. Surround them…with the great and noble forms of genius, and encompass them about with the symbols of perfection, until Semblance conquer Reality, and Art triumph over Nature" by refining it (*AEM* 61).

Schiller grounds his view of the necessity for aesthetic education on a basic theory of human nature. Man has two fundamental drives: a sensuous or material drive (*Stofftrieb*) that "proceeds from the physical existence of man, or his sensuous nature", and "the formal drive" (*Formtrieb*) which "proceeds from the absolute existence of man, or from his rational nature" (*AEM* 79–81). The sense-drive impels us to experience the changing world to satisfy our material needs. And, as bound to this changing material world, it is coarser and constantly "pressing for change" so as to experience "the most manifold contacts with the world" (*AEM* 85–7). By contrast, the form-drive, reflecting man's "rational" and "absolute existence," aims at "changelessness." Since, in the changing world of sensation, absolute changelessness is impossible, our formal rational nature "insists on unity and persistence" in change and aims to attain this by partly retreating from the changing world to achieve more stable forms which it then seeks to impose on experience. For Schiller, the very notion of a stable, persisting "Person...amid all the changes of Condition" constitutes, through its unity of form, the model and indeed condition of human rationality and freedom that morality requires (*AEM* 73–5).

Schiller cannot allow that the conflicting drives of sense and form are completely incompatible, for that would mean our human nature is doomed to division. But he insists on their tendency to conflict with and encroach on each other; hence it is "the task of culture...to do justice to both drives equally" (*AEM* 87). Here, art comes to the rescue with Schiller's introduction of a third mediating drive "in which both the others work in concert" (*AEM* 97). This drive he calls the play-drive (*Spieltrieb*), and it is at the core of art and the aesthetic. As "the object of the sense-drive...we call life,...and the object of the form-drive...we call form, [so the] object of the play-drive...may therefore be called living-form: a concept serving to designate all the aesthetic qualities of phenomena and, in a word, what in the widest sense of the term we call beauty" (*AEM* 101). The play-drive's efforts at harmonizing the principles of life and form are rarely perfectly successful. The result, therefore, is that beauty tends to be either "energizing" or "melting," depending on the dominance of life or form in the "living-form" (*AEM* 111–15).

Nevertheless, since it is only in play that man's two basic drives are somehow harmonized, "man...is only fully a human being when he plays." Play thus becomes the foundation for "the whole edifice of the art of the beautiful and of the still more difficult art of living" (*AEM* 107–9). Schiller concludes that we must introduce art and beauty into all dimensions of life and at the core of our education, "since it is only out of the aesthetic, not out of the physical, state that the moral can develop" (*AEM* 165). For it is beauty which best "works upon our feeling" to inspire "lofty sentiments" and make us "desire more nobly" (*AEM* 127, 163, 169). Art's role in creating a more civil society lies not only in its moral education of the individual by developing a harmonious psyche and noble feelings, but also in its great communicative power. "A-social appetite must renounce its self-seeking" in the grace of art's beauty.

> Though it may be his needs which drive man into society, and reason which implants within him the principles of social behaviour, beauty alone can confer upon him a social character. Taste alone brings harmony in society, because it fosters harmony in the individual. All other forms of perception divide man, because they are founded exclusively either upon the sensuous or upon the spiritual part of his being; only the aesthetic mode of perception makes of him a whole, because both his natures must be in harmony if he is to achieve it. All other forms of communication divide society, because they relate exclusively either to the private receptivity or private proficiency of its individual members, hence to what distinguishes man from man; only the aesthetic mode of communication unites society because it relates that which is common to all....No privilege, no autocracy of any kind, is tolerated where taste rules, and the realm of aesthetic semblance extends its sway. (*AEM* 215–17)

Against this romantic idea that art develops our sensibility and thus enhances our capacities for moral feeling and human understanding, we find two chief lines of argument which revive the charges advanced earlier in this chapter. The first is that preoccupation with art will make our feeling artificial, that devotion to aesthetic education generates decadent aestheticism. Our natural human sympathies tend to be dismissed as ordinary or vulgar rather than artistically refined. Moreover, there is the danger that our great human potential for feeling and deep emotion will be directed not at fellow humans but at works of art. Art's aesthetic emotions serve, then, not as an effective stimulant to real moral feeling and action but as a facile and self-deceptive substitute for them. We cannot be reminded too often of the aesthetically refined Nazi officers who would weep at Beethoven to express their human emotions while inhumanly orchestrating the wholesale slaughter of innocent children. And this paradox constantly repeats itself in less extreme forms, as when we emerge from the theater emotionally wrought with concern for society's victims there portrayed, and then hurriedly bypass the real victims begging for concern on the frozen streets which are their home. Art's semblance is neither as innocent nor as morally effective as Schiller suggests it must be. Beauty as semblance and art as imaginative play encourage the compartmentalization of the aesthetic as an escape from reality, an idea which helps legitimate the ugly brutality of the real, non-aesthetic world.

Secondly, art's universal and democratic appeal and taste's freedom from "privilege" and "autocracy" can no longer be given much credence. What Schiller (and also Hume and Kant) meant by universality was not the natural taste of all people in all classes, including the common taste of the vulgar, but was basically the shared taste of culturally privileged society. Rather than unequivocally uniting society, fine art, through its privileging distinction from craft, entertainment, and popular art, divides society and communicates that division. And through the added distinction between privileged and ordinary or vulgar modes of interpretive appreciation, art can divide society still further into the privileged elite who *tastefully* appreciate it and those others who may like art but are not supposed to understand it properly. Both these arguments against art's moral and social value can be seen most clearly in Eliot's poem, to which we now return.

IV

The older sentimental hostess represents the good and bad of aesthetic education. She seems deeply devoted to the joys of art and the pleasures of friendship, the two pillars of G. E. Moore's ideal life and Bloomsbury's ethics.[20] Moreover, her feeling for the young man is steady, unchanging, and expressed in aesthetic form. Indeed, her unchanging stability and withdrawal from the world (captured in her poignant refrain, "I shall sit here serving tea to friends") makes her representative of Schiller's stable idea of form. And her tea-pouring ritual aptly captures Schiller's notion of "melting beauty" (*AEM* 113), which is dominated by forms whose life energies are largely sapped, as the heroine later confesses her "buried life" has been. Further, just as the form-drive is the active shaping principle, so the hostess is the formative directing figure of the drama. In regard to her will for friendship, the young man remains the more passive (and evasive) reactor, as befitting the sense-drive, which, for Schiller, is fundamentally receptive and reactive.

But the hostess's taste for art and the aesthetic has overtones of affectation, cloying sentimentalism, and snobbery, at least to the ironic eye of the young narrator. She stages their encounter as a romantic "scene": "With 'I have saved this afternoon for you'; / And four wax candles in the darkened room, / Four rings of light upon the ceiling overhead, / An atmosphere of Juliet's tomb." Though the scene evokes both art's form and aura (in the four candles and four rings of light), we recognize her romantic staging as artificial and ludicrously inappropriate to their relationship. She is no young Juliet entertaining her Romeo, and her ironic portrait is not simply of an older woman but "of a Lady," which links both her and the art of portraiture to class distinctions of privilege. Similarly, her musical comments (mockingly described by the narrator as sentimental "tones of violins mingled with remote cornets," later "violins" and "cracked cornets") indicate not so much perceptive appreciation as aesthetic posturing and elitism. "So intimate, this Chopin, that I think his soul / Should be resurrected only among friends / Some two or three, who will not touch the bloom / That is rubbed and questioned in the concert room."

This snobbery is immediately linked, through the shared theme of "friends", to her quest for friendship, thereby suggesting that this quest is not a wide moral quest for general community but likewise involves elitist snobbery, accepting only such "a friend who has these qualities" of distinction which makes friendship as special and refined as art. More closely representing the form-drive, she gives art primacy over life ("For indeed I do not love it"), since she finds "life composed so much...of odds and ends" rather than composed aesthetically as she tries to compose hers. The very depiction of her artistically staged room as "Juliet's tomb" strongly links her principle of art to life-stifling death; and the young man, a symbol of life's energy, not surprisingly feels anxious and threatened there.

In his restless reactive nature, his coarser desires, impatient sense of time and events, and drive for change and life, the young man represents the sense-drive. He is the moving visitor, who "will go on" more than others, who "is going abroad," and who is too restive to sit still within the formal space of his visit, instead suggesting:

> – Let us take the air, in a tobacco trance,
> Admire the monuments,
> Discuss the late events,
> Correct our watches by the public clocks.
> Then sit for half an hour and drink our bocks.

His role as a symbol of sensuous, changing life is later made more manifest in the woman's complaint: "Ah, my friend, you do not know, you do
not know / What life is, you who hold it in your hands"; and the subhuman nature of his sense-drive for life is captured in the changing animal
imagery in which his reaction to her human feeling is expressed:

> And I must borrow every changing shape
> To find expression…dance, dance
> Like a dancing bear,
> Cry like a parrot, chatter like an ape.
> Let us take the air, in a tobacco trance –

The last line is his refrain for outside movement, which sharply contrasts
with the interior tea ceremony of the woman's refrain.

As readers, we share the narrator's distaste for the snobby artificiality
of the woman's aesthetic life of elitist art and aestheticized friendship,
and we empathize with his bored "prelude" of rhythmically primitive
protest:

> Among the windings of the violins
> And the ariettes
> Of cracked cornets
> Inside my brain a dull tom-tom begins
> Absurdly hammering a prelude of its own,
> Capricious monotone
> That is at least one definite 'false note.'

His false note is in scare quotes, which, given the narrator's irony,
suggests that its savage and capricious monotone is false only by the very
stylized and artificial standards of "true" music endorsed by the woman's
romantically rarefied taste for high art. Yet, since such taste and standards are not natural but are rather the product of elaborate cultural
conditioning (if not also posturing) in a very artificial society, the primitive "false note" of the tom-tom seems more natural, true, and "definite"
than the "windings of violins" and "ariettes / Of cracked cornets" which
convey her aesthetically refined overtures of friendship. These attempts
at aesthetically educating his feeling are exposed more clearly as false
notes in the next section, degenerating to "the insistent out-of-tune / Of a
broken violin on an August afternoon" as she tries to move his heart,
aided by the beauty of lilacs, and "twists one in her fingers while she
talks." Rather than powerfully and universally communicating, the

aesthetic in her contorting hands is both elitistly selective and hopelessly ineffective. All that the narrator can receive from her is the urge to "take [his] hat" and flee.

The woman's uncritically romantic aesthetic education seems a phony failure. But if the traditional forms of high art and the aesthetic are too artificial to communicate and educate human feeling and thus enhance our life, does the critical narrator have anything better to offer? It clearly seems not. Though repelled and apparently frightened by her aesthetic realm of semblance, of beauteous art and friendship, he seems no happier in the "real life" to which he escapes and in some sense represents. For what is his life but the solitary roving consumption of the disjointed sensational events and low entertainments that alienated modern life typically provides? These sensational odds and ends, consumed to feed his sense-drive, are experienced not directly and in integrated form but only vicariously through what Walter Benjamin recognized as the further disjointing medium of the newspaper.

> You will see me any morning in the park
> Reading the comics and the sporting page.
> Particularly I remark
> An English countess goes upon the stage.
> A Greek was murdered at a Polish dance,
> Another bank defaulter has confessed.

These events are such meaningless "odds and ends" and such dismally unsensational sensations as to undermine the narrator's anti-romantic jibe at hearing "the latest Pole / Transmit the Preludes, through his hair and fingertips" (rather than through his soul). For even the cloying romanticism of Chopin seems superior to the grim, lifeless, and, in a sense unreal realism of standard mass-media fare – newspaper scandals, comics, and sports. But these lines on scandal suggest more than social degradation and corruption. There is a hint in the murder of the Greek at a Polish dance (recalling the Polish Chopin) of how the earlier Greek aesthetic – where art was much more robust, democratic, and so very integrated into the real life of society – has been killed by an alien and artificial romanticism, in which art is spirited away to an ethereal realm of pure aestheticism.[21]

In any case, the disjointed and meaningless real life of the narrator hardly seems better than the affected aesthetic semblance of the lady. He himself is clearly not thrilled by it, though this indifference seems to him preferable to the threat of real feeling that beauty can generate. Beauty and feeling constitute a threat because they endanger his selfish self-sufficiency, suggesting that there are perhaps more rewarding (though also more risky) projects of fulfillment than those dictated by the sense-drive of calculative self-interest. In that everyday worldly routine, he remarks:

> I keep my countenance,
> I remain self-possessed
> Except when a street-piano, mechanical and tired
> Reiterates some worn-out common song
> With the smell of hyacinths across the garden
> Recalling things that other people have desired.
> Are these ideas right or wrong?

Armed with Laforguian irony against the familiar phalanx of aestheticism – the romantically wrought and rarefied purple Preludes of Chopin and the presumably purple lilacs of sophisticated sentiment in the hostess – the young narrator is, however, vulnerably moved by the more natural music and beauty of the street and garden. These are not sequestered for the elite but are communally open and shared. The song is common and on the street, while the garden is obviously in the open air. Though rendered mechanically or less artfully than the Pole's performance and the woman's staging, these aesthetic things are at least more honest, direct, and open than "the windings of the violins" and the woman's "twisting [of] the lilac stalks." They are therefore more emotionally effective.

Aesthetic experience is a deep and natural human need, which if frustrated in the realm of high art will seek satisfaction elsewhere. As Dewey complained, "When, because of their remoteness, the objects acknowledged by the cultivated to be works of fine art seem anemic to the mass of people, esthetic hunger is likely to seek the cheap and vulgar" (*AE* 12). This complaint against the elitist and spiritualizing compartmentalization of fine art is shared here by Eliot, who is neither praising common street songs as great art nor condemning them (and the narrator who is moved by them) as worthlessly vulgar. We can tell by the imagery of the piano song – "mechanical and tired," "worn-out," and "common" (this last being ambiguous as to positive "sharing" or negative "vulgarity") – that such art does not represent the aesthetic ideal. The same goes for the young man's primitive rhythm formed in reactive protest to the woman's artificial strains. It is a "dull tom-tom," "absurdly hammering," a "Capricious monotone."[22] It obviously does not represent (even for the young narrator) what good art should be, even if it seems more vivid and compelling than the woman's decadent romanticism. Eliot seems to be suggesting here that though art must not altogether abandon its more primitive roots, rhythms, and life energies, a full return to primitivism is not a viable solution for western aesthetics. Though we may despise sophisticated decadence, we cannot be fully satisfied by naive primitivism, which is ultimately false to our socio-cultural experience and thus, for us, involves a sophisticated posturing and escapism of its own.

This dilemma, reflected in the negative imagery of the tom-tom and the worn-out song, can also be grasped in the narrator's person. We know that he must be a cultivated man of parts, if not by his language and apparent career as a poet, then at least by the attention and praise the sophisticated lady bestows on him. His perceptively ironic critique of late romantic art and aestheticism suggests an aesthetic refinement far beyond the woman's sentimental gush, a cultural conditioning which seems to render him incapable of full gratification through the primitive and "worn-out common" forms of popular art.

Nor is the young man stupidly insensitive to feeling. He acutely discerns the woman's feelings without being sympathetically moved by them, as a connoisseur might remark an aesthetic quality or emotion without really feeling it. His insensitivity is a fault of human feeling, not perception. He is afraid that feeling will undermine his "self-possession" and perhaps eventually plunge him into the woman's sentimental excess and friendship-hungering weakness. So self-absorbed and self-seeking, he can only see the woman's motives for friendship as threateningly selfish as well, and he therefore recoils in fear from them. Schiller almost seems to be describing this young man when he wrote: "Proud self-sufficiency contracts the heart of the man of the world, a heart which in natural man still often beats in sympathy....Only by completely abjuring sensibility can we, so it is thought, be safe from its aberrations" (*AEM* 27). Such a man, who can be found even "among the most cultivated," is close to the state of ethical savagery. "Unacquainted as yet with his own human dignity, he is far from respecting it in others; and, conscious of his own savage greed, he fears it in every creature which resembles him. He never sees others in himself but only himself in others; and communal life, far from enlarging him into a representative of the species, only confines him ever more narrowly within his own individuality" (*AEM* 173). His "self-seeking" life of sense amounts to a "monotonous round of ends, a constant vacillation of judgements" (*AEM* 171), which very clearly suggests not only the young narrator's daily routine of morning reading and proposed "tobacco trance" rounds to the public monuments, "public clocks," and public houses, but also his vacillating uncertainty about ideas being "right or wrong."

Yet, as Schiller argues, aesthetic charm can touch and eventually tenderize even the hardened heart; and Eliot's young man of the world is genuinely, though not adequately, moved by the street song and hyacinths. Though not fully stirred to human desire and sympathy by such common and simple beauty (nor by his earlier primitive tom-tom), he is at least nudged far enough out of his self-possession to consider what "other people have desired" and the validity or value of such desires: "Are these ideas right or wrong?" Such questioning, however, is still far short of ethical self-criticism and reform. For "right and wrong" need not even be ethically "right or wrong" but could mean merely "true or false" or simply "instrumentally right or wrong" (as in the "right way" to cheat or torture).

Moreover, we can see in the third, climactic meeting that the young man remains committed to self-possession and to the denial of those human feelings of sympathy which so frighten him in the woman. However, his self-possession seems already somewhat weakened by the aesthetic experience of the last stanza. For, in approaching the woman's apartment, he confesses "a slight sensation of being ill at ease", feeling as if he had mounted the stairs on his "hands and knees." In paying his farewell call to the woman before he goes abroad, the young man must face the full force of her feeling, her continued desire for friendship (now through correspondence), and her disappointment that her feelings of friendship have not been returned.

> 'Perhaps you can write to me.'
> My self-possession flares up for a second;
> *This* is as I had reckoned.
> 'I have been wondering frequently of late
> (But our beginnings never know our ends!)
> Why we have not developed into friends.'
> I feel like one who smiles, and turning shall remark
> Suddenly, his expression in a glass.
> My self-possession gutters; we are really in the dark.

If we read closely, we see that it is not her request and plaintive feelings which so completely unhinge the young man's self-possession. It is rather his perception of his falsely and cruelly smiling response, which is likened to the critical self-awareness one gets from catching one's embarrassed smile in the mirror, "his expression in a glass." But the metaphor of catching an image in a mirror is precisely the oldest and most transparent metaphor for art and its *mimesis*. Eliot, then, is suggesting metaphorically that art can overturn a hardened man's self-possession and can do so by critically representing his image or action. Art, one might say, can help us criticize the evils of life and society simply by representing them, and such criticism is a necessary step toward ethical and social improvement. Aesthetic education is possible only if it involves criticism; art edifies only when its mirror images are not merely produced or consumed, but when they are critically grasped and appropriated. This theme will be recursively reinforced in the poem's final stanza.

Before that, in the penultimate stanza, we see art not only mirroring but intensifying the image it captures. The intensification of artistic rendering appears in the poignantly repeated rhyme and rhythm of the woman's final plea.

> We must leave it now to fate.
> You will write, at any rate.
> Perhaps it is not too late.
> I shall sit here, serving tea to friends.

Here again it seems that the artistry of the feeling, rather than the feeling itself, is what overcomes the narrator's self-possession and reveals him to himself as less than human. His response can match neither the humanity nor the aesthetic power of the woman's plea; his graceless and changing attempts to find expression are but the ludicrous subhuman antics of a circus animal.

> And I must borrow every changing shape
> To find expression...dance, dance
> Like a dancing bear,
> Cry like a parrot, chatter like an ape.
> Let us take the air, in a tobacco trance —

The final stanza finds the young narrator alone and abroad, envisaging the possible death of the sentimental lady. For she had already plaintively spoken of her "buried life" when she offered him "the friendship and the sympathy / Of one about to reach her journey's end." Imagining her death with vivid, detailed artistry, while he sits "pen in hand" apparently to recall and record the memory of her repeated offer and his repeated denial of sympathy, the young man is revealed as the poet who has inscribed the poem's retrospective narrative, and as the man who has exploited the suffering of others as material for his art. Art can prey on human feeling rather than develop it; indeed, it can deny and contort it in order better to prey upon it. But, on the other hand, his poetic representation of her death finally stirs the young man to question the validity of his own feelings and the ethical legitimacy of his posture of cold, smiling irony toward the human sentiments of others. Here the high art of poetry seems to succeed in inducing real moral feeling, for which the primitive tom-tom and worn-out street song were inadequate. But does it really? The poem's complex conclusion demands the closest scrutiny.

> Well! and what if she should die some afternoon,
> Afternoon grey and smoky, evening yellow and rose;
> Should die and leave me sitting pen in hand
> With the smoke coming down among the housetops;
> Doubtful, for a while
> Not knowing what to feel or if I understand
> Or whether wise or foolish, tardy or too soon...
> Would she not have the advantage, after all?
> This music is successful with a 'dying fall'
> Now that we talk of dying –
> And should I have the right to smile?

It is true that the vividly artistic rendering of her death makes him critically address his own feeling, or indeed lack of it. Moreover, this aesthetic artistry does indeed suggest to him the advantage of the woman's flow of sentiment which he scorned as embarrassing weakness. By freeing feeling from the yoke of self-possession to follow its own course, one is spared "not knowing what to feel." One does not need to know; one simply feels. Further, it is undeniable that the artistic portrait of her imagined death (not only in its richly painted "grey and smoky,... yellow and rose" atmosphere, but also in its musically styled "dying fall") evokes, in the poem's last line, the narrator's first truly ethical question. Indeed the "should" and "right" of "And should I have the right to smile?" are the poem's first and only clearly ethical terms, since "right or wrong" ideas, as we saw, may well have non-ethical import.

On the other hand, the poem can be read to suggest that the woman's final advantage is not in her feeling but in her death, which means the end of feeling. The young man, now clearly revealed as a poet and hence under the aegis of art, could then be construed as affirming artistic death over the life of real feeling. Art, of course, has always been contrasted to life, and death is undeniably so contrasted. In writing this poem about the woman, he is trying once again to escape from really feeling for her; and art provides this escape. Moreover, since late romanticism and "art for art's sake," one often finds an insistence on the separation and purification of art from ordinary real-life concerns and emotions, a view that aesthetic emotions must not be confused with those of real life. Clive Bell, for instance, advocated this,[23] and so (for a short time) did Eliot himself, though only several years after this poem had been completed. In 1920, at the height of his phase of objectivist criticism, he asserted that "a literary critic should have no emotions except those immediately provoked by a work of art – and these...are, when valid, perhaps not to be called emotions at all."[24]

Perhaps, then, the young narrator-poet is not truly moved by his art to real emotion and sympathy but merely to aesthetic emotion. Perhaps art does not arouse or nourish real ethical sympathy and praxis, but rather provides an easy escape from it through the surrogate satisfaction of imagined artistic sympathy, which can be shaped in a pleasing form and requires no real action or immediate confrontation with raw feeling. One could then say that the young narrator-poet remains morally savage by being aesthetically refined, by not letting human feelings interfere with the pure aesthetic appreciation of the lady's death. For he appreciates her death in clearly and merely aesthetic terms, as simply "music...with a 'dying fall'," rather than in terms of real death – of suffering, loss, sorrow, or ethical remorse. This suggests that aesthetic education rather than opening us up to real moral feeling and human sympathy, indurates us into an aesthetically refined but morally insensitive attitude, where we tend to regard everything, even people, as objects for aesthetic use. Even in this closing stanza, where the narrator is most powerfully stirred, he seems to treat the lady as an aesthetic object (the object for his "Portrait of a Lady") and not as an end in itself having human dignity. It is very questionable whether he is at all moved by her actual fate or instead, in narcissistic aestheticism, by his own artistic representation of it. Indeed, the genuineness of his feeling – and with it the whole aestheticization of life which makes even the grim brutality of death a moment for aesthetic delectation rather than suffering sympathy – seems to be questioned by the poet-narrator himself. The poem's concluding question "And should I have the right to smile?" makes this point powerfully and is so complexly rich and layered in meaning that it goes on reverberating long after the words are read.

The question is not only whether the young narrator should have the right to smile ironically at the folly of the woman's past emotional weakness and to smile with relief at his final escape, through her death, from her demands of real feeling and friendship. It is also the question of whether the narrator-poet has the right to smile with satisfaction at the fine way he has transfigured her threateningly real emotion and suffering into a well-wrought and pleasingly digestible work of art which provides vicarious living and feeling through aesthetic emotion. But he seems very aware of his tendentious aestheticization of her death; and given his capacity for self-criticism (witnessed in his descriptions of his awkwardness when not "self-possessed"), he may be smiling ironically at the recognition that this aesthetic posture toward human life and death is an immoral one. Should I have the right to smile, he is also asking, at my cruel, inhuman aestheticism, and even at my superior "intellectual" perception of this moral fault? Do we have a right to laugh in criticism at ourselves and our ethical foibles, if they are, in fact, no laughing matter?

This final, echoing question does not stop here for an answer but pushes us still further, beyond the narrator-poet to the actual poet and finally to the reader and critic. Identifying the young narrator-poet with the young Eliot who completed this work at the age of 23, we then see Eliot as asking whether he himself has the right to smile with critical superiority at the young narrator's aestheticism and self-deception that life can be treated as art. Or is he smiling in affirmation at such self-deception? For what is Eliot himself doing in writing this poem but committing the very same act. In criticizing art's problematic aestheticization of evils which need to be taken more than aesthetically, he has simply reproduced the problem by producing another aesthetic object, an object which will satisfy our aesthetic emotions and even the high-minded aesthetic taste that some of us have for "moral content" in art. But the refined artistic rendering or aestheticization of that content shifts attention from the root problem itself which is and needs to be solved in life, not art. Here art reveals part of its fundamentally aporetic character in persistently distracting us from the problem precisely in the act of directing us to it.

Finally, the reader-critic is not immune from this question and threat of self-deception. Should I have the right to smile at Eliot's paradoxical aestheticization of the ethical in attempting to criticize precisely that error? For does he not suggest his own awareness of the difficulty in this final echoing question, which can thus be taken as directed at himself as ultimate author of the poem – that is, as someone devoted to creating art rather than engaging in more direct social criticism and moral praxis. If we reader-critics simply appreciate the poem's moral message and conundrum as aesthetic fare, we have no more right to smile and rest content in our noble sentiments and subtleties of reading than Eliot or the young narrator had in the skill of writing.

If there is the trace of an answer to this moral paradox of art, it seems to be this: We need to bring our criticism of artworks and their moral content to a critical awareness of the social role of art itself, and further to the wider criticism of our social world where high art can be so foreign to life and human sympathy. Such critical awareness art can stimulate but not in itself provide. Art, as we see in "Portrait of a Lady," can at best issue in a captivating and ambiguous question which criticism – taken widely to include also philosophical, moral, and social criticism – must clarify and try to answer.

And should we have the right, then, to end here? Instead, we have the duty to pursue the critique of our unhappy socio-cultural fragmentation, where friendship founders in fear, flight, and isolation, and where beauty and feeling are realized not in happy communion but in the artistic illusion of a lady's lonely death and a young man's solitary regret. Our socio-cultural fragmentation finds expression and support in the sharp separation of high art from popular forms of artistic expression which are even denied the status of art. In our culture, to achieve full aesthetic legitimacy, one must mount a steep staircase of spiritualization and elitist refinement, much as the young man must mount the stairs to reach the artistic sanctum of the lady. And if it seems uncomfortably stifling and somber up there, one dare not thrust open the windows to let in the fresh air and popular song from the street. One is instead made to feel like a savage or animal ("a dancing bear") incapable of breathing the pure air of art and thus impelled to flee to a wholly different cultural domain.

If the young man represents more popular forms of artistic expression, while the lady stands for high art, their failure to communicate or stay together symbolizes a grave cultural problem. Exiled from aesthetic respectability and acceptance in our artistic tradition, popular art is deprived of the artistic care and control that could render it more aesthetically satisfying and sensitive. Abandoned to deformation through life's pressures, which are largely the dehumanizing pressures of economic profit, it grows robust, technically sophisticated, but brutally crude in sensibility. In contrast, high art, like the lady, is left to die alone in its suffocating purity and lifeless spirituality, divorced from the invigorating life energies (the Schillerian "energizing beauty") which belong to popular expressive forms as much as they belong to the young man.

This lamentable cultural dichotomy between genuine high art and illegimate popular culture seems to leave us with an unacceptable aesthetic dilemma: between the stiflingly moribund artificiality of the high and the dehumanizing dull primitivism of the popular. This dilemma and dichotomy must be challenged by continued critique of our institutional ideology of art for its blanket rejection of popular art as aesthetically illegitimate and socio-culturally corruptive.

7

Form and Funk: The Aesthetic Challenge of Popular Art

I

Popular art has not been popular with aestheticians and theorists of culture, at least not in their professional moments. When not altogether ignored as beneath contempt, it is typically vilified as mindless, tasteless trash.[1] The denigration of popular art or mass culture (the debate over the proper term is significant and instructive[2]) seems particularly compelling since it is widely endorsed by intellectuals of violently different socio-political views and agendas. Indeed, it provides a rare instance where right-wing reactionaries and Marxian radicals join hands and make common cause.

It is difficult to oppose such a powerful coalition of thinkers by defending popular art. Yet this is precisely my aim in this chapter, and for a variety of reasons. My Deweyan pragmatism makes me not only critical of the alienating esotericism and totalizing claims of high art, but acutely suspicious of any essential and unbridgeable divide between its products and those of popular culture. Moreover, history itself clearly shows us that the popular entertainment of one culture (e.g. Greek or even Elizabethan drama) can become the high classics of a subsequent age. Indeed, even within the very same cultural period, a given work can function either as popular or as high art depending on how it is interpreted and appropriated by its public. In nineteenth-century America, Shakespeare was both high theater and vaudeville.[3]

Because the boundaries between high and popular art seem neither clear nor uncontested (much film, for example, apparently straddling the two), to speak of them simply and generally, as I shall be doing, involves a great deal of philosophical abstraction and simplification. But since the global condemnations of popular art are made in such simplifying, binary terms, I feel justified in using them for its defense, even if I hope that such defense will eventually lead to the dissolution of the high/popular art dichotomy and to a more fine-grained and concrete analysis of the various arts and the differing forms of their appropriation.[4]

The strongest and most urgent reason for defending popular art is that it provides us (even us intellectuals) with too much aesthetic satisfaction to accept its wholesale denunciation as debased, dehumanizing, and aesthetically illegitimate. To condemn it as fit only for the barbaric taste and dull wit of the unenlightened, manipulated masses is to divide us not only against the rest of our community but against ourselves. We are made to disdain the things that give us pleasure and to feel ashamed of the pleasure they give. Thus, while conservative and Marxian critics of popular culture repeatedly bemoan our contemporary societal and personal fragmentation (blaming it on such forces as modernization, industrialization, secularization, and capitalism), the rigid line of legitimacy they draw between high and popular culture both reinscribes and reinforces those same painful divisions in society, and still more deeply in ourselves. Similarly, while the delegitimating critique of popular art is typically pursued under the banner of safeguarding our aesthetic satisfaction, it actually represents a form of ascetic renunciation, one of many forms that intellectuals since Plato have employed to subordinate the unruly power and sensual appeal of the aesthetic.

For such reasons, even if the defense of popular art can hardly achieve the socio-cultural liberation of the dominated groups who consume this art, it can at least help liberate those dominated parts of ourselves which are similarly oppressed by the exclusive claims of high culture. And such liberation, with its recognition of the pain of cultural oppression, can perhaps provide both stimulus and hope for wider social reform.[5]

Four factors make it particularly difficult to defend popular art against its formidable intellectual critics. First, the defense must be waged more or less on enemy territory, since the very attempt to meet the intellectualist critique involves both accepting the power of its claim to require an answer and accepting the terms of its indictment, terms which are hardly neutral. Defenses of popular art are not common, partly because most pop culture enthusiasts don't consider the intellectual critique either relevant or powerful enough to be worthy of response. They see no need to defend their taste against the claims of alienated "uptight" intellectuals, just as they see no need to justify it by anything more than the satisfaction it gives to them and so many others.

A second but related difficulty is that intellectual apologists of popular art tend to be too apologetic about its aesthetic shortcomings. Uncritically subscribing to the aesthetic ideology of high art and its aesthetic critique of popular culture, they defend popular art by appeal to "extenuating circumstances" of social needs and democratic principles, rather than making a case for its aesthetic validity. Thus Herbert Gans, a staunch defender of popular culture, admits its relative aesthetic poverty and inferiority to high culture. High art provides "greater and perhaps more lasting aesthetic gratification" because of its creative "innovation," "experimentation in form," exploration of deep "social, political and philosophical questions," and its capacity to be "understood on several levels"; while popular culture is deficient in these aesthetic features (*PH* 76–9, 125). However, Gans argues that since the lower classes "lack the socioeconomic and educational opportunities prerequisite for choosing the higher cultures," they cannot be condemned for choosing and enjoying the only cultural products they are capable of enjoying, and that a democratic society which fails to supply them with adequate education and leisure for high culture "must permit the creation of cultural content which will meet...[their actual] needs and standards" of taste (*PH* 128, 129).

Though admirably humanitarian, this defense of popular art will not work for readers of this book. It excuses only those who lack the education and leisure to appreciate high culture. Gans makes it clear that we "should be expected to choose the [cultural] content that fits [our] educational levels...and...should be judged negatively" if we "consistently choose below these levels" but praised if we choose above them (*PH* 126–7). Popular culture, then, is good only for those who can do no better; it is not something in which very different social classes (and human faculties) can unite in aesthetic pleasure and appreciation. It is not to be celebrated, but only tolerated until we can provide enough educational resources "to permit everyone to choose from higher taste cultures" (*PH* 128). Such social apologies for popular art undermine its genuine defense, since they perpetuate the same myth of abject aesthetic poverty as the critiques they oppose, just as they foster the same sort of social and personal fragmentation.

A proper defense of popular art requires its aesthetic vindication, but a third reason why such defense seems so unlikely is that we tend to think of high art only in terms of its more celebrated works of genius, while popular art is typically identified with its most mediocre and standardized products. Yet, unfortunately, there are many mediocre and even bad works of high art, as even the most avid advocates of high culture will admit. And just as high art is no unblemished collection of master-pieces, so, I shall argue, popular art is not an undifferentiated abyss of tastelessness where no aesthetic criteria are displayed or exercised. In both these types of art, the distinction between them being flexible and historical rather than rigid and intrinsic, there is room and need for aesthetic discriminations of success and failure.

Finally, perhaps the greatest problem is the tendency in intellectual discourse for the term "aesthetic" to be appropriated exclusively as a term of high art and sophisticated style, as if the very notion of a popu-lar aesthetic were almost a contradiction in terms. This tendency has prevented some who are sympathetic to popular needs for culture and who see through the "disinterested," "non-commercial" ideology of high culture from recognizing the existence of a popular aesthetic that is not wholly negative, dominated, and impoverished. The most striking example of this regrettable bias is Pierre Bourdieu, who rigorously exposes the hidden economy and veiled interests of the so-called disin-terested aesthetic of high culture, but nonetheless remains too enchanted by the myth he demystifies to acknowledge the existence of any legitimate popular aesthetic. He insists on referring to this notion only with disclaiming scare quotes and repeatedly stresses that the so-called popu-lar aesthetic is nothing more than "a foil or negative reference point" from which any legitimate aesthetic must distance itself to establish legitimacy.[6]

We must admit that the term "aesthetic" originated in intellectual discourse and has been most frequently applied to high art and the most refined appreciation of nature. But its application is certainly no longer so narrowly confined. One need only consider the many fashion schools and cosmetic salons which are called "aesthetic institutes" and whose professional staff are termed "aestheticians." Moreover, traditional aesthetic predicates such as "grace," "elegance," "unity," and "style" are regularly applied to the products of popular art with no apparent equivo-cation. No one appreciates more than Bourdieu the great socio-political stakes of such highly valued classificatory terms as "art" and "aesthetic," so it is surprising and troubling that he so readily concedes them to high culture's exclusive possession. It is therefore all the more necessary to secure their freedom from such monopolistic domination by defending the aesthetic legitimacy of popular art.

To provide such defense, I shall be challenging the major aesthetic indictments against popular art; and since I cannot pretend to treat all the popular arts here, I shall focus mainly on rock music, particularly the funky sort inspired by Afro-American culture. My study will become still narrower, but also more concrete, in the subsequent chapter, which is devoted to the aesthetics of rap and an analysis of one of its works. Together these chapters aim to demonstrate by a combination of general argument and detailed concrete analysis that popular art not only can satisfy the most important standards of our aesthetic tradition, but also has the power to enrich and refashion our traditional concept of the aesthetic, so as to liberate it more fully from its alienating association with class privilege, socio-political inaction, and the ascetic denial of life. But before undertaking the aesthetic defense of popular art, a more general problem must be considered.

II

Since the most bitter and damaging indictments of popular art are directed not at its aesthetic status but at its pernicious socio-cultural and political influence, one might object that an aesthetic defense could do very little indeed to legitimate popular art. Though I have no wish to discount the serious socio-political effects of popular art, the objection can be met by showing that the apparent extra-aesthetic dangers of popular art are directly linked to and largely based on its presumed aesthetic faults. This response should neither surprise us nor be seen as a formalist reduction of the socio-political to the aesthetic, once we recognize that aesthetic taste as a cultural product is itself socially and politically inflected. We can see how the more general indictments of popular art rest on the aesthetic by analyzing the rather comprehensive list of socio-cultural and political charges compiled by Herbert Gans, which he divides into four groups.

The first group concerns the intrinsically "negative character of popular culture creation" – more particularly, that it is produced by a large-scale commercial industry purely "for profit" and is "imposed from above" on its helplessly "passive consumers" (*PH* 19–20). But behind and motivating these charges of commercialism and manipulatory imposition, we find essentially aesthetic complaints. The charge is not simply that popular art makes a profit (for so does high art), but that in order to be profitable "it must create a homogeneous and standardized product that appeals to a mass audience" (*PH* 20), thereby sacrificing rigorous aesthetic aims of personal artistic expression to sell out to .mass taste. This is an aesthetic indictment against the creativity, originality, and artistic autonomy of popular art.

Similarly, it cannot be the mere use of industrialized technologies that makes popular art undesirable, since high culture's musical, literary, and plastic arts also employ them. The charge again is a fundamentally aesthetic one, that industrialization leads to standardization of techniques and uniformity of products, which both stifle the free expression of the creative artist and narrowly limit the aesthetic choice of the audience. The former is reduced from a self-determining creator to a wage-laborer in an assembly-line process, while the latter are compelled to enjoy what does not really satisfy them because they are systematically programmed to think it enjoyable and because there is no real alternative on the market. Finally, Dwight Macdonald's charge that "Mass Culture is imposed from above"[7] can hardly be the simple charge of cultural indoctrination, for high culture has always so imposed itself (whether from the court, the Church, the academy, or the powerful sanctums of the artworld). The real complaint is that the imposition is not worthwhile, because the products imposed are worthless – once again, an aesthetic claim.

The second group of socio-cultural indictments against popular culture concerns its "negative effects on high culture" (*PH* 19). Gans sees only two basic charges here: "that popular culture borrows content from high culture with the consequence of debasing it; and that, by offering economic incentives, popular culture is able to lure away potential high culture creators, thus impairing the quality of high culture" (*PH* 27). Again, though not explicitly directed at the aesthetic value of popular art, such charges imply and rely on its denial. Since Gans concedes the aesthetic inferiority of popular art, he must respond to these charges by arguing that the instances of borrowing have not in fact produced a general "debasement of high culture *per se* or of its vitality" and that the market for high art is too small to accommodate all the potential creators who are economically lured into popular art (*PH* 28–9). His fundamental argument here and throughout is that popular culture should be tolerated, since it "poses no genuine threat to high culture or its creators" (*PH* 51). This rather dubious assertion denies the power of popular culture and treats high culture's reactive attack as a paranoid fantasy. One could respond more radically to Gans's charges by questioning their underlying aesthetic assumptions. One could even admit that popular art's borrowing of themes and creators does challenge and perhaps diminish the power of high culture, but then go on insist that it compensates by having real aesthetic worth of its own.

First, we should realize that, culturally, there is nothing intrinsically wrong with borrowing content. Within the arts of high culture, content has always been borrowed, and very often from popular sources.[8] Such borrowing provides part of the thick sense of interconnectedness which enriches a cultural tradition. Obviously, what legitimates high art's borrowing is that its works have aesthetic merit, while popular art presumably has none. Similarly, the charge that popular art drains creative talent away from high-art production derives its accusatory power from the premise that such diverted talent is put to no good use, since popular art is aesthetically worthless as compared to high culture and has no other compensating value.

The presumed aesthetic worthlessness of popular art also underlies Gans's third group of socio-cultural charges, which concern "the negative effects on the popular culture audience" (*PH* 19). Three such effects are specified: "popular culture is emotionally destructive because it produces spurious gratification…it is intellectually destructive because it offers meretricious and escapist content which inhibits people's ability to cope with reality; and…it is culturally destructive, impairing people's ability to partake of high culture" (*PH* 30). Such criticisms, which Gans rejects as inconclusively supported by empirical evidence, all clearly rely on the assumed aesthetic poverty of popular art. The charge of spurious gratification implies an inability to produce genuine aesthetic pleasure. It cannot mean that the gratification is only a sublimated surrogate for more direct or primitive pleasure, since such a charge would be truer of the more refined pleasures of high art. Similarly, the claim that popular art can entertain only through sensational escapist content presumes its aesthetic impotence to move us through meaningful form and realistic content. And the charge that popular art destroys the intellect and corrupts our capacity for genuine culture likewise presupposes that it has no subtleties which could either stimulate or reward intellectual and aesthetic attention. All these assumptions of the intrinsically negative aesthetic character of popular art can be contested.

Finally, the fourth group of "non-aesthetic" charges concerns popular culture's "negative effects on the society" – specifically that it "not only reduces the level of cultural quality – or civilization – of the society, but also encourages totalitarianism by creating a passive audience peculiarly responsive to the techniques of mass persuasion" (*PH* 19). Gans counters the first charge mainly by pointing to its lack of empirical proof, arguing that at least in statistical terms of consumption there has been a rise in high culture interest (probably through improved education) since the advent of mass-media popular art (*PH* 45). But he further insists that people's freedom and pleasure are more important than "cultural quality" *per se*, "that the overall taste level of a society is not as significant a criterion for the goodness of a society as the welfare of its members" (*PH* 130). As to the second charge, Gans denies that popular culture has either the power to promote a dictatorship or the duty to "be a bulwark against such dangers as totalitarianism." Both these denials are questionable, as is Gans's related assumption that the media are merely responsive to public opinion, providing at most "the reinforcement of existing social trends," rather than shaping or transforming them (*PH* 46–7).[9]

If we find Gans's defense inadequate, we can once again find an alternative response by exposing and challenging the aesthetic assumption which underlies the two charges. The idea that society's cultural quality must be lowered by the presence of popular culture (rather than raised and enriched through its introduction of cultural and aesthetic variety) simply presumes that the products of popular culture are invariably and intrinsically of negative aesthetic value, and so necessarily "lower...the [cultural quality and] taste level of society as a whole" (*PH* 43–4). But why accept this necessitarian assumption, particularly when we recognize the traditional intellectualist bias which motivates it?

Secondly, to charge that popular art fosters totalitarian conformism because it demands a mindless, passive response is once again to assume that popular art can neither inspire nor reward any aesthetic attention beyond cretinized, uncritical passivity. The charge would be effectively undermined if it were shown that such art can be not only intellectually stimulating but acutely critical of "existing social trends." My subsequent account of rap music will try to show this and reveal other aesthetic features whose presence in popular art has been resolutely denied by the denouncing critics of mass culture. But in preparation for this task, and having shown that the apparently non-aesthetic indictments of popular art largely depend on aesthetic ones, I should first investigate these aesthetic charges in greater detail.

In defending popular art against them, I am not attempting a full-scale aesthetic whitewash. I admit that the products of popular art are often aesthetically wretched and lamentably unappealing, just as I recognize that their social effects can be very noxious, particularly when they are consumed in a passive, all-accepting way. What I shall contest are the philosophical arguments that popular art is always and necessarily an aesthetic failure, inferior and inadequate by its intrinsic constitution, that (in the words of Dwight Macdonald) "there are theoretical reasons why Mass Culture is not and can never be any good."[10]

In the debate over popular art, my defense needs to be located between the poles of condemnatory pessimism (characteristic of reactionary high-culture elitists but also of the Marxian Frankfurt school and its present-day disciples) and celebratory optimism (exemplified by the Popular Culture Association and the *Journal of Popular Culture*). If the former pole denounces popular art in near paranoid terror as maniacal manipulation devoid of redeeming aesthetic or social merit, the latter embraces it with ingenuous optimism as the free expression of the best of American life and ideology, an optimism which might well be regarded as the most cynical of pessimisms. My intermediary position is a *meliorism*, which recognizes popular art's grave flaws and abuses but also its merits and potential. It holds that popular art *should be* improved because it leaves much to be desired, but that it *can be* improved because it can and often does achieve real aesthetic merit and serve worthy social goals. This position insists that popular art deserves serious aesthetic attention, since to dismiss it as beneath aesthetic consideration is to consign its evaluation and future to the most mercenary pressures of the marketplace. The long-range aim of meliorism is to direct inquiry away from general condemnations or glorifications so that attention may be better focused on more concrete problems and specific improvements. But for the moment, the general philosophic arguments for popular art's intrinsic aesthetic worthlessness are too influential to leave unanswered. They are at once diverse and deeply imbricated, so my ensuing treatment of them in terms of six distinct basic charges will risk some simplification and overlapping repetition.

III

(1) Perhaps the most basic aesthetic complaint against popular art is that it simply fails to provide any real aesthetic satisfaction at all. Of course, even the most hostile critics know that movies entertain millions and that rock music makes audiences dance and throb with pleasure. But such obvious and discomforting facts are neatly sidestepped by denying that these satisfactions are genuine. The apparent gratifications, sensations, and experiences that popular art provides are dismissed as spurious and

fraudulent, while high art, in contrast, is held to supply something genuine.

Leo Lowenthal, for example, sees "the differences between popular culture and [true] art" in terms of the difference "between spurious gratification and a genuine experience," and Clement Greenberg likewise condemns the popular arts (which he collectively and pejoratively labels "kitsch") for supplying only "vicarious experience and faked sensations."[11] Adorno, who similarly inveighs against the "washed-out" and "fake" satisfactions of popular art, explains that it is only "because the masses are denied real enjoyment [that] they, out of resentment, enjoy the substitutes that come their way...[through] low art and entertainment."[12] Moreover, critics like Bernard Rosenberg and Ernest van den Haag further insist that the pseudo-pleasures and "substitute gratifications" of "the entertainment industry" prevent us from achieving "any really satisfying experience," because the "diversion" they provide "distracts [us] from life and real gratification."[13]

Scrutiny of these citations will reveal that the anxious zeal to strip popular art of anything positive like pleasure has led its critics not merely to deny that its experiences and enjoyments are *aesthetically* genuine, but more radically to deny that they are real or genuine at all. In short, the claim of spuriousness, a strategy of imperious intellectualist presumption, implies that the cultural elite not only has the power to determine, against popular judgement, the limits of aesthetic legitimacy, but also the power to legislate, against empirical evidence, what can be called real experience or pleasure. Yet how can such a radical claim be substantiated? It in fact never is, but instead is sustained by the authority of its proponents and the virtual absence of opposition. Quite understandably, it faces no strong challenge either from the intellectuals whom it flatters or from non-intellectuals, who lack the strength or interest to contest it and who typically just ignore it as "abstract bullshit" that has no practical effect on their world.

What in fact is meant in asserting that "the gratifications offered by popular culture are spurious", and what arguments serve to support this claim?[14] Is it anything more than a rhetorical gesture of denying the legitimacy and value of these gratifications by challenging their reality? Perhaps the most straightforward interpretation and justification of the charge of spuriousness is that popular art's alleged gratifications are not real because they are never deeply felt, that they are spurious because they are merely "washed-out," "faked sensations." But the experience of rock music, which can be so intensely absorbing and powerful that it is likened to spiritual possession, surely gives the lie to such a charge. Even rock's severest critics recognize the passionately real potency and intoxicating satisfactions of its experience, just as they mourn the dire educational consequences and the ruthlessly commercialized exploitation of this power. Distressed by its unrivaled power to engage and express the longings and experience of today's youth, Allan Bloom blasts rock music as a "gutter phenomenon." It belongs in the gutter not because it fails to please, but because the intense pleasure it gives young people "makes it very difficult for them to have a passionate relationship to the art and thought that are the substance of a liberal education," an education which Bloom conceives in extremely traditionalist and intellectualist terms.[15]

Obviously and threateningly real in their intensity and appeal, the gratifications of popular art are sometimes scorned as spurious in another sense, that of ephemerality. They are not real because they are fleeting. "We are diverted temporarily...but not gratified." "What you consume now may please you for the moment;...in another moment it will leave you ravenous again."[16] Such an argument, however, will not withstand analysis. First, on the logical level, it is simply false to conclude the unreality of something from its ephemerality. This *non sequitur* may seem convincing not only because it has a grand philosophical pedigree extending back to Parmenides, but also because it serves an equally strong psychological motive – our deep desire for stability, which is typically misconstrued as requiring the certainty of total permanence. But despite this support from such powerful and longstanding prejudices, the inference is clearly wrong. Something which exists only for a time nonetheless really exists, and a temporary gratification is a gratification all the same.

Moreover, the argument that transience entails spuriousness, that gratifications are unreal and fraudulent if they later leave us hungering for more, cannot serve to discredit popular art in contrast to high culture. For if accepted, the argument would be equally effective against the gratifications of high art. Are we permanently or even lastingly satisfied by the reading of a single sonnet or the viewing of a dozen paintings? Does the passing of these gratifications imply that they are somehow fraudulent? Not at all, because one of the positive features of genuine aesthetic pleasure is that, while it gratifies, it also stimulates the desire for more such pleasure. If your aesthetic pleasure in an object leaves you wanting no more, you have probably not been pleased at all.[17] Indeed, the whole insistence on lasting gratification needs to be questioned. It seems too theological and otherworldly. In our world of continuous change and desire, there are no gratifications that are permanent, and the only end to the passing of pleasure and the desire for more is death.

A somewhat different charge of ephemerality commonly made against popular art refers not to the transience of the gratifications themselves but to the fleetingness of its capacity to gratify. Works of popular art do not weather the test of time. They may top the charts for a season, but they quickly lose the power to entertain us and soon fade into oblivion; their charms and pleasures are thus revealed as ultimately illusory. High art, on the other hand, retains its power to gratify. The works of Homer and the drama of ancient Greece, we are too often told, demonstrate the legitimacy of the gratifications they provide by having provided them to multitudes for centuries and by still providing them today. There is nothing in popular art to match this history of durability, not even in the classics of film and the "golden oldies" of popular music.

But even granting all this, the argument remains badly flawed. First, it is too early to conclude that none of our classics of popular art will survive as objects of aesthetic enjoyment. And it is easier to believe some will than to believe that many people still read Homer for pleasure. Moreover, we tend to forget the socio-cultural and institutional reasons which underwrite the continued pleasurability of the classics of high art. Education and availability of choice play an enormous but often forgotten role in determining the objects of our pleasure. To a large extent we enjoy what we are trained and conditioned to enjoy and what the options of our circumstances allow us to enjoy. Since the classics have long been systematically disseminated and their appreciation rigorously inculcated through powerful institutions of education, while (at least until the age of mass media) there was no such organized or effective framework for transmitting and preserving works of popular art, it should be no surprise that the former have better survived as objects of attention and hence as objects of aesthetic enjoyment.

Critics of popular art are fond of arguing that TV viewers don't really like the programs they watch but that they "enjoy" them nevertheless because there is nothing better available on the other channels; that the consumer of popular art is like "the prisoner who loves his cell because he has been left nothing else to love."[18] But this same argument from paucity of options can be turned on the "eternal" enjoyment of Homer, which today is so negligible that it seems almost as mythical as his gods and heroes. Indeed, it is precisely because the mass media now provide an alternative system of dissemination and education that the exclusive adoration of the classics inculcated by the traditional scholastic system has been largely undermined by interest in the popular arts. Again, this is not to argue that the classics and high art no longer deserve and reward aesthetic interest, but only to reject their traditional monopoly of legitimate aesthetic attention.

The argument that popular art is spurious because ephemeral is also flawed in forgetting that many of the great classics of high art were originally produced and consumed as popular art. Greek drama was a very popular and raucous affair, as was the Elizabethan theater; and many now esteemed novels (like *Wuthering Heights*) were once condemned as sensationalist commercial trash in much the same way that movies, TV, and rock music have been condemned in more recent times. To deny that works of popular art survive by simply ignoring the popular origins of those that in fact do is more than an innocent error. It is an exploitative expropriation of the cultural resources of the dominated majority by a dominant elite. For once these works are exclusively reclassified as high art, their mode of appropriation is redefined so that their popular appreciation will be demeaned and discounted, thus essentially reserving them for the more distinguished delectation of the cultural elite.

Finally, even if we concede that works of popular art are transient and their power to please relatively brief, this neither renders them valueless nor their gratifications spurious. To presume that it does is to equate all pleasure and value with permanence. But there is value in transient things, and indeed sometimes in their very transience. Brief encounters may sometimes be sweeter and better than abiding relationships. To reject the value of the ephemeral has been a rather permanent prejudice of our intellectual culture, and perhaps it was a very serviceable one for past conditions where survival was so insecure that attention and value had to be fixed on the most enduring. But it is a prejudice, nonetheless, which blights and blunts our pleasures. Indeed, it even blocks a major path for constructing a more stably satisfying life. For once ephemeral pleasures are discounted as relatively valueless and unworthy of attention, serious thinking is not devoted to how they can best be achieved, repeated, and securely integrated into life. Consequently, such pleasures and their sometimes explosive effect on life are dangerously left to the vagaries of chance, blind desire, and the indoctrinating pressures of advertising.

Popular art's gratifications have been censured as spurious in yet another sense: as mere substitutes for pleasures that are somehow more basic or real. Adorno, who rightly protests the social conditions which deny us "real gratification in the sphere of immediate sense experience," complains that popular art purveys false surrogates for such enjoyment as a form of narcotic escape. "Because the masses are denied real enjoyment, they, out of resentment, enjoy the substitutes that come their way" (*AT* 19, 340). Yet the pleasures of high art, as Adorno must admit, are no less mediated and removed from actual living; and they can also serve escapist ends.

But just as often, the charge of surrogacy locates genuine satisfaction in the ultimate rather than the immediate, in a deferred and consequently more complete gratification. Explicitly likening popular art to masturbation, as providing mere discharge of tension rather than real satisfaction, van den Haag condemns it for glutting us with energy-draining "substitute gratifications [that] incapacitate the individual for real ones" and thus prevent us from any "ultimate gratification."[19] In much the same style of prurient innuendo, Allan Bloom implies the fraudulence of rock's satisfactions by associating them with undeferred and deviant sexual pleasure: "Rock music provides premature ecstasy" to children and teens "as though they were ready to enjoy the final or complete satisfaction."[20]

Certainly deferral and resistance frequently augment satisfaction, but where is the "complete" and "final" satisfaction to be found? Hardly in this world, which knows no end to desire. Real satisfaction is rather relegated to some transcendental domain – for Bloom the realm of platonistic ideals, for Adorno a Marxian utopia, and for van den Haag the Christian afterlife. The only pleasures they seem willing to legitimate are those we cannot attain, at least not in this world. Even the aesthetic pleasures of high art cannot be spared sanction. "In a false world," Adorno bitterly avows, "all *hedone* is false. This goes for aesthetic pleasure too." And van den Haag somberly intones the same message of abject anguish: "As for the pleasures of this life, they are not worth pursuing."[21] Thus, as suggested earlier, the critique that popular art provides only spurious pleasures is less a defense of real pleasure than a mask for the wholesale denial of all worldly pleasure, a strategy adopted by ascetic minds who fear pleasure as a dangerous diversion from their transcendental goals or simply as a discomforting threat to their fundamentally ascetic ethos.

Two final reasons are sometimes offered for the spuriousness of popular art's satisfactions. The first maintains that since "genuine experience... presupposes effortful participation," popular art cannot provide any such "really satisfying experience." The second insists that its experience cannot be genuine because it fails "to involve the whole individual in his relation to reality."[22] Both these arguments, however, lead beyond the charge of spurious satisfaction to two other criticisms of popular art which are important enough to demand individual attention: the charges of effortless passivity and empty superficiality.

(2) Popular art is often condemned for not providing any aesthetic challenge or active response. In contrast to high art, whose appreciation demands aesthetic effort and thus stimulates aesthetic activity and resultant satisfaction, popular art both induces and requires a lifeless and unrewarding passivity. Its "simple and repetitive structures," says Bourdieu, only "invite a passive, absent participation" (*D* 386). This effortless passivity is thought to explain not only its wide appeal but its failure to truly satisfy. Its "effortlessness" easily captivates those of us who are too weary and beaten to seek what is challenging. But since enjoyment (as Aristotle realized) is a by-product attendant upon and essentially bound to activity, our lack of active effort ultimately translates into joyless boredom. Rather than energetically and acutely responding to the work (as we can in high art), we lazily and languidly receive it in a passive, listless torpor. Nor could it tolerate more vigorous scrutiny and response. Thus the audience of popular art is necessarily reduced from active participants to "passive consumers" who must be "as passive as possible."[23]

Adorno and Horkheimer explain how "all amusement suffers from this incurable malady."

> Pleasure hardens into boredom because, if it is to remain pleasure, it must not demand any effort and therefore moves rigorously in the worn grooves of association. No independent thinking must be expected from the audience: the product prescribes every reaction: not by its natural form (which collapses under reflection), but by signals. Any logical connection calling for mental effort is painstakingly avoided.[24]

Much popular art may indeed conform to Horkheimer and Adorno's analysis. But their critique also betrays the simplistic conflation of all legitimate activity with serious thinking, of "any effort" with "mental effort" of the intellect. Critics of popular culture are loath to recognize that there are humanly worthy and aesthetically rewarding activities other than intellectual exertion. So even if all art and aesthetic enjoyment do indeed require some active effort or the overcoming of some resistance, it

does not follow that they require effortful "independent thinking." There
are other, more somatic forms of effort, resistance, and satisfaction.

Rock songs are typically enjoyed through moving, dancing, and singing
along with the music, often with such vigorous efforts that we break a
sweat and eventually exhaust ourselves. And such efforts, as Dewey
realized, involve overcoming resistances like "embarrassment, fear,
awkwardness, self-consciousness, [and] lack of vitality."[25] Clearly, on the
somatic level, there is much more effortful activity in the appreciation of
rock than in that of high-brow music, whose concerts compel us to sit in
a motionless silence which often induces not mere torpid passivity but
snoring sleep. The term "funky", used to characterize and commend
many rock songs, derives from an African word meaning "positive sweat"
and is expressive of an African aesthetic of vigorously active and
communally impassioned engagement rather than dispassionate judg-
mental remoteness.[26] The much more energetic and kinesthetic response
evoked by rock exposes the fundamental passivity of the traditional
aesthetic attitude of disinterested, distanced contemplation – a contemplative attitude that has its roots in the quest for philosophical and
theological knowledge rather than pleasure, for individual enlightenment
rather than communal interaction or social change. Popular arts like rock
thus suggest a radically revised aesthetic with a joyous return of the
somatic dimension which philosophy has long repressed to preserve its
own hegemony (through that of the intellect) in all realms of human
value. No wonder the aesthetic legitimacy of such art is vehemently
denied and its embodied and embodying efforts are ignored or rejected as
irrational regression from art's true (i.e. intellectual) purpose. The fact
that such art and its appreciation have their roots in non-Western
civilization renders them even more unacceptably retrograde.

For Adorno, pop music is "regressive" and aesthetically invalid because it "is a somatic stimulus" (*AT* 170); for Allan Bloom, the problem
with rock is its deep appeal to "sensuality" and "sexual desire," which
renders it "*alogon*." "It is not only not reasonable, it is hostile to reason."
Mark Miller makes the same mistake of inferring aesthetic illegitimacy
and intellectual corruption from the mere fact of rock's more immediate
sensuous appeal. "Rock n' Roll music," he complains in quoting John
Lennon, "gets right through to you without having to go through your
brain"; and this sensuous immediacy is negatively misconstrued as
entailing effortless nullity and passive "immobility," so that "all rock
aspires to the condition of Muzak." In short, since rock can be enjoyed
without intellectual "interpretation," it is therefore not sufficiently

"cerebral" to be aesthetically legitimate, and its so-called "artists and listeners are anti-intellectual and usually stoned." Rock's only and short-lived value was the critical consciousness induced by its first transgressional challenge; and in a remark which betrays the body-despising Cartesianism of popular culture's critics, Miller laments that rock's "body went on dancing...[after] it had lost its soul" of original protest.[27]

Along with their anti-somatic animus, the arguments of Adorno, Bloom, and Miller share two vitiating logical blunders. First, the sensuous appeal of rock does not entail anti-intellectualism (in either its creators or its audience). Only if the sensuous were essentially incompatible with the intellect would this follow; and why should we sensuous intellects suppose this? It is only the presumption of intellectualist exclusiveness, a powerful philosophical prejudice with a platonic pedigree, that leads these thinkers to regard the two as mutually exclusive. A second fallacy is to infer that because rock music can be enjoyed without hard thinking or interpretation, its enjoyment therefore cannot sustain or reward reflective analysis. If it *can* be enjoyed on an intellectually shallow level, it still does not follow that it *must* be so enjoyed and has nothing else to offer.

(3) Let us, then, face the charge that popular art is in fact too superficial to engage the intellect. For if it can engage and satisfy only the somatic and mentally jejune dimensions of human experience, its value would be seriously limited, though still, I believe, far from negligible. The charge of intellectual shallowness typically breaks down into two more specific claims.

(a) The first is that popular art cannot deal with the deep realities and real problems of life, and therefore strives to distract us with an escapist dream world of pseudo-problems and easy, clichéd solutions. In contrast to high (or true) art, which "tends to engage life at its deeper levels" and treats "the essential" in reality, popular art "distracts from life" and from life's "real and most important problems"; in particular, its works "distract the masses from becoming more clearly aware of their real needs."[28] Popular art, Dwight Macdonald explains, is obliged to ignore or "void...the deep realities (sex, death, failure, tragedy)...since the realities would be too real...to induce...[the] narcotized acceptance" that it seeks.[29] But this again presumes without argument that the aim of popular art is always a drugged quiescent stupor, while in fact there is ample evidence to the contrary. Long before Woodstock, rock music had often been a strident, mobilizing voice of protest; and in recent years, through such rock concert projects as Live Aid, Farm Aid, and Human Rights Now, it has proven an effective source of collaborative social action for worthy political and humanitarian causes.

Van den Haag provides the most common argument why reality cannot be handled by mass-media products. Popular art must appeal to a larger than high-brow audience and so must tailor its products to the comprehension of this wider public. But this, for van den Haag and other culture snobs, means tailoring them too small to encompass any real issues or significant experience.

> They must omit, therefore, all human experience likely to be mis-understood – all experience and expression the meaning of which is not obvious and approved. Which is to say that the mass media cannot touch the experiences that art, philosophy and literature deal with: relevant and significant human experience presented in relevant and significant form. For if it is such, it is new, doubtful, difficult, perhaps offensive, at any rate easily misunderstood....[Hence] the mass media...cannot touch real prob-lems or real solutions.[30]

At least two fundamental fallacies invalidate this argument. First, there is the mistaken presumption that popular art cannot be popular unless its form and content are completely transparent and totally approved. But there is no justification for this view except the equally false presumption that consumers of popular art are just too stupid to understand more than the obvious and too psychologically naive to appreciate the presentation of views with which they may ultimately disagree. Recent studies of tele-vision drama demonstrate that the mass-media audience can take a criti-cal and complex attitude to the "heroes" and views there presented;[31] and the point is reinforced by the evidence of rock enthusiasts who enjoy songs suggestive of drug-taking and violent living while in fact dis-approving of such behavior. Moreover, even assuming its audience is largely simple-minded, we still cannot conclude that popular art's content must be fully obvious and approved in order to please. For there remains the possibility that it may please even when only partially understood or indeed misunderstood. Certainly the middle-class white youth who first took to rock 'n' roll had no real understanding of the lyrics they thrilled to, many of whose words bore hidden Afro-American meanings like the term "rock 'n' roll" itself, which meant "to fuck."

Secondly, van den Haag's argument falsely conflates the "relevant and significant" in human experience and expression with the new and the difficult. No grounds are given for equating these clearly distinct notions, and any such equation is refuted by the abiding significance that our more familiar experiences and traditional forms (e.g. falling in love, kissing our children good-night, holiday prayers and meals) often have in our lives. Van den Haag and others make this false equation through their blind allegiance to the high modernist aesthetic of originality and difficulty, which is unconsciously smuggled in as a general standard of experiential relevance and significance. Still worse, it becomes the standard of "the real," so that the ordinary problems treated by popular art – disappointed love, economic hardship, family conflicts, alienation, drugs, sex, and violence – can be denied as unreal, while the "real problems" worthy of artistic expression are only those novel and esoteric enough to escape the experience and comprehension of the general public. This is surely a convenient strategy for the privileged and conservative to ignore and suppress the realities of those they dominate by denying the artistic legitimacy of their expression, a strategy which vividly exemplifies Bourdieu's point that aesthetic conflicts are often fundamentally "political conflicts...for the power to impose the dominant definition of reality, and social reality in particular."[32] But however unattractively banal they are to the cultural aesthete, such "unreal" problems (and the common "unreal" people whose lives they exhaust) constitute an important dimension of our world. Poverty and violence, sex and drugs, "spare parts and broken hearts" (to quote Bruce Springsteen) "keep this world turnin' around"; and they have a way of reasserting their repressed reality with a brutal vengeance, as one departs the theater and is hit by the street.[33]

(b) Popular art has been condemned as superficial and empty in another sense which makes no appeal to "deep realities" and "real problems." Here the charge is simply that works of popular art lack sufficient complexities, subtleties, and levels of meaning to be in any way mentally stimulating or capable of "sustaining serious interest." In contrast to high art, which "tends to be complex" so that its "content can be perceived and understood on several levels," popular art must gain its wide popularity by dealing only in "broad, easily recognizable images," flat stereotypes, and empty clichés.[34] Hence, unable to exercise our intelligence, it can only (in Adorno's words) "fill empty time with more emptiness" (*AT* 348).

Certainly, too many mass-media products are boringly superficial and one-dimensional, but culture critics wrongly conclude that all must be.

Implicitly appealing to the homogenizing prejudice that "all mass culture is identical,"[35] they resolutely ignore the subtle complexities that can in fact be found in popular artworks. Yet even Adorno came to recognize that popular works often "consist of various levels of meanings, superimposed on one another, all of which contribute to the effect."[36] And John Fiske's study of television narratives shows that their popularity often indeed depends on their being multileveled, multivocal, and polysemic so that they can simultaneously be read differently by and thus appeal to a wide "variety of groups with different, often conflicting interests." For, as media and marketing experts realize, the popular TV audience is "not a homogeneous mass" but a shifting constellation of many different social groups who "actively read television in order to produce from it meanings that connect with their social experience."[37]

Intellectualist critics typically fail to recognize the multilayered, multivocal, and nuanced meanings of popular art because they are "turned off" from the outset and unwilling to give these works the sympathetic attention needed to tease out such complexities. But sometimes they just don't understand the works in question. Rock music has long been the carrier of covert messages. Emerging as it did from oppressive conditions of slavery and cultural suppression, rock's complex levels of meaning (somatic as well as discursive) were necessary for it to dissemble innocuous and mindless quiescence while expressing protest and pride. From black culture to youth culture, the tradition persisted, so that Bob Dylan could tell an interviewer in 1965, "If I told you what our music was really about, we'd probably all get arrested."[38] Today, we still find intelligent adults who are firmly convinced that rock's lyrics are altogether trivial and inane, but who will nonetheless eventually confess that they are unable to grasp their meaning over the raucous sound and nonstandard diction. If most of our adult population is young enough to have been raised on Elvis and Little Richard, and hence hip enough not to complain too much about the noise and nonsense of the classic rock tradition, the charge of meaningless sound and vile empty lyrics is now directed at genres like punk and rap, where both noise and linguistic deviance are consciously thematized to form part of the semantic and formal complexity of certain songs.[39]

(4) Our culture regards art as quintessentially creative and original, as necessarily engaged in innovation and experimentation. This is why many aestheticians claim that an artwork is always unique, and why even

a traditionalist like T. S. Eliot insists that a work which "would not be new...would therefore not be a work of art."[40] By contrast, popular art is globally denigrated not only as unoriginal and monotonous, but as necessarily so because of its motives and methods of production. Its products are inevitably "tepid and standardized", because they are technologically constructed from formulas and "ready-made clichés" by a profit-hungry industry geared to "catering to consumer tastes rather than developing or cultivating autonomous ones."[41] Hence, in contrast to the creative originality and other "features of genuine art,...popular culture proves to have its own genuine characteristics: standardization, stereotypy, conservatism, mendacity, manipulated consumer goods."[42]

The claim that popular art is necessarily uncreative relies on three lines of argument. First, its standardization and technological production preclude creativity, because they put limits on individuality.[43] Second, popular art's group production and division of labor frustrate original expression, because they involve more than one artist's decision.[44] Third, the desire to entertain a large audience is incompatible with individual self-expression and hence with original aesthetic expression. All these arguments rest on the premise that aesthetic creation is necessarily individualistic, a questionable romantic myth nourished by bourgeois liberalism's ideology of individualism, and one which belies art's essential communal dimension. In any case, none of these arguments is compelling; nor will they serve to isolate popular works from high art.

Standardization can be found in high as well as popular art. Both employ conventions or formulas to facilitate communication, to achieve certain aesthetic forms and effects whose value has been proven, and to provide a solid basis from which to develop creative elaborations and innovations. The sonnet's length is just as rigidly standard as the TV sitcom's, and neither limit precludes creativity. What determines the aesthetic validity of formulas, conventions, and generic standards is whether they are imaginatively deployed. If popular art too often exploits them in a routine, mechanical fashion, high art has its own deadly forms of monotonous standardization like academicism, where, in Clement Greenberg's words, "creative activity dwindles" and "the same themes are mechanically varied in a hundred different works."[45] As for the use of technological inventions, it is surely present in high art, and it is less a barrier than an impetus to aesthetic creativity (as the history of architecture clearly demonstrates). The technology of popular art has helped create new artistic forms like the movie, the TV series, and the rock video; and this adventurous and unpredictable creative power, so threatening to the weakening authority of high art and its custodians, is partly what motivates their charge that popular art is creatively impotent.[46]

The second argument is no less problematic. We can grant no contradiction between collective production and artistic creativity without thereby challenging the aesthetic legitimacy of Greek temples, Gothic churches, and the works of oral literary traditions. It is undeniable that creative artistic aims are often frustrated or corrupted by corporate pressures (perhaps most notoriously in Hollywood). But this, as Dewey would say, is something to combat and rectify in practice, not to reify into a principle of necessary contradiction between original expression and group work. Though collective production will no doubt place constraints on the flights of individual fancy, it is also true that the collaboration of several minds can compensate creativity with added imaginative resources. In any case, we must remember that even the individual imagination always works in some sort of collaboration with a larger community, in terms of the tradition's inherited conventions and the audience's anticipated reactions. Thus, even the high-culture artist, as a socially constructed and socially motivated self, may, in the very act of pleasing herself, also be trying to please a large audience – even if it be only the imagined legions of posterity.

Such considerations also relate to the third and most common argument for popular art's intrinsic lack of creativity. This argument asserts that popularity requires artistic form and content to be easily grasped and appreciated by the entire mass audience; and this in turn means denying personal creative expression so as to appeal to the lowest common denominator. Hence only the most basic stereotypes in both content and form can be presented. In short, since "mass media must offer homogenized fare to meet an average of tastes," it can say nothing creative or provocative, but is confined to expressing only "the obvious and approved."[47] We know this conclusion is false, if only by the fact that products of popular art have regularly shocked and offended the sensibilities of "average" people. But we need to expose the fallacies which make the argument seem plausible to so many culture critics.

The first error is confusing a "multitudinous audience" with a "mass audience." Popularity requires only the former, while only the latter implies a homogenized undifferentiated whole. High-brow culture critics falsely assume that the popular art audience is such a mass. They fail to recognize how this audience is actually structured into different taste groups reflecting different social and educational backgrounds and ideologies, and employing different strategies for interpreting works of popular art so as to make them more relevant and pleasurable for the taste group's particular social experience. Media studies show that a work expressing a particular view can be very popular with audiences who reject (or simply do not grasp) it, because such audiences systematically misread the work, creatively "decoding" or reconstituting its meaning to make it more interesting and serviceable to them. This is why feminists, Marxists, and traditionalist Moroccan Jews in Israel can all be devoted fans of *Dallas* and why "*Dynasty* has become a cult show among gays in the USA."[48]

But even if we ignore this argument from creative misreadings, which more democratically locates popular art's creativity in its various consumers and not only in its official creators, there is further reason for distinguishing between a multitudinous and a mass audience. For a particular taste group sharing a distinct social or ethnic background (or a common ideology or artistic tradition) may be clearly distinguishable from what is considered the homogeneous mass audience of average Americans and yet still be numerous enough to constitute a multitudinous audience whose satisfaction will render an art sufficiently popular to count as popular art and reach mass-media coverage. The fact that there are such distinctive large audiences means that popular art need not confine itself to styles, stereotypes, and views that are understood and accepted by the so-called (and perhaps ultimately mythical) general public.

The record scratching, black English, sexually explicit content, and anti-American anger of many hit rap songs are not at all "obvious and approved" for the vast majority of "middle America," but this does not prevent such songs from achieving immense popularity. Indeed, their popularity derives precisely from their distinctive ethnic and ideological focus and their challenge of accepted public standards, from being a "Public Enemy" as the popularly celebrated but publicly denounced rap crew shrewdly named itself. Nor is this distinction-based popularity necessarily confined to the young black ghetto audience. For rap's message of bitter injustice and violent protest against oppressive authority can be taken up by alienated youth from different social backgrounds, or even by marginalized intellectuals who are discontent with the system and willing to be educated in rap's styles, tropes, and vernacular. In short, as rock showed before rap, popularity does not require conformity to a global "average of tastes"; nor does it preclude the creation of meanings only properly understood by initiates in a subculture or countercultural artistic tradition.

Popular artists are also consumers of popular art and form part of its audience. Often they share the tastes of those toward whom their work is directed. Here there can be no real conflict between wanting to express oneself creatively and wanting to please one's large audience. Falsely assuming the necessity of such a conflict is the second error of the third argument. It stems from the romantic myth of individual genius, which insisted that isolation from society and contempt for its common values were crucial to artistic integrity and vision. The historical and socio-economic pressures which fostered this myth are now widely acknowledged. It developed when artists had been cut off from their traditional forms of societal patronage and were uncertain of both their role and their audience in the rapidly changing society of the nineteenth century. Few today would give it credence, and even seemingly elitist artists like T. S. Eliot have explicitly denied it by asserting the necessary connection of the artist to her community and expressing the wish to reach as large a portion of that community as possible.[49]

Finally, the argument that popular art's popularity requires slavish conformity to accepted stereotypes rests on the premise that its consumers are too simple-minded to appreciate the presentation of views they may find unfamiliar and unacceptable. But, as already noted, empirical evidence of media consumption shows this to be false; media viewers are not (in Stuart Hall's phrase) the "cultural dopes" that intellectualist high-brows take them to be.[50] The whole idea that popular art's audience is psychologically too naive and one-dimensional to entertain or be entertained by conflicting ideas and ambiguity of values seems clearly refuted by the baffling experience of postmodern living, where everyday coping frequently requires not only the entertaining but the simultaneous inhabiting of contradictory roles and conflicting language-games. No longer an elite aesthetic luxury, multiplicity of attitude and the vacillating suspension of both belief and disbelief are a necessity of life. For in what can we still commit full faith and total investment without self-deception or irony?

(5) The issue of conformity to public standards introduces a fifth major aesthetic indictment against popular art: lack of aesthetic autonomy and resistance. Aestheticians typically regard autonomy as "an irrevocable aspect of art" (*AT* 1) which is crucial to its value. Even Adorno and

Bourdieu, who recognize that this autonomy is the product of socio-historical factors and serves a social agenda of class distinction, nevertheless insist that it is essential to artistic legitimacy and the very notion of aesthetic appreciation. For art to be created and appreciated *qua* art and not as something else, requires, says Bourdieu, "an autonomous field of artistic production...capable of imposing its own norms on both the production and consumption of its products" and of refusing external functions or "any necessity other than those inscribed in...[its] specific tradition." The core of such autonomous norms is granting "primacy to that of which the artist is master, i.e. the form, manner, style, rather than the 'subject', the external referent, which involves subordination to functions – even if only the most elementary one, that of representing, signifying, saying something" (*D* 3). Similarly, for Adorno, art's norms are exclusive of any function other than the service of art itself. Art "will not play a serving role" and should eschew "even the childish notion of wanting to be a source of pleasure," so that "the autonomous work of art...is functional only with reference to itself" (*AT* 89, 136, 281). By contrast, popular art forfeits aesthetic validity simply by its desire to entertain and serve ordinary human needs rather than purely artistic ends. But why does functionality entail artistic and aesthetic illegitimacy?

Ultimately these inferences rest on defining art and the aesthetic as essentially opposed to reality or life. For Adorno, though art is rooted and informed by material and social life, it defines and justifies itself only "by being different from the ungodly reality" of our world and divorced from its practical functional exigencies. In claiming its own free and imaginative domain, art represents a critique of the world's relentlessly grubbing functionality, so that "if any social function can be ascribed to art at all, it is the function to have no function" (*AT* 322). Bourdieu similarly maintains that the very notion of the aesthetic attitude "implies a break with...the world" and the concerns of ordinary life (*D* 4). Since popular art affirms the "continuity between art and life, which implies the subordination of form to function" (*D* 32), Bourdieu concludes that it cannot count as legitimate art. It cannot be aesthetically legitimated by any so-called popular aesthetic, because such an aesthetic, Bourdieu argues, is not worthy of the name. First, because this aesthetic is never consciously and positively formulated ("for itself"), but merely serves as "a negative reference point" for the legitimate life-opposing aesthetic to define itself by contrast (*D* 4, 41, 57); and second, because by accepting real-life concerns and pleasures and thus challenging art's pure autonomy, the popular aesthetic is disqualified as essentially opposed to art and as engaged in a "systematic reduction of the things of art to the things of life" (*D* 5).

These anti-functionalist arguments against popular art all hang on the premise that art and real life can and should be essentially opposed and separated. But though a hoary dogma of aesthetic philosophy, why should this view be accepted? Its provenance and motivation should certainly make us suspicious. Originating in Plato's attack on art as doubly removed from reality, it has been sustained by a philosophical tradition which was always eager, even in defending art, to endorse its distance from the real, so as to insure philosophy's sovereignty in determining reality, including the real nature of art.

But if we look at matters free from philosophical prejudice and historical parochiality, we see that art surely forms part of life, just as life forms the substance of art and even constitutes itself artistically in "the art of living."[51] Both as objects and as experiences, works of art inhabit the world and function in our lives. Music is used to lull babies to sleep and to rouse patriotic feeling. Poetry is used for prayer and courtship, fables to inculcate moral lessons. Certainly in ancient Athenian culture the arts were intimately integrated into everyday life and its ethos. Paintings and sculptures were not put in museums for pure visual delectation but served (like architecture) definite religious, social, and political purposes. Music and song were part of the religious rites and civic ceremonies of the people. The classics of Greek drama were aimed at reinforcing social unity and civic pride through retelling communal myth and were performed at festivals alongside athletic competitions. They constituted popular culture, and behavior at them was no more formal and refined than what we find at today's rock concerts.[52] In short, while Greek art lacked the modern notion of artistic autonomy, this lack did not rob it of aesthetic potency.

Bourdieu, of course, knows this well, and his own work insists on the historical evolution of the nineteenth century, in which art was transformed into *autonomous* art and the aesthetic into a *pure* aesthetic. But his purist definitions suggest that history's changes are irrevocably permanent and that, once transfigured into pure autonomy, art and the aesthetic can no longer be legitimate in a less pure and life-denying form. History, however, continues its transformations; and recent developments in postmodern culture suggest the disintegration of the purist ideal and the increasing implosion of the aesthetic into all areas of life. Moreover, although Bourdieu penetratingly exposes the deeper material conditions and concealed social interests involved in aesthetic purity (which render it far from pure, though it be globally misperceived as pure), he seems unwilling to entertain the idea that we can break through this collective misperception of pure autonomy and still maintain a viable aesthetic. He rejects the possibility of an alternative aesthetic where life is given centrality, and popular art and experience can be redeemed. But such an aesthetic is not only possible; it is powerfully presented in Dewey's pragmatist theory of art, which makes the energies, needs, and pleasures of "the live creature" central to aesthetic experience.

Art's autonomy is expressed not simply in its difference from life but in its sense of self-worth and self-asserting resistance to society. Adorno, for example, insists that "Art will live on only as long as it has the power to resist society." If it fails to assert its autonomous distinction through this resistance, it degenerates to a mere "commodity" (*AT* 321). Thus, even if high art has been largely commodified, it at least proudly claims autonomous value, whereas popular culture does not even "pretend to be art" but proclaims itself a "business" or "industry." Still worse, its products reinforce this lack of resistance by purveying a conservative, conformist " 'message' of adjustment and unreflecting obedience."[53] Such remarks reflect a familiar line of critique: since genuine art must be oppositional and "differ from the accepted," popular art's necessary conformity to average tastes and hence conservative attitudes must invalidate as art.[54]

But both premises of the argument have been shown to be untenable. Opposition to society is not an eternal essence of art but a particular aesthetic ideology which emerged in the nineteenth century as a result of socio-economic developments which removed the traditional forms of social connection and support that art and artists had earlier enjoyed. Not only before but during the dominance of this "art for art's sake" ideology, esteemed works of high art were often far from oppositional and anti-conservative in form and content.[55] Moreover, works of popular art need not be conservative or conformist to achieve their popularity.

Bourdieu advances a more subtle argument: popular art cannot be aesthetically legitimate because it essentially denies its own aesthetic validity or autonomy by implicitly accepting the domination of the high-art aesthetic which haughtily denigrates it. Our culture is one in which high art's aesthetic of "the pure disposition is so universally recognized...that no voice is heard pointing out that the definition of art, and through it the art of living, is an object of struggle among the classes." Hence, simply by existing in this culture, the popular aesthetic (which he links to the working class) must be "a dominated aesthetic which is constantly obliged to define itself in terms of the dominant aesthetics" (*D* 41, 48). Since by these dominant standards popular art fails to qualify as art, and since it fails to assert or generate its own independent legitimation, Bourdieu concludes that in a sense "there is no popular art" and that popular culture is "a paradoxical notion which imposes, willy-nilly, the dominant definition of culture" and hence its own invalidation (*D* 395). Such self-delegitimation can take the form of either resigned "degradation or self-destructive rehabilitation" through hopeless copying of high culture (*D* 48).

However compelling this argument may be for the French culture Bourdieu studies, it fails as a global argument against popular art. For, at least in America, such art does assert its aesthetic status and provide its own forms of aesthetic legitimation. Not only do many popular artists regard their role as more than mere entertainment, but the artistic status of their art is frequently thematized in their works. Moreover, awards like Oscars, Emmies, and Grammies (which are neither wholly determined by nor reducible to box-office sales) confer in the eyes of most Americans not only aesthetic legitimation but a degree of artistic prestige. There is also a large and growing array of aesthetic criticism of the popular arts, including some aesthetically oriented historical studies of their development. Such criticism, disseminated not only in journals and books but in the mass media, is clearly a form of legitimating discourse; and it employs the same sort of aesthetic predicates that are applied to high art (though it also uses new ones, like "funky"). This sharing of predicates and critical discourse does not entail its submission to high art, unless we presume from the outset that the high-art aesthetic has exclusive control of the legitimate use of aesthetic discourse; and this already begs the question of exclusive aesthetic legitimacy, which is precisely what popular art is contesting.

Similarly, it is wrong to assume that popular art's apparent lack of an articulated philosophical aesthetic somehow precludes its aesthetic legitimacy. Legitimation takes other, and more powerful, forms than philosophical theory, and popular art can be aesthetically legitimated through the experiences it provides and the listening, viewing, and critical practices it so widely engenders. Moreover, just as it is wrong to confuse legitimation with philosophical legitimation, so it is wrong to confine socially accepted aesthetic legitimacy to that which is granted by the socially marginalized intellectual community. Certainly we Americans take neither philosophy nor the cultural hegemony of intellectuals as seriously as the French and other Europeans do. This insouciantly rebellious attitude embodied in American popular culture is, I believe, a large part of its captivating appeal and genuine value for Europeans, particularly for the young and culturally dominated. For it provides an invaluable tool for their growing liberation from a long entrenched and stifling cultural domination by an oppressive tradition of disembodied, intellectualist philosophy and high courtly art.

In criticizing Bourdieu's global claim by appeal to American cultural difference, I am, however, only reinforcing his more general view that art and the aesthetic are not universal, timeless essences but cultural products essentially informed and transformed by social and historical conditions. For certain socio–historical factors could well explain why it is in America that the popular arts have best thrived and most successfully challenged the stranglehold of high art on aesthetic and cultural legitimacy. To properly demonstrate and map these factors would require detailed socio–historical research beyond the scope of this chapter. But the following explanatory factors seem the most promising.

First, though America is far from a classless society, its social structure has arguably been more flexible and decentered than those of traditional European societies; and its dominant ideology has been more outspokenly egalitarian and anti-aristocratic. Secondly, as a New World nation that had to fight for political and economic independence from Europe, America was more inclined to resist European cultural domination; and high culture was clearly perceived as an aristocratic European import, sometimes inciting violent patriotic protest.[56] Third, as a nation of immigrants from different cultures, there was no unique national tradition of high art which could be unproblematically imported from the Old World and held as binding; nor was there a centralized educational system to enforce cultural uniformity. The liberating effect of cultural plurality for popular art can be seen most dramatically in the development of blues, jazz, and rock from African cultural sources by Afro-Americans who were so brutally excluded from the dominant society that they could be largely free from the grip of its dominant aesthetic.[57]

But perhaps the most important reason for its greater cultural freedom is that American society lacked the two traditional institutions which largely structured European high culture and sustained its dominating power: an aristocratic court and a national church. As many have argued, the notion of high art was in large part an invention by aristocrats to insure their continued social privilege over the increasingly prosperous bourgeoisie, a strategy of distinction that was later aped by the socially aspiring burghers.[58] The ecclesiastical tradition, on the other hand, provided a powerful and institutionally entrenched ideal of highly spiritualized experience, as well as a habit of pious attention to works of art. It further provided an intellectual priestly class to direct and regulate the propriety of such transcendent experience and its discourse. When theological faith was lost but religious sentiments and somber spiritualizing habits were still enormously potent, these were projected into the religion of high art, a new realm of unworldly experience and devotional seriousness with a new priestly class of intellectual artists and critics. America's religious tradition was much weaker, and its dominant, dour puritanism was markedly uncongenial to aesthetic appropriation. As a secular republic having no traditional aristocracy and embracing many religious denominations, America could better resist what Bourdieu describes as the essential "aristocracy of culture" (*D* 11–96), and thus it could aesthetically affirm popular arts which claim neither aristocratic distinction nor quasi-religious value.[59]

(6) Finally, popular art is condemned for not achieving adequate form. As Abraham Kaplan sharply puts it: "what is unaesthetic about popular art is its formlessness. It does not invite or even permit the sustained effort necessary to the creation of an artistic form."[60] In contrast to high art's deep concern with form, popular art is generally assumed to be so totally preoccupied with content that form can play only a negligible and subservient role, and thus can never adequately express or thematize itself.

The arguments against the formal adequacy of popular art are themselves multiform. Both the unity and complexity of its formal structure have been strictly denied. For Macdonald and Adorno, popular works necessarily lack formal unity, not only because they are group productions rather than the creation of autonomous individuals, but also because they cater to a regressive audience of unintegrated non-individuals who have lost the synthesizing ability to grasp "the multilevel unity" of genuine works of art. Rather than form, they have only simplistic formulas, which merely serve as a background vehicle for superficially provocative individual effects.[61]

More often it is not unity but formal complexity that is denied to popular works and used to distinguish them from genuine art. Bourdieu, who defines the aesthetic attitude as a capacity to regard things as "form rather than function," sees this detached, life-distancing attitude as the key to high art's achievement of "formal complexity." It is only through this attitude that we can reach ("as the final stage in the conquest of artistic autonomy") "the production of an 'open work', intrinsically and deliberately polysemic" (*D* 3, 34–5). For Bourdieu, popular art's close connection with the content of life "implies the subordination of form to function" and the consequent failure to achieve formal complexity. In popular art we are more immediately engaged in the content or substance of the work; and this, Bourdieu argues, is incompatible with genuine aesthetic appreciation, "given the basic opposition between form and substance" (*D* 4, 197). Aesthetic legitimacy comes only "by displacing the interest from the 'content', characters, plot, etc., to the form, to the specifically artistic effects which are only appreciated relationally, through a comparison with other works which is incompatible with immersion in the singularity of the work immediately given" (*D* 34).

Such comparative relationality with other works and styles in the given artistic tradition is undeniably a rich source of formal complexity in high art. But this intertextuality can also be present in works of popular art, many of which self-consciously allude to and quote from each other to produce a variety of aesthetic effects, including a complex formal texture of implied art-historical relations. Nor are these allusions unappreciated by the popular-art audience, who are generally more literate in their artistic traditions than are the audiences of high art in theirs.[62]

What is more disturbing about Bourdieu's argument is the apparent assumption that form and content are somehow necessarily opposed, so that we cannot properly experience (or create) a work formally unless we distance ourselves from any investment or enthusiasm in content. Not only does this seem to beg a very contested form/content distinction, but it confuses two senses of "formal": that which displays formality and that which simply has form, structure, or shape. It is only the former which entails a posture of distance, ceremonious restraint, and denial of life's investments. Rather than something essentially opposed to life, form is an ever present part of the shape and rhythm of living; and aesthetic form (as Bourdieu well knows) has its deep but denied roots in organic bodily rhythms and the social conditions which help structure them.[63] It can be found in more immediate and enthusiastic bodily investment as well as through intellectual distance; form can be funky as well as austerely formal.

Related to the issues of formal complexity and art-historical inter-textuality are two other formalist charges against popular art. While high art is praised for its acute awareness of and thematized concern for the aesthetic medium, its artists often deriving their "chief inspiration from the medium they work in,"[64] popular art is thought to be so

dominated by content that it neglects its status as medium and representational form, thus performing (in Bourdieu's words) "a systematic
reduction of the things of art to the things of life" (*D* 5). Secondly, while
high art is distinguished by "innovation and experimentation in form"
(*PH* 76), popular art's inadequate attention to the formal medium
coupled with its desire to entertain through subject matter means that
such art lacks "the taste for formal experiment" (*D* 4). Again implying a
fundamental opposition between form and substance, Bourdieu holds
that popular art and its audience can accept "formal experiments and
specifically aesthetic effects only to the extent that they can be forgotten
and do not get in the way of the substance of the work" (*D* 33).

But many works of popular art show concern with form by explicitly
foregrounding their style and medium. Many, moreover, self-consciously
exhibit their status as representation (as in TV's *Moonlighting* and *Monty
Python's Flying Circus* or even in some of the "low" comedy films of Mel
Brooks). This is done not only through dialogue and visual narrative that
self-referentially points to the work's status as fictional text, but also, as
Fiske argues, through formal "devices such as excessive stylishness, self-
conscious camera work, unmotivated editing, and the occasional breaking
of the 180° rule."[65] As for experimentation, the popular mass-media arts
are indeed products of experiments in media and form; and though the
bulk of popular art is formalistically conservative, there are continuing
efforts of formal innovation in the creation of new genres or styles (like
the rock video and rap) and sometimes also within established ones.

Talking in such generalities and briefly mentioning examples will
hardly constitute convincing proof that popular art has those formal
qualities thought to distinguish high art as aesthetic: unity and complexity, intertextuality and open-textured polysemy, experimentation and
foregrounded attention to medium. Perhaps the only good way to prove
this and answer all the previous charges is by showing concretely that
works of popular art do in fact display the aesthetic values its critics
reserve exclusively for high art. And this can only be done by careful
study of actual works in specific genres. The next chapter takes up this
challenge with the study of rap and a close reading of one of its works.

8

The Fine Art of Rap

> ...rapt Poesy,
> And arts, though unimagined, yet to be.
>> Shelley, *Prometheus Unbound*

I

Rap is today's fastest growing genre of popular music, and the most maligned and persecuted. Its claim to artistic status is drowned under a flood of abusive critique, acts of censorship, and commercializing cooptation.[1] This should not be surprising. For rap's cultural roots and prime following belong to the black underclass of American society; and its militant black pride and thematizing of the ghetto experience represent a threatening siren to that society's complacent status quo. Given this political incentive for undermining rap, one can readily find aesthetic reasons which seem to discredit it as a legitimate art form. Rap songs are not even sung, only spoken or chanted. They typically employ neither live musicians nor original music; the soundtrack is instead composed from various cuts (or "samples") of records already made and often well-known. Finally, the lyrics seem crude and simple-minded, the diction substandard, the rhymes raucous, repetitive, and frequently raunchy. Yet, as this chapter's title suggests, these same lyrics insistently claim and extol rap's status as poetry and fine art.[2]

I wish to examine more closely the aesthetics of rap, or "hip hop" as the *cognoscenti* often call it.[3] Since I enjoy this music, I have a personal stake in defending its aesthetic legitimacy.[4] But the cultural issues and aesthetic stakes are much larger. For rap, I believe, is a postmodern popular art which challenges some of our most deeply entrenched aesthetic conventions, conventions which are common not only to modernism as an artistic style and ideology but to the philosophical doctrine of modernity and its sharp differentiation of cultural spheres. Yet, while challenging such conventions, rap still, I believe, satisfies the most crucial conventional criteria for aesthetic legitimacy, which are generally denied to popular art. It thus defies any rigid distinction between high and popular art made on purely aesthetic grounds, just as it puts into question the very notion of such pure grounds. To substantiate these claims, I shall first consider rap in terms of postmodern aesthetics. But since aesthetic legitimacy is best demonstrated by actual critical perception, I shall devote most of the chapter to a close reading of a representative rap, which shows how the genre can answer the major aesthetic indictments against popular art.

Postmodernism is a vexingly complex and contested phenomenon, whose aesthetic consequently resists clear and unchallengeable definition.[5] Nonetheless, certain themes and stylistic features are widely recognized as characteristically postmodern, which is not to say that they cannot also be found to varying degrees in some modernist art. These characteristics include recycling appropriation rather than unique originative creation, the eclectic mixing of styles, the enthusiastic embracing of the new technology and mass culture, the challenging of modernist notions of aesthetic autonomy and artistic purity, and an emphasis on the localized and temporal rather than the putatively universal and eternal. Whether or not we wish to call these features postmodern, rap not only saliently exemplifies but often consciously highlights and thematizes them. Thus, even if we reject the whole category of postmodernism, these features are essential for understanding rap.

Appropriative Sampling

Artistic appropriation is the historical source of hip-hop music and still remains the core of its technique and a central feature of its aesthetic form and message. The music is composed by selecting and combining parts of prerecorded songs to produce a "new" soundtrack. This soundtrack, produced by the DJ on a multiple turntable, constitutes the musical background for the rap lyrics. These in turn are frequently devoted both to praising the DJ's inimitable virtuosity in sampling and synthesizing the appropriated music and to boasting of the lyrical and rhyming power of the rapper (called the MC). While the rapper's vaunting self-praise often highlights his sexual desirability, commercial success, and property assets, these signs of status are all presented as secondary to and derivative from his verbal power.

Some whites may find it difficult to imagine that verbal virtuosity would be greatly appreciated in the black urban ghetto. But sociological study reveals that it is very highly valued there, and anthropological research shows that asserting superior social status through verbal prowess is a deeply entrenched black tradition which goes back to the griots in West Africa and which has long been sustained in the New World through such conventionalized verbal contests or games as "signifying" or "the dozens."[6] Failure to recognize the traditional tropes, stylistic conventions, and constraint-produced complexities of Afro-American English (such as semantic inversion and indirection, feigned simplicity, and covert parody – all originally designed to conceal the real meaning from hostile white listeners)[7] has induced the false belief that all rap lyrics are superficial and monotonous, if not altogether moronic. But informed and sympathetic close reading will reveal in many rap songs not only the witty vernacular expression of keen insights but also forms of linguistic subtlety and multiple levels of meaning whose polysemic complexity, ambiguity, and intertextuality can sometimes rival those of high art's so-called open work.

Like its stylized aggressively boasting language, rap's other most salient feature – its dominant funky beat – can be traced back to African roots, to jungle rhythms which were taken up by rock and disco and then reappropriated by rap DJs – the musical cannibals of the urban jungle. But for all its African heritage, hip hop was born in the disco era of the mid-seventies in the grim ghettos of New York: first the Bronx and then Harlem and Brooklyn. As it appropriated disco sounds and techniques, it undermined and transformed them, much as jazz (an earlier black art of appropriation) had done with the melodies of popular songs. But in contrast to jazz, hip hop did not take mere melodies or musical phrases – that is, abstract musical patterns exemplifiable in different performances and thus bearing the ontological status of "type entities." Instead, it lifted concrete sound events, prerecorded token performances of such musical patterns. Thus, unlike jazz, its borrowing and transfiguration did not require creative skill in composition or in playing musical instruments, but only in manipulating recording equipment. DJs in ordinary disco clubs had developed the technique of cutting and blending one record into the next, matching tempos to make a smooth transition without violently disrupting the flow of dancing. Dissatisfied with the tame sound of disco and commercial pop, self-styled DJs in the Bronx reapplied this technique of cutting to concentrate and augment those parts of the records which could provide for better dancing. For them the important part of the record was the break – the part of a tune in which the drums took over. It could be the explosive Tito Puente style of Latin timbales to be heard on Jimmy Castor records; the loose funk drumming of countless '60s soul records by legends like James Brown or Dyke and the Blazers; even the foursquare bass-drum-and-snare intros adored by heavy metal and hard rockers like Thin Lizzy and the Rolling Stones. That was when the dancers flew and DJs began cutting between the same few bars on the two turntables, extending the break into an instrumental.[8]

In short, hip hop began explicitly as dance music, to be appreciated through movement not mere listening. It was originally designed only for live performance (at dances held in homes, schools, community centers, and parks), where one could admire the dexterity of the DJ and the personality and improvisational skills of the rapper. It was not intended for a mass audience, and for several years remained confined to the New York City area and outside the mass-media network. Though rap was often taped informally on cassette and then reproduced and circulated by its growing body of fans and bootleggers, it was only in 1979 that rap had its first radio broadcast and released its first records. These two singles, "Rapper's Delight" and "King Tim III (Personality Jock)," which were made by groups outside the core rap community but who had connections with the recording industry, provoked competitive resentment in the rap world and the incentive and example to get out of the underground and on to disc and radio. However, even when the groups moved from the street to the studio, where they could use live music, the DJ's role of appropriation was not abandoned and continued to be thematized in rap lyrics as central to the art.[9]

From the basic technique of cutting between sampled records, hip hop developed three other formal devices which contribute significantly to its sound and aesthetic: "scratch mixing," "punch phrasing," and simple scratching. The first is simply overlaying or mixing certain sounds from one record to those of another already playing.[10] Punch phrasing is a refinement of such mixing, where the DJ moves the needle back and forth over a specific phrase of chords or drum slaps of a record so as to add a powerful percussive effect to the sound of the other record which is all the while playing on the other turntable. The third device is a more wild, rapid, back and forth scratching of the record, too fast for the recorded music to be recognized but productive of a dramatic scratching sound which has its own intense musical quality and crazed beat.

These devices of cutting, mixing, and scratching give rap a variety of forms of appropriation, which seem as versatile and imaginative as those of high art – as those, say, exemplified by Duchamp's mustache on the *Mona Lisa*, Rauschenberg's erasure of a De Kooning canvas, and Andy Warhol's multiple re-representations of prepackaged commercial images. Rap also displays a variety of appropriated content. Not only does it sample from a wide range of popular songs, it feeds eclectically on classical music, TV theme songs, advertising jingles, and the electronic music of arcade games. It even appropriates non-musical content, such as media news reports and fragments of speeches by Malcolm X and Martin Luther King.[11]

Though some DJs took pride in appropriating from very unlikely and arcane sources and sometimes tried to conceal (for fear of competition) the exact records they were sampling, there was never any attempt to conceal the fact that they were working from prerecorded sounds rather than composing their own original music. On the contrary, they openly celebrated their method of sampling. What is the aesthetic significance of this proud art of appropriation?

First, it challenges the traditional ideal of originality and uniqueness that has long enslaved our conception of art. Romanticism and its cult of genius likened the artist to a divine creator and advocated that his works be altogether new and express his singular personality. Modernism, with its commitment to artistic progress and the avant-garde, reinforced the dogma that radical novelty was the essence of art. Though artists have always borrowed from each other's works, the fact was generally ignored or implicitly denied through the ideology of originality, which posed a sharp distinction between original creation and derivative borrowing. Postmodern art like rap undermines this dichotomy by creatively deploying and thematizing its appropriation to show that borrowing and creation are not at all incompatible. It further suggests that the apparently original work of art is itself always a product of unacknowledged borrowings, the unique and novel text always a tissue of echoes and fragments of earlier texts.

Originality thus loses its absolute originary status and is reconceived to include the transfiguring reappropriation and recycling of the old. In this postmodern picture there are no ultimate, untouchable originals, only appropriations of appropriations and simulacra of simulacra; so creative energy can be liberated to play with familiar creations without fear that it thereby denies itself the opportunity to be truly creative by not producing a totally original work. Rap songs simultaneously celebrate their originality and their borrowing.[12] And, as the dichotomy of creation/

appropriation is challenged, so is the deep division between creative artist and appropriative audience. Transfigurative appreciation can take the form of art.

Cutting and Temporality

Rap's sampling style also challenges art's traditional ideal of unity and integrity. Since Aristotle, aestheticians have often viewed the artwork as an organic whole so perfectly unified that any tampering with its parts would destroy the whole. Moreover, the ideologies of romanticism and "art for art's sake" have reinforced our habit of treating artworks as transcendent and virtually sacred ends in themselves, whose integrity we should respect and never violate. In contrast to this aesthetic of austere organic unity, rap's cutting and sampling reflect the "schizophrenic fragmentation" and "collage effect" characteristic of the postmodern aesthetic.[13] In contrast to an aesthetic of devotional worship to a fixed, untouchable work, hip hop offers the pleasures of deconstructive art – the thrilling beauty of dismembering (and rapping over) old works to create new ones, dismantling the prepackaged and wearily familiar into something stimulatingly different.

The DJ's sampling and the MC's rap also highlight the fact that the apparent unity of the original artwork is often an artificially constructed one, at least in contemporary popular music where the production process is frequently quite fragmented: an instrumental track recorded in Memphis, combined with a back-up vocal from New York, and a lead voice from L.A. Rap simply continues this process of layered artistic composition by deconstructing and differently reassembling prepackaged musical products and then superimposing the MC's added layer of lyrics so as to produce a new work. But rap does this without the pretense that its own work is inviolable, that the artistic process is ever final, that there is ever a product which should be so fetishized that it could never be submitted to appropriative transfiguration. Instead, rap's sampling implies that an artwork's integrity as object should never outweigh the possibilities for continuing creation through use of that object. Its aesthetic thus suggests the Deweyan message that art is more essentially process than finished product, a welcome message in our culture, whose tendency to reify and commodify all artistic expression is so strong that rap itself is victimized by this tendency while defiantly protesting it.

In defying the fetishized integrity of artworks, rap also challenges traditional notions of their monumentality, universality, and permanence. No longer are admired works conceived in Eliotic fashion as "an ideal order" of "monuments" timelessly existing and yet preserved through time by tradition.[14] In contrast to the standard view that "a poem is forever," rap highlights the artwork's temporality and likely impermanence: not only by appropriative deconstructions but by explicitly thematizing its own temporality in its lyrics. For example, several songs by BDP include lines like "Fresh for '88, you suckers" or "Fresh for '89, you suckers."[15] Such declarations of date imply a consequent admission of datedness; what is fresh for '88 is apparently stale by '89, and so superseded by a new freshness of '89 vintage. But, by rap's postmodern aesthetic, the ephemeral freshness of artistic creations does not render them aesthetically unworthy; no more than the ephemeral freshness of cream renders its sweet taste unreal.[16] For the view that aesthetic value can only be real if it passes the test of time is simply an entrenched but unjustified presumption, ultimately deriving from the pervasive philosophical bias to equate reality with the permanent and unchanging.

By refusing to treat artworks as eternal monuments for permanent, hands-off devotion, by reworking works to make them work better, rap also questions their assumed universality – the dogma that good art must be able to please all people and all ages by dealing with universal human themes. Hip hop does treat universal themes like injustice and oppression, but it is proudly localized as "ghetto music," thematizing its roots and commitment to the black urban ghetto and its culture. While it typically avoids excluding white society – and there are white rappers and audiences[17] – rap focuses on features of ghetto life that whites and middle-class blacks would rather ignore: pimping, prostitution, and drug addiction, as well as rampant venereal disease, street killings, and oppressive harassment by white policemen. Most rappers define their local allegiances in quite specific terms, often not simply by city but by neighborhood, like Compton, Harlem, Brooklyn, or the Bronx. Even when rap goes international, it remains proudly local; we find in French rap, for example, the same targeting of specific neighborhoods and concentration on local problems.[18]

Though localization may be a salient aspect of the postmodern breakdown of modernism's international style, rap's strong local sense is probably more the product of its origins in neighborhood conflict and competition. As Toop notes, hip hop helped transform violent rivalries between local gangs into musical-verbal contests between rapping crews.[19] By now it is difficult to point to sharp stylistic differences between the music of the various locales, for local distinctiveness is hard to maintain once the music begins circulating through the mass-media system and is subjected to its commercializing pressures. For such reasons, rap lyrics often complain about its commercial expansion just as they celebrate it.

Technology and Mass-Media Culture

Rap's complex attitude toward mass circulation and commercialization reflects another central feature of postmodernism: its fascinated and over-whelming absorption of contemporary technology, particularly that of the mass media. While the commercial products of this technology seem so simple and fruitful to use, both the actual complexities of technological production and its intricate relations to the sustaining socio-economic system are, for the consumer public, frighteningly unfathomable and unmanageable. Mesmerized by the powers technology provides us, we postmoderns are also vaguely disturbed by the great power it has over us, as the all-pervasive but increasingly incomprehensible medium of our lives. But fascination with its awesome power can afford us the further (perhaps illusory) thrill that in effectively employing technology, we prove ourselves its master. Such thrills are characteristic of what Jameson calls the "hallucinatory exhilaration" of the "postmodern or technological sublime."[20]

Hip hop powerfully displays this syndrome, enthusiastically embracing and masterfully appropriating mass-media technology, but still remaining unhappily oppressed and appropriated by that same technological system and its sustaining society. Rap was born of commercial mass-media tech-nology: records and turntables, amplifiers and mixers. Its technological character allowed its artists to create music they could not otherwise have made, either because they could not afford the musical instruments required or because they lacked the musical training to play them.[21] Technology constituted its DJs as artists rather than consumers or mere executant technicians. "Run-DMC first said a deejay could be a band / Stand on its own feet, get you out your seat," exclaims a rap by Public Enemy.[22] But without commercial mass-media technology, the DJ band would have had nothing to stand on.

The creative virtuosity with which rap artists have appropriated new technology is indeed exhilarating, and it is often acclaimed in rap lyrics. By acrobatically juggling the cutting and changing of many records on multiple turntables, skillful DJs showed their physical as well as artistic mastery of commercial music and its technology. From the initial disco equipment, rap artists have gone on to adopt more (and more advanced) technologies: electronic drums, synthesizers, sounds from calculators and touch-tone phones, and computers which scan entire ranges of possible sounds and then replicate and synthesize the desired ones.

Mass-media technology has also been crucial to rap's impressively growing popularity. As a product of black culture, an essentially oral rather than written culture, rap needs to be heard and felt immediately, through its energetically moving sound, in order to be properly appreciated. No notational score could transmit its crazy collage of music, and even the lyrics cannot be adequately conveyed in mere written form, divorced from their expressive rhythm, intonation, and surging stress and flow. Only mass-media technology allows for the wide dissemination and preservation of such oral performance events. Both through radio and TV broadcasting and through the recording media of records, tapes, and CDs, rap has been able to reach out beyond its original ghetto audience and thus allow its music and message a real hearing, even in white America and Europe. Only through the mass media could hip hop become a very audible voice in our popular culture, one which middle America would like to suppress since it often stridently expresses the frustrating oppression of ghetto life and the proud and pressing desire for social resistance and change. Without such systems, rap could not have achieved its "penetration to the core of the nation" (Ice-T) or its opportunity to "teach the bourgeois" (Public Enemy).[23] Similarly, only through the mass media could hip hop have achieved artistic fame and fortune, its commercial success enabling renewed artistic investment and serving as an undeniable source of black cultural pride.

Rap not only relies on mass-media techniques and technologies, it derives much of its content and imagery from mass culture. TV shows, sports personalities, arcade games, and familiar name-brand commercial products (e.g. Adidas sneakers) are frequently referred to in the lyrics, and their musical themes or jingles are sometimes sampled. Such items of mass-media culture help provide the common cultural background necessary for artistic creation and communication in a society where the tradition of high culture is largely unknown or unappealing, if not also oppressively alien and exclusionary.

But for all its acknowledged gifts, the mass media are not a trusted and unambiguous ally. They are simultaneously the focus of deep suspicion and angry critique. Rappers inveigh against the media's false and superficial fare, its commercially standardized and sanitized but unreal and mindless content. "False media, we don't need it, do we? It's fake," urge Public Enemy,[24] who also lament (in "She Watch Channel Zero") how standard TV shows undermine the intelligence, responsibilities, and cultural roots of black women. Rappers are constantly attacking the radio for refusing to broadcast their more politically potent or sexually explicit raps and instead filling the air with tame "commercial pap" (BDP). "Radio suckers never play me," complain Public Enemy, a line which gets sampled and punch-phrased by Ice-T in an eponymous rap condemning the radio and the FCC for a censorship which denies both freedom of expression and the hard realities of life so as to insure the continuous media fare of "nothin' but commercial junk."[25] Scorning the option of a "sell-out," Ice-T raises (and answers) the crucial "media question" troubling all progressive rap: "Can the radio handle the truth? Nope." But he also asserts his assurance that even with a radio ban he can reach and make millions through the medium of tapes, suggesting that the media provide their own ways of subverting attempts at regulatory control ("They're makin' radio wack, people have to escape / But even if I'm banned, I'll sell a million tapes").[26]

Finally, apart from their false, superficial content and repressive censorship, the media are linked to a global commercial system and society which callously exploit and oppress hip hop's primary audience. Recognizing that those who govern and speak for the dominating technological-commercial complex are indifferent to the enduring woes of the black underclass ("Here is a land that never gave a damn about a brother like me...but the suckers had authority"), rappers protest how our capitalist society exploits the disenfranchized blacks both to preserve its socio-political stability (through their service in the military and police) and to increase its profits by increasing their demand for unnecessary consumer goods.[27] One very prominent theme of hip hop is how the advertised ideal of conspicuous consumption – luxury cars, clothes, and high-tech appliances – lures many ghetto youths to a life of crime, a life which promises the quick attainment of such commodities but typically ends in death, jail, or destitution, thus reinforcing the ghetto cycle of poverty and despair.

It is one of the postmodern paradoxes of hip hop that rappers extol their own achievement of consumerist luxury while simultaneously condemning its uncritical idealization and quest as misguided and dangerous for their audience in the ghetto community to which they ardently avow their solidarity and allegiance. In the same way, self-declared "underground" rappers at once denigrate commercialism as an artistic and political sell-out, but nonetheless glorify their own commercial success, often regarding it as indicative of their artistic power.[28] Such paradoxes reflect more fundamental contradictions in the socio-cultural fields of ghetto life and so-called non-commercial art.[29]

Certainly there is a very deep connection in Afro-American culture between independent expression and economic achievement, which would impel even non-commercial rappers to tout their commercial success and property. For, as Houston Baker so well demonstrates, Afro-American artists must always, consciously or unconsciously, come to terms with the history of slavery and commercial exploitation that forms the ground of black experience and expression.[30] Just as slaves were converted from independent humans into property, so their way to regain independence was to achieve sufficient property of their own to buy their manumission (as in the traditional liberation narrative of Frederick Douglass). Having long been denied a voice because they were property, Afro-Americans could reasonably conclude "that *only* property enables expression."[31] For underground rappers, then, commercial success and its luxury trappings may function essentially as signs of an economic independence which enables free artistic and political expression and which itself is conversely further enabled by such expression. A major dimension of this celebrated economic independence is its independence from crime.[32]

Autonomy and Distance

If rap's free-wheeling eclectic cannibalism violates high-modernist conventions of aesthetic purity and integrity, its belligerent insistence on the deeply political dimension of culture challenges one of the most fundamental artistic conventions of modernity: aesthetic autonomy. Modernity, according to Weber and others, was bound up with the project of occidental rationalization, secularization, and differentiation, which disenchanted the traditional religious world-view and carved up its organic domain into three separate and autonomous spheres of secular culture: science, art, and morality, each governed by its own inner logic of theoretical, aesthetic, or moral-practical judgement.[33] This tripartite division was of course powerfully reflected and reinforced by Kant's critical analysis of human thinking in terms of pure reason, practical reason, and aesthetic judgement.

In this division of cultural spheres, art was distinguished from science as being not concerned with the formulation or dissemination of knowledge, since its aesthetic judgement was essentially non-conceptual and sub-jective. It was also sharply differentiated from the practical activity of ethics and politics, which involved real interests and appetitive will (as well as conceptual thinking). Instead, art was consigned to a dis-interested, imaginative realm which Schiller later described as the realm of play and semblance.[34] As the aesthetic was distinguished from the more rational realms of knowledge and action, so it was also firmly differentiated from the more sensate and appetitive gratifications of embodied human nature, aesthetic pleasure rather residing in distanced, disinterested contemplation of formal properties.

Hip hop's genre of "knowledge rap" (or "message rap") is dedicated to the defiant violation of this compartmentalized, trivializing, and evis-cerating view of art and the aesthetic. Such rappers repeatedly insist that their role as artists and poets is inseparable from their role as insight-ful inquirers of reality and teachers of truth, particularly those aspects of reality and truth that get neglected or distorted by establishment history books and contemporary media coverage. KRS-One of BDP claims to be not only "a teacher and artist, startin' new concepts at their hardest," but a philosopher (indeed, according to the jacket notes on the *Ghetto Music* album, a "metaphysician") and also a scientist ("I don't drop science, I teach it. Correct!").[35] In contrast to the media's political whitewash, stereotypes, and empty escapist entertainment, he proudly claims: "I'm tryin' not to escape, but hit the problem head on / By bring-ing out the truth in a song.... / It's simple; BDP will teach reality. / No beatin' around the bush, straight up; just like the beat is free. / So now you know a poet's job is never done. / But I'm never overworked, 'cause I'm still number one."[36]

Of course, the realities and truths which hip hop reveals are not the transcendental eternal verities of traditional philosophy, but rather the mutable facts and patterns of the material, socio-historical world. Yet this emphasis on the temporally changing and malleable nature of the real (reflected in rap's frequent time tags and its popular idiom of "knowing what time it is"[37]) constitutes a respectably tenable metaphysical position associated with American pragmatism. Though few may know it, rap philosophers are really "down with" Dewey, not merely in metaphysics but in a non-compartmentalized aesthetics which highlights social func-tion, process, and embodied experience.

For knowledge rap not only insists on uniting the aesthetic and the cognitive; it equally stresses that practical functionality can form part of artistic meaning and value. Many rap songs are explicitly devoted to raising black political consciousness, pride, and revolutionary impulses; some make the powerful point that aesthetic judgements (and particularly the issue of what counts as art) involve political issues of legitimation and social struggle in which rap is engaged as progressive praxis and which it advances by its very self-assertion as art. Other raps function as street-smart moral fables, offering cautionary narratives and practical advice on problems of crime, drugs, and sexual hygiene (e.g. Ice-T's "Drama" and "High Rollers," Kool Moe Dee's "Monster Crack" and "Go See the Doctor," BDP's "Stop the Violence" and "Jimmy"). There are raps which challenge the univocal claims of white history and education and suggest alternative black historical narratives – from biblical history to the history of hip hop itself (e.g. BDP's "Why is That?," "You Must Learn," and "Hip Hop Rules"). Finally, we should note that rap has been used effectively to teach writing and reading skills and black history in the ghetto classroom.[38]

Jameson suggests that the disintegration of traditional modernist boundaries could provide the redemptive option of "a new radical cultural politics," a postmodern aesthetic which "foregrounds the cognitive and pedagogical dimensions of political art and culture."[39] He regards this new cultural form as still "hypothetical"; but perhaps it is evolving in rap, whose artists explicitly aim at teaching and political activism, just as they seek to undermine the socially oppressive dichotomy between legitimate (i.e. high) art and popular entertainment by simultaneously asserting the popular and artistic status of hip hop.

However, like most culture critics, Jameson worries whether postmodern art can provide effective social criticism and political protest, because of its "abolition of critical distance." Having undermined the fortress of artistic autonomy and enthusiastically appropriated the content of workaday and commercial living, postmodern art seems to lack the "minimal aesthetic distance" necessary for art to stand "outside the massive Being of capital" and thus represent an alternative to (and hence critique of) what Adorno called "the ungodly reality." Though those tuned in to Public Enemy, BDP, or Ice-T can hardly doubt the authenticity and power of their oppositional energy, the charge that all contemporary "forms of cultural resistance are secretly disarmed and reabsorbed by a system of which they themselves might be considered a part" might well be directed at rap. For while it condemns media stereotypes, violence, and the quest for luxurious living, rap just as often exploits or glorifies them to make its points. While denouncing commercialism and the capitalist system, even rap's "underground" lyrics simultaneously celebrate its own commercial success and business histories, some songs, for example, describing and justifying the rapper's change of record company for commercial reasons.[40]

Hip hop surely does not lie wholly outside what Jameson (in a questionable organicistic presumption) regards as the "global and totalizing space of the new world system" of multinational capitalism – as if the congeries of contingent events and chaotic processes of our world could ever be fully totalized in one space or system! But granting for the moment that there is this all-embracing system, why should rap's profitable connection with some of its features void the power of its social critique? Do we need to be fully outside something in order to criticize it effectively? Does not the postmodern and poststructuralist decentering critique of definitive, ontologically grounded boundaries put the whole notion of being "fully outside" seriously into question?

With this challenging of a clear inside/outside dichotomy, we should likewise ask why proper aesthetic response traditionally requires distanced contemplation by a soberly disinterested subject. This presumed necessity of distance is yet another manifestation of the modernist ideology of artistic purity and autonomy which hip hop repudiates. Indeed, rather than an aesthetic of distanced, disengaged, formalist judgement, rappers urge an aesthetic of deeply embodied participatory involvement, with content as well as form. They want to be appreciated primarily through energetic and impassioned dance, not through immobile contemplation and dispassionate study.[41] Queen Latifah, for example, insistently commands her listeners, "I order you to dance for me." For, as Ice-T explains, the rapper "won't be happy till the dancers are wet" with sweat, "out of control" and wildly "possessed" by the beat, as indeed the captivating rapper should himself be possessed so as to rock his audience with his God-given gift of rhyme.[42] This aesthetic of divine yet bodily possession recalls Plato's account of poetry and its appreciation as a chain of divine madness extending down from the divine Muse through the artists and performers to the audience, a seizure which, for all its divinity was criticized as regrettably irrational and inferior to true knowledge.[43] More important, the spiritual ecstasy of divine bodily possession should remind us of Vodun and the metaphysics of African religion, to which the aesthetics of Afro-American music has indeed been traced.[44]

What could be further from modernity's project of rationalization and secularization, what more inimical to modernism's rationalized, disembodied, and formalized aesthetic? No wonder the established modernist aesthetic is so hostile to rap and to rock music in general. If there is a viable space between the modernist rationalized aesthetic and an altogether irrational one whose rabid Dionysian excess must vitiate its cognitive, didactic, and political claims, this is the space for a postmodern aesthetic. I think the fine art of rap inhabits that space, and I hope it will continue to thrive there.

II

Thus far I have presented rap as a challenging violator of traditional artistic conventions. Why, then, still call it art? Rap's lyrics proudly claim it is art, performative self-assertion being a crucial means to achieve such status. But mere self-assertion is not enough to establish the arthood or aesthetic character of an expressive form; the claim must be convincing. Primarily, of course, conviction must come from experience; we must feel a work's artistry and aesthetic power impress itself on our senses and intelligence. Socio-cultural acceptance of some sort is also necessary. There must be a possible space for the work or genre in the socio-cultural field of art. But theoretical justification can help create that space and extend art's limits by assimilating previously unaccepted forms into art's honorific category. One proven strategy for such assimilation is showing that, despite obvious deviance from established conventions, an expressive form still meets enough of the more crucial criteria to warrant recognition of its artistic or aesthetic legitimacy. Popular art is often refused such legitimacy because of alleged failure to meet such criteria, particularly those of complexity and depth, creativity and form, artistic self-respect and self-consciousness.

While rap may be the most denigrated of popular arts, its better works can, I think, satisfy these central artistic criteria. The best way to demonstrate this is not by general polemics and pleading but by looking closely at a concrete specimen of the genre. I therefore turn to a close reading of "Talkin' All That Jazz," recorded in 1988 by the Brooklyn crew "Stetsasonic." It is neither my favorite rap nor the one I think most artistically sophisticated. I choose it for its popularity and representative character (proved by its selection in a number of rap anthologies[45]) and because it highlights some of the central aesthetic issues that rap raises.

Though the aim of my reading is to show this rap's aesthetic richness, the very method of reading – that is, presenting and analyzing this rap as inscribed text – must involve ignoring some of its most important aesthetic dimensions and its intended mode of aesthetic appreciation. For I shall be abstracting from its crucial dimensions of sound, since the printed page captures neither the music nor the oral phrasing and intonation of the lyrics (a point of pride and style among rappers). Nor can it convey the complex aesthetic effects of the multiple rhythms and tensions between the driving musical beat and the word stress of the rap delivery, which in contrast to popular songs maintains its own speech rhythms.[46] A full appreciation of a rap's aesthetic dimensions would require not merely hearing it but dancing to it, feeling its rhythms in movement, as the genre emphatically means us to. The printed medium of our written culture precludes this, thereby suggesting more generally the inherent difficulties in appreciating and legitimating oral culture by academic means so deeply entrenched and locked in the written.

Nonetheless, if rap can satisfy aesthetic standards in its impoverished form as written poetry, *a fortiori* it can meet them in its rich and robust actuality as music and rhythmic speech. Recognizing, then, that a rap is aesthetically much more than its text, let us see how the text itself can sustain a claim to aesthetic status in terms of the central criteria we have mentioned.

TALKIN' ALL THAT JAZZ

Well, here's how it started.
Heard you on the radio
Talk about rap,
Sayin' all that crap
About how we sample.
Give an example.
Think we'll let you get away with that.
You criticize our method
Of how we make records.
You said it wasn't art,
So now we're gonna rip you apart.
Stop, check it out my man.
This is the music of a hip-hop band.
Jazz, well you can call it that,
But this jazz retains a new format.
Point, when you misjudged us,
Speculated, created a fuss,

You've made the same mistake politicians have,
Talkin' all that jazz.

[musical break]

Talk, well I heard talk is cheap.
Well, like beauty, talk is just skin deep.
And when you lie and you talk a lot,
People tell you to step off a lot.
You see you misunderstood,
A sample's just a fact,
Like a portion of my method,
A tool. In fact,
It's only of importance when I make it a priority,
And what we sample of is a majority.
But you are a minority, in terms of thought,
Narrow-minded and poorly taught
About hip hop's aims and the silly games
To embrace my music so no one use it.
You step on us and we'll step on you.
You can't have your cake and eat it too.
Talkin' all that jazz.

[musical break]

Lies, that's when you hide the truth.
It's when you talk more jazz than proof.
And when you lie and address something you don't know,
It's so whacked that it's bound to show.
When you lie about me and the band, we get angry.
We'll bite our pens and start writin' again.
And the things we write are always true,
Sucker, so get a grip now we're talkin' about you.
Seems to me that you have a problem,
So we can see what we can do to solve them.
Think rap is a fad; you must be mad,
'Cause we're so bad, we get respect you never had.
Tell the truth, James Brown was old,
Till Eric and Rak came out with "I got soul."
Rap brings back old R & B,
And if we would not,
People could have forgot.
We want to make this perfectly clear:

We're talented and strong and have no fear
Of those who choose to judge but lack pizazz,
Talkin' all that jazz.

[musical break]

Now we're not tryin' to be a boss to you.
We just wanna get across to you
That if you're talkin' jazz
The situation is a no win.
You might even get hurt, my friend.
Stetsasonic, the hip-hop band,
And like Sly and the Family Stone
We will stand
Up for the music we live and play
And for the song we sing today.
For now, let us set the record straight,
And later on we'll have a forum and
A formal debate.
But it's important you remember though,
What you reap is what you sow.
Talkin' all that jazz.
Talkin' all that jazz.
Talkin' all that jazz.

Complexity

At first glance this song seems simple enough, perhaps too simple to
warrant aesthetic consideration. It lacks the trappings of erudite allusion,
opaque elision, and syntactico-semantic obscurity which constitute the
characteristic complexity of modernist poetry. Its straightforward statement, paucity of metaphor, and repeated clichés suggest that it is devoid
of any complexity or depth of meaning. But rich semantic complexity and
polysemy are deeply enfolded into its seemingly artless, simple language.
The song's multiple levels of meaning are detectable from the very title
and indeed encapsulated in its key word "jazz." Jazz has, of course, at
least two relevant but radically different and differently valorized meanings in the poem's context. The first concerns jazz as a musical art
form originating in Afro-American culture and long opposed and discredited by the cultural establishment, but by now culturally legitimated throughout the world. The second sense concerns the most

common slang use of jazz as "lying and exaggerated talk; also idle and foolish talk."[47]

This ambiguity and privileging opposition within the very meaning of jazz – its positively valorized standard usage as a musical art over its slang (hence less "legitimate") usage as lies and pretentious talk – is developed into a central theme of this rap and seems central to rap in general. "Talkin' All That Jazz" simultaneously exploits and questions this privileging opposition, presenting rap as a force involved with legitimating the illegitimate, exposing the socio-political factors involved in such legitimation, and challenging the legitimacy of the powers denying legitimacy to rap. In confronting these issues, the song in turn raises deeply philosophical questions about the nature of truth and art and their sources of authority. For art, we should remember, though now culturally sacralized, was itself sometimes delegitimated as pretentious lies and idle foolishness.

To dismiss this kind of reading from the outset, one might be tempted to argue that the term "jazz" is adequately disambiguated by the context of the title and certainly by the complete song. For the phrase "talkin' all that jazz" seems to suggest that we are concerned not at all with jazz as positive music but only with negative *talk* and lies, specifically the pretentious, foolish lies which constitute the uninformed criticism of hip hop and whose personified source is the confrontational target, or "you," of the poem. "Heard you on the radio / Talk about rap, / Sayin' all that crap." The identification of "talkin' jazz" with lies and foolish talk is confirmed by linking it with the discourse of politicians ("You've made the same mistake politicians have, / Talkin' all that Jazz"); and it certainly seems clinched by the lines "Lies, that's when you hide the truth, / It's when you talk more jazz than proof. / And when you lie and address something you don't know, / It's so whacked that it's bound to show."

But just as it is identified with negative lies, so "talkin' jazz" is also positively identified as musical art by the very topic of the song – rap as an art. For, we must ask, what is rap but talking jazz? It is not mere jazz-related instrumental music, nor even lyrics sung to jazz rhythms or tunes. The most obvious feature of rap music is that it is defiantly talk rather than song, the word "rap" being a slang synonym for talk. And the linking of rap music with jazz is confirmed in the first stanza: "This is the music of a hip-hop band. / Jazz, well you can call it that. / But this jazz retains a new format."

These lines embody even more semantic complexities of valorization.

The band accepts its identification with jazz, as the most respected black cultural form and tradition to which hip hop is genealogically attached. But the acceptance is somewhat hesitant. For rap does not want to be seen as a mere variety of established jazz, not even of progressive jazz; it rather insists on its originality. Rap's jazz, unlike standard jazz already appropriated by the establishment, "retains a new format," sustains novelty and freshness by maintaining a closer link to changing popular experience and vernacular expression (to the "majority" of the street). There is the hint that hip hop is thus truer to the original spirit of jazz; and there is also the hint that jazz has somehow been tainted through its past treatment by the cultural establishment and through its accommodating compliance with that treatment.[48] For surely the establishment's initial rejection of jazz as wildly exaggerated and foolish music helped give the term its negative slang meaning of foolish pretension and untruth. And this abiding negative meaning maintains a sense of the original rejection, which seems to introduce a troublingly negative trace in even its standard meaning as music, thus raising the lingering question of whether this music is truly art in the standard sacralized sense in which classical music obviously is.

These deep ambiguities of jazz are most cleverly manipulated by Stetsasonic to make the case for rap as an art. The meaning of jazz as pretentious lies, based both on its identification with art rather than truth and on its further rejection as serious art, is in turn used to dismiss as pretentious lying the renewed rejection of new jazz in the form of rap. The rappers reject as "talkin' jazz" the allegedly legitimate discourse of those who ignorantly reject rap as degenerate, appropriative "talkin' jazz." The band at once employs and reverses the jazz/serious truth distinction by asserting that their talking jazz is true (and true art), while the supposedly serious discourse of the anti-rap, anti-jazz critics is really "talkin' jazz" in the negative sense; for the latter are altogether misinformed, "narrow-minded and poorly taught." Their allegedly true talk about true art is neither truth nor art but ignorant palaver devoid of critical understanding or creative pizazz. In contrast to the weak, "whacked" lies of its bigoted critics, rap's lines "are always true." Moreover, they are not mindlessly and carelessly uttered like the "cheap" condemnatory "crap" of radio talk, but instead thoughtfully composed in writing[49] and then performed by artists who are "talented and strong" and committed to original expression in this "new format." Thus, in contrast to its denunciatory criticism, rap is claimed to display both truth and artistry – a claim which this rap artfully demonstrates by its ingeniously double-edged and inversive method of asserting it.[50]

Though complexity of meaning and witty twists of argument are undeniably found here, it may be denied that they are actually intended or exist for the real rap audience. Perhaps they are merely the product of our academic habit of reading – indeed, even torturing – texts to find ambiguities. Reading rap in this complex way, one might argue, is unfaithful to the spontaneity and simplicity of the genre and its audience. Moreover, by suggesting that simpler responses are inferior understandings, it serves to expropriate the art from its popular use and from the people who use it. Such a process, where intellectualized modes of appropriation are used to transform popular into elite art, is quite common in cultural history.[51]

This line of objection to my reading is strong enough to demand an immediate response. First, there is no compelling reason to limit the rap's meaning to explicit authorial intentions; for its meaning is also a function of its language and readers, a social product beyond the determining control of the individual author. The ambiguities of "jazz" and the cultural conflicts and history they embody are already there in the language through which the author must speak, whether he intends them or not. Secondly, since art can be appreciated in many ways and on many levels, new modes of appreciation by new audiences cannot be outlawed as *necessarily* disenfranchizing those of the original audience. This happens only when the new intellectualized forms insist on imposing their privileged or exclusionary status as legitimate. Rap can be validly appreciated simply through dance, which is not to say that its typical audience typically appreciates it only in such a narrow and non-intellectual fashion. Indeed, whatever our view on the intentional fallacy and the primacy of intended audience, I think the ambiguities and inversions are too prominent and pointed here to be unintended; and the prime rap audience is very well equipped to understand them. For precisely this sort of ambiguity and inversion is basic to the black linguistic community.

Afro-American English is saliently ambiguous. For example, while "nigger" in white English is univocally a term of abuse, in black speech it is just as "often a term of affection, admiration, approval."[52] The reasons for this greater ambiguity should be obvious. "Negro slaves were compelled to create a semi-clandestine vernacular" to express their desires while disguising them from the hostile scrutiny of their overseers, and they did so by giving ordinary English words specific black meanings along with their standard ones.[53] One crucial method of multiplying meanings was by inverting them. Since language both embodies and sustains societal power relations, this method of inversion is particularly significant, both as a source of protest and as a source of extremely subtle linguistic skill. As G. S. Holt explains:

> Blacks clearly recognized that to master the language of whites was in effect to consent to be mastered by it through the white definitions of caste built into the semantic/social system. Inversion therefore becomes the defensive mechanism which enables blacks to fight linguistic, and thereby psychological, entrapment....Words and phrases were given reverse meanings and functions changed. Whites, denied access to the semantic extensions of duality, connotations, and denotations that developed within black usage, could only interpret the same material according to its original singular meaning..., enabling blacks to deceive and manipulate whites without penalty. This protective process, understood and shared by blacks, became a contest of matching wits...[and a] form of linguistic guerilla warfare [which] protected the subordinated, permitted the masking and disguising of true feelings, allowed the subtle assertion of self, and promoted group solidarity.[54]

It also, of course, helped make the black community especially adept and familiar with the encoding and decoding of ambiguous and inverted messages. Rap fans, then, through their ordinary linguistic training, have typically mastered a wittily indirect communicative skill which one researcher regards as "a form of verbal art,"[55] and which enables them to readily process texts of great semantic complexity if the content is relevant to their experience. Thus, Stetsasonic's ambiguous, inversive play on the notion of "talkin' jazz" is hardly beyond the reach of the rap audience, even if it is far less obvious than the text's most transparent and by now commonplace inversion of "bad" to mean good ("Think rap is a fad; you must be mad, / 'Cause we're so bad we get respect you never had").

The phrase "To embrace my music so no one use it" is a much more difficult ambiguity. While the term "embrace" typically carries the favorable sense of to accept or adopt, here we seem to have the privileging of its secondary meaning of "to encircle, surround, or enclose," thus in a sense to quarantine and deny the music's use. Yet we can still make good sense of the phrase with the former meaning, by reading it as a protest against the silly game of accepting the music as mere faddish entertainment devoid of any real artistic or political use. Finally, there is the narrowly legal sense of "embrace": "to attempt to influence (a judge or jury) through corrupt means."[56] Whether or not this rather unfamiliar meaning was explicitly intended (or is generally understood by the rap audience, which I doubt), it fits the line perfectly, expressing the rappers' protest at the corrupt falsehoods through which their radio critics seek to influence the judging public. The legal sense and context are particularly appropriate, since the rap is largely about "sampling," the appropriative method which has embroiled rap groups in endless legal wrangles about copyright.

The most famous and relentless prosecutor of the rappers is James Brown, who is represented here somewhat critically: "Tell the truth, James Brown was old, / Till Eric and Rak came out with "I got soul." / Rap brings back old R & B, / And if we would not, / People could have forgot." This provides yet another ambiguous inversion. For while James Brown is typically praised as the source of rap's best beats and its aesthetic of funk and black pride (a historical role which this rap affirms), he is here simultaneously criticized for being old and not sufficiently progressive. His inspiring delivery of "I got soul," it is thus suggested, not only *was* sampled by Eric and Rak (the rap duo Eric B. and Rakim), but it had to be in order to make it fresh and not forgotten. The old must be respected, but not at the expense of obstructing the new, for such obstruction of the living tradition will only end in the loss of its past. We have here the complex message of T. S. Eliot's "Tradition and the Individual Talent," updated and adapted for the black musical tradition and formulated with subtle and self-conscious intertextuality.

Philosophical Content

I want now to maintain that rap can be intellectually rewarding not merely because of the stimulation of its polysemic complexity, but also because of its philosophical insights. For just as popular art has been condemned as inevitably superficial because of its simplistic semantic structures, it is similarly denounced for being devoid of any deep content.

Since popular art's use of clichés is often held to be a prime cause of its bland shallowness, something should be said to vindicate the obvious clichés in "Talkin' All That Jazz." For the song is studded with some of the tritest, most commonplace proverbs: "talk is cheap"; "beauty…is just skin deep"; "You can't have your cake and eat it too"; "What you reap is what you sow." However, within the particular context of this rap, these proverbs acquire new meanings which not only depart from but challenge the clichés of cultural thought that they standardly embody. Indeed, by their very use in arguments against the cultural cliché that rap is not art, these proverbs lose some of their bland commonplace character. Moreover, their use is aesthetically justifiable as a reinforcing verbal counterpart to the method of appropriative sampling which forms the major theme of this rap. For just as rap DJs cannibalize familiar prepackaged musical phrases to create an original sound by placing them in new contexts, so the MC can appropriate old proverbs and give them new significance by his recontextualizing application of them in his rap.

Consider the first two clichés about truth and beauty which together form a couplet: "Talk, well I heard talk is cheap. / Well, like beauty, talk is just skin deep." So conjoined in this rap's specific context, these clichés are anything but simplistic and commonplace in meaning. Instead, they undermine with ambiguity the simple common truths they standardly express, while also suggesting philosophical theses on the nature of language, beauty, and aesthetic judgement which radically diverge from and challenge commonplace dogma on these issues.

Of course, "talk is cheap" can be understood here in its standard sense: that is, it costs nothing and requires no effort, knowledge, or talent to blast rap with ignorant criticisms. Such uninformed "talkin' jazz" is worthless, cheap talk. The proverb's standard sense also suggests the commonplace opposition between mere talk (which is easy but effects nothing) and real action or performance which not only costs effort but actually does something. And Stetsasonic employ this opposition in the contrast they draw between the "narrow-minded" critics who, lacking the pizazz to create art, simply talk about and "judge" it and, on the other hand, the rap artists who are "talented and strong" and fearless enough to act and create, rather than merely "speculate" with "cheap" talk.

However, over and against these standard senses, the contextual content of this rap more strikingly insists that so-called cheap talk is not really so cheap at all. It is instead very costly. First, its ignorant maligning of rap deceives the public, insults and persecutes rap artists and their audience, and thereby creates a confusing "fuss" about the nature of hip hop. The clichéd distinction between talk and action is thus challenged by showing that mere talk can constitute an action having costly consequences. This argument is painfully confirmed by the actual facts of rap's condemnation and persecution by people totally unfamiliar with the music, who therefore rely on the hearsay of others who are themselves as disinclined to listen to rap as to let it be heard.[57] Moreover, as "Talkin' All That Jazz" also argues, the seemingly cheap condemnatory talk of the critics will end up costing them dearly as well; for "when you lie and you talk a lot, / People tell you to step off a lot." Injured by their "Talk about rap / Sayin' all that crap," Stetsasonic violently warn rap's denouncers of the high price of such cheap talk: "You said it wasn't art, / So now we're gonna rip you apart."

If uninformed "cheap" talk can have such powerful effects, what is the source of discourse's power and authority? If "talkin' jazz" can be false criticism or true art, if discourse in general can be taken as lies or truth, what determines discursive truth and aesthetic legitimacy? These heady philosophical issues are ingeniously linked in the same clichéd couplet, where talk (or discourse) is identified with beauty as being "just skin deep." Here again we see how the specific rap context provides a bland old cliché with radically new meaning. Given rap's ghetto roots and its aesthetic rejection and persecution as black music, the complaint that beauty is just skin deep is transformed from the hackneyed critique of beauty's superficiality (its concern with surface appearance) and comes to embody the powerfully provocative charge that beauty is connected with racial bias, with reactions linked to the surface color of skin. In more general terms, aesthetic judgement is not the pure, lofty, and disinterested contemplation of form that it is standardly taken to be; instead, it is profoundly conditioned and governed by socio-political (including racial) prejudices and interests.

Thus, in contrast to the clichéd view that sees truth and beauty as altogether independent of power relations, this rap emphasizes the different power relations involved in determining truth and aesthetic legitimacy. Two sources of discursive authority are located. The first is socio-political power, as manifested and exercised, for example, by the control of the media and political institutions. Though uninformed and inimically biased, the anti-rap critics deliver their verdicts through the pervasive, legitimating medium of radio. Their condemnation that rap is devoid of aesthetic merit and unworthy of artistic status can therefore pass for truth, since it is broadcast without challenge by the dominant media and thus receives the aura of expertise and authority typically associated with views propagated through privileged channels of mass communication. Rappers, on the other hand, particularly those with an underground political message, are denied similar radio access, let alone equal time, to present and defend their art. Truth and artistic status are thus in large part issues of socio-political control.

The song reinforces this message when it links rap's artistic denunciation by the media with the mistakes of politicians who disvalue and disenfranchize the black community. With an implied pragmatist epistemology which puts no store in social truths no one believes or in artistic status no one recognizes, the song suggests that the truth of rap's artistic status is not something independently there to be discovered, but rather something which must be made; and it can be made only by challenging and overcoming the established establishment's truth of rap's artistic illegitimacy. The song urges and itself represents such a challenge. Given the serious socio-political interests and stakes involved in the struggle for artistic legitimation, the rappers realize that this struggle is an essentially violent one; and to defend hip hop against its media critics, they are prepared to use violence: "You said it wasn't art, / So now we're gonna rip you apart." The threat of violence is seriously intended, for it is repeated later in the song, warning anyone who sounds off against rap: "You might even get hurt, my friend."[58]

Aware of the connection between artistic status and socio-political power, the rappers also realize that the establishment's rejection of hip hop can be opposed by attacking the contradictions and weaknesses of its socio-political base. While American society claims to be a liberal democracy with free speech and majority rule, this is contradicted by its censorship of rap and, more generally, by its cultural leaders' tendency to identify true art only with high art, even though the majority of Americans find more aesthetic satisfaction in the arts of popular culture. In defending their music against its media critics, Stetsasonic argue that those elitist cultural czars are overstepping the democratic power base which empowers their judgements. In terms of taste, they "are a minority"; just as "in terms of thought," they are "Narrow-minded and poorly taught / About hip hop's aims" for a more democratic and emancipatory popular art.[59] By contrast, the rappers defend their art by aligning it with the majority. Their insistence that "what we sample of is a majority" aims to justify not only their method of sampling but also their resultant musical creation by suggesting that they reflect popular taste and majority interests.

How valid is this claim? Jon Pareles, the *New York Times* rock critic, describes rap as "the fastest growing genre in popular music and the chosen soundtrack for millions of fans." Moreover, the fact that its daily show on MTV "consistently draws the cable channel's largest audiences" suggests that rap has moved well beyond its black urban origins.[60] Certainly in America's largest cities, many of which have black majorities, rap's popularity is unquestionable. Its growing dominance on the street is defiantly audible, booming loudly through car radios and "ghetto blasters." Its popularity in terms of concerts and record sales (despite the harassment of censorship) is already vast and steadily growing, far out of proportion to the cultural recognition it has so far been granted. If the hip-hop audience does not (yet) represent a majority of the big city radio audience, it constitutes an extremely large constituency which has been badly served by radio's treatment of rap.

"Talkin' All That Jazz" not only appeals to rap's majoritarian power base within its primary urban setting, but, through its own polemic, seeks to mobilize and expand rap's popular support. One of its polemical strategies involves the politics of personal pronouns. The whole song is structured on the opposition between "you" and "us." On the narrowest, literal level, the "us" is simply Stetsasonic, the hip-hop band that is singing this song. Ordinarily this could suggest that the listening audience was part of the "you" to whom the song is addressed. However, since the song is an angry protest, it takes care to address its audience not as a "you," but instead distinguishes them, at the very outset, from the confrontational "you" of its hostile message – the radio's anti-rap critic(s). For the vast majority of the song's audience are not radio speakers but only listeners.

The audience is further encouraged to assimilate themselves to the celebrated "we" of the song by their opposition to the confrontational "you" that is aggressively attacked as an ignorant and untalented but powerfully oppressive and hypercritical minority. The "we" thus comes to mean not only Stetsasonic, but the whole hip-hop community whose cause they are advocating. And it reaches still further by appealing to those who are not yet fans of hip hop but can identify with it because of their common opposition to the media and political authorities against which this song, and hip hop in general, are defiantly struggling. Anyone resentful of the weak "whacked" babblings of media figures and politicians, anyone angry with our society's authoritative spokesmen and their iniquitous exercise of power, any artist (or athlete or laborer) incensed at being negatively judged by critics lacking the talent, strength, or pizazz to perform what they haughtily criticize; to all such people – and their number is legion – this song should appeal through its impassioned spirit of protest and thus should enlist increasing support for rap, outside its original, core ghetto audience.

This strategy of gaining acceptance for rap by widening the sociocultural base of its support is shrewdly pursued through at least three other rhetorical devices. First, in the third stanza, rap is linked to the music of rhythm and blues ("R & B"), arguably the source of all rock music and a genre which achieved great popularity among white audiences not only in America but throughout the world. If "Rap brings back old R & B" (not only through the sampling of its driving rhythms but through rap's deep expression of the blues' concern with poverty and oppression), then, the song implicitly argues, rap is surely worth having. If rap's recycling, reshaping return to R & B helps keep it alive and creatively remembered ("And if we would not, / People could have forgot"), then rap's artistic value should be recognized and protected from censorship and harassment. In other words, even if we don't like rap itself, we should accept it for its instrumental value in keeping alive the tradition of innovative black music which generated rhythm and blues, jazz, and rock – forms whose popularity with the general white audience is uncontestable.

This implicit appeal to a wider and also white audience is subtly developed in the last stanza's invocation of "Sly and the Family Stone," with whom Stetsasonic, the hip-hop band, explicitly identify themselves. Sly Stone, who started out as a San Francisco DJ, is recognized along with James Brown as one of the prime progenitors and inspirations of hip hop. But, unlike James Brown, from whom he borrowed but whose music and persona had a more exclusively black character and appeal, Sly achieved a style that, though rooted in black music and committed to black pride, completely captured the white rock audience and the socio-cultural acceptance it provides. Sly's crossing and breaking of racial (and gender) barriers was strikingly exemplified in the composition of his band "The Family," which included blacks and whites, men and women. As Greil Marcus observed, it was Sly who broke the color line at Woodstock, "emerging as the festival's biggest hit."[61] Moreover, it was Sly who had the cultural confidence and courage to claim artistic status for his songs by describing himself as a "poet,"[62] showing the way for Stetsasonic and other rappers to insist that rap be recognized as art and poetry, and showing that such aesthetic manifestoes and socio-cultural protest can be successfully made through song. His hit, "Stand," insistently exhorts the oppressed and disenfranchised to struggle for their beliefs, rights, and culture; to "stand for the things you know are right." It prophetically warns later rappers that the oppressive authorities "will try to make you crawl," when they learn "what you're sayin' makes sense at all"; but it nonetheless encourages them to continue the struggle, since "a midget

standing tall" can help bring down the "giant beside him about to fall."
In a semantically rich and artfully subtle use of intertextuality, Sly's hit
is cited by Stetsasonic, with the word "stand" at once fully integrated
into their text, yet clearly marked and emphasized as distinct by the
rhythm and the rhyme scheme: "Stetsasonic, the hip-hop band, / And
like Sly and the Family Stone / We will stand / Up for the music we live
and play / And for the song we sing today." With the same rich subtlety,
these lines, through their invocation of Sly, simultaneously express a
gesture of openness and appeal to the white audience, together with an
unflinching spirit of black pride and protest.

Sandwiched between the invocations of Sly and of "R & B," we find a
third strategy for making rap more acceptable to the general audience: a
reassurance that rap's claim for artistic legitimacy is not a demand for
hegemony. In promising "we're not tryin' to be a boss to you," the
"Stets" reassure the unconverted audience of hip hop that their aim is
simply to be heard, not to silence others, even if they are prepared to
"hurt" those whose "talkin' jazz" seeks to censure and censor rap. In
proposing the goal of peaceful pluralistic coexistence (as opposed to the
"no-win" situation of violent cultural strife), the rappers are cleverly
appealing to one of American society's most widely held and deeply
cherished tenets, the freedom of pluralist tolerance. If we are tempted to
dismiss this ideal as bourgeois liberal ideology, it remains effective as an
argument to those who share that ideology; and its scope is actually far
wider. For it also reemerges in the utopian visions of Marxians like
Adorno, whose socio-political (and aesthetic) ideal is difference without
domination. The advocacy of such ideals, of course, adds yet another
aspect to the rich philosophical content of this song.

Let me conclude discussion of this content by briefly noting the second
source of discursive and aesthetic authority that the song recognizes. This
is the charismatic authority of artistic and rhetorical power. If truth and
artistic status depend on a socio-cultural power structure, this structure
is not permanently fixed but is rather a changing field of struggle. And
one way a population's beliefs and tastes can be transformed is by the
expressive power of the discourse or art presented to them, though of
course their appreciation of this power will always rest on some of their
antecedent beliefs and tastes.[63] Thus, the song suggests, we listeners can
come to reject the critics' "talkin' jazz" as lies yet recognize rap's "talkin'
jazz" as art, truth, and proof by sensing their comparative expressive
power. While the critics' discourse is palpably weak ("so whacked that

it's bound to show") and lacks "pizazz," rap's discourse proves its truth and artistic status by its punch and power, by being "talented and strong."

Such proof through perceptual persuasion is not a confused aberration but an important form of argument in aesthetics and elsewhere;[64] and this song, a rap manifesto in rap, is clearly meant as such a perceptually persuasive proof of rap's artistic status by its own specific artistic power. Stetsasonic do not pretend to provide an exhaustive survey or extended "formal debate"; they claim to "set the record straight" about rap and its record-sampling distortions within the mere space of a record by the convincing and exemplary appeal of "the song [they] sing today": a self-consciously self-asserting and arguably self-validating declaration of the truth that rap is art.

Artistic Self-Consciousness, Creativity, and Form

This self-conscious self-assertion of artistic status is more important than it might seem, for artistic self-consciousness is regarded by many aestheticians as an essential feature of art.[65] Thus, one reason why popular arts have been denied artistic status is that they fail to claim it. They do not, Horkheimer and Adorno argue, even "pretend to be art" but rather accept their status as entertainment industries. They do not, Bourdieu argues, insist on their own aesthetic legitimacy, but instead meekly accept the dominant high-art aesthetic which essentially denies them.[66] Lacking the requisite artistic self-consciousness and self-respect to claim artistic status, popular art does not merit or achieve it. However true this may be for other popular arts, it cannot be said for rap. Stetsasonic, like countless other rappers, "stand / Up for the music [they] live and play," aggressively claiming and proudly celebrating rap as an art.

"Talkin' All That Jazz" evinces at least five aspects of proud artistic self-consciousness, apart from its firm assertion of artistic status. First, as art is something which stands out from ordinary conduct and humdrum experience by its superior skill and quality, this song insists on rap's superior talent, strength, and "pizazz" vis-à-vis ordinary cheap talk. Second, if art's essentially historical character means that to be a work of art is to belong to an artistic tradition, the song underlines rap's connection to such tradition. It does this most pointedly by first describing itself as a new kind of jazz, thus aligning itself with the black musical form most widely recognized as legitimate art, and then further connecting itself with "old R & B" whose established popularity is even claimed to be enhanced or insured through rap's "bringing back" of its rhythms. There are also the more specific and intricate intertextual links to Sly Stone, James Brown, and the rap crew Eric B. and Rakim, which give a fuller sense of rap's place in and shaping of a continuing artistic tradition, one that involves both the recognition and contestation that any healthy, fruitful tradition must display.[67]

A very important aspect of recent artistic tradition (and one often regarded as essential to the very nature of art) is art's oppositional stance. Many maintain that art – to qualify as such by displaying its defining originality and distinction from the ordinary – must somehow take a stand against a generally accepted but unacceptable reality or status quo (artistic or societal), even if this opposition be expressed only implicitly by art's fictionality or by the difficulties it poses for ordinary comprehension. Whether or not such oppositional character is indeed essential to art, it is certainly present in rap, not only explicitly but often self-consciously. Violent protest against the status quo – the establishment culture and media, the politicians and police, and the representations and realities they all seek to impose – is, as we have seen, a central and often thematized feature of rap lyrics. But "Talkin' All That Jazz" most clearly exemplifies rap's self-consciousness as *artistic* opposition, attacking and defying the cultural czars who deny rap aesthetic legitimacy or artistic status. Moreover, apart from this explicit content, its very form as dramatic monologue of confrontational discourse is structured by the oppositional stance.

Two other features of modern artistic consciousness are frequently considered essential for any art worthy of the name and are just as frequently denied to the products of popular culture: concern for creativity and attention to form.[68] Both are powerfully present in "Talkin' All That Jazz," and their demonstration will conclude my aesthetic account of this rap and of rap in general.

Though its appropriative sampling challenges romantic notions of pure originality, rap still claims to be creative. It moreover insists that originality can be manifested in the revisionary appropriation of the old, whether this be old records or the old proverbs which "Talkin' All That Jazz" samples but creatively endows with new meanings. Indeed, "Talkin' All That Jazz" is all about rap's acute consciousness of its novelty as an artistic form, a consciousness painfully sharpened by rap's having been persecuted as such. In the economy of two lines, Stetsasonic cleverly establish rap's link to artistic tradition through its connection with jazz, while at the same time reaffirming the genre's creative divergence and importance as a new artistic form. "Jazz, well you can call it that, / But this jazz retains a new format." Moreover, the single phrase that rap "*retains* a new format" (rather than, say, *inventing* one), ingeniously captures the complex paradox of artistic tradition and innovation which Eliot labored to express: the idea that art can and must be novel to be traditional (and traditional to be novel), that one cannot conform to our artistic tradition by simply conforming to it, since this tradition is one of novelty and deviation from conformity.

Rap thus refutes the dogma that concern for form and formal experimentation cannot be found in popular art. Moreover, it displays the thematized attention to artistic medium and method often regarded as the hallmark of contemporary high art. Sampling is not only rap's most radical formal innovation (since some earlier pop songs also experimented with speech rather than singing), it is also the one most concerned with rap's artistic medium – recorded music. And, not surprisingly, it is extremely contested, in the courts of law as well as the court of culture. The aesthetic defense of sampling constitutes the motivating theme of "Talkin' All That Jazz," which from the outset links the issue of rap's artistic legitimacy with that of its sampling method.

> Well, here's how it started.
> Heard you on the radio
> Talk about rap,
> Sayin' all that crap
> About how we sample.
> Give an example.
> Think we'll let you get away with that.
> You criticize our method
> Of how we make records.
> You said it wasn't art,
> So now we're gonna rip you apart.

To defend rap's claim as creative art, sampling must be defended from the obvious and plausible charge that it is just the stealing or copying of already existing songs. The defense is that rap's sampling is not an end in itself, an attempt to reproduce or imitate already popular records. It is rather a formal technique or "method" to transform old fragments into new songs with "a new format" by innovatively manipulating the technical media of the recording industry. As with any artistic method or "tool," sampling's aesthetic significance or value depends on how it is used ("It's only of importance when I make it a priority") and thus needs to be judged within particular concrete contexts; hence Stetsasonic's injunction for the maligning critics to "Give an example" of how their sampling vitiates their artistry. Further, Stetsasonic suggest that sampling is only "a portion" of rap's method, and not always its highest priority. This message and their challenge to "Give an example" are formalistically reinforced by the fact that the actual use of sampling and scratch mixing in "Talkin' All That Jazz" is relatively limited.[69]

Aware that rap's innovative technique of sampling might be dismissed as an ephemeral gimmick, Stetsasonic explicitly answer the "mad" critics who think "rap is a fad" devoid of creative potential and staying power, by pointing to the "strong" talent of its artists and the enduring "respect" it has won among its growing audience. And the Stets are not just "talkin' jazz." For, while the pop culture pundits thought rap would barely survive a season when it first recorded in 1979, it is finally achieving some critical recognition. "Now as the 90's begin," writes *New York Times* critic Jon Pareles, rap "is both the most startingly original and fastest growing genre in popular music."[70]

But while granting its creative originality, Pareles questions rap's achievement of coherent form. Its techniques of sampling and mixing and its fragmented, mass-media mentality prevent the creation of ordered form and logical structure, resulting in songs fractured by "dislocations and discontinuities" where "rhythm is paramount and non sequiturs are perpetual." The songs "don't develop from a beginning to an end," thus giving the sense that "a song could be cut off at any moment." This is certainly true for some rap, and perhaps for that which most immediately attracts attention and hostility by its deviation from accepted form. But it is at best a very partial and exaggerated account of the genre as a whole. For rap is full of songs firmly structured either on clear narrative development or on coherent logical argument. The narrative form includes the frequent celebratory ballads of the rapper's exploits and the many cautionary moral exempla about drugs, venereal disease, and the life of crime. The logical format is exemplifed by many of rap's songs of protest and black pride, including its frequent manifestoes of rap's self-pride. "Talkin' All That Jazz" falls into this last category, and its formal and logical coherence is undeniable.

It is composed of four clearly structured stanzas, which, though of slightly unequal length, are equally framed by the same instrumental interlude which at once distinguishes and connects them. These stanzas are further formalistically united by their closing with the same one-line refrain, which is also the song's title. Finally, we may note that while this closing line appears once in each of the first three stanzas, in the fourth and final stanza it is given three times, as if to recall, reinforce, and sum up the three preceeding stanzas and their arguments.

The song's argument in defense of rap is also coherently structured. The first stanza begins with the condemnation of rap and sampling followed by the threatening, protesting counterclaim of rap's creative artistic status. The second proceeds to refute rap's condemnation by explaining the role of sampling, stressing rap's popular appeal, and pointing to the elitist narrowness and ignorance of its condemnatory critics, while continuing the threat of retaliatory violence ("You step on us and we'll step on you"). The third stanza continues the theme of "angry" retaliation against the maligning lies of rap critics, while further justifing rap's legitimacy both in terms of the truth, talent, and strength it displays and because of its renovating preservation of the artistic tradition of Afro-American music. The final stanza, while reinforcing this traditional link and maintaining the song's proud "stand" of resistance and threat of violence, also extends an invitation of peaceful coexistence to rap's as yet unconverted audience, showing that they need not be afraid of granting rap artistic legitimacy. This closing advocacy of pluralistic tolerance ("of not tryin' to be a boss") does not come from fear of rap's weakness in the face of critical scrutiny. Rap is ready for "a formal debate," but only when it can have an adequate "forum" (i.e. "public space") to express itself, a forum that the media and cultural establishment have so far denied.

Here again we have the insightful and ingeniously telescoped linking of the aesthetic and the political. The struggle for aesthetic legitimacy (a symptom of more general social struggles) can only achieve the form of refined and carefully reasoned debates about form when one can enjoy the security of being heard. The rappers are still struggling for that hearing, and to get it, Stetsasonic must "for now" speak more urgently and violently, so less formally. If the denigration and suppression of rap's voice incite violent protest rather than sweet aesthetic reasonings, the enemies of rap are themselves responsible ("What you reap is what you sow").

This prioritization of getting a hearing before going into a formal debate, of securing expressive legitimacy before concentrating on intricacies of form, can be taken as a critical but defensive self-commentary on this song's own formal status; and it raises a crucial formalist issue which rap must face. For while "Talkin' All That Jazz" achieves formal unity and logical coherence, it remains formalistically more simple and traditional than many other raps, which talk much less about sampling but instead apply it much more extensively, complexly, and emphatically (e.g. "The Adventures of Grandmaster Flash on the Wheels of Steel"). But while such songs produce a far more radically "new format," they seem more susceptible to Pareles' charge of formal incoherence. This may suggest a tension between rap's claims of formal innovation and its satisfaction of the formal coherence required of art. For rap's artistic innovation, particularly its technique of sampling, is closely connected with elements of fragmentation, dislocation, and breaking of forms.[71]

This tension between formal innovation and already appreciable formal coherence constitutes the formal debate in which rap is now actively engaged. It is still in the process of testing the limits of its innovative techniques and the formal sensibilities of its audience in order to find the right balance – a form that is both new and yet somehow assimilable to our changing aesthetic tradition and formal sensibility. Less than twenty years old, rap is still far from a solution and from artistic maturity. It will attain neither if it is not first accorded the artistic legitimacy necessary to pursue its own development and that of its audience, without the oppression and dismissive abuse of the cultural establishment and without the compulsion to sell out to the most immediate and crassest commercial pressures. "Talkin' All That Jazz," a song advocating rap's new format but which still remains comfortably close to traditional form, is an appeal for such legitimacy, and an appealing one because of the way it meets traditional aesthetic criteria. It thus provides us intellectuals with a more inviting invitation to enter the formal debate about rap, a debate which it defers to the future and which only the future will resolve.

9

Postmodern Ethics and the Art of Living

I

In a brief and bracketed interjection in proposition 6.421 of his *Tractatus Logico-Philosophicus*, Wittgenstein asserts that "ethics and aesthetics are one."[1] The message appears as cryptic as it is bold, pronounced parenthetically with no further clarification or justification, in that austere economy of pregnant minimalist expression so characteristic of the modernist style. What the young Wittgenstein meant can best be surmised by looking not only at the Tractarian context but at his earlier *Notebooks*,[2] where the dictum originally appeared along with some sketchy elucidation. Apparently, he wished to convey the idea that ethics and aesthetics were fundamentally the same in at least three significant respects. First, both involve seeing things *sub specie aeternitatis* – that is, transcendentally, "from outside," in "such a way [that] they have the whole world as background." In aesthetics, "the work of art is the object seen *sub specie aeternitatis*;...[while in ethics] the good life is the world seen *sub specie aeternitatis*. This is the connection between art and ethics" (*N* 83). Second, both ethics and aesthetics concern the realm of "the mystical," not only because their statements (being neither empirical nor logical propositions) belong to the unsayable, but also because both employ that transcendental global perspective he associates with the mystical and with "absolute value."[3] Third, both are essentially concerned with happiness. As "the artistic way of looking at things...looks at the world with a happy eye," since "art is gay," so ethics amounts to the question of being "either happy or unhappy; that is all. It can be said: good or evil do not exist" (*N* 74, 86).

These three connections, whatever sense and cogency we find in them, hardly establish the utter unity of ethics and aesthetics. Moreover, though the doctrine is not repudiated (as so many Tractarian doctrines are) in Wittgenstein's later philosophy, neither is it explicitly affirmed or developed. Indeed, one might argue that his later, decentered, non-transcendental, and pluralistic philosophy of language-games, which Lyotard claims as a major source of postmodernist thought,[4] would be hostile to any homogenizing unification of the ethical and aesthetic domains. For these domains surely appear to involve somewhat different language-games.[5] On the other hand, the substantial underlying connection of ethics and aesthetics is strongly implied in Wittgenstein's later account of aesthetic appreciation. For such appreciation is seen as not reducible to isolated, formulizable critical rules and expressions of approval, but rather as deeply and necessarily situated in a complex cultural background, entwined in and shaped by ways of living which cannot but include an ethical dimension.[6] If we had to assign Wittgenstein a final position on the "oneness" of ethics and aesthetics, it would probably be the balanced if uninspiring view that they are neither fully united and identical nor completely distinct.

Let us now leave Wittgenstein aside, having paid what I hope will be sufficient exegetical dues for appropriating his language, and turn to why his parenthetical phrase is today so meaningful. The answer, I believe, is that the dictum "ethics and aesthetics are one" gives pointed expression to important insights and problems of both aesthetic and ethical theorizing in our postmodern age. It denies modernism's aesthetic ideology of artistic purism, common to modernist poetry and to the formalist and abstract movements in plastic art. Instead it implies that such isolationist ideology is no longer viable now that the traditional compartmentalization of knowledge and culture threatens to disintegrate into manifold forms of interdisciplinary activity. In such conditions, there is not only room, but need, for a criticism of art that is morally, socially, and politically motivated, just as there is need for art itself to be so motivated.

I shall speak no more of the ethico–political in art and its criticism, but shall instead devote this final chapter to its no less significant converse, the aestheticization of the ethical. The idea here, to adumbrate its more salient aspects in a phrase, is that aesthetic considerations are or should be crucial and ultimately perhaps paramount in determining how we choose to lead or shape our lives and how we assess what a good life is. It fleshes out Wittgenstein's ambiguous dictum that ethics and aesthetics are one by erecting the aesthetic as the proper ethical ideal, the preferred model and criterion of assessment for the good life. Such aestheticization is understandably directed primarily at what might be called the private ethical realm, the question of how the individual should shape his life to fulfill himself as a person.[7] But it can be very naturally extended to the public realm, to questions of what a good society should be like. At the very least, one could argue that a good society must be such as to insure the possibility, if not the productive fostering, of an aesthetically satisfying life for its constituent individuals. Moreover, it has been quite common and still remains tempting to characterize good societies themselves by aesthetic standards, conceiving them as organic unities with an optimal balance of unity in variety – that classic and still potent definition of the beautiful.

If, as I believe, the aestheticization of the ethical is a dominant (though hardly unprecedented)[8] current in our postmodern age, it is perhaps more evident in our everyday lives and the popular imagination of our culture than in academic philosophy. It is manifested by our culture's preoccupation with glamour and gratification, with personal appearance and enrichment. The celebrated figures of our time are not men of valor or women of virtue but those significantly called the "beautiful people." We are less inclined to the imitation of Christ than to imitating the cosmetics and fashion of Madonna; no one today reads the lives of the saints for edification and example, but the biographies of film stars and the success stories of corporate millionaires are perennial best-sellers.

However, the postmodernist ethics of taste is not without philosophical apologists. It finds clear support in Foucault (with his ideal of "an aesthetics of existence") and in other continental thinkers in the Nietzschean tradition. But I shall be concentrating on its expression in recent Anglo-American philosophy. My major focus will be Richard Rorty, perhaps the most outspoken and outrageous philosophical exponent of America's popular imagination and one who explicitly advocates "the aesthetic life" as the good life. For Rorty, "this aesthetic life" is one of "private perfection" and "self-creation," a life motivated by the "desire to enlarge oneself," "the desire to embrace more and more possibilities" and escape the limiting "inherited descriptions" of oneself – a desire expressed in "the aesthetic search for novel experiences and novel language" (*R* 11, 12, 15; *CIS* xiv, 29). In other words, aesthetic gratification, self-enrichment, and self-creation are sought not only through actual experiments in living, but through the more timid option of employing "new vocabularies of moral reflection" so as to characterize our actions and self-image in a more freshly appealing and richer way (*R* 11).

Rorty's aestheticized ethic of private perfection is coupled with an affirmation of liberalism (with its tolerance of individuality, distaste for cruelty, and its procedural justice which "aims at human equality" (*CIS* 88)) as the best form of public morality and social solidarity. But he does not think that these private and public ideals can be fused in one theory or quest; and it is clearly the aestheticized private ethic which is privileged as giving real content to life, while liberalism merely provides the necessary stable framework of social organization for us to pursue in peace and comfort our individual aesthetic goals. For Rorty explicitly urges us to see the prime value and "aim of a just and free society as letting its citizens be as privatistic, 'irrationalist,' and aestheticist as they please so long as they do it on their own time – causing no harm to others and using no resources needed by those less advantaged" (*CIS* xiv). Rorty's aestheticization of the ethical presents, I believe, a promising direction, even if it needs to be criticized and modified in some important ways. In any case, its assessment requires that it be set in the context of other arguments for and visions of the aesthetic life.

II

Why should postmodern philosophy aestheticize the ethical? The rise of the ethics of taste can be largely explained as the result of the fall of more traditional models of the ethical. Just as, once born, we have to live our lives in some fashion, so once we start reflecting ethically on how to live we must reflect in some fashion. Erosion of faith in traditional ethical theories left an ethical *horror vacui* which the ethics of taste naturally rushed to fill. Rorty seems close to saying this when he argues that after Galileo, Darwin, and Freud "neither the religious nor the secular and liberal morality seems possible, and no third alternative has emerged" – except, it would seem, for the aesthetic one that he goes on to advocate.[9] The most powerful reasons impelling contemporary philosophers to reject traditional ethics appear to derive from two general philosophical attitudes. The first is a historicist and pluralist anti-essentialism as to human nature, while the second expresses a perception of severe limitations in morality which make it clearly inadequate for a full-blown satisfying ethic. We might describe this second view as the underdetermination of ethics by morality. Each of these attitudes involves a number of aspects or levels which merit attention.

(1) Traditionally, ethical theories have sought to justify not only themselves but the whole ethical enterprise from what Bernard Williams calls
"an Archimedean point: something to which even the amoralist or skeptic
is committed but which, properly thought through, will show us that he
is irrational, or unreasonable, or at any rate mistaken."[10] Typically, such
foundationalist theories base themselves on general theories of human
nature, trying to derive what life is essentially good for man from what is
essential to or essential in humankind, and recognizing that any ethical
"ought" depends on some non-ethical "can." The desire for pleasure or
happiness and the capacity for and exercise of rational thought and action
have been the most familiar and compelling candidates for such essential
features. In synthesizing the two, as well as in giving a much more
concrete and substantial picture of what constitutes the good life for man
(though not for women and slaves), the ethical theory of Aristotle enjoys
an advantage over that of Kant. For while Kant's epistemology fully
recognizes both the sensuous and the rational nature of man, his distinctive ethic rests on a very purified and eviscerally abstract concept of man
as rational agent. Such an agent, to realize his rational essence, requires
some freedom of choice in action, and he properly exercises it ethically by
choosing on the basis of rational, universalizable principles without regard to contingent considerations of prudential expediency and sentiment.

The particular problems with the Aristotelian and Kantian enterprises,
many of which Williams neatly outlines, need not concern us here. The
more basic problem which pervades these and similar attempts to ground
ethics in an account of man's intrinsic or essential nature is our strong
postmodernist suspicion that there really is no such thing. We have an
even stronger suspicion that there is no ahistorical essence that is both
universally found and ontologically fixed in humankind and yet is also
determinate and substantial enough to generate or justify, by mere logical
derivation or elaboration, a definite ethical theory. We have come to see
that even our best candidates for essential status, like rationality and
happiness, seem promising only as long as we don't probe too deeply into
the culturally and historically divergent accounts of what in fact really
constitutes these things.

The lack of an ahistorical, ontologically given human essence does
not, however, foreclose all possibility of deriving an ethical theory from
essential human nature. For that project could perhaps get by with some
non-ontological but still transhistorical, cross-cultural human essence;
some sort of amalgam of linguistic, cultural, and biological universals

found to be present in and necessary to human life whenever and wherever it has flourished, and one from which could be projected a definite
and coherent picture of what constitutes the good life. But scepticism
here is no less potent in the face of obvious historical and cultural divergence. Even in what we conceive as the same cultural tradition – say, that
which Eliot once personified as "the mind of Europe"[11] – we find very
different answers to the question of what is essential to or desirable for a
properly human life. Moreover, given what Lyotard diagnosed as our
postmodern suspicion of grand legitimating narratives,[12] we cannot try
to explain away such divergence by appeal to the variant but progressive manifestation of the human spirit in search of liberation and/or
perfection.

Yet, though we may reject both ahistorical and transhistorical human
essence as a ground for some universal ethic there still remains the more
modest option of generating an essential ethical theory for our own
specific age and culture. This "limited" aim is surely what we most want,
since what we want to know is how to live our own lives rather than those
of our ancestors or descendants, which are obviously not ours to live. But
even drastically narrowing the focus to contemporary American society,
we find there is just too much significant variety to talk confidently of any
formative essence which could tell us what to seek in seeking the good
life. We are perhaps unified in a commitment to freedom and the opportunity for pursuit of happiness. But such notions, as communitarian
critics of liberalism frequently complain, are helplessly vague and abstract; and the unity they apparently provide quickly disintegrates into
rival visions of what freedom, happiness, and opportunity really mean.

There are at least two good reasons why not even such localized
human essences can be found. First, not only in America but in any
advanced civilization, there is a very high order of division of labor, a
division of occupational roles. The notion of a general functional essence
of man such as Aristotle and other ethical theorists assumed and built on
seems no longer viable when men *and women* have so many different
functional occupations which are so difficult to reconcile. How do we
reconcile the functional essence of the farmer and the stockbroker, the
creative artist and the factory hand, the priest and the cosmetician, the
scientist and the casino operator? More disturbing is the fact that we not
only collectively experience a conflict of divergent functional essences,
we feel it just as powerfully within our individual selves. The conflict
between a woman's functional essence as defined by her profession and

that defined by her role as mother is perhaps the most familiar and acute of such contemporary problems of identity. But there are countless other examples of how our professional roles or self-definitions sharply conflict or simply do not coherently mesh with our self-definition as friends, family, or political agents, thus making it seem impossible to find a functional essence for the individual in some coherent amalgam of his or her social roles.

To say that a postmodern cannot generate a general or even a personal ethic from his or her specific functional role because we all inhabit collectively and individually a plurality of inadequately integrated roles is to say with Wittgenstein and Lyotard that we inhabit such a motley variety of language-games and are shaped by so many forms of discourse that we no longer can say definitively who we are. We cannot tell what is the good life for us, because the nature of us is so questionable and unsteady with our changing roles and self-representations. It is questionable, Rorty would argue, because it is not definitively there to be discovered, but instead open to be made and shaped, and should therefore be shaped aesthetically.

Moreover, according to Rorty, not only is it pointless to try to penetrate our social roles to find a common human essence which is not there, but even the idea of an underlying coherent individual essence of particular personhood (one's own true self) is a myth which Freud effectively exploded. One's own self or personality is instead revealed as an uneasy combination of a number of conflicting (conscious and unconscious) "quasi persons" formed through historical contingencies and composed of "incompatible systems of belief and desire," a view which discredits the whole idea of a person's one "true self" (*R* 5, 9, 19). Rather than something unified and consistent emerging from an autonomous, stable, and rational core, the self is "centerless," a collection of "quasi selves," the product of "random assemblages of contingent and idiosyncratic needs," shaped and modified by "a host of idiosyncratic, accidental episodes" transformed by distorting memory and multiple vocabularies (*R* 4, 12, 14). "Anything from the sound of a word through the color of a leaf to the feel of a piece of skin can, as Freud showed us, serve to dramatize and crystallize a human being's sense of self-identity. ...Any seemingly random constellation of such things can set the tone of a life" (*CIS* 37). For Rorty, this Freudian decentering, multiplication, and randomization of the self "opened up new possibilities for the aesthetic life" as an ethic. For if there is no true self to discover and conform to, then the most promising models of "moral reflection and sophistication" become "self-creation" and "self-enlargement" rather than "self-knowledge" and "purification" (*R* 11–12).

Anti-essentialism as to human nature thus leads to an ethics of taste. It would be wrong, however, to see this as a logical derivation. If human nature's absence of essence means it implies no determinate ethic, it therefore cannot imply an aesthetic one. But it still can lead to an ethics of taste, since in the absence of any intrinsic foundation to justify an ethic, we may reasonably be encouraged to choose the one that most appeals to us; and it is plausible to think that such appeal is ultimately an aesthetic matter, a question of what strikes us as most attractive or most perfect.

(2) It is time to turn from anti-essentialism to the second general attitude which has worked to undermine traditional ethical theories and thereby promote an aestheticized ethics of taste. I called this attitude "the underdetermination of ethics by morality," and it has two aspects, which respectively concern the extension and dominance of moral considerations in ethical thought. The first aspect finds its most general expression in contemporary philosophy's increasing recognition that morality as traditionally conceived does not really cover the full gamut of ethical concern. For the ethical involves a very wide range of considerations of value and goodness in respect to how one should live. Many of these considerations are clearly personal and egoistic, or at least not universalized (e.g. special concern for one's own interests or one's family's), and many are non-obligational (e.g., munificence and uncalled-for acts of kindness or heroism). But the traditional project of morality, as Williams and Wollheim maintain, constitutes a much narrower special "subsystem" of the ethical, governed by obligation and universalizability. Taking "morality in the narrow sense...to be that which has obligation as its core," Wollheim contrasts it sharply with the realm of value and goodness in terms of their differing psychological genealogy and consequent potential for human satisfaction. "One (morality) derives from introjection [of a menacing figure], the other (value) derives from projection ['of archaic bliss, of love satisfied']. One is in its origins largely defensive and largely coercive, the other is neither. One tries to guard against fear, the other to perpetuate love."[13] And if Wollheim's account of morality emphasizes its menacing beginnings and baneful aspects, Williams is still more explicit (and perhaps more extreme) in asserting with insouciant bluntness that "we would be better off without it" (*ELP* 174).

Williams's critique of "morality, the peculiar institution" or "special system," (*ELP* 174) concentrates less on its distressing psychological sources and effects than on its logical peculiarities and insufficiency in accounting for our ethical thinking. What makes this insufficiency so vitiating is that while morality clearly underdetermines ethics, it constitutes and sees itself as a system which is globally exhaustive in its determinations. It presents itself as a consistent system of obligations (and consequent rights) which can tell us what we should do in any instance. That we should or ought to do something implies that we *can* do it, and therefore these obligations will be hierarchically ordered so as to prevent their conflicting in any final or irresolvable sense, since they cannot be allowed to issue in contradictory actions, which, as incompatible, cannot be performed. "Moral obligation is inescapable," and whether you want to subscribe to the system or not, it includes you in its categorical universalizing logic and imputes you moral blame if you do not act according to its comprehensive system of obligations (*ELP* 177–8).

Williams is chiefly occupied with challenging two of morality's globally categorical presumptions: its claim to exhaustive extension of application and its supreme, overriding potency wherever applied. He shows how morality cannot defend the first claim against obvious cases of kindness and generosity that are non–obligatory or even in clear conflict with some prior definite obligation. And he exposes the failures of philosophical efforts to salvage the claim through the unconvincing positing of an elaborate hypothetical system of differently ordered obligations (particular obligations, general obligations, negative obligations, *prima facie* obligations, obligations to self, to others, etc.) so that any action we might look upon with favor or distaste will be seen as deriving or deviating from some relevant (or ordered complex of) obligation.

Closely connected with morality's assumption that it exhausts all ethical action and choice, that any worthy act can ultimately be justified only in terms of some obligation, is the presumption that in any ethical question moral considerations should always override all others and determine how one should act or live. Thus, if the performance of a noble unobliged act of kindness prevents me from meeting a trivial obligation, say arriving to dinner on time, then a vague general obligation relating to kindness must be posited to justify my act's obvious worth. The idea that certain things can be good regardless of obligation and can even outweigh obligation in ethical deliberation is utterly foreign and intolerable to the system of morality. Williams calls this morality's maxim "that only an obligation can beat an obligation" (*ELP* 187), and its perceived falsity constitutes the second part of the postmodern case for the under-determination of ethics by morality. Ethics, as distinguished from morality, recognizes that there is more to the good life than the ful-fillment of obligations and even "can see that things other than itself are important...[to life] as part of what make it worth living" (*ELP* 184). This does not mean that ethics need reject moral considerations entirely, only that it must reject their claim to entirety and overridingness. What is denied (and this time in Wollheim's words) is "the view that morality is ultimate or overruling" (*TL* 225).

Demoting moral obligation to merely one significant factor in ethical deliberation on how to live the good life makes such deliberation much more like aesthetic judgement and justification than syllogistic or legal-istic discourse. Finding what is right becomes a matter of finding the most fitting and appealing gestalt, of perceiving the most attractive and harmonious constellation of various and variously weighted features in a given situation or life. It is no longer the deduction of one obligation from another more general obligation or group of obligations; nor is it the outcome of a logical calculation based on a clear hierarchical order of obligations. Likewise, ethical justification comes to resemble aesthetic explanation in appealing not to syllogism or algorithm but to perceptual-ly persuasive argument (through well-wrought narrative, tendentious rhetoric, and imaginative examples) in its attempt to convince. Such justification relies on and aims to sustain and extend some basic consen-sus (a vague *sensus communis*) on the bounds of appropriate action, yet also recognizes and serves to promote a tolerance of difference of per-ception or taste within these (revisable) bounds. As with aesthetic interpretation and evaluation, we want our friends and associates to understand our ethical perspectives and choices and to see them as reasonable; but no longer is it so crucial that they accept them as universally right and valid for all. Ethical judgements can no more be demonstratively proved categorically true through unexceptionable principles than can aesthetic ones. For ethical decisions, like artistic ones, should not be the outcome of strict application of rules but the product of creative and critical imagination. Ethics and aesthetics become one in this meaningful and sensible sense; and the project of an ethical life becomes an exercise in living aesthetically. Perhaps this is what Wollheim has in mind when for one brief moment he very vaguely and tentatively suggests that ethics be viewed "like art" (*TL* 198).[14]

III

Though this aestheticization of the ethical seems a solid step in the right direction, Rorty's explicit advocacy of the aesthetic life is far more radical and substantive. Rejecting traditional moral theory on the grounds that we have no common essence but are products of random and idiosyncratic contingencies, Rorty urges the conclusion that we must create ourselves and must do so by self-enriching aesthetic redescription. One might argue that a self could be created by one's choice of even the most traditional or ascetic of moralities, so the necessity of self-creation in no way entails or prescribes the pursuit of a distinctively aesthetic life. But, as we shall see, Rorty insists on identifying the life of self-creation as an aesthetic life; even if the specific life he urges does not do justice to the varieties of aesthetic life advocated by philosophers over the ages and even in this century alone.

What then is Rorty's vision of the aesthetic life, and how does it compare to others? It rejects any "search for purity" and focused simplicity based on stable self-knowledge and affirms instead "a search for self-enlargement," "self-enrichment," and "self-creation" (*R* 11, 15; *CIS* 41). "The desire to enlarge oneself," says Rorty, "is the desire to embrace more and more possibilities, to be constantly learning, to give oneself over entirely to curiosity, to end by having envisaged all the possibilities of the past and of the future," an end which is obviously endless (*R* 11). This quest for self-enrichment and self-creation involves a dual "aesthetic search for novel experiences and [for] novel language" to redescribe and thereby enrich those experiences and their experiencer (*R* 15). Similarly, "the development of richer, fuller ways of formulating one's desires and hopes" makes "those desires and hopes themselves – and thereby oneself – richer and fuller" (*R* 11). The aesthetic aim is no longer to "see things steadily and see them whole" but to see them and ourselves through ever new "alternative narratives and alternative vocabularies [designed] as instruments for change" (*R* 9). Those "exceptional individuals" who can take the breathless pace and confusion of producing and inhabiting these multiple vocabularies bent on continuous change will be able "to make their lives works of art," where such works of self-creation must be strongly original, neither a "copy or replica of something which has already been identified" nor even "elegant variations" on previous creations (*R* 11; *CIS* 28).

Rorty identifies such masters of the aesthetic life in the seemingly different figures of the curious intellectual "ironist" (perhaps best personified as the sceptical, wide-ranging literary critic) and "the strong poet." Yet he wants to assimilate the two as essentially the same in their ethico-aesthetic quest, as both adventurously aiming at self-enrichment and self-creation through the use of novel language to redescribe the self. But the aims of self-creation and of enrichment through endlessly curious self-redescription are not at all identical. Not only can we achieve one without the other, but the two goals can be in deep tension. Boundless seeking for change can threaten the concentration necessary for creating oneself in a strong and satisfying way. The curious ironist and the self-creating strong poet can represent, in fact, two quite different forms of aesthetic life that Rorty unfortunately runs together as the aesthetic life he advocates. Besides being problematically conflated, each genre presents difficulties in its Rortian formulation.

The aesthetic life of "the curious intellectual" or "ironist" is "the life of unending curiosity, the life that seeks to extend its own bound rather than to find its center." Its "desire to embrace more and more possibilities" by embracing more and more different vocabularies for self-redescription comes with the injunction to be "increasingly ironic, playful, free, and inventive" with regard to whatever vocabulary one currently chooses or regards as determining one's self-description and ethical identity (*R* 11, 12). Rorty calls this determining vocabulary one's "final vocabulary"; and he defines the ironist as one who "has radical and continuing doubts about the final vocabulary she currently uses" and is thus constantly looking for new and better ones through wide reading. "Ironists are afraid that they will get stuck in the vocabulary in which they were brought up" or indeed in any single vocabulary. Having abandoned the idea of any essential self, final vocabulary, or grand narrative on which they should converge, they are bent on "diversification and novelty" of self-description, continuously enlarging their "own moral identity by revising [their] own final vocabulary." The ever curious, self-enriching ironist "reminds herself of her rootlessness" as she restlessly tries to take the most tricks in as many new language-games as she can learn to play (*CIS* 73, 75, 77, 80).

By contrast, the strong poet must know and respect limitation in order to create herself as a distinctive individual. She cannot give herself "over entirely to curiosity" to embrace as many narratives and vocabularies as possible, ideally experimenting with "all the possibilities of the past and of the future." For to do so, she risks losing the focus necessary to fix and firmly imprint a sense of what is special and distinctive to her life and language; and this is the very core of Rorty's poetic life of self-creation. The strong poet's fear is that, even if her words survive, "nobody will find anything distinctive in them." "One will not have impressed one's mark upon the language but, rather, will have spent one's life shoving about already coined pieces. So one will not really have had an I at all" (*CIS* 24). Yet this fear implies a powerful critique of the ironist's aesthetic life of self-enrichment.

That life is essentially romantic picaresque in genre, a tireless, insatiable, Faustian quest for enriching titillation through curiosity and novelty, a quest that is as wide-ranging as it is unstructured through the lack of center it so celebrates. However, the absence of any structuring center (which need be neither universally human, statically permanent, nor given rather than made) prevents it from being the sort of *Bildungsroman* it seems to want to be. For the maximized spawning of alternative and often inconsistent vocabularies and narratives of the self, which aims to deconstruct any stable self into a changing, growing multiplicity of selves or self-descriptions, makes the whole prospect of an integral enduring self seem altogether empty and suspect. But without such a self that is capable of identity through change or changing description, there can be no self capable of self-enrichment or enlargement, and this would nullify the Rortian aesthetic life of self-enrichment by rendering it meaningless. Similarly, to abandon the notion of a firmly distinctive self, one that is not continuously supplanted by endless redescription in new vocabularies acquired from others, is to render the prospect of distinctive self-creation problematic at the least. This need for self-centering, self-distinguishing limitation – the very opposite of the quest for all possibilities – is forcefully expressed in the lines from Larkin which Rorty uses to introduce the aesthetic ideal of self-creation:

> And once you have walked the length of your mind, what
> You command is as clear as a lading-list.
> Anything else must not, for you, be thought
>   To exist.
> And what's the profit? Only that, in time
> We half-identify the blind impress
> All our behavings bear, may trace it home.

The argument for self-limiting self-definition is not an appeal to an essential self that exists at the foundational core of every one of us, but rather an appeal to unity and coherence. For, having rightly abandoned essentialism, we can only constitute the self in terms of narrative about it, as Rorty himself urges. It follows that the unity and coherence of the self will depend on the unity and coherence of its narratives. Thus, though he rejects MacIntyre's nostalgia for Aristotelian narratives, Rorty cannot quarrel with his insistence on "a concept of a self whose unity resides in the unity of a narrative."[15] For without any unity and coherence of narrative, there is no intelligible self for the aesthetic ironist to enrich, enlarge, or perfect. If we abandon the aim of a unified, coherent self-narrative for Rorty's chorus of inconsistent "quasi selves" constituted by alternative, constantly changing, and often incommensurable narratives and vocabularies, with no complex narrative "able to make them all hang together" (*R* 5, 8), then the project of self-enrichment becomes mythical and incoherent with the myth and incoherence of a single self collecting these riches together.

The self-unity needed to speak meaningfully of self-enrichment or perfection is, however, something pragmatically and often painfully forged or constructed, rather than foundationally given. It surely involves developmental change and multiplicity, as all narrative unity must, and it can display conflict in its unity, just as interesting narratives do. A unified self is not a uniform self; but neither can it be an unordered collection of incompatible "quasi selves" inhabiting the same corporeal machine.

Rorty seems to recognize the necessity for self-unity when he asserts that the only post-Freudian version of human dignity is "a coherent self-image" and when he tries to appropriate MacIntyre's unifying virtue of "integrity or constancy" as part of his aesthetic life's "search for perfection" (*R* 17, 19). But he implicitly denies coherence in advocating a self composed of "a plurality of persons...[constituted by] incompatible systems of belief and desire" (*R* 19); and the only constancy that he in fact prescribes for the ironist aesthete is the constancy of change, of novel alternative self-descriptions and narrations, the constancy of inconstancy, which essentially nullifies the coherence of the self.

In learning so much from Freud, Rorty might have probed why Freud seemed much less eager to dispense with a unified, integrated self. Why, for example, did he prefer to posit a dominated unconscious rather than simply multiple consciousnesses or personalities residing in the same body? Why did he never portray our psychological constituents in Rortian fashion as ideally "egalitarian," as "rational" quasi-persons engaging in free conversation (*R* 7–9), unordered by repression and censorship, which of course imply some organizational hierarchy? One reason may be that Freud realized what a pricelessly important, yet fragile achievement the unity of self is, how difficult and painful such a unified self or self-narration is to construct, and yet how necessary it is for leading any plausible version of a good or satisfying life in human society. It is certainly presupposed in Rorty's ideal of the ironist's aesthetic life, no matter how much his postmodern theory of multiple selves claims to reject it. In fact, what makes his portrayal of this life seem not only coherent but perhaps attractive to us is that it in fact centers around one kind of self-vocabulary and narrative, that of the curious intellectual and her quest.

The other strand of Rortian aesthetic life, that of self-creation as personified by the strong poet, is free from the theoretically self-vitiating denial of self-coherence. We already saw how this life requires focusing limitation. It also implies some sort of central narrative or unifying pattern – contingent, idiosyncratic, developing, and actively shaped as it may be – which organizes the crazy congeries of experience into "the drama of an individual human life...as a whole," so that it is not an endlessly expanding hodge-podge of incompatible narratives in incommensurable vocabularies (*CIS* 29). Thus, in the words of Larkin's poem, "all our behavings" may come to be understood and structured in terms of that pattern which may become "clear as a lading-list," even though it be based on "the blind impress" of certain contingent factors in our lives which we can only "half-identify." Moreover, while the blind impress is irrevocably given, the pattern is *not*; and Rorty rightly insists on self-creation as the felicitous weaving of the pattern, the artistic construction of a narrative that will render our lives and selves more satisfying.

Rorty, however, gives us too narrow a picture of what constitutes aesthetically satisfying life and self-creation. For even when the ideal of the endlessly changing ironist is supplemented by the ideal of the strong poet who creates a firm and distinctively original identity, the possibilities of aesthetic life remain too limited. Critique of these limitations might be furthered by noting two other versions of aesthetic life which have found cultural expression and philosophical advocacy.

IV

Perhaps the most familiar one is a life devoted to the enjoyment of beauty: beautiful objects of nature and of art, as well as those hybrid products of nature and art we are loath to regard as objects of either –

beautiful people. This aesthetic life was very influential in the early part of our century through the fashionable Bloomsbury coterie who confess to having imbibed it from G. E. Moore's account of the ideal in human life. For Moore (who, like Rorty, repudiates any ethics based on the idea of an essential "true self"), the ideal consists of "certain states of consciousness, which may be roughly described as the pleasures of human intercourse and the enjoyment of beautiful objects." This is because "personal affections and aesthetic enjoyments include *all* the greatest, and *by far* the greatest, goods we can imagine" in life.[16] Both these components of the aesthetic life are constituted by very complex and rewarding organic unities (composed of countless and changing variables) which cannot be reduced to algorithmic prescription. However, Moore does affirm that the highest pleasures of personal affection require "that the object must be not only truly beautiful, but also truly good in a high degree," and that a proper appreciation of human beauty must include appreciation of its "purely material" form and the "corporeal expression" of its mental qualities (*PE* 203–4).

If this Moorean-Bloomsbury aesthetic life strikes us as distinctively and even chicly contemporary in engaging with our hedonistic penchant for beautiful things and beautiful people, we should remember that it represents (like Rorty's ironist quest) a familiar romantic genre, more particularly a late romantic ideal of aestheticism. Unwilling to accept the universal dominance of the mechanized world picture, unable to accept the traditional religious and moral claims to spirituality, and unready to be sullied by philistine politics and the grubby toil of social reform, the aesthetes sought individual salvation through the satisfying gemlike flame of art and sensation rather than through God or State. Their ideal of the aesthetic life differs from Rorty's not only in being less preoccupied with the ceaseless strivings of intellectual curiosity and the strenuous struggle of original self-creation, but in being more appreciative of beauty, pleasurable sensation, and the leisurely luxury of satisfaction. It is essentially the ethic of Pater and Wilde, an exquisite flower of aestheticist decadence which remains undeniably and captivatingly sweet, and may be the only flower still capable of growing in our postmodern wasteland of social hope.

However, as versions of the aesthetic life tend somewhat to overlap and be compounded, we find in Wilde's Nietzschean maxim that "life itself is an art" a clear suggestion of another form of aesthetic life, which can be called, for contrast, the classical.[17] The idea here is not so much a life of aesthetic consumption, but a life which is itself a product worthy of aesthetic appreciation for its structure and design as an organic unity. Like many old ideas, it is reclaimed and recycled in postmodern thought. Foucault, for example, returns to it through an analysis of ancient Greek culture, whose "ethics...was an aesthetics of existence," the expression of "the will to live a beautiful life, and to leave to others memories of a beautiful existence."[18]

The Greeks, as Williams and Wollheim both note in discussing ethical reflection, were strongly inclined to conceive and assess the good life holistically, as a unified whole. The idea that an individual's life needs to be seen, organized, and evaluated in terms of such an organic (rather than merely aggregative) unity gave Solon's famous injunction to "call no man happy until he is dead" its special force. For a disastrously inappropriate end could distort beyond repair the satisfying unity of the life led thus far. One of the basic projects of Greek ethics was to try to find a satisfyingly well-structured life that is maximally free from the threat of disunifying misfortune; and one general strategy to achieve such unity is to establish a center and contours for life by a kind of overarching aim or interlocking set of aims, a limiting concentration on a narrower range of goods (naturally those less susceptible to misfortune).

This kind of slimmed-down, centered, limit-respecting life of unity is labeled by Rorty "the ascetic life" (*R* 11) in unfavorable contrast to "the aesthetic life" he advocates. But such characterization is misleading and unfair. It is simply wrong to assume that a life emphasizing strong unity and thus adopting the limits this requires cannot be an aesthetic life, that it cannot be enjoyed and praised as aesthetically satisfying or even recommended for its aesthetic appeal. One could well choose the life of an earth-rooted, family-bound farmer over a jet-hopping, spouse-swapping academic simply in terms of its aesthetic joys of order, coherence, and harmony, which stem from a centrally structured and limited project of development, whose unity is both enhanced and largely constituted by cyclical and developmental variations on its central theme or narrative. As Foucault realized in his study of Greek ethics, one can pursue still greater simplicity and purity of life in order to stylize oneself as an extraordinary individual through a distinctively unified concentration on a narrow project. Even real asceticism can be recommended as aesthetically effective, not simply through a style of minimalist distinction where less becomes more since it is beyond the taste of the masses, but also because of the positive pleasures of self-limiting self-mastery.[19]

While the classical perspective on aesthetic living can accommodate asceticism, it is not confined to ascetic narrowness. It instead embodies the classical definition of beauty as unity in variety and thus is far from opposed to richness and diversity. What it maintains is that variety must not be maximized beyond the limit it can be coherently held together in some satisfying unity. The ascetic aims at a very narrow focus of unity through the unavoidable variety of life's vicissitudes. But the classical ideal of aesthetic life can endorse a rich variety of experience, if our aesthetic taste, psychological needs, and material and social conditions allow the forging of more complex and looser unities. Such unity would be neither foundationally given nor static. It could even be the sort of genealogical, self-constituted, and self-projected unity in variety that Nietzsche (surely a classically steeped romantic) seems to be offering us as the ideal life or character.[20] Such unity can even accommodate a self of multiple narratives, as long as these can be made somehow to hang together as a higher unity from the right narrative perspective, one which makes that self more compellingly rich and powerful as an aesthetic character.

Just as one need not be a rootless ironist to live the aesthetic life, so one need not take the path of the strong poet to create oneself aesthetically. Here, too, Rorty confuses the aesthetic with the radically novel, just as he conflates artistic creation with unique originality and autonomy with distinction. Aesthetic self-creation, for Rorty's strong poet, must be strikingly novel and distinctive. Her goal is "to make something that never had been dreamed of before," highlighting her idiosyncrasy and describing herself "in a new language," "in words never used before," so as to create "a self to be which her predecessors never knew was possible." We fail in this aesthetic quest if our creations and our selves are simply "better or worse instances of familiar types," even "elegant variations on previously written poems" (*CIS* 13, 24, 28–9). But even if the ethical goal of narrative self-creation be modeled on the creation of an aesthetic work of art, it still does not follow that such creation must be radically novel and altogether unique. For neither do artworks require such radical and idiosyncratic originality in order to be aesthetically satisfying, as we can see most clearly in classical and medieval art. To think that true artistic creation precludes established types and variations on familiar formulas is to confuse art with the artistic ideology of romantic individualism and the modernist avant-garde, a historically parochial confusion to which Rorty falls victim. One can style oneself aesthetically, create one's life as a work of art, by adopting and adapting familiar roles and life-styles, adjusting these generic forms to one's individual contingent circumstances.

This, as Foucault recognized, was the Greek manner of the aesthetic construction of life, a stylized construction of the ethical subject not in terms of categorical moral prescriptions but through a sense of the art of living based on certain generic formulas and ideals already socially entrenched as appropriate. There was no need to invent an entirely new formula; there was nothing inartistic about elegant variations on the familiar. Today, of course, we find a much wider range of recommended life-styles and much less consensus on the most appropriate. But this merely provides us with more materials and models for artistic self-fashioning; and though we still suffer from the modern habit of identifying art too narrowly with radical originality and individualistic uniqueness, postmodernism is increasingly putting this aesthetic into question.

As Rorty's notion of the strong poet conflates artistic creation with innovative uniqueness, it similarly confuses between autonomy and original self-definition, freedom and uniqueness. The only way Rorty thinks we can define ourselves as free individuals is to escape from inherited self-descriptions by redescribing and thus reconstituting the self in new ways and new language which "the past never knew." But why can't our autonomy be expressed in the freedom to define ourselves through an already existing life-style or language? There is no reason why the freedom to be oneself should be incompatible with being like others, unless we conflate autonomy with radical individualism. Indeed, the Rortian compulsion to create oneself in novel fashion can itself be seen as a form of non-autonomy, a bondage to the new and individualistic. Its motivating fear of being a replica suggests, in fact, a very tenuous sense of self, one desperately needing to assert itself by unique individuality and concentration on personal distinction. Its vision of self and self-perfection as "standing out" in one's private dimension rather than as being expressed and enriched through enveloping folds of social solidarity seems a very one-sided and phallocentric concept of selfhood.[21]

Moreover, it is a form of autonomy and aesthetic living which is limited to a narrow elite. "It is something which certain particular human beings hope to attain by self-creation, and which a few actually do" (*CIS* 65). Given its elitist distinction, the project of radically innovative self-creation is difficult to recommend as a general model for aesthetic living, as a direction that all should take in their search for private perfection and happiness. But instead of taking the promising pluralist option of recognizing a variety of forms of aesthetic life, some not requiring original distinction,[22] Rorty tries to universalize and democratize the strong poet's quest by making everyone an innovative and ambitiously individualistic strong poet in their unconscious. Building on Freud, he argues that since even the most prosaic person has an imaginative fantasy life which seeks expression, we should "see the conscious need of the strong poet to *demonstrate* that [she] is not a copy or replica as merely a special form of an unconscious need everyone has" (*CIS* 35–6, 43). But the fact that everyone's idiosyncratic unconscious seeks expression does not mean that what it seeks is the expression of its idiosyncracy, one's self-presentation as something distinctively original and innovative.

V

Rorty's emphasis on personal distinction reflects his view of the aesthetic life as a distinctly private ethic, essentially independent of the public ethics of social life; and he indeed claims that no philosophy or theory can synthesize the "private" goal of self-creation with the public one of social solidarity (*CIS* xiii–xiv). This claim could be challenged as the misguided product of our deeply entrenched liberal ideology and romantic aesthetics. Only when the former defines the self as essentially private and the latter regards aesthetic creation as, by necessity, radically individualistic do the making of self and society seem inherently at odds. We must be careful not to interpret a given socio–cultural structure of division into an intrinsic philosophical divide. Still, as long as our society shares these liberal and romantic commitments, Rorty may be right about the impossibility of a satisfactory synthesis. To construct an aesthetic life which unites private and public would require rethinking not only our ethics and politics but the nature of artistic creation and its demand for radical originality. The shape of such a synthesis is at present hard to envisage, but liberating our concept of art from its bondage to avant-garde individualism would seem a propitious preparation for its exploration.

In any case, even granting that within our liberal society the goals of self-perfection and social solidarity cannot be adequately fused in a single ethical vision, we should still criticize Rorty's vision of the aesthetic life for its excessively privatized character. It rests "on a firm distinction between the private and public" (*CIS* 83) that occludes the latter's formative influence on the former. For, given the familiar dialectic of self and other, the private self that Rorty wants to create and perfect is always largely the product of a public field; it is always already social and must be so as soon as it has a language for its private thoughts. Indeed, not only Rorty's particular private morality but his privatization of morality are obviously reflective of the particular public and wider society which shape his thinking – the intellectual field and the consumerist world of late-capitalist liberalism.

Consider first the essential public dimension of the strong poet's putatively private quest. First, as Rorty admits, her new language must borrow from the shared language of the past to develop and highlight its novelty, just as it depends on the shared language of the future if it is to remain comprehensible. Moreover, the success of her putatively private quest depends essentially on public recognition; for this, Rorty notes, is what makes the difference between original "genius" and mere aberrational "eccentricity" (*CIS*, 29, 37). Most important, her very ideal of private self-creation, the desire for individual distinction and originality, is itself the product of the pressures of a given public field. It is the field of artistic and intellectual competition, whose social logic of increasing individuation to secure legitimation, distinction, and marketability has been closely analyzed by Pierre Bourdieu.[23] One is not a genuine thinker or artist unless one succeeds in producing one's own particular brand of thought or art; so there are pressures to distinguish one's position by marking, affirming, and highlighting one's differences within the shared field of endeavor. The fact that these social pressures have been internalized by individual agents does not render them essentially private in character, and the so-called private ethical project they structure cannot be said to swing clear of public influences and consequences.

The privatized quest of the ironist aesthete is no less informed by public pressures and ethos. One does not need a very penetrating or subversive eye to see in its glorification and quest of the new, in its "aesthetic search for novel experience and novel language," precisely that old worship of the new which fuels the rapid and relentless pace of commodity consumption in our late-capitalist consumer society. As critics of commodity aesthetics have shown, the demand for constant aesthetic innovation, urged in the noble names of creativity and progress, is also a cunningly systematic program to increase exchange-value by masking or distorting use-value, by making the already purchased and still very much usable item seem outdated and in need of change, thereby stimulating new purchasing.[24] This programmatic, profit-driven innovation pervades our whole consumer society and thus, inevitably, its ethical thinking. The ironist's quest to acquire more and more new vocabularies is the philosophical counterpart of the consumer's quest to maximize consumption. Both seem narcotic dreams of happiness induced by capitalism's master dream (a grimly real one) of greater sales and greater profits.

Moreover, the very privatization of morality into a matter of mere personal enrichment clearly reflects the public morality whose privileging of the autonomous private individual (property owner or consumer) was so central to the collective rise of capitalism and liberalism. Yet, in apparent paradox or perhaps as its own immanent critique, this autonomy of self is precisely what is stricken and undermined by late capitalism's fragmented society. Competitive individualism and its attendant societal deformations have dissolved the stable and interlocking social roles which once afforded some integrity and solid structure to the self. In this socio-ethical void and in the absence of serious thinking as to how best to structure life aesthetically, the shaping of the self and its career is simply left to the whims of market forces. We are abandoned to the changing sway of well-advertised, profit-motivated notions of self-fulfillment and gratification, while lacking any stable sense of a self to fulfil. The advertised idea that everyone should fashion himself as a unique individual through the free personal choice of life-styles cannot hide the fact that not only the range of viable life-style options but the individual's very awareness and choice are severely constrained and relentlessly programmed by societal forces that are usually far beyond his power (as individual) to resist, let alone control.

This late-capitalist paradox of the privatized quest for self-fulfillment issuing in loss of real autonomy and integrity of self is perfectly reflected in Rorty's deep contradiction of exhorting the ironist's self-enrichment while effectively denying her the existence of a self to be enriched. The Rortian non-self of incompatible "quasi selves" intent on multiple shifting vocabularies seems indeed the ideal self for the powers governing a consumer society: a fragmented, confused self, hungrily acquiring as many new commodities as it can, but lacking the disciplined integrity to challenge either its habits of consumption or the system which manipulates and profits from them.

In its extreme privatization of morality, in failing to recognize how deeply and ineluctably the public ethos structures the very conception of our diverse quests for private perfection, Rorty's vision of the aesthetic life needs to be expanded to embrace more of the social. It needs a similar expansion, as we saw, to embrace a wider variety of genres of aesthetic living and self-creation. I wish to close my critique by pointing to another dimension where Rorty's vision of human nature and self-fulfillment seems much too narrow – his reductive linguistic essentialism.

Though Rorty is vehemently outspoken in repudiating essentialism, and though he specifically denies that we share a human essence by sharing a common thing called language, his view of the self as nothing but a complex web of vocabularies and narratives seems uncomfortably close to an essentialist view of human nature as exclusively linguistic. All that seems to matter for selfhood and human being-in-the-world is language: "human beings are simply incarnated vocabularies"; it is simply "words which...made us what we are" (*CIS* 88, 117). Thus, Nietzsche is praised as one who "by describing himself in his own terms...created himself, [since] he...created the only part of himself that mattered by constructing his own mind. To create one's mind is to create one's own language" (*CIS* 27). For humans are "nothing more than sentential attitudes – nothing more than the presence or absence of dispositions toward the use of sentences phrased in some historically conditioned vocabulary" (*CIS* 88).

Such remarks clearly suggest that man is essentially mind and that mind is essentially linguistic. But more troubling than their apparent essentialism is the fact that they endorse a fundamentally mentalistic view of human nature against Nietzsche's own emphasis on the formative role and value of the body, even in the shaping of the mind. This linguistic mentalism and dismissive neglect of the body is particularly counter-productive in a philosopher intent on advancing the aesthetic life. For aesthetics' connection with bodily senses and pleasures and with non-linguistic perceptions should be obvious were it not for the rationalizing bias which has enthralled so much traditional aesthetic theory and which still seems to ensnare Rorty's.

But though he strives to exclude the subsentential from the significantly human and aesthetic, when Rorty turns to expounding his notion of liberalism as the "desire to avoid cruelty and pain," the non-discursive returns with a vengeance in the form of pain, which "is non-linguistic" and all but threatens to oust language as the most common human factor. "What unites ...[an individual] with the rest of the species is not a common language but *just* susceptibility to pain, and in particular that special sort of pain which the brutes do not share with the humans – humiliation," a pain which Rorty linguistically identifies, however, as the loss of language (*CIS* 65, 92, 94, 177–8). Indeed, pain, together with brute power, seems to constitute for Rorty the fundamental unchangeable reality of the world which cannot be vanquished by our transformative narratives.

> For our relation to the world, to brute power and to naked pain, is not the sort of relation we have to persons. Faced with the nonhuman, the nonlinguistic, we no longer have an ability to overcome contingency and pain by appropriation and transformation [of language], but only the ability to *recognize* contingency and pain. The final victory of poetry in its ancient quarrel with philosophy – the final victory of metaphors of self-creation over metaphors of discovery – would consist in our becoming reconciled to the thought that this is the only sort of power over the world which we can hope to have. For that would be the final abjuration of the notion that truth, and not just power and pain, is to be found "out there." (*CIS* 40)

That the bottom-line, untransformable reality is "just power and pain" seems a sweepingly metaphysical statement rather out of character with Rorty's repudiation of metaphysics. But whether we read this as a regressive slip to bad metaphysics (through a metaphysics of badness) or instead as just an empirical generalization about our non-linguistic experience, it betrays a deep and particularly troubling absence in the Rortian vision of aesthetic living. For it is a very sad and unsatisfying aestheticism which affirms the pervasive presence of non-linguistic pain but ignores the sensual bodily pleasures. Such pleasures are "out there" as well; and not only do they form a large part of what makes life worth living, but they can be cultivated to make life more aesthetically rich and rewarding. Rorty's neglect of such pleasures makes his aestheticism unsatisfyingly eviscerate and tame. It remains too much the product of a puritan and capitalist America; for it is aimed not at rich sensual satisfaction or even more generally at pleasure (a notion he hardly mentions), but rather at the breathless production and accumulation of new vocabularies and new narratives. It is more a poetics, a theory of industrious making, than an aesthetics of full-bodied enjoying.

The aesthetic life should also cultivate the pleasures and disciplines of the body. Though such somatic experience may be irreducible to linguistic formulation, its contribution to the formation of mind and selfhood cannot be denied and indeed reveals the fundamental wrongheadedness of considering mind and body as separate entities and of identifying the self narrowly with the former. Though Rorty correctly insists that the self is structured by the vocabulary it inherits, Foucault is equally right in stressing that it is also the product of disciplinary practices inscribed on the body. And if we can emancipate and transform the self through new language, we can also perhaps liberate and transfigure it through new bodily practices.

I do not want to suggest that working through the body can provide an altogether autonomous route to private perfection and self-creation. Like the language of the strong poet, the body is not a wholly private affair. It has been significantly shaped and repressively scarred by history's dominant social practices and ideologies, which also means that it is not free from linguistic markings. But the fact that the somatic has been structured by body-punishing ideologies and discourse does not mean that it cannot serve as a source to challenge them through the use of alternative body practices and greater somatic awareness. We may have to read and listen to the body more attentively; we may even have to overcome the language-bound metaphorics of reading and listening, and learn better how to feel it. Of course, working on one's self through one's body is not in itself a very serious challenge to the socio-political structures which shape the self and the language of its description. But it could perhaps instill attitudes and behavioral patterns that would favor and support social transformation.

Ideally, pursuit of the aesthetic life would involve enrichment of self and society through somatic, linguistic, cognitive, psychological, and social change that is mutually supportive if not collaborative. Some, however, fear that social reform can only be stymied by attention to the body because this focus must be narrowly individualistic. As Fredric Jameson argues, attention to the body only concerns "my individual relationship with my own body...and not that very different relationship between myself or my body and other people," and it therefore can only promote the dangerous privatism and individualism on which unhappy bourgeois society rests.[25] But viewing the somatic as essentially private seems itself a problematic piece of bourgeois ideology. Not only is the body shaped by the social, it contributes to the social. We can share our bodies and bodily pleasures as much as we share our minds, and they can be as public as our thoughts.

Talk of self-transformation through body practices is likely to evoke some dangerously simplistic and standardized images: the callow confidence acquired by the 90lb weakling through muscles developed in a body-building program or the fragile self-esteem that the formerly flabby achieve through aerobic slimming and toning. The idea that somatic self-transformation must fit the model of Arnold Schwartzenegger and

Jane Fonda is a very pernicious presumption which reflects the poverty of thinking on the aesthetics of the body.[26] For when it is assumed that the body is not a proper locus for seriously critical and imaginative aesthetic thought, the pursuit of somatic well-being is left to the domination of market forces plying standardized ideals of superficially impressive body contours.

Advocating a more embodied pragmatist aesthetic does not mean confining aesthetic fulfillment to lean, tan, athletic youth. This is not simply because it recognizes other dimensions of aesthetic achievement, but because the aesthetics of the body is not limited to its surface form and ornamental cosmetics; it also concerns how the body moves and experiences itself. If our rationalist aesthetic tradition privileged firm external forms and distanced appreciation, a more Deweyan approach is needed to recognize and encourage the dynamic and experiential in bodily aesthetics. Such an approach would consider how factors like better-balanced breathing and posture, greater kinesthetic harmony, and, more generally, greater somatic consciousness can aesthetically enrich our lives in terms of an enhanced quality and awareness of felt experience. It would also explore the ways in which bodily practices that achieve these effects can help transform the self emotionally, cognitively, and ethically by instilling greater psychological balance, perceptual receptivity, and open, patient tolerance.

If all this sounds excessively "New Age," it must be remembered that many of these ideas can trace themselves back to ancient Asian traditions like yoga and T'ai chi ch'uan. If the different goals, methods, and traditions of somatic philosophy are worth exploring, it will have to wait for another book. Here our idea of a more embodied aesthetic aimed at living beauty realizes the pragmatist function of theory advocated by William James[27]: rather than a final solution, it offers "a program for more work." To see just how much and what kind of work on the body is called for, readers of this second edition can consult the next chapter on somaesthetics.

10

Somaesthetics:
A Disciplinary Proposal

I

"Beauty is a great recommendation," wrote Montaigne, "and there is no man so barbarous and sturdy as not to be somewhat struck by its charm. The body has a great part in our being, it holds a high rank in it; so its structure and composition are well worth consideration."[1] The focus of Montaigne's somatic interest here is obviously not the body's physiological components but its aesthetic functioning, its potential for beauty.

This aesthetic potential, I have elsewhere argued, is at least twofold. As an object grasped by our external senses, the body (of another or even one's own) can provide beautiful sensory perceptions or (in Kant's famous terminology) "representations." But there is also the beautiful experience of one's own body from within – the endorphin-enhanced glow of high-level cardiovascular functioning, the slow savoring awareness of improved, deeper breathing, the tingling thrill of feeling into new parts of one's spine.[2] If my appeal to the proprioceptive beauty of personal somatic experience seems strangely idiosyncratic or weirdly "New Age," consider the 1884 remark of Jean-Marie Guyau, the once renowned author of *Les problèmes de l'esthétique contemporaine*: "To breathe deeply, sensing how one's blood is purified through its contact with the air and how one's whole circulatory system takes on new activity and strength, this is truly an almost intoxicating delight whose aesthetic value can hardly be denied."[3]

Rather than denying it, my aim is to affirm Montaigne's and Guyau's aesthetic attention to the body but also to render it more systematic. In exploring the body's crucial and complex role in aesthetic experience, I previously proposed the idea of a body-centered discipline that I called "somaesthetics."[4] Timidly tentative, my proposal remained very vague.

Suggesting somaesthetics as a possibility worth exploring, I dared not presume to define it by offering a systematic account of what topics, concepts, aims, and practices it would comprise. After almost three millennia of philosophy, to propose a new philosophical discipline might seem a reckless act of arrogance; to suggest one centered on the body could only add absurdity to hubris. Nonetheless, and at the risk of ridicule, this chapter shall outline the basic aims and elements of somaesthetics and try to explain how it could promote some of philosophy's most crucial concerns. The purpose is to show its potential utility, not its radical novelty. *If* somaesthetics is radical, it is only in the sense of reviving some of the deepest roots of aesthetics and philosophy. Yet, new names like "somaesthetics" can have a special efficacy for reorganizing and thus reanimating old insights, as William James shrewdly recognized in defining pragmatism as "a new name for some old ways of thinking," a definition that aptly fits my sense of somaesthetics.[5]

To show how somaesthetics is grounded in aesthetic tradition, I begin by examining the philosophical text that founded modern aesthetics, Alexander Baumgarten's *Aesthetica* (1750/1758). Baumgarten's original aesthetic project will be shown to have far greater scope and practical import than what we recognize as aesthetics today, implying an entire program of philosophical self-perfection in the art of living. I then outline the discipline of somaesthetics, explaining how it shares the same enlarged scope, multiple dimensions, and practical element that Baumgarten urged, and also promotes precisely those aims that philosophy traditionally defines as central to its own project: aims such as knowledge, virtue, and the good life. But in pursuing Baumgarten's broad practical vision of aesthetics, somaesthetics goes even further by also embracing a crucial feature that Baumgarten unfortunately omitted from his program – cultivation of the body. Modern philosophy too often displays the same sad somatic neglect. I conclude, however, by considering two contemporary philosophers, John Dewey and Michel Foucault, who differently exemplify my idea of somaesthetics, though without properly thematizing or articulating this field as such. The chapter ends by raising an important theoretical issue that somaesthetics must face: the possibility of assessing individual body tastes and practices in terms of more general somatic values or norms.

II

When Alexander Baumgarten coined the term *aesthetica* to ground a formal philosophical discipline, his aims for that discipline went far beyond the focus of what now defines philosophical aesthetics: the theory of fine art and natural beauty.[6] Deriving its name from the Greek *aisthesis* (sensory perception), Baumgarten intended his new philosophical science to comprise a general theory of sensory knowledge. Such an aesthetic was meant to complement logic, the two together designed to provide a comprehensive theory of knowledge he termed *Gnoseology*.

Though following his Leibnizian teacher, Christian Wolff, in calling such sensory perception a "lower faculty," Baumgarten's aim was not to denounce its inferiority. Instead, *Aesthetica* argues for the cognitive value of sensory perception, celebrating its rich potential not only for better thinking but for better living. In the book's "Prolegomena," Baumgarten asserts that aesthetic study will promote greater knowledge in several different ways: by supplying better sensory perception as "good material for science" to work with; by presenting its own special sort of sensory perception as a "suitable" object of science; by therefore "advancing science beyond the limits of treating only clear [i.e., logical] perception"; and by providing "good foundations for all contemplative activity and the liberal arts." Finally, the improvement of sensory perception through aesthetic study will "give an individual, *ceteris paribus*, an advantage over others" not just in thought but "in the practical action of common life" (A §3).

The wide-ranging utility that Baumgarten claims for aesthetics is implicit in his initial definition of the discipline: "Aesthetics (as the theory of the liberal arts, the science of lower cognition, the art of beautiful thinking, and the art of analogical thought) is the science of sensory cognition" (A §1). This vaster scope of all sensory perception allows Baumgarten to distinguish aesthetics from the already established scientific disciplines of poetics and rhetoric. Like these disciplines (and like its austere "sister," logic), aesthetics is not merely a theoretical enterprise, but also a normative practice – a discipline that implies practical exercise or training that is aimed at achieving useful ends. "The end of aesthetics," writes Baumgarten, "is the perfection of sensory cognition as such, this implying beauty," while the contrasting "imperfection" (identified as "deformity") is to be avoided (A §14).

Aesthetics as a systematic discipline of perfecting sensory cognition ("*artificialis aesthetices*") is both distinguished from and built upon what Baumgarten calls "natural aesthetics" ("*aesthetica naturalis*"), which he defines as the innate workings of our sensory cognitive faculties and their natural development through non-systematic learning and exercise. The aesthetic goal of systematically perfecting our sensory perception requires, of course, the crucial natural gifts of our "lower" (i.e., sense-related) cognitive faculties. Baumgarten insists especially on "keenness of sensation," "imaginative capacity," "penetrating insight," "good memory," "poetic disposition," "good taste," "foresight," and "expressive talent." But all of these, he argues, must be governed by "the higher cognitive faculties [of] understanding and reason" (*"facultates cognoscitivae superiores... intellectus et ratio,"* A §§30–8).

The perfectionist project of aesthetics must, however, go beyond all these (high and low) naturally developed faculties. It further requires a systematic program of instruction that includes two branches. The first (*askesis* or *exercitatio aesthetica*) is a program of practical exercise or training. Here, through repetitive drill of certain kinds of actions, one learns to instill harmony of mind with respect to a given theme or thought (A §47). Contrasting such aesthetic drill to the mechanical drill of soldiers, Baumgarten defines it as including also the systematic practicing of improvisation and even the playing of games, as well as exercises in the more erudite arts (A §§52, 55, 58).

The second part of aesthetic instruction is distinctively theoretical. To this theoretical study (which Baumgarten characterizes as *mathesis* [μάθησις] and *disciplina aesthetica*) belong all the fine forms of knowledge (*pulchra eruditio*), whose "most important parts are the sciences of God, of the universe, and of man," especially those sciences of man dealing with "his moral stature, history, not excluding myth, ancient cultures and displays of his signifying genius" (A §§62–4). But the theoretical discipline of aesthetics must also include a general "theory of the form of beautiful cognition" (*"theoria de forma pulchrae cognitionis"*) to complement the already established rules and theories in the specific aesthetic disciplines of oratory, poetry, music, etc. (A §§68, 69).

The major aims, concepts, and structural components of Baumgarten's founding project of aesthetics deserve far more detailed attention than this brief account provides. (If it is shocking how little today's aestheticians know Baumgarten's work, it seems even more scandalous that his *Aesthetica* is still not translated into English.)[7] My skeletal sketch of Baumgarten's aesthetics should, nonetheless, suffice both to suggest its pragmatic potential and to highlight a theme that is astoundingly absent, yet logically required, from his project: *cultivation of the body*.

Baumgarten defines aesthetics as the science of sensory cognition and as aimed at its perfection. But the senses surely belong to the body and are deeply influenced by its condition. Our sensory perception thus depends on how the body feels and functions; what it desires, does, and suffers. Yet, Baumgarten refuses to include the study and perfection of the body within his aesthetic program. Of the many fields of knowledge therein embraced, from theology to ancient myth, there is no mention of anything like physiology or physiognomy. Of the wide range of aesthetic exercises Baumgarten envisages, no distinctively somatic exercise is recommended. On the contrary, he seems keen to discourage vigorous body training, explicitly denouncing what he calls "fierce athletics" ("*ferociae athleticae*"), which he puts on a par with other presumed somatic evils like "lust," "licentiousness," and "orgies" (A §50).

This neglect of bodily training and theory for aesthetics appears even more shocking when we realize that Baumgarten essentially identifies the body with the lower faculties of sense, precisely those faculties whose cognition forms the very object of aesthetics. "The lower faculties, the flesh" ("*facultates inferiores, caro*"), he writes (A §12), should not be "stirred up" in their corrupt state but rather controlled, improved, and properly directed through aesthetic training. To designate the body by the sinfully charged term "flesh" shows Baumgarten's theological distaste for the somatic, and the Latin connotations of *caro* (as opposed to the more standard *carnis*) are especially negative.[8]

Such clues suggest a religious motive for Baumgarten's exclusion of the body from his aesthetic project of sensory science.[9] More specific philosophical reasons can also be surmised. In the rationalist tradition that Baumgarten inherited from Descartes through Leibniz to Wolff, the body was regarded as a mere machine. It could therefore never truly be a site of sentience or sensory perception, let alone knowledge. On the other hand, these philosophies that sharply divide the body from the perceiving mind were themselves largely inspired by religious doctrines that denigrated the body to save and celebrate the immaterial soul.

Whatever Baumgarten's precise reasons for neglecting the body in aesthetics, they do not justify its continued omission. Very interesting genealogical inquiries could be directed to tracing this persistent tradition of somaesthetic neglect and to explaining why the scope of post-Baumgartenian aesthetics was reduced from the vast field of sensory cognition to the narrow compass of beauty and fine art. We might further inquire why the initial pragmatic and meliorative aspect of aesthetics (i.e., its Baumgartenian definition as a discipline for perfecting perception and thus action) has likewise disappeared. How, in other words, has aesthetics, like philosophy itself, shrunk from a noble art of living into a minor, specialized, university discipline?[10]

Intriguing as these inquiries are, my prime goals here are reconstructive rather than historical: (1) to revive Baumgarten's idea of aesthetics as a life-improving cognitive discipline that extends far beyond questions of beauty and fine arts and that involves both theory and practical exercise; (2) to end the neglect of the body that Baumgarten disastrously introduced into aesthetics (a neglect intensified by the great idealist tradition in nineteenth-century aesthetics); and (3) to propose an enlarged, somatically centered field, *somaesthetics*, that can contribute significantly to many crucial philosophical concerns, thus enabling philosophy to more successfully redeem its original role as an art of living.

III

Somaesthetics can be provisionally defined as the critical, meliorative study of the experience and use of one's body as a locus of sensory-aesthetic appreciation (*aisthesis*) and creative self-fashioning. It is, therefore, also devoted to the knowledge, discourses, practices, and bodily disciplines that structure such somatic care or can improve it. If we put aside traditional philosophical prejudice against the body and simply recall philosophy's central aims of knowledge, self-knowledge, right action, and its quest for the good life, then the philosophical value of somaesthetics should become clear in several ways.

(1) Since knowledge is largely based on sensory perception whose reliability often proves questionable, philosophy has always been concerned with the critique of the senses, exposing their limits and avoiding their misguidance by subjecting them to discursive reason. Philosophy's work here (at least in Western modernity) has been confined to the sort of second-order critical analysis of sensory propositions that constitutes traditional epistemology. The complementary route offered by somaesthetics is, instead, to correct the actual functional performance of our senses by an improved direction of one's body, since the senses belong to and are conditioned by the soma.

This somaesthetic strategy has ancient philosophical roots. Socrates himself affirmed the crucial role of somatic care, and "took care to exercise his body and kept it in good condition" by regular dance training and simple living. "The body," he declared, "is valuable for all human activities, and in all its uses it is very important that it should be as fit as possible. Even in the act of thinking, which is supposed to require least assistance from the body, everyone knows that serious mistakes often happen through physical ill-health."[11]

Socrates was far from heterodox here. Many ancient Greek philosophers likewise advocated somatic training for the pursuit of wisdom and virtue. Aristippus, founder of the Cyrenaic school, insisted that "bodily training contributes to the acquisition of virtue," since fit bodies provide sharper perceptions and more discipline and versatility for adapting oneself in thought, attitude, and action. Zeno, founder of Stoicism, likewise urged regular bodily exercise, claiming that "proper care of health and one's organs of sense" are "unconditional duties." Cynicism's founder was even more outspoken in advocating bodily training as essential for the sensory knowledge and discipline that wisdom and the good life demanded. Practicing the somatic discipline he preached, Diogenes experimented with a variety of body practices to test and toughen himself: from eating raw food and walking barefoot in the snow to masturbating in public and accepting the blows of drunken revelers.[12]

Recognition of somatic training as an essential means toward philosophical enlightenment lies at the heart of Asian practices of Hatha yoga, Zen meditation, and T'ai chi ch'uan. As Japanese philosopher Yuasa Yusuo insists, the concept of "personal cultivation," or *shugyo*, is presupposed in Eastern thought as "the philosophical foundation." Such *shugyo* training has an essential bodily component, since "true knowledge cannot be obtained simply by means of theoretical thinking," but only "through 'bodily recognition or realization' (*tainin* or *taitoku*)."[13] Like these ancient Asian practices, contemporary Western body disciplines, such as the Alexander Technique, the Feldenkrais Method, and Bioenergetics, seek to improve the acuity, health, and control of our senses by cultivating heightened attention to and mastery of their somatic functioning, while also freeing us from bodily habits and defects that impair sensory performance.[14] From this somaesthetic perspective, knowledge of the world is improved not by denying our bodily senses but by perfecting them.

(2) If self-knowledge (rather than mere knowledge of worldly facts) is philosophy's prime cognitive aim, then knowledge of one's bodily dimension must not be ignored. Concerned not simply with the body's external form or *representation* but also with its lived *experience*, somaesthetics works at improving awareness of our bodily states and feelings, thus providing greater insight into both our passing moods and lasting attitudes. It can, therefore, reveal and improve somatic malfunctions that normally go undetected even though they impair our well-being and performance.

Consider two examples. We rarely notice our breathing, but its rhythm and depth provide rapid, reliable evidence of our emotional state. Consciousness of breathing can therefore make us aware that we are angry, tense, or anxious when we might otherwise remain unaware of these feelings and thus vulnerable to their misdirection. Similarly, a chronic muscular contraction that not only constrains movement but results in tension and pain may nonetheless go unnoticed because it has become habitual. As unnoticed, this chronic contraction cannot be relieved, nor can its resultant disability and discomfort. Yet, once such somatic functioning is brought to clear attention, there is a chance to modify it and avoid its unhealthy consequences, which include not only pain but a dulling of the senses, a diminution of aesthetic sensitivity and pleasure.

(3) A third central aim of philosophy is virtue and right action, for which we need knowledge and self-knowledge, but also effective will. Since action is only achieved through the body, our power of volition – the ability to act as we will to act – depends on somatic efficacy. Through somaesthetics' exploration and discipline of our bodily experience, we can gain a practical, "hands-on" grasp of the actual workings of effective volition – a better mastery of the will's concrete application in behavior. Knowing and desiring the right action will not avail if we cannot will our bodies to perform it; and our surprising inability to perform the most simple bodily tasks is matched only by our astounding blindness to this inability, these failures resulting from inadequate somaesthetic awareness.

Just think of the struggling golfer who tries to keep his head down and his eyes on the ball and who is completely convinced that he is doing so, even though he, in fact, miserably fails. His conscious will is unsuccessful because deeply ingrained somatic habits override it; and he does not even notice this failure because his habitual sense perception is so inadequate and distorted that it feels as if the action intended is indeed performed as willed. In too much of our action, we are like the "head-lifting" golfer whose will, however strong, still remains impotent, since it lacks the somatic sensibility – the corporeal *aisthesis* – to make it effective. Such somatic misperception and weakening of the will stunts our efforts at virtue; hence, virtue itself demands somatic self-perfection. Today's proponents of such reasoning are body therapists outside the current bounds of legitimized philosophy, but their argument has ancient philosophical credentials. Diogenes the Cynic was not alone in employing it to advocate rigorous body training as "that whereby, with constant exercise, perceptions are formed such as secure freedom of movement for virtuous deeds."[15]

(4) Pursuit of virtue and self-mastery is traditionally integrated into ethics' quest for better living. If philosophy is concerned with the pursuit of happiness, then somaesthetics' concern with the body as the locus and medium of our pleasures clearly deserves more philosophical attention. Even the joys and stimulations of so-called pure thought are (for us embodied humans) influenced by somatic conditioning and require muscular contraction. They can therefore be intensified or better savored through improved somatic awareness and discipline. A very sad curiosity of recent philosophy is that so much inquiry has been devoted to the ontology and epistemology of pain, so little to its psychosomatic management, to its mastery and transformation into tranquillity or pleasure.[16]

(5) These four neglected points do not exhaust the ways that somatics is central to philosophy. Michel Foucault's seminal vision of the body as a docile, malleable site for inscribing social power reveals the crucial role somatics can play for political philosophy. It offers a way of understanding how complex hierarchies of power can be widely exercised and reproduced without any need to make them explicit in laws or to officially enforce them. Entire ideologies of domination can thus be covertly materialized and preserved by encoding them in somatic norms that, as bodily habits, typically get taken for granted and therefore escape critical consciousness. For example, the presumptions that "proper" women speak softly, stay slim, eat dainty foods, sit with their legs close together, and assume the passive role or lower position in (heterosexual) copulation all function as embodied norms that sustain women's social disempowerment while granting them full official liberty. However, if oppressive power relations can impose onerous identities that get encoded and sustained in our bodies, these oppressive relations can themselves be challenged by alternative somatic practices. Fruitfully embraced by recent feminist and queer body theorists, this Foucauldian message has long been part of the program of body therapists like Wilhelm Reich and Moshe Feldenkrais.

(6) Beyond the essential epistemological, ethical, and socio-political issues already mentioned, the body plays a crucial role in ontology. Nietzsche and Merleau-Ponty show its ontological centrality as the focal point from

which our world and reciprocally ourselves are constructively projected, while analytic philosophy examines the body as a criterion for personal identity and as the ontological ground (through its central nervous system) for explaining mental states.[17]

(7) Finally, outside the legitimized realm of academic philosophy, somatic therapists like Reich, F. M. Alexander, and Feldenkrais affirm deep reciprocal influences between one's body and one's psychological development. Somatic malfunctioning is explained as both a product and a reinforcing cause of personality problems, which themselves may require body work for their proper remedy. Similar claims are made by yogis and Zen masters, but also by bodybuilders and martial arts practitioners. In these diverse disciplines, somatic training forms the heart of ethics' care of the self, a prerequisite to mental well-being and psychological self-mastery.

These seven points may remind us that there is already an abundance of discourse on the body in contemporary theory. But such body talk tends to lack two important features. First, it needs a structuring overview or architectonic to integrate its very different, seemingly incommensurable, discourses into a more productively systematic field. It would be useful to have a comprehensive framework that could connect the discourse of biopolitics with the therapies of Bioenergetics and might even link analytic philosophy's ontological doctrines of psychosomatic supervenience to bodybuilding's principles of supersets.[18] The second thing lacking in most current philosophical body talk is a clear pragmatic orientation – something that the individual can directly translate into a discipline of improved somatic practice. Both of these deficiencies can be remedied by the proposed field of somaesthetics, a discipline of theory and practice.

IV

Somaesthetics has three fundamental dimensions.

(1) *Analytic somaesthetics* describes the basic nature of bodily perceptions and practices and their function in our knowledge and construction of reality. This theoretical dimension involves traditional ontological and epistemological issues of the body but also includes the sort of sociopolitical inquiries Foucault and Pierre Bourdieu have made central: how the

body is both shaped by power and employed as an instrument to maintain it, how bodily norms of health, skill, and beauty, and even the most basic categories of sex and gender, are constructed to reflect and sustain social forces.[19]

Foucault's approach to these somatic issues was typically *genealogical*, portraying the historical emergence of various body doctrines, norms, and practices. Bourdieu's work extends this descriptive approach with a sociologically detailed synchronic analysis of the social constitution and deployment of body norms, which can be further complemented by comparative analyses that contrast the somatic views and practices of two or more synchronic cultures. The value of such historical-social analysis does not preclude a place for somaesthetic analytics of a more universalist bent, like the kind found in Merleau-Ponty and in more traditional ontological theorizing about the mind–body relationship that has issued in such doctrines as: dualism, epiphenomenalism, eliminative materialism, functionalism, emergentism, and their respective subvarieties.

(2) In contrast to analytic somaesthetics, whose logic (whether genealogical or ontological) is descriptive, *pragmatic somaesthetics* has a distinctly normative, prescriptive character – by proposing specific methods of somatic improvement and engaging in their comparative critique. Since the viability of any proposed method will depend on certain facts about the body (whether ontological, physiological, or social), this pragmatic dimension will always presuppose the analytic dimension. But it transcends mere analysis not simply by evaluating the facts that analysis describes, but by proposing various methods to improve certain facts by remaking the body and society.

Over the long course of human history, a vast variety of pragmatic disciplines have been recommended to improve our experience and use of the body: diverse diets, body piercing and scarification, forms of dance and martial arts, yoga, massage, aerobics, bodybuilding, various erotic arts (including consensual sadomasochism), and such modern psychosomatic therapies as the Alexander Technique, the Feldenkrais Method, Bioenergetics, Rolfing, etc. These diverse methodologies of practice can be roughly classified in terms of *representational* and *experiential* forms. Representational somaesthetics emphasizes the body's external appearance, while experiential disciplines prefer to focus on the aesthetic quality of its "inner" experience. Such experiential methods aim to make us "feel better" in both senses of this ambiguous phrase (which reflects the ambiguity of the very notion of aesthetics): to make the quality of our experience more satisfyingly rich, but also to make our awareness of somatic experience more acute and perceptive. Cosmetic practices (from make-up and hair-styling to plastic surgery) exemplify the representational side of somaes-thetics, while practices like yoga, *zazen* meditation, or Feldenkrais's "Awareness Through Movement" are paradigmatic of the experiential mode in its senses of both heightened quality and perceptual acuity.[20]

Some popular body practices (like aerobics) do not fall exclusively into either category. But the representational/experiential distinction remains useful, particularly for refuting certain arguments that would condemn somaesthetics as intrinsically superficial and devoid of the spiritual. Hork-heimer and Adorno's famous critique of somatics provides a good example of such arguments. Any attempt "to bring about a renaissance of the body" must fail, they claim, because it implicitly reinforces our culture's "distinc-tion . . . between the body and the spirit." As an object of care, the body will be representationally exteriorized as a mere physical thing ("the dead thing, the '*corpus*' ") in contrast to the inner living spirit.[21] Attention to the body is thus always *alienated* attention to an external representation outside one's spiritual self. Moreover, as external representation, it is inescapably dominated and deployed by society's corrupt masters of the image – adver-tising and propaganda.

> The idolizing of the vital phenomena from the "blond beast" to the South Sea islanders inevitably leads to the "sarong film" and the advertising post-ers for vitamin pills and skin creams which simply stand for the immanent aim of publicity: the new, great, beautiful, and noble type of man – the Führer and his storm troopers.[22]

Enthusiasts of bodily beauty and bodily training are not merely superfi-cial; they are more sinisterly linked to fascist exterminators, who treat the human body as a mere "physical substance,"[23] a malleable mechanical tool whose parts must be shaped and sharpened to make it more effectively serve whatever power controls it. By such Nazi logic, if bodies are no longer in good repair, they should be melted down into soap or converted into some other useful thing, like a lamp shade.

> Those who extolled the body above all else, the gymnasts and scouts, always had the closest affinity with killing. . . . They see the body as a moving mech-anism, with joints as its components and flesh to cushion the skeleton. They

use the body and its parts as though they were already separated from it. . . . They measure others, without realizing it, with the gaze of a coffin maker [and so call them] tall, short, fat or heavy. . . . Language keeps pace with them. It has transformed a walk into motion and a meal into calories.[24]

Formulated more than fifty years ago, Horkheimer and Adorno's critique remains a powerful summary of today's major indictments against aesthetics of the body. By promoting seductive images of bodily beauty and excellence, somaesthetics stands accused as a tool of capitalist advertising and political repression. It alienates, reifies, and fragments the body, treating it as an external means and mechanism that is anatomized into separate areas of intensive labor for ostentatious, measurable results and the sale of countless commodities marketed to achieve them. Hence we find our preoccupation with body measurements and with specialized "fitness" classes devoted to "abs," thighs, butts, and so forth; hence the billion-dollar cosmetics industry with its specialized products for different body parts. A somatic aesthetics, the argument continues, must therefore undermine individuality and freedom by urging conformity to standardized bodily measures and models as optimally instrumental or attractive. These models, moreover, reflect and reinforce oppressive social hierarchies (as, for example, the North American somatic ideal of tall, lean, blond, blue-eyed looks obviously serves the privilege of its dominant ethnic groups).

Potent as such indictments may be, they all depend on construing somaesthetics as a theory that reduces the body to an external object – a mechanical instrument of atomized parts, measurable surfaces, and standardized norms of beauty. They ignore the body's subject-role as the living locus of beautiful, personal experience. But somaesthetics, in its *experiential* dimension, clearly refuses to exteriorize the body as an alienated thing distinct from the active spirit of human experience. Nor does it necessarily impose a fixed set of standardized norms of external measurement (e.g., optimal pulse) to assess good somaesthetic experience.[25]

The blindness of culture critics to the somatics of experience is understandable and still widespread. For the somatics of representation remains far more dominant in our culture, a culture largely built on the division of body from spirit, and economically driven by the capitalism of conspicuous consumption that is fueled by the marketing of body images. But precisely for this reason, the field of somaesthetics, with its essential experiential dimension, needs more careful, reconstructive attention from philosophers.

The representational/experiential distinction is thus useful in defending somaesthetics from charges that neglect its interior, experienced depth. But the distinction must not be taken as rigidly *exclusive*. For there is an inevitable complementarity of representations and experience, of outer and inner. As commercial advertising rightly reminds us, how we look influences how we feel; but also vice versa. Practices such as dieting or body-building that are initially pursued for purposes of attractive representation often end up generating special feelings that are then sought for their own sake. The dieter becomes an anorexic craving the inner feel of hunger; the bodybuilder becomes an addict of the experiential surge of "the pump."

Conversely, somatic methods aimed at inner experience often employ representational means as cues to effect the body posture necessary for inducing the desired experience: whether by consulting one's image in a mirror, focusing one's gaze on a body part like the tip of the nose or the navel, or simply visualizing a body form in one's imagination. But, by the same token, a representational practice like bodybuilding also utilizes acute awareness of experiential clues (e.g., of optimal fatigue, body alignment, and full muscle extension) to serve its sculptural ends of external form.

If the representational/experiential distinction is not logically exclusive, neither does it seem entirely exhaustive. A third category of *performative* somaesthetics might be introduced for disciplines devoted primarily to bodily strength or health; perhaps, for example, to disciplines like the martial arts, athletics, gymnastics, and weightlifting (which needs to be distinguished from bodybuilding). However, to the extent that such performance-oriented practices aim either at the external exhibition of one's strength and health or, alternatively, at one's inner feelings of those powers, we might assimilate them into either the dominantly representational or experiential mode.

Another useful way of classifying somaesthetic practices may be in terms of whether they are directed primarily at the individual practitioner herself or instead primarily at others. A masseuse or a surgeon, for example, typically works on others' bodies, but in doing T'ai chi chu'an or cross-country training, one is working more on one's own body. Clearly, the distinction between self-directed and other-directed somaesthetics cannot be rigid, since many practices belong to both. As cosmetic practices of "make up" can be performed on oneself or on others, so in sexual practices one typically seeks both one's own experiential pleasures and one's partner's by maneuvering the bodies of both self and other. Moreover, even self-directed somaesthetic work often seems motivated by the desire to please others, while other-directed practices (like massage) can have its own self-oriented pleasures. But despite its vagueness (partly due to the interdependence of the very concepts of self and other), the distinction between self-directed and other-directed somaesthetics can at least be useful in combating the common prejudice that to focus attention on the body implies a selfish retreat from the social.

(3) However we classify the different methodologies of pragmatic somaesthetics, they need to be distinguished from their actual practice. I call this third dimension *practical somaesthetics*. It is not a matter of producing theories or texts, not even texts that offer pragmatic methods of somatic care. It is instead all about actually practicing such care through intelligently disciplined body work aimed at somatic self-improvement (whether in a representational, experiential, or performative mode). Concerned not with saying but with *doing*, this practical dimension is the most neglected by academic body philosophers, whose commitment to the discursive *logos* typically ends in textualizing the body. For practical somaesthetics, the less said the better, *if* this means the more work actually done. But, unfortunately, it usually means that actual body work simply gets left altogether out of philosophical practice. Unfortunately, in philosophy, what goes without saying typically goes without doing, so the concrete activity of body work must be emphatically named as the crucial practical dimension of somaesthetics, conceived as a comprehensive philosophical discipline concerned with self-knowledge and self-care.

V

Having explained what somaesthetics means by outlining its three main dimensions and its representational and experiential modes, I turn to issues raised by the rest of this chapter's title. If somaesthetics is introduced as "a disciplinary proposal," what sort of discipline could it be? How would it, or should it, relate to the traditional disciplines of aesthetics and philosophy?

The first question is more easily answered. In proposing somaesthetics as a discipline, I deliberately play on discipline's double meaning: as *a branch of learning or instruction* and as *a corporal form of training or exercise*. Clearly, the analytic dimension of somaesthetics could contain systematic structures of knowledge, for example, historical and anthropological studies of body norms, ideals, and practices, or psychological and ontological theories of mind-body relations, etc. These various forms of knowledge, which can illuminate the body's use as a site of beauty, are typically lodged on very different and often non-intersecting disciplinary branches. Part of the point of proposing somaesthetics as a discipline is to constitute a disciplinary framework that structurally links and can fruitfully unify the many body-related studies that are presently pursued in unconnected inquiries and seemingly incommensurable disciplinary forms.

The same argument can be made with respect to what I call pragmatic somaesthetics. From diet books to yoga manuals, from "make-over" and exercise videos to handbooks of bodybuilding and guides to psychosomatic therapies, we find a confusingly vast array of theories for improving the use, health, and experience of our bodies. Linking them together under the disciplinary rubric of somaesthetics can help us bring a more productive order to this confusing profusion by encouraging the search for basic common principles and differentiating criteria in terms of which these diverse practices can be classified and related. In contrast, the kind of activity I identify as *practical somaesthetics* captures the second sense of disciplinarity – its pursuit as not mere theory but actual corporal training or practice.

Where, then, can this threefold, double-jointed discipline of somaesthetics find a place in the wider disciplinary matrix of knowledge? Could it find a comfortable nest in an already established branch of learning or must it struggle to form its own special limb to climb out on? Its name implies that somaesthetics might best be nested as a subdiscipline within the already well-established discipline of aesthetics, which, in turn, would be expanded and somewhat transformed by the inclusion of somaesthetics.

To make this option more convincing, I began by showing how somaesthetics, though omitted from Baumgarten's founding program of modern aesthetics, seems necessary for its full success. In any case, long before Baumgarten's aesthetics, the appreciation of bodily beauty and sensory acuity was central to the concerns we now call aesthetic, not only among the Greeks and Romans but also in Asian philosophical traditions.[26] This attitude still survives in Western modernity, though it has been largely eclipsed by our dominant idealist aesthetic tradition. Consider David Hume (a contemporary of Baumgarten) and Friedrich Nietzsche. With his normative notion of "the perfection of every sense," Hume's insistence on practice as a method for sharpening the sensory appreciation required by good critics points surely in the direction of somaesthetics. So does Nietzsche's celebration of the body with his advocacy of "an ever-greater spiritualization and multiplication of the senses" to realize the body's aesthetic potential for life-enhancing value.[27] Such examples also show that, given the multiplicity of the body's aesthetic uses and pleasures, there is no reason to exclude our tiny eye muscles or invisible taste buds from the domain of somaesthetic exercise, which must not be confined to the brute image of building bulk for bulging biceps.

Somaesthetics, then, seems easiest to construe as a subdiscipline of aesthetics, a counterpart of already established subdisciplines, such as "musical aesthetics," "visual aesthetics," or "environmental aesthetics," though one more centered on the body. But this idea could raise two objections. First, while the other subdisciplines seem defined by a specific artistic genre or a special category of aesthetic objects (e.g., natural and constructed environments), somaesthetics seems to cut across the whole range of aesthetic genres. This is because it treats the body not only as an *object* of aesthetic value and creation, but also as a crucial sensory *medium* for enhancing our dealings with all other aesthetic objects and also with matters not standardly aesthetic. We can easily see, for example, how somaesthetics' improvement of sensory acuity, muscular movement, and experiential awareness could fruitfully contribute to the understanding and practice of traditional arts like music, painting, and dance (a somaesthetic art par excellence), and how it could also enhance our appreciation of the natural and constructed environments that we navigate and inhabit. Moreover, by addressing enterprises not typically taken as aesthetic – not only martial arts, sports, meditative practices, and psychosomatic therapies, but the core philosophical tasks of self-knowledge and self-mastery, somaesthetics threatens to burst the bounds of a narrowly aesthetic discipline.

There is a blunt reply to this first objection: So much the worse for narrow definitions of aesthetics! As an open, essentially contested concept, aesthetics can absorb new topics and practices. Moreover, some of these "imported" topics are not really new to the field of aesthetics. Far older and grander than the recent interest in sports aesthetics, there looms an illustrious tradition of exploring aesthetics as a key to ethics and the art of living, a tradition powerfully exemplified in Schiller's *Letters on the Aesthetic Education of Man* and in the writings of Kierkegaard, Nietzsche, and the later Foucault.[28]

A second objection to subsuming somaesthetics as a branch of aesthetics might go as follows: If aesthetics is a subdiscipline of philosophy and somaesthetics purports to be a subdiscipline of aesthetics, then by the transitivity of subsumption, somaesthetics should also be a subdiscipline (or a sub-subdiscipline) of philosophy. But, though it clearly involves philosophy, somaesthetics seems to include too much other stuff to be contained as a philosophical subdiscipline. It claims to address not only anthropological, sociological, and historical research on the body, but also physiological and psychological research. Moreover, through its practical dimension, somaesthetics even engages in bodily practices that seem foreign, if not inimical, to the tradition of philosophy: martial arts, fashion, cosmetics, bodybuilding, dieting, etc. If philosophy is defined as theory, then does not somaesthetics' crucial practical dimension bar its entry as a philosophical subdiscipline?

To these objections I see two possible responses. One is to argue for a wider conception of philosophy. Such a conception not only admits the valuable role of historical, anthropological, sociological, and other empirical science for philosophical research but further insists on philosophy as more than mere theory, recalling the ancient idea of philosophy as an embodied practice, a way of life. The ideal of philosophy as informed by all the pertinent sciences and directed toward the improved conduct of life may seem alien to our academic training and professional self-image as specialists of conceptual analysis. Its full achievement may be beyond our powers, and it surely seems impossible to realize through ordinary classroom instruction. Just imagine what would happen to the philosophy professor who asked his seminar in somaesthetics to study Wilhelm Reich's body therapy by lying down in class and practicing the Reichian orgasm reflex. Would asking students to lift weights or perform yoga postures and breathing exercises be much easier? Even asking them to dance or sing or keep a special diet would seem a shock to today's philosophical posture of pure theory. But ancient philosophical schools, like later religious orders (and military academies), have often been very different in this regard, applying the institutional discipline of instructing disciples in a far more holistic sense. For all the difficulties it presents for conventional academia, this ideal remains a venerable and appealing model of philosophy, one into which somaesthetics could nicely fit as a subdiscipline.[29]

There is, of course, another way to admit the very wide range of somaesthetic inquiry and also embrace its concrete performance of bodily practice, while still keeping this discipline as a subdiscipline of aesthetics. We can simply regard aesthetics as much more than a subdiscipline of philosophy. Such a broad conception of aesthetics that transcends standard philosophy by more closely engaging the human and natural sciences was in fact advocated by some influential twentieth-century theorists, like Max Dessoir and Thomas Munro. Arguing against the limits of traditional philosophy of art and beauty, they sought to create aesthetics as an interdisciplinary field of knowledge that would be independent of philosophy, a discipline with its own special journals and "distinct departments."[30] By further broadening this idea, we could construe aesthetics as a discipline that, besides its theoretical pursuits, also involves instruction in the production, performance, and criticism of art and other aesthetic practices. Though foreign to most philosophy departments, this broad conception of aesthetic discipline is familiarly at work in other academies – of music, art, dance, and cooking.

Of these two options for nesting somaesthetics, which should be favored? As a philosopher keen to promote broader and more practical conceptions of his discipline, I prefer to absorb the swell of somaesthetics within the philosophical fold, thus enhancing the discipline of philosophy. I also worry whether aesthetics as an autonomous discipline independent of philosophy is institutionally sturdy enough to bear the challenge of nurturing somaesthetics. But, I am happy to leave these precise questions of affiliation provisionally open, for at least three reasons. As a new, still schematic proposal, somaesthetics should not yet let its disciplinary bonds be tied too tightly. It should be allowed enough freedom to grow in the directions (and under the larger disciplines) that prove most fruitful for its progress. Second, in order to develop, somaesthetics must be the collaborative work of a community of thinkers and practitioners, not the pronouncement of an individual voice. That community, not this individual, will best define its precise disciplinary home and limits. The third reason why I readily leave open such detailed questions of affiliation and demarcation is that there are far more pressing, and more interesting, issues to pursue in the field of somaesthetics than the drawing of its precise boundaries.

VI

Some of these important issues can be introduced by contrasting two twentieth-century philosophers, John Dewey and Michel Foucault, who are exemplary for working in all three dimensions of somaesthetics. Prompted by Darwin and James, Dewey developed a naturalist "emergent" account of what he called "body-mind." But this ontological theory was likewise guided by his study of the pragmatic "body-mind" methodology of F. M. Alexander, to which Dewey devoted several celebratory essays. And Dewey's commitment to body-mind unity was perhaps most inspired by his concrete practical exercises in the Alexander Technique, in which he trained himself for more than twenty years and to which (at the age of almost ninety) he attributed his good health and longevity.[31]

Foucault's avid pursuit of somaesthetics in all its three major branches is no less remarkable than Dewey's, though radically different. The analytic genealogist, who showed how "docile bodies" were systematically shaped by seemingly innocent body-disciplines in order to advance certain socio-political agendas, emerges also as the pragmatic methodologist proposing alternative body practices to overcome the repressive ideologies entrenched in our docile bodies. Foremost among these alternatives were practices of consensual, gay sadomasochism, whose experiences, he argued, challenged not only the hierarchy of the head but the privileging of genital sexuality, which, in turn, privileged heterosexuality. Foucault also repeatedly advocated strong "drugs which can produce very intense pleasures," insisting that they "must become a part of our culture."[32] Bravely practicing the somaesthetics he preached, Foucault tested his favored methodologies by experimenting on his own flesh and with other live bodies.

In *Practicing Philosophy*, I probe the limits of Foucault's choices while affirming somaesthetic alternatives that he neglects and I prefer to practice.[33] But one can hardly deny the value of drugs and consensual sadomasochism for the precise projects of somaesthetics that Foucault was personally most concerned with, projects of radical innovation, gay liberation, and his own problematic quest for pleasure. Indeed, "different strokes for different folks" affirms a vernacular wisdom apt for more than S/M's disciples. To some extent, must not this pluralism be a maxim not only for somaesthetics but for the whole idea of philosophy as a way of life, a disciplined creative practice whose greatest artwork is our reconstructed self? If Emerson and Nietzsche are right that each self is essentially unique (the unrepeatable product of myriad contingencies), should not each self require its own special philosophy and body practice?[34] "Every man," says Thoreau, "is the builder of a temple, called his body, to the god he worships, after a style purely his own, nor can he get off by hammering marble instead. We are all sculptors and painters, and our material is our own flesh and blood and bones. Any nobleness begins to refine a man's features, any meanness or sensuality to imbrute them."[35] But, on the other hand, don't our embodied selves share significant commonalities of biological make-up and societal conditioning that would allow some interesting generalizations about the values and risks of different somatic methods? How could philosophy or science (or even practical life) be possible without such generalization?

Somaesthetics must reconcile the claims of bodily difference and free-dom of taste with the contrasting claims of objective bodily norms and bodily needs that straddle the much contested nature/culture distinction. If it can appeal to no fixed definition of bodily beauty or pleasure, somaes-thetics must, nonetheless, grapple with justifying judgments that certain somatic forms, functions, and experience can be better or worse than oth-ers. These are thorny problems, but they should not strike us aestheticians as very peculiar, for they essentially embody the familiar theoretical ten-sions between aesthetic subjectivity and normative standards, between in-dividual taste and *sensus communis*, that form the heart of modern aesthetics since Hume and Kant. Here again, somaesthetics remains firmly rooted in the problematics of traditional aesthetic theory.

But there are also more practical (and more existentially pressing) ques-tions of somaesthetics that deserve greater attention. In the postmodern pluralist confusion of our culture, we are steeped in the ideology of life-styles and saturated with a bewildering variety to choose from. How, then, should we shape and care for our embodied selves? With hallucinogenic drugs or vegetarian diet, with shaved heads or dreadlocks, with prick rings and leather masks or with steroids and silicone implants, through piercing or aerobics or through yogic exercises of *pranayama*? Are there useful cri-teria for choosing between the very different somaesthetic programs on offer? Are there any good ways of combining them? Why do those philo-sophically rich and critically reflective somaesthetic disciplines that are central to Asian philosophy remain so foreign to our Western philosophical work?

These questions suggest only a minute fraction of the issues pointedly collected and posed by somaesthetics as a disciplinary proposal. If such issues still lack systematic treatment but are implied in Baumgarten's origi-nal "mission statement" of aesthetics; if they are likewise implied by the classic idea of philosophy as an embodied way of life, then somaesthetics deserves to be named and pursued as a branch of philosophical inquiry. The precise place it will eventually find in the wider field of philosophy is not something we can guarantee at its initial proposal, for such issues de-pend not only on the dominant directions that future somaesthetic inquir-ies will take, but also on the changing, essentially contested field of philosophy itself, with its equally changing and contested subdisciplines.

Initially, however, somaesthetics seems best situated within an expanded discipline of aesthetics. Such an enlarged aesthetics would give more sys-tematic attention to the body's crucial roles in aesthetic perception and experience, including the aesthetic dimensions of body therapies, sports, martial arts, cosmetics, etc., that remain marginalized in academic aesthetic theory. But to incorporate somaesthetics' practical dimension, the field of aesthetics must also expand its notion of disciplinary attention to actual, hands-on training in specific body practices that aim at somaesthetic improvement. Inclusion of such body work may make aesthetics more difficult to teach or practice in the standard university classroom, but it certainly could make the field more exciting and absorbing, as it comes to engage more of our embodied selves.

Notes

Introduction to the Second Edition

1   The translations include French, German, Finnish, Polish, Portuguese, and Japanese; with Korean, Slovak, and Hungarian versions in preparation. Outside of philosophy, most criticism of the book came from sociology, anthropology, literary and cultural studies, and art and music journalism.

2   See, for example, Richard Shusterman, "Note sur *L'art à l'état vif*," *Etudes Littéraires* 25 (1992), 215–8 "Sur *L'art à l'état vif*," *Gradhiva* 12 (1992), 66–74; "Too Legit to Quit?: Popular Art and Legitimation," *Jerusalem Philosophical Quarterly* 42 (1993), 215–24; "Art in a Box," in M. Rollins (ed.), *Danto and His Critics* (Oxford: Blackwell, 1993), 161–74; "Die Sorge um den Korper in der Heutigen Kultur," in A. Kuhlmann (ed.), *Philosophische Ansichten der Kultur der Moderne* (Frankfurt: Fischer, 1994), 241–77; "L'expérience comme forme de l'art," *Revue d'esthétique* 25 (1994), 179–86; "Breaking out of the White Cube," in Suzi Gablik (ed.), *Conversations Before the End of Time* (London: Thames and Hudson, 1995), 247–65; "Soma und Medien," *Kunstforum International* 132 (1996), 210–5; "Style et styles de vie," *Littérature* 105 (1997), 102–9; "A House Divided," *Documenta X – the Book* (Kassel: Cantz, 1997), 650–2; "The Self As a Work of Art," *The Nation*, 30 June 1997, 25–8; "Interpretation, Pleasure and Value in Aesthetic Experience," *Journal of Aesthetics and Art Criticism* 56 (1998), 51–3; "Transforming Art and Philosophy," in M. Hannula (ed.), *Stopping the Process? Contemporary Views on Art and Exhibitions* (Helsinki: Nordic Institute for Contemporary Art, 1998), 35–44; "Provakation und Erinnerung," *Deutsche Zeitschrift für Philosophie* 47 (1999), 127–37. But also see my publications cited more specifically in the following notes.

3   I have, however, corrected the few misprints in the first edition and revised some of the last paragraph of chapter 9 to improve the transition to the new chapter which follows.

4 See Richard Shusterman, *Practicing Philosophy: Pragmatism and the Philosophical Life* (New York: Routledge, 1997), chs. 1–4.

5 See Richard Shusterman, "The End of Aesthetic Experience," *Journal of Aesthetics and Art Criticism* 55 (1997), 29–41; "Popular Art and Education," *Studies in Philosophy and Education* 13 (1995), 203–12; "Légitimer la légitimation de l'art populaire," *Politix* 24 (1993), 153–67; and *Practicing Philosophy*, ch. 6.

6 See, for example, Richard Shusterman, "Rap Remix: Pragmatism, Postmodernism, and Other Issues in the House," *Critical Inquiry* 22 (1995), 150–8; *Practicing Philosophy*, ch. 5, and "Pragmatism, Art and Violence: The Case of Rap," in T. Yamamoto (ed.), *Philosophical Designs for a Socio-Cultural Transformation* (New York: Rowman and Littlefield, 1998), 667–774.

7 See Richard Shusterman, "Moving Truth: Affect and Authenticity in Country Musicals," *Journal of Aesthetics and Art Criticism* 57 (1999), 221–33.

8 I provide a detailed case for Dewey's aesthetic affinities (and likely debt) to Emerson and to Alain Locke in, respectively, "Emerson's Pragmatist Aesthetics," *Revue Internationale de Philosophie* 207 (1999), 87–99; and "Pragmatist Aesthetics: Roots and Radicalism," in Leonard Harris (ed.), *The Critical Pragmatism of Alain Locke* (New York: Rowman and Littlefield, 1999), 97–110.

9 In the following discussion, I respond to the most pervasive and interesting arguments against the views expressed in *Pragmatist Aesthetics*. These arguments are culled chiefly from the following useful critical accounts (but also from a long critical dialogue with Pierre Bourdieu, in whose series the book appeared in French, as *L'art à l'état vif*, Paris: Minuit, 1992). See Daniel Soutif, "L'or du rap," *Libération*, 23 April 1992, 29; Rainer Rochlitz, "Esthétiques Hédonistes," *Critique* 540 (May 1992), 353–73; Jean-Pierre Cometti, "Note de lecture sur *L'art à l'état vif*," *Les Cahiers du Musée National d'Art Moderne* 40 (1992), 119–21; Louis Pinto, "Note de lecture sur *L'art à l'état vif*," *Politix* 20 (1992), 169–74; Tom Holert, "Der Philosoph als Fan," *Texte zur Kunst* (June 1992), 149–51; Jerrold Levinson, "Review of *Pragmatist Aesthetics*," *Mind* 102 (1993), 682–6; Paul Mattick, "Review of *Pragmatist Aesthetics*," *Transactions of the Charles S. Peirce Society* 29 (1993), 480–8; Tim Brennan, "Off the Gangsta Tip: A Rap Appreciation, or Forgetting About Los Angeles," *Critical Inquiry* 20 (1994), 663–93; William Earle, "Review of *Pragmatist Aesthetics*," *Poetics Today* 16 (1995), 375–82; Simon Frith, *Performing Rites: On the Value of Popular Music* (Cambridge: Harvard University Press, 1996), ch.1; Alexander Nehamas, "Richard Shusterman on Pleasure and Aesthetic Experience," *Journal of Aesthetics and Art Criticism* 56 (1998), 49–51; Wolfgang Welsch, "Rettung durch Halbierung? Zu Richard Shustermans Rehabilitierung ästhetischer Erfahrung," *Deutsche Zeitschrift für Philosophie* 47 (1999), 111–26; Theodore Gracyk, "Valuing and Evaluating Popular Music," *Journal of Aesthetics and Art Criticism* 57 (1999), 205–20;

Charles Altieri, "Practical Sense – Impractical Objects: Why Neo-Pragmatism Cannot Sustain an Aesthetics," *REAL: Yearbook of Research in English and American Literature* 15 (1999), 113–36; Herbert Grabes, "The Renovation of Pragmatist Aesthetics," ibid., 15 (1999), 137–50. This volume also contains a response to Altieri's and Grabes's papers, where I explore in more detail the advantages (and practical limits) of pragmatism's pluralist stance: "The Uses of Pragmatism and its Logic of Pluralism," ibid., 151–60.

10   For more detailed argument on this point, see "Popular Art and Education."

11   T. S. Eliot, "The Frontiers of Poetry," in *Of Poetry and Poets* (London: Faber, 1957), 115. For a detailed account of Eliot's views on these matters of pleasure and aesthetic understanding, see my study, *T. S. Eliot and the Philosophy of Literary Criticism* (New York: Columbia University Press, 1988), ch. 6.

Chapter 1   Placing Pragmatism

1   I discuss Moore's aesthetics and its relation to subsequent analytic philosophy of art in "Analysing Analytic Aesthetics," in Richard Shusterman (ed.), *Analytic Aesthetics* (Oxford: Blackwell, 1989), 1–19. A concise overview of Wittgenstein's writings and influence in aesthetics can be found in my "Wittgenstein and Critical Reasoning," *Philosophy and Phenomenological Research* 47 (1986), 91–110. See also Richard Eldridge, "Problems and Prospects of Wittgensteinian Aesthetics," *Journal of Aesthetics and Art Criticism* 45 (1987), 251–61.

2   I shall be using the new scholarly edition published as vol. 10 of the *Late Works of John Dewey* (Carbondale: Southern Illinois University Press, 1987). Page references will appear parenthetically with the abbreviation *AE*.

3   Its impact extended beyond philosophy to such artists as Robert Motherwell, Thomas Hart Benton, and Jackson Pollock. See Stewart Beuttner, "Dewey and the Visual Arts," *Journal of Aesthetics and Art Criticism* 33 (1975), 383–91.

4   See Richard Rorty, *Philosophy and the Mirror of Nature* (Princeton: Princeton University Press, 1979), 130–69, and "Dewey's Metaphysics," in *Consequences of Pragmatism* (Minneapolis: University of Minnesota Press, 1982), 72–89. Nicholas Wolterstorff makes a good case for analytic philosophy of art as a species of neo-Kantianism but does not consider pragmatist aesthetics. See N. Wolterstorff, "Philosophy of Art after Analysis and Romanticism," in Shusterman (ed.), *Analytic Aesthetics*, 32–58.

5   See, for example, Stephen Pepper's critique of its Hegelian organicism in "Some Questions on Dewey's Aesthetics," in P. A. Schilpp, *The Philosophy of John Dewey* (La Salle, Ill.: Open Court, 1989), 369–89. For a contemporary defense of Dewey with respect to this critique, see Thomas Alexander, *John*

Dewey's Theory of Art, Experience, and Nature: The Horizons of Feeling (Albany: SUNY Press, 1987), 1–13.

6　See, for example, W. B. Gallie, "The Function of Philosophical Aesthetics," in William Elton (ed.), *Aesthetics and Language* (Oxford: Blackwell, 1954), 13–35. The Elton volume contains many other criticisms of Croce. For a general account of analytic aesthetics' early development through opposition to Croceanism, see my "Analytic Aesthetics, Literary Theory, and Deconstruction," *Monist* 69 (1986), 22–38.

7　See Arnold Isenberg, "Analytical Philosophy and the Study of Art," *Journal of Aesthetics and Art Criticism* 46 (1987), 128.

8　G. E. Moore, *Principia Ethica* (Cambridge: Cambridge University Press, 1903; repr. 1959), 201.

9　See Margaret Macdonald, "Some Distinctive Features of Arguments Used in Criticism of the Arts," in Elton (ed.), *Aesthetics and Language,* 114. Sibley's paper first appeared in *Philosophical Review* 68 (1959), 421–50, and has been widely anthologized.

10　Immanuel Kant, *The Critique of Judgement,* trans. J. C. Meredith (Oxford: Oxford University Press, 1952), 116. The other citations in this paragraph are from 64, 65, 67, 212–13.

11　For Kant the aesthetic judgement is essentially characterized by disinterested attention to form, where disinterestedness presupposes freedom from "want" (*Critique of Judgement,* 49). But who, then, can afford to be disinterested? Who can take the time and trouble to peruse things with exclusive regard to their form and ignore their instrumentality in satisfying one's wants and needs? Obviously only those who have the ease, leisure, and means to do so, those whose essential wants and needs are most adequately satisfied – in short, the socio-economically and culturally privileged. Not only does taste in art require the right education, but even the aesthetic appreciation of nature turns out for Kant to be dependent on the right socio-cultural conditions and training. The sublime cannot be appreciated without a secure distance from the "terrifying" ravages of nature and without culture's "development of moral ideals." Hence, "culture is requisite for the judgement of the sublime (more than for that upon the beautiful)" (115–16). But even appreciation of beauty in nature "is not in fact common" or natural to the uncultured. "It is peculiar to those whose habits of thought are already trained to the good or else are eminently susceptible of such training" (160) and whose taste for form can disregard nature's emotional and sensual charms, which render a judgement of taste impure (65).

　　It is revealing to note that in introducing the notion of disinterestedness by distinguishing it from various "interested" reactions, Kant employs characters who clearly underscore the link of taste with socio-cultural privilege and distinction. Those who fail to adopt the disinterested aesthetic attitude to a palace are the "Iroquois *sachem* who said nothing in Paris pleased him more than the eating houses," "a *Rousseau*" who demonstrates concern for the underprivileged by protesting "against the vanity of the great who spend the sweat of the people on such superfluous things," and someone "on an uninhabited island" totally deprived of society and thus deprived of the opportunity to assert his social status to and over others through his judgement of taste (43). My arguments against Kant's naturalism are developed in much greater detail in "Of the Scandal of Taste: Social Privilege as Nature in the Aesthetic Theories of Hume and Kant," *Philosophical Forum* 20 (1989), 211–29.

12　See Peter Strawson, "Aesthetic Appraisal and Works of Art," in *Freedom and Resentment* (London: Methuen, 1974), 187, and Stuart Hampshire, "Logic and Appreciation," in Elton (ed.), *Aesthetics and Language*, 162, 164.

13　For him, "a philosophy of art is sterilized unless it makes us aware of the function of art in relation to other modes of experience" (*AE* 17).

14　The quotes from Nietzsche are from his *Birth of Tragedy* and *The Genealogy of Morals* (New York: Doubleday, 1956), 143, 240, 247. Foucault speaks of the "aesthetics of existence" in *The History of Sexuality*, vol. 2 (New York: Vintage, 1986), 89–93, and his view of aesthetic life will be discussed in ch. 9. Dewey's naturalism cannot be accused of ignoring how history's social structures crucially inform the body and its modes of pleasure. Such structures, for Dewey, belong to the environing nature which helps shape the individual organism interacting with it. Dewey's recognition of how social and historical factors shape our aesthetic perception, how "the institutional life of mankind" affects "our different senses" (*AE* 26–76), forms part of his socio-historical critique of the museum conception of art, which I discuss below. Far from any narrowly physicalist naturalism, Dewey insists, "Neither the savage nor the civilized man is what he is by native constitution but by the culture in which he participates" (*AE* 347).

15　See Maurice Merleau-Ponty, *Signs* (Evanston: Northwestern University Press, 1964), 70. Compare Dewey: Since "the movements of the individual body enter into all reshapings of material . . . something of the rhythm of vital natural expression . . . must go into carving, painting, and making statues, planning buildings, and writing stories" (*AE* 231–2). "Art is thus prefigured in the very processes of living" (*AE* 30).

16　John Dewey, *Experience and Nature* (La Salle, Ill: Open Court, 1929), 290; hereafter abbreviated *EN*.

17　In clear rejection of the Kantian differentiation of the aesthetic from the practical and cognitive, Dewey asserts: "The enemies of the aesthetic are neither the practical nor the intellectual. They are the humdrum; slackness of loose-ends; submission to conventions in practice and intellectual procedure" (*AE* 47).

18　For those interested in following Dewey's critique of these dualisms, see *AE* 26–8, 267, for body/mind; 34, 38, 109 for material/ideal; 40, 125, 161,

251–2, 263, for thought/feeling; 112–14, 123, 133, for form/substance; 152–5, 163, 190, 336, 341, for man/nature; 109, 252, 254, 274–5, 286, for self/world; 251, 281, 292, for subject/object; and 201–2 for means/ends.

19   The citations here are from John Passmore, "The Dreariness of Aesthetics," in Elton (ed.), *Aesthetics and Language,* 50, 55. This point is elaborated in my "Analytic Aesthetics, Literary Theory, and Deconstruction."

20   J. O. Urmson, "What Makes a Situation Aesthetic?", in F. J. Coleman (ed.), *Contemporary Studies in Aesthetics* (New York: McGraw-Hill, 1968), 359, 368.

21   I discuss the aesthetic visuality of the text in "Aesthetic Blindness to Textual Visuality," *Journal of Aesthetics and Art Criticism* 41 (1982), 87–96; "The Anomalous Nature of Literature," *British Journal of Aesthetics* 18 (1978), 317–29; and "Ingarden, Inscription, and Literary Ontology," *Journal of the British Society for Phenomenology* 18 (1987), 103–19.

22   Morris Weitz, "The Role of Theory in Aesthetics," *Journal of Aesthetics and Art Criticism* 16 (1955), 27–35; repr. in Coleman (ed.), *Contemporary Studies,* 90.

23   The non-evaluational orientation is sometimes quite explicit, as when Nelson Goodman complains that preoccupation with evaluation has caused "constriction and distortion of aesthetic inquiry" (*Languages of Art* (Oxford: Oxford University Press, 1969), 261–2).

24   T. W. Adorno, *Aesthetic Theory* (London: Routledge & Kegan Paul, 1984), 19, 460. Adorno's insistence on the entangled "dialectic of culture and barbarism" echoes Benjamin's famous remark that "there is no document of civilization which is not at the same time a document of barbarism." See T. W. Adorno, *Prisms* (Cambridge, Mass.: MIT Press, 1981), 34, and Walter Benjamin, *Illuminations: Essays and Reflections* (New York: Harcourt, Brace & World, 1968), 256.

25   Dewey is not recommending a narrowly political or moralistic art, which he, like Adorno, disfavors (*AE* 186, 194, 348–51). But what exactly does the importation of art and its aesthetic principle into the realm of ordinary living actually mean for Dewey? This is perhaps not sufficiently clear. Part of the story would be a more energetic and attentive cultivation of the diverse practical arts of living (which include the social, political, and technological arts), with greater emphasis on qualities of harmony, creativity, and imagination and with a better integration of means and ends, so that more of life's activities are pursued with immediate satisfaction rather than under the mere hope of remotely deferred and externally related enjoyment (*AE* 87). Another part might be restructuring our ethical, social, and political life through his aesthetic notion of unity, where "there is no sacrifice of the self-identity of the parts" in composing an integrated whole (*AE* 43), again an ideal advocated by Adorno. If such clarifications of the integration of art and ordinary living seem still too vague, my treatment of popular art and the aesthetic life (ch. 7–9) can be seen as an attempt to provide more concrete elaboration of this idea.

26 "The story of the severance and final sharp opposition [in the concept of art] of the useful and the fine is the history of that industrial development through which so much production has become a form of postponed living and so much of consumption a superimposed enjoyment of the fruits of the labor of others" (*AE* 34). To this painful rift between industrial production and aesthetic enjoyment, an expression of the conceptual gap between art and practical life, "No permanent solution is possible save in a radical social alteration, which affects the degree and kind of participation the worker has in the production and social disposition of the wares he produces" (*AE* 345).

27 See Moore, *Principia Ethica*, 187–8; M. C. Beardsley, *Aesthetics: Problems in the Philosophy of Criticism* (New York: Harcourt, Brace, 1958), 457–61; and Clive Bell, *Art* (New York: Capricorn, 1958), 73. Beardsley's isolating "fallacy" theories, co-authored with the New Critic William K. Wimsatt, formed the explicit ahistorical ideology of the New Criticism, which dominated the fifties and sixties, and whose critical practice in turn served as the model and justificatory base for analytic aesthetics.

28 See Arthur Danto, "The Artworld," *Journal of Philosophy* 61 (1964), 581.

29 See Arthur Danto, *The Philosophical Disenfranchisement of Art* (New York: Columbia University Press, 1986), 97–111, 204, and Roger Scruton, *The Aesthetic Understanding* (London: Methuen, 1983), 166–78.

30 See Pierre Bourdieu, *Distinction: A Social Critique of the Judgement of Taste* (Cambridge, Mass.: Harvard University Press, 1984).

31 G. W. F. Hegel, *Philosophy of Right*, trans. T. M. Knox (Oxford: Oxford University Press, 1952), 11.

32 For Dewey, art is a qualitative mode of experience rather than a substantive kind or compartmental category of experience. "Art is a quality that permeates an experience; it is not, save by a figure of speech, the experience itself" (*AE* 329). Dewey just as often speaks of art as "a quality of action" or "a quality of activity" (*AE* 218, 227, 233). But since action and activity are forms of experience, this involves no inconsistency in his theory.

33 Adorno, *Aesthetic Theory*, 263.

34 Ibid. 252, 253. Adorno's view that "the work of art is a mode of behaviour" (257) clearly parallels Dewey's definition of art as "a quality of action" or of experience. But Adorno is, nonetheless, much more favorable than Dewey to art's reification into objects. This is because high art's sacralized objects help sustain the compartmental conception of art and because, in sharp contrast to Dewey, he is keen on preserving this notion of art as a domain which remains separated from life and thus more effectively free to criticize life's impurities.

35 Ibid. 255–6.

36 Dewey argues that atomistic empiricism falsely confuses the results of its *analysis* of the given in experience with what is actually given in experience *as experienced*, such confusion being an example of "the intellectualist fallacy"

(*EN* 18–23). Like his fellow pragmatist James, Dewey thought we experienced whole things and their relations, not merely individual, independent sensations which were then related and synthesized into objects through some additional mental faculty.

37 The Deweyan distinction between mere experience and "*an* experience" clearly parallels the Diltheyan distinction between *Erfahrung* and *Erlebnis* common in continental heremeneutic theory, though Dewey does not refer to Dilthey in *Art as Experience*.

38 See George Dickie, "Beardsley's Phantom Aesthetic Experience," *Journal of Philosophy* 62 (1965), 129–36, which also criticizes Dewey for treating aesthetic experience as some idealistic "metaphysical" thing (134–5).

39 Danto, *Philosophical Disenfranchisement of Art*, xiv–xv, 13.

40 See John Dewey, *Reconstruction in Philosophy* (New York: Mentor, 1952), 32–3, and *EN*, 67–9, where the "preoccupation with direct enjoyment" through "feasting and festivities, ornamentation, dance," etc., is discussed approvingly as one of humanity's "most striking features." Moreover, as he adds in *AE*, "pleasures are not to be despised in a world full of pain" (23).

41 Goodman, an analytic aesthetician with strong pragmatist leanings, makes an excellent case for the pervasive cognitive dimension and value of aesthetic experience. But his case is marred by reducing aesthetic value to cognitive value, a reduction which reflects the philosopher's occupational prejudice for knowledge. See his *Languages of Art*, 259, where he speaks of the "subsumption of aesthetic under cognitive excellence." He confirms this view more recently in *Of Mind and Other Matters* (Cambridge, Mass.: Harvard University Press, 1984), 138, 148.

42 See W. K. Wimsatt, *The Verbal Icon* (Lexington: University of Kentucky Press, 1954).

43 M. C. Beardsley, *The Possibility of Criticism* (Detroit: Wayne State University Press, 1970), 16. For Beardsley's earlier emphasis on aesthetic experience as the metacritical foundation of critical evaluation, see his *Aesthetics*, 524–43.

44 See Goodman, *Languages of Art*, 120, 186, 209–10. For a more detailed criticism of Goodman's method of definition from a pragmatist perspective, see Richard Shusterman, *The Object of Literary Criticism* (Amsterdam: Rodopi, 1984) 130–9.

45 Dewey, *Reconstruction in Philosophy*, 101. Influential statements of poststructuralism's move from fixed "object-work" to changing textual activity can be found in Roland Barthes, "From Work to Text," in *Image, Music, Text* (New York: Hill and Wang, 1977), 155–64, and Jacques Derrida, *Of Grammatology* (Baltimore: Johns Hopkins University Press, 1976).

46 Dewey is more a philosopher of vision than of careful logical detail. His unnuanced remarks here about the work being always experienced differently and being identified with its experience not only raise the fear of subjectivism, but raise a real problem about the work's self-identity. This problem is

not at all resolved by his suggestion that identity of experience is something monotonous that aesthetically we should be glad to avoid. For the problem is a logical one of how we can speak of the same work providing different experiences without according it some functional self-identity through these different experiences that is not reducible to the art product. Though Dewey provides no clear answer to this question, he has the materials to do so; and I try to outline an answer in ch. 4.

47 See Victor Turner, *From Ritual to Theatre* (New York: Performing Arts Journal Press, 1982), 17–18.

Chapter 2   Art and Theory between Experience and Practice

1 On this point, see John Dewey, *Experience and Nature* (La Salle, Ill.: Open Court, 1929), 74–7, hereafter *EN*; and *Art as Experience* (Carbondale, Ill.: Southern Illinois University Press, 1987), 298, 331, hereafter *AE*. References to these two works will appear parenthetically in the body of the text. See also Arthur Danto, *The Philosophical Disenfranchisement of Art* (New York: Columbia University Press, 1986), 1–21.

2 Morris Weitz, "The Role of Theory in Aesthetics," *Journal of Aesthetics and Art Criticism* 16 (1955), 27–35. This influential paper has been widely anthologized. My page references are to its reprinting in F. J. Coleman (ed.), *Contemporary Studies in Aesthetics* (New York: McGraw-Hill, 1968), 84–94; citations from 90, 94.

3 Weitz hastily assumes that philosophy must eschew evaluative issues, since he presumes both the fact/value dichotomy and the view that philosophy is concerned only with mirroring truths or facts. Both presumptions are highly questionable. Some values are facts (certainly in the social and experiential domain); evaluative statements can be descriptively true and informative, while certain descriptions virtually entail evaluations (particularly with regard to negative judgements). The second presumption will be challenged below. Its quietistic philosophical ideal of perspicuously representing the status quo can be found even in a thinker as emancipated as Wittgenstein, who maintains: "Philosophy may in no way interfere with the actual use of language; it can in the end only describe it. For it cannot give it a foundation either. It leaves everything as it is." Ludwig Wittgenstein, *Philosophical Investigations* (Oxford: Blackwell, 1968), para. 124.

4 George Dickie, *Aesthetics* (Indianapolis: Bobbs-Merrill, 1971), 101. Dickie has subsequently reformulated his institutional theory in *The Art Circle* (New York: Haven, 1984). But the essential approach has not changed, and for my genealogical purposes the early influential version is more appropriate.

5 I develop these analogies and analogous criticisms in more detail in "Positivism: Legal and Aesthetic," *Journal of Value Inquiry* 16 (1982), 319–25.

6   See Arthur Danto, *The Transfiguration of the Commonplace* (Cambridge, Mass.: Harvard University Press, 1981), 5–6, 94; citation from 125.

7   Ibid. 135; the other citation in this paragraph is from 208.

8   Ibid. vii. Although Danto's definition of art in terms of artistic interpretation is supplemented by further specification in terms of representation, expression, metaphor, rhetoric, and style, the application of all these notions always falls back on the central category of the artworld which is defined through its history.

9   Danto, *Philosophical Disenfranchisement of Art*, 204, 209.

10 Richard Wollheim, *Art and its Objects* (Harmondsworth: Penguin, 1975), 120–1, 142, 167. Jerrold Levinson is another analytic philosopher who defines art historically. See his "Defining Art Historically," *British Journal of Aesthetics* 19 (1979), 232–50.

11 T. W. Adorno, *Aesthetic Theory* (London: Routledge & Kegan Paul, 1984), 3–4, 371, 418–19.

12 See Noël Carroll, "Art, Practice, and Narrative," *Monist* 71 (1988), 140–56, and Nicholas Wolterstorff, "Philosophy of Art after Analysis and Romanticism," in Richard Shusterman (ed.), *Analytic Aesthetics* (Oxford: Blackwell, 1989) 32–58. Carroll defines art as a "cultural" practice, while Wolterstorff treats it as a "social" practice. Both adjectives are perhaps redundant. For, since all practices in the relevant sense are norm-related, they must (by an analogue of Wittgenstein's private-language argument) be social; and social practices are always in some sense practices of a culture, even so called anti-social and anti-cultural practices. Both Carroll and Wolterstorff base their theories on the influential account of practice given by Alisdair MacIntyre, *After Virtue* (London: Duckworth, 1981).

13 Carroll, "Art, Practice, and Narrative," 152.

14 John Dewey, "Philosophy and Civilization," in *Philosophy and Civilization* (New York: Capricorn, 1963), 3–12. For Dewey a major source of such perplexities are "scientific tendencies and political aspirations which are novel and incompatible with received authorities" (3–4).

15 It may be suggested that the practice's past history can serve as an "external" critique for its present misdirection. But since the very shape and relevance of that history are largely determined by present practice and its narrative inclinations, the force of this "external" critique is questionable.

16 The power of aesthetic experience can be so compelling as to undermine competing values, and Habermas, for instance, blames the Nietzschean and postmodern critique of reason on the bewitching attraction of aesthetic experience as an alternative normative ground (see Jürgen Habermas, *The Philosophical Discourses of Modernity* (Cambridge, Mass.: MIT Press, 1987), 92–105).

17 Indeed, even their artistic status derives from their functioning in such experience. Dewey is not alone in suggesting this. Nelson Goodman makes much

the same point by arguing that in defining art, "the real question is not 'What objects are (permanently) works of art?' but 'When is an object a work of art?'" and by answering the latter question in terms of the object's functioning as such in aesthetic experience, where such "aesthetic functioning . . . provides the basis for the notion of a work of art." See Nelson Goodman, *Ways of Worldmaking* (Indianapolis: Hackett, 1978), 66–7, and *Of Mind and Other Matters* (Cambridge, Mass.: Harvard University Press, 1984), 145. Goodman characterizes aesthetic experience and functioning in terms of the prevalence of certain features of symbolization: syntactic and semantic density, relative repleteness, exemplification, and multiple and complex reference (ibid. 135–6); and he locates its value in wholly cognitive terms, which Dewey would find much too narrow.

18 Habermas relies on this argument when he insists on "the modern origin of aesthetic experience" (*Philosophical Discourses of Modernity*, 307). Moreover, he further builds on it to argue that radical critiques of modernist reason by appeal to aesthetic experience as an alternative "other" involve a deep contradiction, since aesthetic experience itself depends for its existence on art as a product of modernist reason's differentiating development of cultural spheres (339–40). In similar but more explicit fashion, Richard Wollheim (*Art and its Objects*, 112–15) argues that our aesthetic feelings and attitude toward nature are only derivative from those of art, and thus we cannot properly consider such feelings "outside, or antecedent to, the institutions of art" (115). But he warily dodges the question of whether these institutions existed in premodern societies.

19 Kant, for example, insisted that aesthetic experience existed more purely in regard to nature, whose appreciation could be totally free of concepts, whereas the experience of art's objects necessarily refers us to the concept of art. See Immanuel Kant, *The Critique of Judgement*, trans. J. C. Meredith (Oxford: Oxford University Press, 1952), 34, 158–60, 172–3, 183–4.

20 We see this in Kant's distinction of art proper as "free" or "fine" art from mere "handicraft" or industrial art. The latter is "labor, i.e. a business, which on its own account is disagreeable (drudgery), and is only attractive by what it results in (e.g. the pay), and which is constantly capable of being a compulsory imposition" (ibid. 164).

21 For Dewey's criticism of the traditional separation of means and ends, and of the confusion of means with mere external causal conditions, see *AE* 201–4. See also *EN* 296–300, where Dewey traces the error of the means/end dichotomy and the false perception of means as coerced external material conditions back to the conditions of production and the class system in ancient Athens.

22 Danto, *Philosophical Disenfranchisement of Art*, 108–9. Danto, however, thinks that art has finally completed its historical mission in Hegelian fashion by turning itself into philosophy of art. But since art and the artworld are, for

Danto, essentially defined by history, the end of its history means the end of art. Danto's prognosis that "the institutions of the artworld . . . which are predicated upon history and hence marking what is new, will bit by bit wither away" is wistfully tempered by the thought of "the immense privilege to have lived in [the] history" of the artworld (115), a confession which speaks with silent eloquence of the many underprivileged who were excluded from its realm and hence from the legitimated experience of art. Nonetheless, in hoping that the end of its history "will return art to human ends" and "abiding human needs" (xv, 115), Danto converges promisingly with pragmatist aesthetics.

23 Adorno, *Aesthetic Theory*, 51. Throughout this work Adorno insists on the "authority of the new" in modern art as "an historical inevitability"; and he links it (as does Dewey) to the capitalist demand for the new to stimulate consumption (30–1). The other citations in this paragraph are from 334 and from Ortega y Gasset, *The Dehumanization of Art* (Princeton: Princeton University Press, 1968), 5, 6.

24 Kant, *Critique of Judgement*, 43.

25 *AE* 329–30. See also Dewey's assertion that "all the elements of our being that are displayed in special emphases and partial realizations in other experiences are merged in esthetic experience" (278).

26 See, for example, A. E. Housman, *The Name and Nature of Poetry* (Cambridge: Cambridge University Press, 1933), 45–50, and T. S. Eliot, *Of Poetry and Poets* (London: Faber, 1957), 97–9.

27 The same argument can be made with respect to Dewey's related description of art as "a quality of activity," since qualities, being "concrete and existential," cannot be captured in general discursive formulas (*AE* 218–19, 227). For Dewey, "Quality is quality, direct, immediate and undefinable" (*EN* 93).

28 Monroe C. Beardsley, *Aesthetics: Problems in the Philosophy of Criticism* (Harcourt, Brace, 1958), 530–1. Sensing perhaps that experience itself cannot do all the necessary critical work, Beardsley also insists on the three evaluative canons of unity, complexity, and intensity, which, though they pertain to experience, can also be demonstrated in the art product (456–70, 534).

29 Yet, even if aesthetic experience is not an epistemologically useful notion, it does not follow that such experience is trivially void of cognitive value. For whether or not its nondiscursive immediacies can be known, having them can still be essential for wide varieties of knowledge and provides the structuring background for properly epistemological critical efforts.

30 This applies not only to art and its subconcepts, but also to beauty, a term which appears in the title of my book but which I make no effort to define. Beauty seems as qualitatively immediate and indefinable as aesthetic experience, and Dewey in fact regarded it as "at the furthest remove" from a conception that could or should be formally defined by philosophy (*AE* 195). In any case, I think contemporary aesthetics has more urgent issues to address.

31 See Stanley Fish, "Consequences," in W. J. T. Mitchell (ed.), *Against Theory* (Chicago: University of Chicago Press, 1985), 110, 115. More recently, Fish has somewhat softened his anti-theoretical stance. While still insisting that "real" theory (by which he means foundationalist theory) has no consequences because it cannot exist, he recognizes that "theory-talk" (the practice of theoretical discourse – what in fact we typically mean by the practice of theory) can be "consequential." For Fish, "the distinction between theory and theory-talk is a distinction between a discourse that stands apart from all practice (and no such discourse exists) and a discourse that is itself a practice" ("Introduction: Going Down the Anti-Formalist Road," in *Doing What Comes Naturally* (Durham, N.C.: Duke University Press, 1989), 14). But this distinction, clearly drawn to insure that theory is so narrowly and foundationally defined as to render it impossible, is a hopeless distinction by Fish's own textualist standards. Since there is no way even to imagine theory without theory-talk, what, then, is the point of distinguishing what cannot even be conceived to exist apart? Rather than introduce this questionable distinction between theory and theory-talk, it is much more useful (hence more reasonable by pragmatist lights) to preserve and improve the theory/practice distinction by reinterpreting theory in non-foundational terms, as a form of discursive, critically persuasive practice. Fish himself seems close to this when he later seeks to demote theory to "a practice," so that "theory becomes what it always was anyway, one among many rhetorical forms whose impact and sway are a function of contingencies (of institutional history, perceived needs, emergent crises, etc.) it can neither predict nor control" (ibid. 25, 26).

32 Apart from its greater optimism, pragmatism seems to differ from deconstruction and Frankfurt-school critical theory in emphasizing that theory helps transform practice not only through critique and rhetorical persuasion but through the proposal of concrete alternatives which are to be tested in experience. Because of its commitment to concrete criticisms and proposals for change, non-foundational pragmatist theory should not be confused with what Fish calls mere "anti-foundationalist theory hope," the idea that merely by the negative gesture of showing in general that the foundations for belief are all contingent, anti-foundationalist theory enables us to release from our beliefs and change them (*Doing What Comes Naturally*, 322, 346, 593n).

33 This point is well argued in Joseph Margolis, *Pragmatism without Foundations* (Oxford: Blackwell, 1986), 42.

34 Stanley Fish, "Dennis Martinez and the Uses of Theory," in *Doing What Comes Naturally*, 386–9.

35 Fish, "Consequences," 121. Fish has more recently called into question the very possibility of critical self-consciousness, arguing that it impossibly "requires . . . a mind capable of standing to the side of its own ways of thinking in order to critique them" from a neutral, interest-free perspective (Stanley Fish, "Critical Self-Consciousness, or Can We Know What We're Doing?,"

in *Doing What Comes Naturally,* 437). But, as he often does, Fish leads us astray by a totalizing move. For all that critical self-consciousness requires is being able to stand aside from *some* of our mind's ways of thinking in order to critique them from the perspective of others. These other ways, for the pragmatist, are of course neither neutral nor interest-free; but they need not be either to have potential for helping us change our minds with respect to a particular practice. It is wrong to identify critical reflection and self-consciousness merely with what Fish calls "anti-foundationalist theory hope," for these can include not mere general awareness of the defeasibility of our views but concrete critical reflection on what is actually wrong with them.

36   Fish, "Consequences," 125. Fish repeats this point in calling for "the demoting of theory to a practice no different from any other [and] ... the elevation of practice to a new, if ever-changing universal in relation to which there is nothing higher ... that can be evoked" (*Doing What Comes Naturally,* 26). But the fact that there is no deep epistemological gap of cognitive privilege between theory and practice does not render them identical or incapable of reciprocal influence, no more than epistemological parity renders different practices identical. Such confusion derives from two totalizing tendencies in Fish: from assimilating all important differences capable of providing critical guidance into a narrowly dominational and rigid "relationship of superiority or governance" (ibid. 377) and from totalizing the notions of theory and practice instead of looking for the difference between them within a particular context of practice and its theoretical reflection. Ultimately the distinction between theory and practice is a functional and contextual one: what counts as a historical theory becomes a first-order practice for a theory of history.

37   Stanley Fish, "Change," in *Doing What Comes Naturally,* 154. The further argument about the mind not being "able to take into account something not already presupposed by its assumptions" is most focused at 145–7.

Chapter 3   *Organic Unity: Analysis and Deconstruction*

1   This emphasis on unity as a foundation or criterion of aesthetic value is perhaps most evident in Moore, Osborne, Richards, Beardsley, and the New Criticism; and we have already seen it in Dewey's account of aesthetic experience. Dewey also speaks of the work of art as an "organism" so "unified" that its "different elements and specific qualities ... blend and fuse in a way which physical things cannot emulate" (*Art as Experience* (Carbondale: Southern Illinois University Press, 1987), 196). For the other examples: see G. E. Moore, *Principia Ethica* (Cambridge: Cambridge University Press, repr. 1959), 27–30, 189–208, henceforth referred to as *PE*. Osborne treats organic unity as the defining characteristic of beauty and works of art: "a work of art is an organic whole of interlocking organic wholes" (Harold Os-

borne, *The Theory of Beauty* (London: Routledge & Kegan Paul, 1952), 203). Richards defines the aesthetic experience with which he identifies the work of art in terms of its distinctive unity and completeness (see I. A. Richards, *Principles of Literary Criticism* (London: Routledge & Kegan Paul, 1976), 142–3, 184–7). Beardsley's organicism is evident in his definition of the aesthetic experience as a complete and coherently unified experience and in his insistence on unity as one of the three objective canons of aesthetic criticism (M. C. Beardsley, *Aesthetics: Problems in Philosophy of Criticism* (New York: Harcourt, Brace, 1958), 462–3, 527–30). Apart from Richards's and Beardsley's connection with New Criticism, Cleanth Brooks's "The Heresy of Paraphrase" can provide an example of New Criticism's commitment to the idea of a richly complex unity of parts, all of which help constitute the poem as a well-wrought whole. For Brooks this essential unity which informs the good poem is a matter of "imaginative" rather than strictly "logical coherences," "of balancing and harmonizing connotations, attitudes, and messages ... [which] unite the like with the unlike" in a polyphonic "achieved harmony" (see C. Brooks, *The Well Wrought Urn* (New York: Harcourt, Brace, 1947), 195, 202).

2   See, for example, Michel Foucault, *The Archaeology of Knowledge* (New York: Harper and Row, 1976), 4–38, and Pierre Macherey, *A Theory of Literary Production* (London: Routledge & Kegan Paul, 1970), 78–9.

3   See Jacques Derrida, "Structure, Sign, and Play in the Discourse of the Human Sciences," in R. Macksey and E. Donato (eds), *The Structuralist Controversy* (Baltimore: Johns Hopkins University Press, 1972), 247–72; citation from 260.

4   See Aristotle's *Poetics*, VII–VIII. I use the translation of S. H. Butcher, in his *Aristotle's Theory of Poetry and Fine Art* (London: Macmillan, 1911); citations from 31, 35. Plato to some extent adumbrated this idea of organic unity in his *Phaedrus*, where he says that "every discourse ought to be a living creature, having a body of its own and a head and feet; there should be a middle, beginning and end, adapted to each other and to the whole" (see *The Dialogues of Plato*, ed. B. Jowett, vol. 3 (Oxford: Clarendon Press, 1953), 172–3).

5   See Paul de Man, "Form and Intent in the American New Criticism," in *Blindness and Insight*, 2nd edn (Minneapolis: University of Minnesota Press, 1983), 20–35; citations from 28. Christopher Norris follows de Man's critique of New Criticism's "formalist" organicism in *Deconstruction: Theory and Practice* (London: Methuen, 1982), 103–5; while Jonathan Culler's attack on the aesthetic idea of organic unity, as expounded in his *On Deconstruction: Theory and Criticism after Structuralism* (Ithaca: Cornell University Press, 1982), will be given detailed attention later in this chapter, with future references to his book designated *OD*.

6   Heraclitus clearly advocates a unity embracing difference and conflict when

he states: "Opposition unites. From what draws apart results the most beautiful harmony. All things take place by strife" (see fragment 46 in Milton Nahm, *Selections from Early Greek Philosophy* (New York: Crofts, 1934), 91). Moreover, Coleridge, who introduced the term "organic unity" into English criticism, spoke of its expression in the imagination of poetic genius as a "unity that . . . reveals itself in the balance or reconciliation of opposite or discordant qualities; of sameness with difference" (S. T. Coleridge, *Biographia Literaria* (London: Dent, 1965), 174). Most strikingly, Heidegger – an avowed influence on de Man – describes artistic unity as a conflictual striving between "world" and "earth," where "the unity of the work comes about in the fighting of the battle" (Martin Heidegger, "The Origin of the Work of Art," in *Poetry, Language, Thought* (New York: Harper and Row, 1971), 49–50).

7   I have elsewhere explored other points of deep opposition and surprising convergence between deconstruction and analytic aesthetics. See Richard Shusterman, "Analytic Aesthetics, Literary Theory, and Deconstruction," *Monist* 69 (1986), 22–38, and "Deconstruction and Analysis: Confrontation and Convergence," *British Journal of Aesthetics* 26 (1986), 311–27.

8   Both these works were first published the very same month, October 1903; so the conflicting valencies and applications of organic unity must have been very clear in Moore's mind. Page references to "The Refutation of Idealism," henceforth *RI*, will be to its reprinting in Moore's *Philosophical Studies* (London: Routledge & Kegan Paul, 1922), 1–30.

9   This argument, however, was enough for Moore's teacher McTaggart to maintain that all wholes are organic wholes and, from this, to conclude that the universe must ultimately be one necessary monistic whole, all of whose so-called different, independent parts are actually, intrinsically, internally related. See J. McTaggart, *The Nature of Existence* (Cambridge: Cambridge University Press, 1921), ch. 20.

10 See James Benziger, "Organic Unity: Leibniz to Coleridge," *PMLA* 66 (1951), 24–48.

11 For Hegel's views on this, see, for example, *The Phenomenology of Mind* (New York: Harper and Row, 1967), 171–8.

12 F. de Saussure, *Course in General Linguistics* (London: Peter Owen, 1960), 120. Deconstructors would rightly insist, however, that one of Derrida's aims is precisely to undermine the whole Saussurian project of explaining language as a closed and totalizable differential system. Derrida might also dispute my talk of the "concept of *différance*," since he repeatedly insists that it is "neither a word nor a concept." See Jacques Derrida, "Différance," in *Speech and Phenomena and Other Essays on Husserl's Theory of Signs* (Evanston: Northwestern University Press, 1973), 129–60, and also his *Positions* (London: Athlone, 1981), 39–40, henceforth *Pos.* With respect to this second point, I would reply with Rorty that authorial fiat cannot immunize an ex-

pression against concepthood, that all that it takes for an expression to be a concept is "a place in a language-game," and that *différance* clearly has such a place in the language-game(s) of deconstruction (see Richard Rorty, "Deconstruction and Circumvention," *Critical Inquiry* 11 (1984), 18). As to the first point (and as my ensuing discussion will argue), it is not clear that the strategy of *différance* can be fully decisive against analytic philosophy and aesthetic unity without an appeal to some sort of totalizing move regarding objects as differential relations.

13 See Derrida, "Différance," 141, and *Pos* 58.
14 G. W. F. Hegel, *Hegel's Logic*, trans. W. Wallace (Oxford University Press, 1975), 191.
15 See Friedrich Nietzsche, *The Will to Power* (New York: Vintage Press, 1968), para. 559, 584, 635. For the ways in which Nietzsche's organicistic dissolution of things into differential relations within a whole underlies his doctrines of the will to power and the eternal recurrence, see Alexander Nehamas, *Nietzsche: Life as Literature* (Cambridge, Mass: Harvard University Press, 1985). For a recent critique of Moore which builds on Nietzsche and my own earlier work on organic unity but which takes a more deconstructionist line than I do, see Thomas Leddy, "Moore and Shusterman on Organic Wholes," *Journal of Aesthetics and Art Criticism* 49 (1991), 63–73. For further clarification of my position on this issue, see Richard Shusterman, "Pragmatism and Perspectivism on Organic Wholes," *Journal of Aesthetics and Art Criticism,* 49, 1991.
16 J. Derrida, "The Parergon," *October* 9 (1979), 26.
17 See Andrew Harrison, "Works of Art and Other Cultural Objects," *Proceedings of the Aristotelian Society* 68 (1967–8), 125; and Nelson Goodman, *Languages of Art* (Oxford: Oxford University Press, 1969), 115–21. Their theorizing reflects the discourse and practice of traditional criticism, which characteristically seeks to determine not simply what is in the work but what is its central and most formative dimension – in Helen Gardner's words "a work's centre, the source of its life in all its parts" (see H. Gardner, *The Business of Criticism* (Oxford: Oxford University Press, 1970), 230.
18 I have elsewhere argued that in many literary works, particularly in poetry, the visual features of the written or printed text are aesthetically very relevant and sometimes essential. The dogma that poetry is only sound and sense but never sight is largely the product of an ancient philosophical bias for the phonocentric and the spiritual as non-physical, coupled with a misguided metaphysical superstition which sees the oral as somehow less physical than the written. On this issue, see Richard Shusterman, "The Anomalous Nature of Literature," *British Journal of Aesthetics* 18 (1978), 317–29; "Aesthetic Blindness to Textual Visuality," *Journal of Aesthetics and Art Criticism* 41 (1982), 87–96; and "Ingarden, Inscription, and Literary Ontology," *Journal of the British Society for Phenomenology* 18 (1987), 103–19.

19 P. de Man, "Foreword" to Carol Jacobs, *The Dissimulating Harmony* (Baltimore: Johns Hopkins University Press, 1978), ix–x.

20 See J. Culler, *Roland Barthes* (New York: Oxford University Press, 1983), 98–100; *OD* 132n., citations from 221, 225, 240; and Norris, *Deconstruction: Theory and Practice*, 92–108, and *The Deconstructive Turn* (London: Methuen, 1983), 6–7, citation from 7.

21 See Richard Shusterman, "Convention: Variations on a Theme," *Philosophical Investigations* 9 (1986), 36–55. The common confusion of the conventional with the superficial is nourished by the conflation of two different senses of "arbitrary": contingent or not ontologically necessary versus capricious, haphazard, unreasoned, and easily reversible.

22 See Hans-Georg Gadamer, *Truth and Method* (New York: Crossroad, 1982), 261; and John Dewey, *Logic: The Theory of Inquiry* (New York: Irvington, 1982), 104–5.

23 De Man, "Form and Intent in the American New Criticism," 31–2.

24 J. Derrida, "Interpreting Signatures (Nietzsche/Heidegger): Two Questions," *Philosophy and Literature* 10 (1986), 256–7.

25 A distinction can be made between being an individual (i.e. a one) and being a distinctively unified individual (i.e. a unified one), between having mere "unicity" and having unity in a stronger sense.

26 For the present discussion I am using "interpretation" in its widest philosophical sense as any perspectival understanding or construal of things. I believe, however, that not all such understanding should be regarded as interpretation, for reasons that I set out in ch. 5.

27 W. James, *Pragmatism and Other Essays* (New York: Simon and Schuster, 1963), 76.

28 The analyst might also object that without foundational essences to constitute identity there could be no shared and stable objects of reference, hence no effective discourse. Pragmatism's response to this has already been suggested: the shared normative regularities necessary for effective individuating reference and speech need not be based on any unchanging ontological referent outside a culture's social practices and can admit of some change or divergence without necessarily incurring a breakdown of communication. The shared referents of our language could be traditionally shared and pragmatically constituted "unities" or "individuals" rather than foundational substances.

29 J. Derrida, "Limited Inc.," *Glyph* 2 (1977), 236.

30 They are also clearly recognized by analytic philosophy's sympathetic exponents and historians. See, for example, J. O. Urmson, *Philosophical Analysis: Its Development between the Two World Wars* (Oxford: Oxford University Press, 1969), 45–7.

31 Hegel's *Logic*, 191; Nietzsche, *Will to Power*, 584, 634, 635.

32 Derrida, "Interpreting Signatures," 258–61. Derrida's specific target is Hei-

degger's interpretation of Nietzsche, one which recognizes and emphasizes this totalization. It should be mentioned, however, that this interpretation is not only Heidegger's, but is present in Nehamas and, more important, is eminent in Nietzsche's text. Nietzsche's notion of organic unity and, in particular, Nehamas's application of it are criticized in more detail in my paper "Nietzsche and Nehamas on Organic Unity," *Southern Journal of Philosophy* 26 (1988), 379–92.

33　See W. V. Quine, *From a Logical Point of View* (New York: Harper and Row, 1963), 4, 16–19, 46.

34　For detailed elaboration of this distinction, see ch. 5 below.

35　W. James, *Collected Essays and Reviews* (New York: Longmans, 1920), 18, and *Pragmatism*, 36, 98.

36　Derrida, "Structure, Sign, and Play," 260, my emphasis.

37　James, *Pragmatism*, 36, 98.

38　Ibid. 71. John Dewey makes the same pragmatist point of mediation: "The need . . . is to find a viable alternative to an atomism which logically involves a denial of connections and to an absolutistic block monism which, in behalf of the reality of relations, leaves no place for the discrete, for plurality, and for individuals" (see Dewey, "Experience, Knowledge, and Value," in P. Schilpp (ed.), *The Philosophy of John Dewey* (LaSalle, Ill.: Open Court, 1989), 544). For both James and Dewey the insistence on ontological individuality and pluralism had a distinct ethico-political motivation.

39　Richard Rorty, *Contingency, Irony, and Solidarity* (Cambridge: Cambridge University Press, 1989), 26.

Chapter 4　*Pragmatism and Interpretation*

1　I should mention that other new pragmatist accounts of interpretation are starting to surface. Joseph Margolis begins to develop one in his "Reinterpreting Interpretation," *Journal of Aesthetics and Art Criticism* 47 (1989), 237–51; and I find it much more congenial than his earlier analytic theory criticized below.

2　See William K. Wimsatt and Monroe C. Beardsley, "The Intentional Fallacy," repr. in Joseph Margolis, *Philosophy Looks at the Arts* (New York: Scribner, 1962), 91–104, and Roland Barthes, "The Death of the Author," in *Image, Music, Text* (New York: Hill and Wang, 1977), 142–8.

3　How elusive and spectral this notion of intention is can be seen in the evasive formulation of its most forthright exponent, E. D. Hirsch. On the one hand, he suggests its pragmatic value as a definite criterion or touchstone which would rule out interpretations inconsistent with what the historical author could have intended. But, afraid of psychologism and aware that literary (if not all) intentions can be too complex to be mechanically deduced from the known historical and biographical facts alone, Hirsch retreats from locating the requisite authorial intention in an empirical individual and instead turns the author into an imaginative construct, "the speaking subject," which "is not . . . identical with the subjectivity of the author as an actual historical person." And this authorial-subject abstraction, far from providing a clear factual touchstone for interpretation, needs to be interpretively constructed itself in terms of the text. See E. D. Hirsch, *Validity in Interpretation* (New Haven: Yale University Press, 1967), 242–4.

4 See, for instance, E. D. Hirsch, *The Aims of Interpretation* (Chicago: University of Chicago Press, 1978), 12–13.

5 Monroe C. Beardsley, *The Possibility of Criticism* (Detroit: Wayne State University Press, 1970), 31, 33, 41–3.

6 Hirsch, *Aims of Interpretation*, 1, 12, and "On Justifying Interpretive Norms," *Journal of Aesthetics and Art Criticism* 43 (1984), 91.

7 Hirsch, *Aims of Interpretation*, 7.

8 Joseph Margolis, *Art and Philosophy* (Atlantic Highlands, N.J.: Humanities Press, 1980). Citations in this paragraph are from 111, 150, 159, 161–2. I provide a more detailed critical account of Margolis's theory in my "Interpretation, Intention, and Truth," *Journal of Aesthetics and Art Criticism* 46 (1988), 399–411.

9 This problem of the circular interdependence of description and interpretation is a manifestation of the perhaps more basic interdependence of work-identity and interpretation, where adequacy of interpretation is measured against the work's substantive identity, but where the latter can only be determined through the former. I discuss this problem further in "Four Problems in Aesthetics," *International Philosophical Quarterly* 22 (1982), 21–33, and *The Object of Literary Criticism* (Amsterdam: Rodopi, 1984), 50–64.

10 See Harold Bloom, *Agon: Towards a Theory of Revisionism* (New York: Oxford University Press, 1982), 16, 17.

11 Harold Bloom, *A Map of Misreading* (New York: Oxford University Press, 1975), 3.

12 Jacques Derrida, *Positions* (London: Athlone, 1981), 27, 45.

13 See Jonathan Culler, *On Deconstruction: Theory and Criticism after Structuralism* (Ithaca: Cornell University Press, 1982), 176. The other citations from Culler in this paragraph are from 123, 128, 176.

14 For Wittgenstein's views on meaning and understanding, see especially his *Philosophical Investigations* (Oxford: Blackwell, 1968), para. 143–242. For further elaboration and clarification of Wittgenstein's position, see G. P. Baker and P. M. S. Hacker, *Wittgenstein: Meaning and Understanding* (Oxford: Blackwell, 1983), 29–45, 321–46. The idea of oral reading as a means to or criterion of correct understanding of poetry is suggested in Ludwig Wittgenstein, *Lectures and Conversations on Aesthetics, Psychology and Religious Belief* (Oxford: Blackwell, 1970), 4–5, 40.

15   Hirsch, *Aims of Interpretation*, 1–3.
16   A distinction may be made between the correspondence theory of truth and that of knowledge, where only the correspondence theory of knowledge is said to require that the correspondent reality "as in itself it really is" be available for comparison and assessment of the knowledge claim. This distinction, however valuable, does not affect the theories we are considering here, which are concerned with claims to interpretive knowledge rather than mere interpretive truth.
17   This position, as I argue in the next chapter, is not tantamount to reducing the world and its experience to the linguistic.
18   Richard Rorty, "Texts and Lumps," *New Literary History* 17 (1985), 3.
19   See Gilbert Ryle's discussion of 'knowing how' in *The Concept of Mind* (London: Hutchinson, 1949), 26–60; Wittgenstein, *Philosophical Investigations*, para. 179; and John Dewey, *Experience and Nature* (LaSalle, Ill.: Open Court, 1989), 352. The idea that there is more to knowledge, even scientific knowledge, than scientific truth is a theme recently highlighted by philosophers as different as Putnam and Lyotard. See Hilary Putnam, *Meaning and the Moral Sciences* (London: Routledge & Kegan Paul, 1979), 72–3, and Jean-François Lyotard, *The Postmodern Condition* (Minneapolis: University of Minnesota Press, 1984), 31–53.
20   I bring evidence for this (from intentionalists, New Critics, structuralists, and deconstructors) in my *T. S. Eliot and the Philosophy of Criticism* (New York: Columbia University Press, 1988), 122–3.
21   Joseph Margolis makes essentially the same point in his new account of interpretation, in "Reinterpreting Interpretation."
22   John Dewey, *Art as Experience* (Carbondale, Ill.: Southern Illinois University Press, 1987), 327; cf. "The Practical Character of Reality," in *Philosophy and Civilization* (New York: Capricorn, 1963), 36–55, where Dewey argues that since "all existences are in transition," the function of knowledge is not "impossible copying" but "to make a *certain* difference in reality" (40, 46–7).
23   See Stephen Knapp and W. B. Michaels, "Against Theory," in W. J. T. Mitchell (ed.), *Against Theory* (Chicago: University of Chicago Press, 1985), 11, hereafter abbreviated *AT*. There are good reasons for denying this narrow construal of theory and their related presumption that theory cannot include any "essentially empirical" account, no matter how general (ibid.). For this view sharply departs from ordinary usage in a way that begs the question against theory by making theory seem much more narrow, rigid, and objectionable than it has to be. Moreover, Knapp and Michaels seem caught in a reflexive contradiction, since their own allegedly anti-theoretical position on interpretation – that "the meaning of a text is simply identical to the author's intended meaning" – is itself non-empirical and theoretical, despite their protestations to the contrary (*AT* 12, 98–100).
24   This question of whose intentions will determine meaning suggests how

meaning and interpretation are also deeply issues of power. One underlying theme of my subsequent critique of Rorty, Fish, and Knapp and Michaels concerns how narrowly they locate this power.

25   In a sequel entitled "Against Theory 2: Hermeneutics and Deconstruction" (*Critical Inquiry* 14 (1987), 49–69), Knapp and Michaels extend their intentionalist critique to the hermeneutic theories of Gadamer and Ricoeur, the semiotic conventionalism of Goodman and Elgin, and the deconstructionist textualism of Derrida. However, their basic line of argument does not change: there is just no way "that a text can mean something other than what its author intends"; nor can there be "any plausible criteria of textual identity [e.g. in terms of syntax, linguistic conventions, or traditions of identification] that can function independent of authorial intention" (50), simply because without some determining intention, texts would neither mean nor be identified as such.

   I should also note that Knapp and Michaels misrepresent Beardsley's anti-intentionalism as maintaining that textual meaning is "permanent and unchanging" (51, 68). On the contrary, the fact that a text's meaning can change (through changes in the meanings of its words) long after its author is dead constitutes one of Beardsley's main arguments to prove that textual meaning is not logically identical to authorial meaning. See Beardsley, *Possibility of Criticism*, 19.

26   William James, *Pragmatism and Other Essays* (New York: Simon and Schuster, 1963), 27, 111. James thinks that those objects and facts we accept as given, regardless of our choice and against our will, are really the product of the past choices and interpretations of our ancestors which we are drilled to accept. "The world *we* feel and live in will be that which our ancestors and we, by slowly cumulative strokes of choice, have extricated out of" raw experience (see William James, *The Principles of Psychology* (New York: Dover, 1950), 289). Peirce and Dewey similarly affirm possibility and pluralistic choice against the necessities of a static universe and of fixed concepts to deal with it. The essentially pluralist spirit of pragmatism has been recently emphasized by Richard Bernstein, "Pragmatism, Pluralism, and the Healing of Wounds," *Proceedings and Addresses of The American Philosophical Association*, 63 (1989), 5–18.

27   James describes pragmatism as essentially facing "forward towards the future" and defines the "pragmatic method" as "*the attitude of looking away from first things, principles, 'categories,' supposed necessities; and of looking towards last things, fruits, consequences and facts.*" His pragmatism similarly insists that the goal of knowledge is not to copy existing reality but "that existing realities may be *changed*" to provide us with more satisfactory experience; see James, (*Pragmatism*, 26–7, 99–100).

28   John Dewey, "The Development of American Pragmatism," in *Philosophy and Civilization*, 24. For Quine's critique of empiricism, to which I subse-

quently refer, see W. V. Quine, *From a Logical Point of View* (New York: Harper and Row, 1963), 20–46.

29 Yet within this frame of fixity in principle, Knapp and Michaels can still allow for the existence of interpretive variety in practice by leaving completely open the so-called empirical question not only of what the historical author intended but who the historical author actually is. It could even be, they say, "the universal muse" (*AT* 103). Thus, like Hirsch, they allow for the professional pressures of interpretive productivity while assuring us that ultimately interpretation converges on a fixed and common object of truth, which preserves the pretense of criticism as a collaborative enterprise aimed at cumulative knowledge.

30 I provide detailed critique of Goodman's textualist definition of identity in *The Object of Literary Criticism,* 130–45, where I treat the concept of work-identity as a "range concept" that is open and pragmatically contextual.

31 I shall be referring to Rorty's works parenthetically, using the following abbreviations: *Consequences of Pragmatism* (Minneapolis: University of Minnesota Press, 1982), *CP*; "Texts and Lumps," *New Literary History* 17 (1985), 1–16, *TL*; "Philosophy without Principles," in Mitchell (ed.), *Against Theory, PP*; *Contingency, Irony, and Solidarity* (Cambridge: Cambridge University Press, 1989), *CIS*.

32 See Donald Davidson, "What Metaphors Mean," in *Inquiries into Truth and Interpretation* (Oxford: Oxford University Press, 1984), 245–64, and "A Nice Derangement of Epitaphs," in E. Lepore (ed.), *Truth and Interpretation* (Oxford: Blackwell, 1986), 433–46.

33 Rorty declares in no uncertain terms: "The vocabulary of self-creation is necessarily private, unshared, unsuited to argument" (*CIS* xiv). His individualist ethic of self-creation is examined at length in ch. 9.

34 Rorty in fact sees pragmatism as "the philosophical counterpart to literary modernism, the kind of literature which prides itself on its autonomy and novelty rather than its truthfulness to experience or its discovery of preexisting significance" (*CP* 153).

35 The citations in this paragraph are from the following works, hereafter abbreviated in the chapter as follows: Stanley Fish, "Change," *South Atlantic Quarterly* 86 (1987), 424, *C*; and "Working on the Chain Gang: Interpretation in the Law and in Literary Criticism," *Critical Inquiry* 9 (1982), 204, 211, *WC*. Fish's other articles to which I shall refer are "Profession Despise Thyself: Fear and Self-Loathing in Literary Studies," *Critical Inquiry* 10 (1983), 349–64, *PD*; and "No Bias, No Merit: The Case Against Blind Submission," *PMLA* 103 (1988), 739–47, *NB*. All these articles are collected in his *Doing What Comes Naturally* (Durham, N.C.: Duke University Press, 1989). I shall also be citing from his *Is There a Text in This Class?: The Authority of Interpretive Communities* (Cambridge, Mass.: Harvard University Press, 1980), ITT.

36 Elsewhere Fish "conceives of persons not as free agents, but as extensions of interpretive communities, communities whose warranting assumptions delimit what can be seen and therefore what can be described" (*C* 435–6).

37 The argument is basically that whatever lies outside the belief structures of an interpretive community cannot be seen, hence believed; and since only a belief can change a belief, no change of belief can come from outside the community. I criticized this argument in ch. 2.

38 See Hans-Georg Gadamer, *Truth and Method* (New York: Crossroad, 1982), 271.

39 I explore some of this variety of interpretive aims (not all of which are cognitive) in "The Logic of Interpretation," *Philosophical Quarterly* 28 (1978), 310–24, and in *T. S. Eliot and the Philosophy of Criticism*, 124–33.

Chapter 5   Beneath Interpretation

1 In an earlier paper ("Beneath Interpretation, Against Hermeneutic Holism," *Monist* 73 (1990), 181–204), I referred to this as "hermeneutic holism." But this term could also suggest a position I do not at all oppose: namely, that the meaning of a word or statement and the justification of a knowledge claim are not simply matters of atomistic reference to foundational objects or atomistic correspondence to privileged representations but instead always depend on a larger context of words, statements, beliefs, etc. – a whole background of social practice and one that is not immune to change. To avoid confusing these positions, "hermeneutic universalism" seems a better term for expressing the ubiquity of interpretation.

2 Friedrich Nietzsche, *The Will to Power* (New York: Vintage Press, 1968), para. 481.

3 See Alexander Nehamas, *Nietzsche: Life as Literature* (Cambridge, Mass.: Harvard University Press, 1985; hereafter abbreviated *N*.

4 Stanley Fish, *Is There a Text in This Class?: The Authority of Interpretive Communities* (Cambridge, Mass.: Harvard University Press, 1980), 350, 352, 355.

5 Stanley Fish, "Working on the Chain Gang: Interpretation in the Law and in Literary Criticism," *Critical Inquiry* 9 (1982), 204.

6 Hans-Georg Gadamer, *Truth and Method* (New York: Crossroad, 1982), 350; hereafter abbreviated *TM*.

7 Susan Sontag, "Against Interpretation," in *Against Interpretation and Other Essays* (New York: Dell, 1966); hereafter abbreviated *AI*.

8 Arthur Danto, *The Philosophical Disenfranchisement of Art* (New York: Columbia University Press, 1986), 45.

9 See Nietzsche, *Will to Power*, para. 556, 557, 559, 560.

10 Immanuel Kant, *The Critique of Judgement*, trans. J. C. Meredith (Oxford:

Oxford University Press, 1952), 64–8; and Clive Bell, *Art* (New York: Capricorn, 1958), ch. 1.

11 T. S. Eliot, "Hamlet," in *Selected Essays* (London: Faber, 1976), 142, and his Introduction to G. W. Knight, *The Wheel of Fire* (London: Methuen, 1962), xix. For a detailed account of the arguments motivating Eliot's hermeneutic turn and for a critical analysis of his mature theory of interpretation, see Richard Shusterman, *T. S. Eliot and the Philosophy of Criticism* (New York: Columbia University Press, 1988), 107–155.

12 I have elsewhere argued that in pragmatic terms we can indeed have complete (albeit perspectival) understanding and that only in pragmatic, contextual terms is the idea of complete understanding at all intelligible. The idea of completeness always presupposes a particular and limited context or purpose of fulfillment, so the foundationalist idea of completeness in and for itself, without aspects or horizons or purpose, is simply a meaningless notion, not a regrettably unreachable ideal. For more on this, see my *T. S. Eliot and the Philosophy of Criticism*, 126–8.

13 John Dewey, *Experience and Nature* (La Salle, Ill.: Open Court, 1929), 21–4.

14 See Dewey's remark that "primary non-reflectional experience . . . has its own organization of a direct, non-logical character" (*Essays in Experimental Logic* (Chicago: University of Chicago Press, 1916), 6).

15 Of course, the hermeneutic universalists would contest such a view of standard usage and insist that even unconscious actions and immediate perceptions must be interpretive, and that they may be so described without gross violation of diction. My point is that the universalists give no compelling reason to extend the use of interpretation this way, and that in recommending linguistic revision or the denial of a useful distinction, the burden of proof lies heavily with them. As should already be clear, the appeal of their case rests on thinking that uninterpreted understanding is impossible because it must be conceived foundationally.

16 Ludwig Wittgenstein, *Philosophical Investigations* (Oxford: Blackwell, 1968), II. xi. 212. Wittgenstein quickly goes on to specify the sort of thinking we do in interpretation: "When we interpret we form hypotheses, which may prove false" (ibid.).

17 Donald Davidson, "Radical Interpretation" and "The Very Idea of a Conceptual Scheme," in *Inquiries into Truth and Interpretation* (Oxford: Oxford University Press, 1984), 125, 185.

18 Hans-Georg Gadamer, "On the Scope and Function of Hermeneutical Reflection," in *Philosophical Hermeneutics* (Berkeley: University of California Press, 1989), 19, 32. Gadamer, however, does not always seem perfectly consistent on this last matter. At one point in *Truth and Method* he speaks of an "understanding of language" which "is not yet of itself a real understanding and does not include an interpretive process but it is an accomplishment of life. For you understand a language by living in it" (346). Could Gadamer

here be acknowledging, albeit in a rather odd and contorted manner, the point I wish to make that interpretation does not go all the way down but always relies on some more primitive linguistic understanding? This alternative (hardly typical) view of Gadamer was suggested to me by John Connolly.

19 See, for example, Ludwig Wittgenstein, *Zettel* (Oxford: Blackwell, 1967), para. 419, and *Philosophical Investigations,* para. 5, 6, 9, 86.

20 See Dewey, *Essays in Experimental Logic,* 4, 6, 9.

21 Moreover, recent work in linguistics and philosophy of language demonstrates how many of our linguistic structures (including some of our more abstract logical principles) seem to be shaped by more basic preconceptual and prelinguistic patterns of bodily experience. See Mark Johnson, *The Body in the Mind* (Chicago: University of Chicago Press, 1987).

22 This is not to deny that our professional activity (e.g. reading, writing, etc.) also relies on uninterpreted (linguistic or kinesthetic) understandings, particularly since such activity clearly depends on our more general non-professional coping and training.

23 See John Lyons, *Semantics* (Cambridge: Cambridge University Press, 1977), vol. 1, 33–50.

24 Martin Heidegger, *Being and Time* (New York: Harper and Row, 1962), 194.

25 Wittgenstein, *Philosophical Investigations,* para. 198, 201.

26 The same can be said for another problematic distinction which much contemporary philosophy seems bent on confusing and then denying – the conventional versus the natural. Convention is always more superficial than the natural which grounds it; but what we regard in one context as conventional in contrast to its more natural background can itself be regarded as natural in relation to something still more superficial or artificial. For more detailed argument of this thesis, see Richard Shusterman, "Convention: Variations on a Theme," *Philosophical Investigations* 9 (1986), 36–55.

27 This is one reason why my rehabilitation of uninterpreted understanding should not be seen as simply a resurrection of what Sellars called "the myth of the given" (Wilfred Sellars, "Empiricism and the Philosophy of Mind," in *Science, Perception and Reality* (New York: Routledge & Kegan Paul), 1963, 127–96); see also Richard Rorty's supportive elaboration in *Philosophy and the Mirror of Nature* (Princeton: Princeton University Press, 1979), 182–92). I agree with Sellars and Rorty that any understanding which functions as epistemological grounding for another understanding must always exist within "the logical space of reasons" and hence be conceptual. But I maintain, first, that such conceptual understandings can still be immediately (though not apodictically) given; they need not be interpretations. Second, I would hold that non-conceptual (e.g. kinesthetic) experiences, though they be beneath the logical space of reasons, may nonetheless be meaningful and constitute a form of understanding. Finally, though I agree with Sellars and Rorty that such experiences cannot provide epistemological grounding or jus-

tification for further understanding unless and until they get conceptualized, they can still provide the practical ground and orienting background for such understanding.

In other words, I am here urging recognition of a category of experienced practice which grounds and guides intelligent activity but which is not at the discursive and epistemological level of the logical space of reasons nor is simply reducible to the physical conditions and causes described by natural science. Nor should this category be seen as epistemologically grounding the categories of reasons and physical causes. Sellars and Rorty would no doubt object that all forms of grounding must necessarily fall into the logical space of reasons or otherwise enter the physical space of causes, spaces which must not be confused and whose dichotomy exhausts the ways of understanding human experience. They are surely right not to confuse logical reasons with physical causes, but to regard the two as constituting an exhaustive dichotomy seems an unnecessary limitation on understanding and an unfortunate vestige of Cartesianism, with its rigid, exhaustive dualism of mind and body, thought and physical extension.

28 Wittgenstein, *Zettel*, para. 234. The imagery of this remark prompts me to hazard the suggestion that our present preoccupation with interpretation is largely the result of our not feeling comfortably at home in the often conflicting worlds of our understanding; that our age is an age of interpretation because it is one of alienation and fragmentation. This may be mourned nostalgically as the loss of unity and certainty, but it is better recognized as the price of our greater freedom and plurality.

29 See Stanley Fish, *Is There a Text in This Class?*, 14, 350; "No Bias, No Merit: The Case Against Blind Submission," *PMLA* 103 (1988), 739; and "Working on the Chain Gang," 211.

30 Bert Dreyfus, in glossing Heidegger's notions of "circumspection" and the "ready-to-hand," aptly describes this smoothly coordinated understanding as "everyday skillful coping" or "absorbed coping." See Hubert Dreyfus, *Being-in-the-World: A Commentary on Being and Time, Division I* (Cambridge, Mass.: MIT Press, 1991), ch. 4. The idea is also central to Dewey's concept of unreflective intelligent behavior versus conscious inquiry. See, for example, John Dewey, "The Practical Character of Reality" and "The Unit of Behavior," in *Philosophy and Civilization* (New York: Capricorn, 1963), 36–55, 233–48.

31 It might seem that artistic interpretation – i.e. interpretive performance – would constitute a refutation of this claim, since Rubinstein's interpretation of Beethoven's *Moonlight Sonata* is not a linguistic text. One need not meet this objection by arguing that "interpretation" is here used in a different, derivative sense. For again we have the translation of one articulated text (the score) into another articulated form (the actual musical performance), and the criterion for having an artistic interpretation is expressing it in such an articulated performance or in explicit instructions for one.

32 Rorty's recent advocacy of aestheticism occasionally comes very close to recognizing the deep value of the sublinguistic, as when he suggests that it is better "to produce tingles than truth" (Richard Rorty, *Contingency, Irony, and Solidarity* (Cambridge: Cambridge University Press, 1989), 152). But he remains more faithful to hermeneutic universalism than to Deweyan pragmatism by asserting that the subsentential is always dependent on the sentential (153n.) and by essentially equating human experience with linguistic experience (e.g. people are "nothing more than sentential attitudes," 88). This residual linguistic essentialism which sadly eviscerates Rorty's promising "aesthetic turn," is criticized in ch. 9 below.

33 Ludwig Wittgenstein, *Tractatus Logico-Philosophicus* (London: Routledge & Kegan Paul, 1963), 6.522 (I depart from the translation of Pears and McGuinness by more simply rendering *zeigt* as "show" rather than "make manifest" and *das Mystiche* as "the mystical" rather than "what is mystical").

Chapter 6   Aesthetic Ideology, Aesthetic Education,
*   and Art's Value in Critique*

1 See Roger Taylor, *Art, an Enemy of the People* (Atlantic Highlands, N.J.: Humanities Press, 1978), 155.

2 See T. S. Eliot, "East Coker," lines 97–8, in *The Complete Poems and Plays of T. S. Eliot* (London: Faber, 1969), 179.

3 This quote from Bogdanov is cited in H. Arvon, *Marxist Aesthetics* (Ithaca: Cornell University Press, 1973), 57.

4 T. W. Adorno, *Aesthetic Theory* (London: Routledge & Kegan Paul, 1984), 131, henceforth abbreviated *AT*.

5 For more on this issue, see my paper "Of the Scandal of Taste: Social Privilege as Nature in the Aesthetic Theories of Hume and Kant," *Philosophical Forum* 20 (1989), 211–29; and see especially Pierre Bourdieu, *Distinction: A Social Critique of the Judgement of Taste* (Cambridge, Mass.: Harvard University Press, 1984), ch. 1.

6 For a more detailed and carefully argued account of the avant-garde's failure to achieve its revolutionary aims, see Peter Bürger, *Theory of the Avant-Garde* (Minneapolis: University of Minnesota Press, 1984). Bürger points out, however, that the avant-garde had the major achievement of exposing with striking clarity art's existence as a distinct bourgeois institution isolated from the praxis of life, thereby opening the way for art's self-criticism.

7 See Bourdieu, *Distinction*, 5, 32–5, and Bürger, *Theory of the Avant-Garde*, 54. The latter insists that although popular art is "integrated into the praxis of life," its practical "aim . . . is to impose a particular kind of consumer behavior"; hence it is not "an instrument of emancipation . . . [but] one of subjection." This is certainly often the case, but, as I shall argue in the next

Notes to Chapter 6

chapter, it is not necessarily so. Moreover, the crassly commercial exploitation of popular art may well be the result of ignoring its aesthetic potential
and abandoning it to the play of market forces.

8 See Bourdieu, *Distinction*, 53–4, 111–15, 291.

9 Herbert Marcuse, "The Affirmative Character of Culture," in *Negations*
(Boston: Beacon Press, 1968), 129, 131, hereafter abbreviated *N*. Through
art's captivating illusion, "men can feel themselves happy even without being
so at all. The effect of illusion renders incorrect even one's own assertion
that one is happy" (122).

10 John Dewey, *Art as Experience* (Carbondale: Southern Illinois University
Press, 1987), 346; hereafter abbreviated *AE*.

11 See, for example, Terry Eagleton, *Literary Theory: An Introduction* (Oxford:
Blackwell, 1983), 51. I treat this and other common distortions of Eliot's
critical theory in my *T. S. Eliot and the Philosophy of Criticism* (New York:
Columbia University Press, 1988), 1–17.

12 T. S. Eliot, *The Use of Poetry and the Use of Criticism* (London: Faber, 1964),
154.

13 Ibid. 152–3.

14 T. S. Eliot, *After Strange Gods* (New York: Harcourt, Brace, 1934), 59–66.
Eliot himself later described his condemnation of Lawrence as the judgement
of "a sick man" (see Helen Gardner, *The Composition of "Four Quartets"*
(London: Faber, 1978), 55). But he never repudiated the idea that literary
criticism needed to be completed by ideological critique.

15 See T. S. Eliot, *Selected Prose of T. S. Eliot*, ed. Frank Kermode (London:
Faber, 1975); 97, 103; *Selected Essays* (London: Faber, 1976), 271; and *Use of
Poetry*, 98, 109.

16 For a detailed account of Eliot's two-stage theory of critical appreciation, see
my *T. S. Eliot and the Philosophy of Criticism*, ch. 6. His theory anticipates
Adorno's, which also insists on the two stages, or standpoints, of sympathetic
immanent understanding (*Verstheen*) and external ideological criticism (see
AT 177–9, 346–7, 387, 477–9). On the one hand, to understand art, one
"must enter into the work," "give . . . himself over to the work" (346, 387).
On the other, "a wholly immanent understanding of works of art is a false and
deficient mode of understanding, because it is under art's spell . . . [Proper
understanding] can be fulfilled only by a twofold approach: specific experience joined to a theory that is able to reflect experience" (177, 179). "The
states of affairs discovered by immanent analysis have to be transcended in
the direction of second reflection and emphatic criticism, . . . [since] narrow-
minded in conception, immanent analysis helps stifle the critical social
thought about art" (477). "Those who have only an inside view of art do not
understand it, whereas those who see art only from the outside tend to falsify
it for lack of affinity with it. Rather than fluctuate randomly between these
two standpoints, aesthetics must unfold their necessary interconnection in
reference to specific works" (479).

17 This important point is made by Stephen Spender, *Eliot* (London: Fontana, 1972), 46.

18 See ibid. 43–6; Hugh Kenner, *The Invisible Poet* (London: Methuen, 1965), 20–6; and A. D. Moody, *Thomas Stearns Eliot: Poet* (Cambridge: Cambridge University Press, 1980), 21–2. The young man's preoccupation with self and the isolation that this involves are already suggested in the atomistic imagery of the phrase "at this *point* many *a one* has failed" (my emphasis).

19 I shall be referring here to the two-language edition, translated and edited by E. M. Wilkinson and L. A. Willoughby: Friedrich Schiller, *On the Aesthetic Education of Man* (Oxford: Clarendon Press, 1982), henceforth abbreviated *AEM*.

20 See G. E. Moore, *Principia Ethica* (Cambridge: Cambridge University Press, repr. 1959), 188–208. Moore's aesthetic ethic is compared with more recent attempts to aestheticize the ethical in ch. 9.

21 This view need not be narrowly ascribed to Eliot's general championing of classicism over romanticism, for the idealization of the Greek aesthetic is far from foreign to romantic thinkers. Indeed, not only did Schiller share it, but had he lived to see the aestheticism of late romanticism and art for art's sake, he would have endorsed the critique of its frequent life-denying escapism. With the Greek integration of life and art as his ideal, Schiller's aesthetic education aims at improving real life in society, not at private, individual aesthetic salvation.

22 I can't resist the idea of a punning identification of Eliot the young poet with the "tom-tom" experience and attitude of the self-possessed young narrator. Eliot was then typically called "Tom" by his friends; and so the criticism of the "dull tom-tom" and the selfishness of the narrator suggests Eliot's critical awareness of these problems in himself.

23 See Clive Bell, *Art* (New York: Capricorn, 1958), ch. 1.

24 Eliot, *Selected Prose*, 56. For Eliot's changing conceptions of critical objectivity, see my *T. S. Eliot and the Philosophy of Criticism*, ch. 3.

Chapter 7   Form and Funk: The Aesthetic Challenge of Popular Art

1 I am pleased to note several exceptions to this general philosophical attitude. The sympathetic studies by Stanley Cavell, Noël Carroll, and Alexander Nehamas on film and television are especially noteworthy. See, for example, Cavell's *The World Viewed* (Cambridge, Mass.: Harvard University Press, 1979); *Pursuits of Happiness* (Cambridge, Mass.: Harvard University Press, 1981); "The Fact of Television," *Daedalus* 111 (1984), 235–68; Carroll's *Philosophical Problems of Classical Film Theory* (Princeton: Princeton University Press, 1988) and *Mystifying Movies* (New York: Columbia University Press, 1988); and Nehamas's works cited in notes 52 and 65 below. See also

David Novitz, "Ways of Art Making: The High and the Popular in Art," *British Journal of Aesthetics* 29 (1989), 213–29.

2　The term "popular" has much more positive connotations, whereas "mass" suggests an undifferentiated and typically inhuman aggregate. For more on this terminological debate, see Herbert J. Gans, *Popular Culture and High Culture: An Analysis and Evaluation of Taste* (New York: Basic Books, 1974), 10, henceforth abbreviated *PH*.

3　See Lawrence W. Levine, *Highbrow/Lowbrow: The Emergence of Cultural Hierarchy in America* (Cambridge, Mass.: Harvard University Press, 1988), 13–81.

4　If one were forced to define the high/popular art distinction, it would be better to do this not simply in terms of different objects but largely in terms of different modes of reception or use. "Popular" usage is contrasted to "high" usage in being closer to ordinary experience and less structured and regulated by schooling and standards inculcated by the system of formal education and dominant intellectual institutions. In French, popular art is accordingly contrasted with "*l'art savant*," and the very idea, or category, of "popular art" may be largely an intellectual invention of devalorizing distinction.

5　Pierre Bourdieu has warned me that the theoretical justification of popular art's legitimacy does not in itself render it legitimate in the real social world. Moreover, since such justification runs the risk of turning our eyes from the social facts of illegitimacy (thereby contributing to their perpetuation), it is a dangerous strategy to adopt. My response is that the risk is worth taking, that justificational polemics do not imply blindness to social realities, and that theoretical advocacy, empirical research, and actual socio-cultural reform can and should be applied to effect the desired legitimation.

6　See Pierre Bourdieu, *Distinction: A Social Critique of the Judgement of Taste* (Cambridge, Mass.: Harvard University Press, 1984), 4, 32, 41, 57, henceforth abbreviated *D*. Roger Taylor makes a similar mistake of concluding that since our concept of art originated with and has been used to serve an oppressive aristocratic elite, it must therefore be forever conceded to elitist powers and hence must necessarily remain an enemy of the people. Taylor also presents an interesting inversion of the standard critique that popular culture corrupts high art, arguing instead that the very idea of art, because of its essential and unchallengeable upper-class character, is a "corrupting influence on popular culture" (see Roger Taylor, *Art, an Enemy of the People* (Atlantic Highlands, N.J.: Humanities Press, 1978), esp. 40–58, 89–155).

7　Dwight Macdonald, "A Theory of Mass Culture," in Bernard Rosenberg and David M. White (eds), *Mass Culture: The Popular Arts in America* (Glencoe, Ill.: Free Press, 1957), 60. The reference in Gans, *PH*, to "passive consumers" cited above is also derived from the same passage of Macdonald.

8　Think, for example, of how impressionist and post-impressionist painting was fond of depicting popular entertainment: cabarets, carnivals, dances, etc. Even as austere a high-culture modernist as Mondrian insists on his popular-culture borrowing by such works as *Broadway Boogie Woogie.* In fact, it can be persuasively argued that the modernist avant-garde relied heavily on popular culture to distance itself from academicism. See Thomas Crow, "Modernism and Mass Culture in the Visual Arts," in B. Buchlosh, S. Guilbaut, and S. Solkin (eds), *Modernism and Modernity* (Nova Scotia: Press of the Nova Scotia College of Art and Design, 1983), 215–64.

9 Todd Gitlin, taking a balanced position between the extremes of manipulation and ingenuous transparency, more correctly argues that while the media cannot, for commercial reasons, ignore existing attitudes, they certainly can and do shape, channel, and to some extent transform them. See Todd Gitlin, "Television's Screens: Hegemony in Transition," in Donald Lazere (ed.), *American Media and Mass Culture: Left Perspectives* (Berkeley: University of California Press, 1987), 240–65.

10 Macdonald, "Theory of Mass Culture," 69.

11 Leo Lowenthal, "Historical Perspectives of Popular Culture," in Rosenberg and White (eds), *Mass Culture,* 51; and Clement Greenberg, "Avant-Garde and Kitsch," ibid. 102.

12 See T. W. Adorno, *Minima Moralia* (London: Verso, 1978), 202, and *Aesthetic Theory* (London: Routledge & Kegan Paul, 1984), 340, henceforth abbreviated *AT.*

13 Bernard Rosenberg, "Mass Culture in America," in Rosenberg and White (eds), *Mass Culture,* 9; and Ernest van den Hag, "Of Happiness and of Despair We Have No Measure," ibid. 533–4.

14 Van den Haag, "Of Happiness," 531.

15 See Allan Bloom, *The Closing of the American Mind* (New York: Simon and Schuster, 1987), 76, 79.

16 The citations are respectively from van den Haag, "Of Happiness," 534, and Rosenberg, "Mass Culture," 9–10.

17 If many claim to be fully satisfied by a monthly concert of classical music, it is probably because they don't really enjoy it very much. For many active people, it is almost as physically unpleasant to be compelled to sit in the stifled, passive immobility of the concert hall as to be coerced to march and stand without respite on those hard museum floors while trying to avoid both the obstructions of other wandering visitors and the unwelcome stares of the surveilling museum guards. In such punishing "pleasures" of high culture, whose experience is required for cultural legitimation even if they are neither understood nor really enjoyed, we find much more cause to speak of "faked sensations" and spurious gratifications than in the entertainment of popular art. But this is not to deny, of course, that high art does provide intensely genuine and invaluable satisfactions.

18 T. W. Adorno, "On the Fetish Character in Music and the Regression of

Listening," in Andrew Arato and Eike Gebhardt (eds), *The Essential Frankfurt School Reader* (New York: Continuum, 1987), 280. The same fundamental argument of coercive conditioning is given by Dwight Macdonald, "Mass Cult and Midcult," in *Against the American Grain* (New York: Random House, 1962), 9–10, and by Donald Lazere, "Media and Manipulation," in Lazere (ed.), *American Media*, 31.

19 Van den Haag, "Of Happiness," 533, 534.

20 Bloom, *Closing of the American Mind*, 77, 80.

21 *AT* 18, and van den Haag, "Of Happiness," 536.

22 The quotations for the first point come from Rosenberg, "Mass Culture," 9; for the second from van den Haag, "Of Happiness," 534.

23 See Rosenberg, "Mass Culture," 5; Macdonald, "Theory of Mass Culture," 60; and Gilbert Seldes, "The People and the Arts," in Rosenberg and White (eds), *Mass Culture*, 85. Adorno also argues that works of popular music "do not permit concentrated listening without becoming unbearable to the listeners" ("On the Fetish Character in Music," 288).

24 Max Horkheimer and T. W. Adorno, *Dialectic of Enlightenment* (New York: Continuum, 1986), 137.

25 John Dewey, *Art as Experience* (Carbondale, Ill.: Southern Illinois University Press, 1987), 162. This is not to deny that rock is often consumed in a rather passive immobility; and its increased television and video consumption may perhaps strengthen this tendency.

26 The African word, from the Ki-Kongo language, is "lu-fuki." See Robert Farris Thompson, *Flash of the Spirit* (New York: Vintage, 1984), 104–5, and Michael Ventura, *Shadow Dancing in the U.S.A.* (Los Angeles: J. P. Tarcher, 1986), 106. This African etymology of "funky" overlaps with a likely English derivation, where the verb "funk" means "to smoke or shake through fear" (see Eric Partridge, *A Dictionary of Slang and Unconventional English* (New York: Macmillan, 1984), 436). In this sense, black funkiness suggests the stinking sweat of the frightened slave – a shameful negative image. Its transformation by contemporary Afro-American culture into a term that can be used to praise is thus especially significant and empowering, and it also exemplifies the semantic complexity characteristic of Afro-American language, which will be discussed further in my study of rap.

27 The quotations are from Bloom, *Closing of the American Mind*, 71, 73; and Mark Crispin Miller, *Boxed In: The Culture of TV* (Evanston: Northwestern University Press, 1989), 175, 181.

28 See Harry Broudy, *Enlightened Cherishing: An Essay on Aesthetic Education* (Urbana: University of Illinois Press, 1972), 111; van den Haag, "Of Happiness," 533, 536; and J. T. Farrell, quoted in Seldes, "The People and the Arts," 81.

29 Macdonald, "Theory of Mass Culture," 72.

30 Van den Haag, "Of Happiness," 516–17.

31   See, for example, the studies on *Dallas* and *Dynasty* discussed in John Fiske, *Television Culture* (London: Methuen, 1987).

32   Pierre Bourdieu, "The Production of Belief," in R. Collins et al., *Media, Culture, and Society: A Critical Reader* (London: Sage, 1986), 154–5.

33   From Bruce Springsteen's "Spare Parts." Finally, apart from these logical fallacies, van den Haag's argument has a very questionable empirical basis. If we look at the history of high art before its romantic and modernist phase, we do not find that experiential novelty and difficulty of comprehension were necessary conditions of aesthetic legitimacy.

34   The citations here are from Broudy, *Enlightened Cherishing*, 111, and Gans, *PH* 77.

35   Horkheimer and Adorno, *Dialectic of Enlightenment*, 121.

36   T. W. Adorno, "Television and the Patterns of Mass Culture," in Rosenberg and White (eds), *Mass Culture*, 478.

37   See Fiske, *Television Culture*, 84, 94.

38   Cited in Ventura, *Shadow Dancing*, 159.

39   Rap's thematization of noise and linguistic deviance can even be seen in the mere titles of some of its songs, e.g. Public Enemy's "Bring the Noise," BDP's "Gimme Dat, (Woy)," and Tone Loc's "Funky Cold Medina."

40   T. S. Eliot, "Tradition and the Individual Talent," in *Selected Essays* (London: Faber, 1976), 15.

41   See *AT* 348; Adorno and Horkheimer, *Dialectic of Enlightenment*, 125; and Ernest van den Haag, "A Dissent from the Consensual Society," in Norman Jacobs (ed.), *Culture for the Millions* (Princeton: Van Nostrand, 1961), 59.

42   Lowenthal, "Historical Perspectives," 55.

43   See, for example, Rosenberg, "Mass Culture," 12, which blames "modern technology" as "the necessary and sufficient cause of mass culture" and its cultural barbarism. Lowenthal ("Historical Perspectives," 55) similarly cites "the decline of the individual in the mechanized working process" of modern technological society.

44   See Macdonald, "Theory of Mass Culture," 65.

45   Greenberg, "Avant-Garde," 98.

46   Behind the attack on popular art's technology also lies the bitter complaint that industrialized technology has dehumanized modern life, and the consequent fear that art will be similarly dehumanized and ultimately incapacitated by technological domination. Technology, for all its regrettable abuses and false ideologies, is a human product which humanity will have to come to grips with and humanize. Popular art can be seen as an expressive arena for negotiation between the technological and the human. We find attempts to playfully humanize the technological machine or assert the artist's human dominance, as when rock performers decorate, juggle, or even destroy their electric guitars or when rap DJs playfully scratch records and switch turntables. However, in today's global technological game, it is far from clear who

is playing and who is being played. This issue is pursued with respect to rap in the next chapter.

47   Van den Haag, "Of Happiness," 517, 529. For more recent expressions of this argument, see Ariel Dorfman, who remarks that "the cultural industry, tailored to answer the simultaneous needs of immense groups of people, levels off its messages at the so-called lowest common denominator, creating only that which everybody can understand effortlessly. This common denominator (as has also been pointed out frequently) is based on a construct of – what else? – the median quintessential North American common man, who has undergone secular canonization as the universal measure for humanity" (Ariel Dorfman, *The Empire's Old Clothes: What the Lone Ranger, Babar, and Other Innocent Heroes Do to Our Minds* (New York: Pantheon Books 1983), 199).

48   See Fiske, *Television Culture,* 71–2, 163–4, 320, and passim, for more on these and other examples. The need for simplistic homogeneous fare to achieve popularity makes sense only when it is assumed that a work's meaning and mode of reception are fixed and uniform for its readers, that its sense is firmly controlled by its author rather than being a dialogical and changing product of its interaction with other texts and socio-historically situated readers.

49   See, for example, T. S. Eliot, *The Use of Poetry and the Use of Criticism* (London: Faber, 1964), 152–3.

50   See Stuart Hall, "The Rediscovery of Ideology: The Return of the Repressed," in M. Gurevitch et al. (eds), *Culture, Society and Media* (London: Methuen, 1982), 56–90.

51   Bourdieu himself employs this notion (*D* 47–8, 57, 254, 370), and I shall explore the ethical idea of aesthetic living in ch. 9.

52   See Alexander Nehamas, "Plato and the Mass Media," *Monist* 71 (1988), 223: "The plays were not produced in front of a well-behaved audience. The dense crowd was given to whistling . . . and the theater resounded with its 'uneducated noise' . . . Plato expresses profound distaste for the tumult with which audiences, in the theater and elsewhere, voiced their approval or dissatisfaction (*Rep.* 492c) . . . Some of their food was used to pelt those actors whom they did not like, and whom they often literally shouted off the stage."

53   Horkheimer and Adorno, *Dialectic of Enlightenment,* 121, 157; Adorno, "Television and the Patterns of Mass Culture," 477.

54   See, for example, van den Haag, "Of Happiness," 517.

55   Adorno, who cannot help but recognize that most works of art have tended to affirm rather than resist the societies which generated them, is driven to defend art's essential oppositional status by construing its mere nonfunctional fictionality or divergence from the real as an act of resistance. But even if we grant this, the same would hold for works of popular art, which are instead typically vilified for their unreal escapism. Adorno elsewhere seems to recog-

nize this, but then condemns popular art for not being adequately escapist to constitute resistance. "It is not because they turn their back on washed-out existence that escape films are so repugnant, but because they do not do so energetically enough" (*Minima Moralia*, 202).

56 In nineteenth-century American theater, for example, a number of English actors were pelted by foodstuffs and shouted off the stage with cries like "Off! Off! Go back to England! Tell them the Yankees sent you back!" Moreover, "audiences in New Orleans often demanded that overtures to Italian operas be augmented by such familiar patriotic tunes as 'Yankee Doodle' and 'Hail Columbia.'" When one conductor chose to ignore these entreaties, "the audience began to tear up chairs and benches." The protest against aristocratic European culture (which was also in large part an expression of anger at European and aristocratic tendencies among upperclass Americans) had its most violent outburst in the Astor Place Riot of 1849, where at least twenty-two people were killed. For more on the American public's resistance (and submission) to the aristocracy, intellectualism, and European-styled elitism of high art, see Levine, *Highbrow/Lowbrow* (my citations are from 62 and 95).

57 Carl Boggs and Ray Pratt, "The Blues Tradition: Poetic Revolt or Cultural Impasse?," in Lazere (ed.), *American Media*, 279, make a similar point: "To the extent that the social conditions that shaped blues were agrarian, precapitalist, and racially defined, the music existed primarily outside the dominant economic system and social relations." For more on black culture as a developed refuge from white socio-cultural domination, see Eugene D. Genovese, *Roll Jordan, Roll: The World The Slaves Made* (New York: Pantheon, 1974), and Lawrence W. Levine, *Black Culture and Black Consciousness* (New York: Oxford University Press, 1977).

58 See, for example, Taylor, *Art, an Enemy of the People*, 43, and Arnold Hauser, *The Social History of Art* (New York: Knopf, 1951), 438ff.

59 This is not to say, however, that such resistance was strong enough to prevent the creation in America of a culturally aristocratic and politically influential high-art establishment, whose formation is well described by Levine. The point is rather that it was (and remains) strong enough to undermine the unquestioned monopoly of high art on aesthetic and cultural legitimacy.

60 Abraham Kaplan, "The Aesthetics of the Popular Arts," in J. B. Hall and B. Ulanov (eds), *Modern Culture and the Arts* (New York: McGraw-Hill, 1972), 53.

61 "The forms of hit songs are so strictly standardized . . . that no specific form appears in any particular piece." This "emancipation of the parts from their cohesion [in any formal unit means] . . . the diversion of interest from the whole . . . to the individual trick" (Adorno, "On the Fetish Character of Music," 281, 289; see also Macdonald, "A Theory of Mass Culture," 65: "Unity is essential in art; it cannot be achieved by a production line of specialists, however competent").

62   Moreover, not only does this audience enjoy formal complexities which de-
     center content and break narrative continuity (as in music video or the styl-
     ized, self-conscious camera work and diegetically disruptive musical-visual
     interludes in *Miami Vice*), but its members are capable of producing their
     own formally complex aesthetic products by segmenting and combining pop-
     ular-art products to create their own original texts. This may be done
     through systematic channel zapping, video-recording and editing, or, as in
     rap, with the segmentational sampling and synthesis of different records. See
     Fiske, *Television Culture*, 103–4, 238, 250–62, for these points with respect
     to TV, and the following chapter with respect to rap.
63   Bourdieu recognizes more than most theorists the deep bodily dimension of
     the aesthetic: "Art is never entirely the *cosa mentale* . . . which the intellectu-
     alist view makes of it. . . . Art is also a 'bodily thing'," related to basic "or-
     ganic" rhythms: "quickening and slowing, crescendo and decrescendo,
     tension and relaxation" (*D* 80). Yet unfortunately, because of his sociologist's
     bias for accepting socially dominant perspectives as positive facts, he confines
     the legitimate aesthetic to the "pure aesthetic" distanced from life and the
     body. This only reinforces the long tradition of intellectualist formalism in
     which the sensory is aesthetically legitimated only as a means to intellectual
     form – as Adorno puts it, "only as the bearer of something intellectual which
     shows itself in the whole" ("On the Fetish Character in Music," 274).
64   Greenberg, "Avant-Garde," 100.
65   Fiske, *Television Culture*, 238. See also the discussion of television's self-re-
     flective style, formal complexity, and self-conscious intertextuality in Alexan-
     der Nehamas's analysis of *St. Elsewhere* in his "Serious Watching," in David
     Hiley, James Bohman, and Richard Shusterman (eds), *The Interpretive Turn:
     Philosophy, Science, Culture* (Ithaca: Cornell University Press, 1991), 260–81.

Chapter 8   The Fine Art of Rap

 1   Rap's censorship became national news when The 2 Live Crew was banned
     and arrested in Florida in the summer of 1990. For details of earlier attempts
     to repress rap, see the pamphlet *You Got a Right to Rock: Don't Let Them
     Take It Away*, written by the editors of *Rock and Roll Confidential* and pub-
     lished by Duke and Duchess Ventures, Inc., New York, in September 1989.
     The censorship of concerts and the "parental" blacklisting of records (vigor-
     ously pursued by the Parents Musical Resource Center) are often thematized
     in rap lyrics and related to issues of aesthetic and political freedom of expres-
     sion, as for instance in Ice-T's "Freedom of Speech" and (albeit with much
     less wit and style) in 2 Live Crew's "Banned in the USA." Of course, more
     recently rap has proven too popular not to be coopted, in its milder forms,
     by the establishment media. Its rhythms and style have been adopted by

mainstream mass-media advertising, and one mild-mannered rapper, Fresh Prince, was given his own primetime major network TV show.

2 I have taken the title from the lyrics of Ice-T's "Hit the Deck," which aims to "demonstrate rappin' as a fine art." There are countless other raps which emphatically declare rap's poetic and artistic status; among the more forceful are: Stetsasonic's "Talkin' All That Jazz," BDP's "I'm Still #1," "Ya Slippin'," "Ghetto Music," and "Hip Hop Rules," and Kool Moe Dee's "The Best."

3 "Hip hop" actually designates an organic cultural complex wider than rap. It includes breakdancing and graffiti, and also a stylized but casual style of dress in which high-top sneakers became high fashion. Rap music supplied the beats for the breakdancers; some rappers testify to having practiced graffiti; and hip-hop fashion is celebrated in many raps, one example being Run-DMC's "My Adidas." For a study of graffiti, see Susan Stewart, "*Ceci Tuera Cela*: Graffiti as Crime and Art," in John Fekete (ed.), *Life After Postmodernism* (New York: St Martin's Press, 1987), 161–80.

4 As a white middle-class Jew, I realize that my interest in rap may be criticized as exploitative and not "politically correct," that I have no right to advocate or study a cultural form whose formative ghetto experience I lack. But though rap's roots lie firmly in the black urban ghetto, it aims (as we shall see) to reach a far wider audience; and its protest against poverty, persecution, and ethnic prejudice should be comprehensible to many groups and individuals who have experienced such things outside the black ghetto. In any case, I think it politically more incorrect to ignore rap's importance for contemporary culture and aesthetics by refusing to treat it simply because of race and socio-ethnic background.

5 I explore the aesthetic dimension of postmodernism in more detail in Richard Shusterman, "Postmodernism and the Aesthetic Turn," *Poetics Today* 10 (1989), 605–22. One very influential account of postmodernism on which I draw is Fredric Jameson's "Postmodernism, or the Cultural Logic of Late Capitalism," *New Left Review* 146 (1984), 53–92.

6 See, for example, Roger Abrahams, *Deep Down in the Jungle* (Chicago: Aldine Press, 1970), whose study of a Philadelphia ghetto reveals that speaking skills "confer high social status" and that even among young males "ability with words is as highly valued as physical strength" (39, 59). Studies of Washington and Chicago ghettos have confirmed this. See Ulf Hannerz, *Soulside* (New York: Columbia University Press, 1969), 84–5, which notes that verbal skill was "widely appreciated among ghetto men" not only for competitive practical purposes but for "entertainment value"; and Thomas Kochman, "Toward an Ethnography of Black American Speech Behavior," in Thomas Kochman (ed.), *Rappin' and Stylin' Out* (Urbana: University of Illinois Press, 1972), 241–64. Along with its narrower use to designate the traditional and stylized practice of verbal insult, black "signifying" has a more general sense

of encoded or indirect communication, which relies heavily on the special background knowledge and particular context of the communicants. For an impressively complex and theoretically sophisticated analysis of "signifying" as such a generic trope and its use "in black texts as explicit theme, as implicit rhetorical strategy, and as a principle of literary history," see Henry Louis Gates, Jr., *The Signifying Monkey: A Theory of Afro-American Literary Criticism* (Oxford: Oxford University Press, 1988), citation from 89.

7   Such linguistic strategies of evasion and indirection, which include "shucking," "tomming," "marking," and "loud-talking," as well as the more generic notions of inversion and signifying, are discussed at length in Kochman, "Toward an Ethnography"; Grace Simms Holt, " 'Inversion' in Black Communication"; and Claudia Mitchell-Kernan, "Signifying, loud-talking, and marking," all found in Kochman (ed.), *Rappin' and Stylin' Out.*

8   See David Toop, *The Rap Attack: African Five to New York Hip Hop* (Boston: South End Press, 1984), 14.

9   See, for example, Ice-T's "Rhyme Pays," Public Enemy's "Bring the Noise," Run-DMC's "Jam-master Jammin'," and BDP's "Ya Slippin'."

10 It is called "scratch mixing," not only because this manual placement of the needle on particular tracks scratches the records but also because the DJ hears the scratch in his ear when he cues the needle on the track to be sampled before actually adding it to the sound of the other record already being sent out on the sound system.

11 Rap historian David Toop (*Rap Attack,* 105) gives a sense of this wild eclecticism: "Bambaataa mixed up calypso, European and Japanese electronic music, Beethoven's Fifth Symphony and rock groups like Mountain; Kool DJ Herc spun the Doobie Brothers back to back with the Isley Brothers; Grandmaster Flash overlayed speech records and sound effects with The Last Poets; Symphonic B Boys Mixx cut up classical music on five turntables." See also 149, 153.

12 See, for example, Public Enemy's "Caught, Can We Get a Witness?," Stetsasonic's "Talkin' All That Jazz," and BDP's "I'm Still #1," "Ya Slippin'," and "The Blueprint." The motivating image of this last rap highlights the simulacral notion of hip-hop originality. In privileging their underground style as original and superior to "the soft commercial sound" of other rap, BDP connects its greater originality with its greater closeness to rap's ghetto origins. "You got a copy, I read from the blueprint." But a blueprint is itself a copy, not an original – indeed, it is a simulacrum or representation of a designed object which typically does not yet (if ever) exist as a concrete original object.

13 See Jameson, "Postmodernism," 73, 75. This is not to deny that rap ever achieves any unity or formal coherence of its own; for I argue below that it does, e.g. in "Talkin' All That Jazz."

14 T. S. Eliot, "Tradition and the Individual Talent," in *Selected Essays* (Lon-

don: Faber, 1976), 15. For a critique of this early view of Eliot's and an explanation of the reasons why he abandoned it in his later theory of tradition, see Richard Shusterman, *T. S. Eliot and the Philosophy of Criticism* (New York: Columbia University Press, 1988), 156–67.

15　See, respectively, "My Philosophy" and "Ghetto Music." The lyrics of "Ya Slippin' " and "Hip Hop Rules" respectively date themselves as 1987 and 1989. Public Enemy's "Don't Believe the Hype" has a 1988 time tag, and similar time tags can be found in raps by Ice-T, Kool Moe Dee, and many others.

16　By the same token, I trust that my present account of rap is worthwhile even though it may soon become outdated by new developments in the genre.

17　There are rap records from white groups like Blondie, Tom Tom Club, Beastie Boys, 3rd Bass, and from the white solo rapper Vanilla Ice.

18　See, for example, the French rap album *Rapattitudes*, in which the rappers refer to their specific neighborhoods in Paris and their problems of housing and social acceptance. French rap, though genuine in spirit, remains very derivative from its American source.

19　Toop, *Rap Attack*, 14–15, 70–1. It might well be argued that hip hop provides an aesthetic field where physical violence and aggression get translated into symbolic form. Certainly, fierce rivalry and aggressive competition are essential to the aesthetic of rap. Perhaps the most common theme in rap lyrics is how the rapper is superior to others in the power of his rhymes and ability to "rock" the audience, how he can take on the challenge of other rappers (who criticize, or "dis," him) and make them look weak and foolish when they duel with him in rap. This dueling is often described in extremely violent terms, as it is in the traditional verbal insult contests of "the dozens" and "signifying" (see sources cited in n. 6). However, together with this uncompromising competitive assertion to be "the best," rappers also express in their lyrics their underlying solidarity with other rap artists who share the same artistic and political agenda.

　　One of the most distressing expressions of rap's symbolic violence is its attitude toward women, which often is not only sexually exploitative but savagely brutal. The best defense rap can provide for its violently misogynist lyrics is that they are self-consciously exaggerated and should be understood as ironic signifying on machoism. This defense (which is problematic at best) is more plausible in the dry wit of Ice-T than in the stark brutality of NWA. The most encouraging sign is that women rappers are rapping back in protest, as, for example, HWA (Hoes Wit Attitude) and BWP (Bytches With Problems), and, most potently, Queen Latifah.

20　Jameson, "Postmodernism," 76, 79.

21　Toop, *Rap Attack*, 151.

22　See Public Enemy's "Bring the Noise."

23　See Ice-T's "Heartbeat" and Public Enemy's "Don't Believe the Hype."

24 In "Don't Believe the Hype."

25 See BDP's "Ghetto Music," Public Enemy's "Rebel Without a Pause," and Ice-T's "Radio Suckers." However, as these rappers admit, some stations on some occasions (usually late at night) will play the "raw reality sound."

26 In "Radio Suckers."

27 See Public Enemy's "Black Steel in the Hour of Chaos." On this theme of black exploitation by white society, see also BDP's "Who Protects Us From You?" and Ice-T's "Squeeze the Trigger."

28 For examples of the former tension, see Ice-T's "High Rollers," "Drama," "6'N the Mornin'," and "Somebody Gotta Do It (Pimpin' Ain't Easy!)," and Big Daddy Kane's "Another Victory"; for the latter, see Ice-T's "Radio Suckers" and BDP's "The Blueprint." Another troubling contradiction is that despite rap's condemnation of minority oppression and exploitation, it frequently adopts the "pimpin' style" which consists of horribly macho celebrations of the (often violent) exploitation of women.

29 Pierre Bourdieu's *Distinction: A Social Critique of the Judgement of Taste* (Cambridge, Mass.: Harvard University Press, 1984) exposes the hidden logic of material, commercial, and class interests and mechanisms which allow for the workings of so-called pure, non-commercial art, and for its effective illusion as pure and non-commercial.

30 Houston Baker, *Blues, Ideology, and Afro-American Literature: A Vernacular Theory* (Chicago: University of Chicago Press, 1984), 34–63.

31 Ibid. 57.

32 See, for example, Ice-T's "Rhyme Pays" and Kool Moe Dee's "They Want Money" and "The Avenue."

33 See, for example, Jürgen Habermas, *The Philosophical Discourses of Modernity* (Cambridge, Mass.: MIT Press, 1987), 1–22.

34 See Friedrich Schiller, *On the Aesthetic Education of Man* (Oxford: Clarendon Press, 1982).

35 See BDP's "My Philosophy" and "Gimme Dat, (Woy)." The lyrics of their knowledge rap "Who Protects Us From You?" describe it as "a public service announcement brought to you by the scientists of Boogie Down Productions."

36 From "I'm Still #1." For BDP's attack on establishment history and media and their stereotypes, see especially "My Philosophy," "You Must Learn," and "Why is That?."

37 This notion, for example, provides the central theme of Kool Moe Dee's "Do You Know What Time It Is?", and it is also given sartorial expression in Public Enemy's Flavor Flav's costume trademark – a huge clock he wears like a necklace.

38 The best example of this is Gary Byrd, a New York radio DJ who developed a literacy program based on rap. For more details on this, see Toop, *Rap Attack*, 45–6.

39 The citations from Jameson in this and the following two paragraphs are from "Postmodernism," 85, 87, 88, 89. Adorno's phrase comes from T. W. Adorno, *Aesthetic Theory* (London: Routledge & Kegan Paul, 1984), 322.

40 See, for example, Ice-T's "409" and BDP's "Nervous." It is noteworthy that even these artists, who identify themselves as non-commercial, bear names that suggest the business world. Ice-T's group or "crew" is called "Rhyme Syndicate Productions," and BDP, of course, stands for "Boogie Down Productions." Commercial rap is often flagrantly such, as when the lyrics advertise the artist's records or his money making commercial phone line (as with LL Cool J's rap "1-900-LL Cool J").

41 Grandmaster Flash complained when, at the novelty and virtuosity of his cutting, "the crowd would stop dancing and just gather round as if it was a seminar. This was what I didn't want. This wasn't school – it was time to shake your ass" (quoted from Toop, *Rap Attack*, 72).

42 See Queen Latifah's "Dance for Me" and Ice-T's "Hit the Deck." For a similar emphasis on the mesmerizing possession and physically and spiritually moving power of rap in both performer and audience, see Kool Moe Dee's "Rock Steady" and "The Best."

43 The point is made most explicitly in Plato's *Ion*. But in Kool Moe Dee's rap "Get the Picture" the direction and valorization of this chain of divine madness is wittily reversed. His hypnotic rapping is identified with "knowledge" and "telling you the truth," which bring the rapper's possessed audience up to the level of the gods, challenging their supremacy and captivating them as well:

> I start to float
> On the rhymes I wrote
> Ascending to a level with the gods and I tote
> Loads and mounds of people
> As they reach new heights
> A half a mile from heaven is the party site
> And I'm the attraction.
> The gods will be packed in
> Coming out of their pockets for me to rock it
> And acting
> Like they've never ever been entertained.
> They try to act godly but they can't maintain.
> . . . .
> And Venus would peak on every word I speak,
> Zeus would get loose
> Fully induced.
> I'll make Apollo's rhymes sound like Mother
> Goose.
> By night's end Mercury is so hyped

> He'd spread the word that there's a god of the mike
> Captivating all the other gods
> By the masses,
> Described as a dark-skinned brother in glasses.

44 See, for example, Michael Ventura, *Shadow Dancing in the U.S.A.* (Los Angeles: J. P. Tarcher, 1986); and Robert Farris Thompson, *Flash of the Spirit* (New York: Vintage, 1984).

45 It is, for instance, the only song to appear in both the popular *Yo! MTV Raps* and *Monster TV Rap Hits* albums. The song is here reprinted with permission from Tee Gee Girl Music (BMI).

46 Nor does my printed transcription of the lyrics convey that they are delivered in antiphonal style by three voices which alternate irregularly between lines and sometimes within the very same line, adding to the rap's jumpy syncopated style and formal complexity.

47 I take these definitions from *Funk and Wagnall's Standard Desk Dictionary* (New York: Thomas Y. Crowell, 1980). *Webster's New Collegiate Dictionary* (Springfield, Mass.: Merriam, 1979) and *The Random House College Dictionary* (New York: Random House, 1984) convey essentially the same meaning of "empty talk: humbug" and "insincere, exaggerated, or pretentious talk."

48 Rap is far more outspoken in its black pride and challenge of white cultural and political domination than jazz. This is not surprising, since the latter evolved in a black experience much closer to slavery.

49 This emphasis on rap as deliberately composed writing rather than mere talk highlights rap's claim to literacy as well as artistry. The song does not, however, draw a dichotomy between talking as lies and writing as truth; for in presenting the truth to their hostile critics, the rappers are not only writing but "talkin' about you." Rappers are generally prone to emphasize their skill in oral improvisation as much as their talent for written composition.

50 This is the song's dominant reading. But, given the ambiguities and inversions on which its case for rap is made, it remains open to alternative, oppositional readings as well. A right-wing critic could argue that the song's musical status as talking jazz, together with its claim to be not only true art but real truth, pathetically confirms its status as mere "talkin' jazz" in the sense of pretentious nonsense or empty "hype." A divergent black activist reading could see the song's *artistic* protest of black socio-cultural oppression as self-vitiatingly implying the false reduction of the political to the aesthetic, suggesting that rap remains just "talkin' jazz" in providing mere artistic protest rather than real political action.

51 See, for example, the study of America's transfiguration of Shakespeare and opera from popular to elite art, in Lawrence Levine, *Highbrow/Lowbrow: The Emergence of Cultural Hierarchy in America* (Cambridge, Mass.: Harvard University Press, 1988).

52 See Holt, " 'Inversion' in Black Communication," 154.
53 Claude Brown, "The Language of Soul," in Kochman (ed.), *Rappin' and Stylin' Out,* 135.
54 Holt, " 'Inversion' in Black Communication," 154.
55 See Claudia Mitchell-Kernan, "Signifying," 326–7. This form of verbal art is one which in fine Deweyan fashion is extremely continuous with and enhancive of ordinary life. We should not forget that rapping was a linguistic style before it went musical, and this sense of rapping, of course, remains.
56 See *The Random House College Dictionary.*
57 An FBI director, for instance, issued an official warning regarding a rap by NWA (Niggers With Attitude), without ever hearing the song; and a survey of the protest mail received by the group revealed that none of these anti-rap critics had in fact heard the song in question or were at all familiar with other rap music. Such hearsay-based animosity has resulted in cancellations of rap concerts and the censoring and confiscation of rap records. For more details on these matters, see Dave Marsh and Phyllis Pollack, "Wanted for Attitude," *Village Voice,* 10 Oct. 1989, 33–7.
58 The violence of this struggle often exceeds the domain of mere symbolic violence. Beyond critique and counter-critique, the establishment exercises the actual violence of censorship and arrest, while rap supporters employ the retaliatory violence of its blasting noise (which is thematized in many rap songs) and the threat of physical violence born of prolonged frustration and oppression. These two forms of retaliatory violence are emphasized and cleverly linked in Spike Lee's *Do the Right Thing,* where the violent silencing of loud rap leads to a neighborhood riot.
59 The contradictions of the democratic establishment's censorship of rap are pointedly expressed in the title song of Ice-T's album *Freedom of Speech... Just Watch What You Say* and are also suggested in the very name of Public Enemy, which mischievously plays on the two different meanings of "public" here in sharp contradiction: the institutionally official versus what truly represents the people or community.
60 See Jon Pareles, "How Rap Moves to Television's Beat," *New York Times,* Sunday, 14, Jan. 1990, sect. 2, Arts & Leisure, 1, 28. MTV indeed does a better job than commercial radio and network TV in presenting rap, but it still concentrates on the commercial sound, while much of the more threatening and interesting underground rap is not adequately represented. In arguing that rap and its popular appeal are essentially shaped by the medium of television, Pareles unfortunately neglects rap's censorship by and critique of TV. It was not until 1989 that TV agreed to include rap in its Grammy Award telecast, a point that has been rapped about, along with critiques of the corruptive illusions that TV propagates (see, e.g., Public Enemy's "Terminator X to the Edge of Panic," which has the revealing line "Who gives a fuck about a Goddamn Grammy," and their "She Watch Channel Zero").

Moreover, it is simplistic to isolate TV as what is responsible for rap's collage effect of rapidly shifting content, self-advertisement, and quickly punctuated bits of information. The same things can be found in commercial radio, which is equally, if not more, part of street culture, and where listeners also jump from station to station to catch more songs than advertisements or news briefs. Radio seems closer to rap's loose, dialogical form, since its format is more flexible and allows more intervention (by DJs and audience phone-ins) than does TV, which is nonetheless an important influence on rap. It is truer to say that rap is a product of our global electronic technology: multiple turntables, tape recorders, "beat boxes" and sound systems, computer games, video, radio, TV, and the rest.

61   Greil Marcus, *Mystery Train: Images of America in Rock 'n' Roll Music* (New York: Dalton, 1982), 82. The book contains an excellent chapter devoted to Sly Stone's career.

62   See the song "Poet" in his album *Riot*, where he sings, "I'm a songwriter, oh yeh, a poet."

63   Hence the song's appeal to the antecedent beliefs in democratic majoritarianism and pluralistic tolerance and to the antecedent tastes for "R & B" and "Sly and the Family Stone."

64   I discuss this form of argument in considerable detail in my articles "The Logic of Interpretation," *Philosophical Quarterly* 28 (1978), 310–24; "Evaluative Reasoning in Criticism," *Ratio* 23 (1981), 141–57; "Wittgenstein and Critical Reasoning," *Philosophy and Phenomenological Research* 47 (1986), 91–110; and in *T. S. Eliot and the Philosophy of Criticism*, 91–106.

65   Wollheim, for instance, speaks of "the perennial and ineradicable self-consciousness of art," in Richard Wollheim, *Art and its Objects* (Harmondsworth: Penguin, 1975), 16.

66   See M. Horkheimer and T. W. Adorno, *Dialectic of Enlightenment* (New York: Continuum, 1986), 121; Bourdieu, *Distinction*, 41, 48, 395; and my discussion of their views in the previous chapter.

67   For an elaboration of this point, see my *T. S. Eliot and the Philosophy of Criticism*, 157–64, 170–90.

68   Both these features can be connected to art's allegedly requisite oppositional character. For art's creative injunction to be new implies at least some opposition to the old and familiar, while preoccupation with form rather than content seems to go against our ordinary cognitive and practical concerns (and thus has come to define for many the specifically aesthetic attitude).

69   I should mention, however, that the song does pointedly sample from jazz, notably from the jazz keyboardist Lonnie Liston-Smith's "Expansions."

70   Pareles, "How Rap Moves," 1. Many rap songs, particularly those that trace and celebrate the history of hip hop, more explicitly flaunt rap's stunning success at outlasting the critics' constant predictions of its early demise, and thereby argue for its value and rich creative potential in terms of its staying power. See, for example, BDP's "Hip Hop Rules."

71 Of course, there is nothing in rap's innovations which logically precludes the achievement of formal coherence and unity. Rhythmic tensions, sampled fragments, and dislocated interjections can be rewoven into compelling artistic wholes, as any reader of works like Eliot's *The Wasteland* should realize. And I think one can also find a complex coherence in "The Adventures of Grandmaster Flash on the Wheels of Steel." However, to some extent, a practical tension does remain. For in giving freest rein to its innovations and artistically revolutionary impulse, rap can end up sounding like formless, senseless noise; and it sometimes does. But abandoning such innovation so as to satisfy traditional demands of form would mean abandoning rap's potential to reshape and extend our sense of form so that we can learn to see and appreciate a pattern where we once saw only formlessness.

Chapter 9   Postmodern Ethics and the Art of Living

1   See Ludwig Wittgenstein, *Tractatus Logico-Philosophicus* (London: Routledge & Kegan Paul, 1963), 146, 147. The English translation in this dual-language edition, "Ethics and aesthetics are one and the same," makes the assertion of identity much stronger than in the German original, which says only "Ethik und Ästhetik sind Eins." Future references to the *Tractatus* will be designated by *T* and the appropriate proposition number.

2   Ludwig Wittgenstein, *Notebooks 1914–1916*, 2nd edn (Chicago: University of Chicago Press, 1979), hereafter abbreviated *N*.

3   See *T* 6.45 and Wittgenstein's "Lecture on Ethics," written sometime between 1929 and 1930 and posthumously published in *Philosophical Review* 74 (1965), 3–12. In this lecture and in *N* 86 Wittgenstein refers to the mystical through the notion of the wonderful or miraculous (*das Wunder*).

4   See Jean-François Lyotard, *The Postmodern Condition* (Minneapolis: University of Minnesota Press, 1984), 10, 40–1.

5   The classic case for the logical differences between ethics and aesthetics is found in Stuart Hampshire, "Logic and Appreciation," repr. in W. Elton (ed.), *Aesthetics and Language* (Oxford: Blackwell, 1954), 161–9.

6   I have discussed this and other aspects of Wittgenstein's later aesthetic theory in "Wittgenstein and Critical Reasoning," *Philosophy and Phenomenological Research* 47 (1986), 91–110.

7   This distinction between "private morality" and "public morality" is a fairly common one and has recently been employed by Rorty in arguing for his own aestheticized ethic. Though the distinction can be useful, I doubt, for reasons discussed later, that the project of private morality is as clearly separable and independent from public morality as Rorty would have us believe. Rorty introduces the public/private morality distinction on pp. 10–11 of his "Freud and Moral Reflection," in J. H. Smith and W. Kerrigan (eds),

Pragmatism's Freud: The Moral Disposition of Psychoanalysis (Baltimore: Johns Hopkins University Press, 1986), 1–27, hereafter abbreviated *R*; and it becomes a very central theme in his *Contingency, Irony, and Solidarity* (Cambridge: Cambridge University Press, 1989), hereafter abbreviated *CIS*.

8 For Plato and generally for the Greeks, the ideas of the good and the beautiful were not so clearly differentiated, as can be seen from the fact that they were frequently referred to collectively in the composite term *kalon-kai-agathon* ("beautiful and good") and that *kalos,* the specific term for the beautiful, was used perhaps as much as *agathos* to denote moral goodness. Once the Greek ethical world governed by the goal of *eudaemonia* gave way to ethics dominated by the ideas of divine commandment and duty or obligation, it was much easier to separate the ethical from the aesthetic and even to regard them as conflicting principles. The famous postclassical connections made between aesthetics and ethics express a salient awareness of their perceived divide. Kant saw beauty as a symbol of morality; Schiller saw an aesthetic education as a means to morality; and Kierkegaard saw an aesthetic attitude to life as an inferior alternative to the ethical life. Postmodernism's ethics of taste is perhaps distinctive only in its attempt at really merging the two spheres in defiant awareness of a long tradition of philosophical bifurcation (which would distinguish it from the Greek overlap), so that the aesthetic is neither a symbol of, means to, or surrogate for an ethic, but rather the constitutive substance of one.

9 Richard Rorty, "Freud, Morality, and Hermeneutics," *New Literary History* 12 (1980), 180.

10 Bernard Williams, *Ethics and the Limits of Philosophy* (London: Fontana, 1985), 29, henceforth abbreviated *ELP*.

11 See T. S. Eliot, "Tradition and the Individual Talent," *Selected Essays* (London: Faber, 1976), 16.

12 See Lyotard, *Postmodern Condition*, 27–41.

13 Richard Wollheim, *The Thread of Life* (Cambridge, Mass.: Harvard University Press, 1984), 215–16; henceforth abbreviated *TL*. Wollheim does not in fact use the term "ethics" here; but he makes the same essential distinction as Williams by speaking of "morality broadly conceived," which includes non-obligational values, versus "morality narrowly conceived," which is dominated by obligation and founded on introjection (e.g. *TL* 221). I should also caution that neither Wollheim nor Williams is a characteristically postmodern philosopher, even if they do challenge modernity's dominant ethic of morality governed by obligational reason. Though their critique no doubt reflects postmodern experience, their philosophical style and general objectivist outlook remain traditionally modern. Rorty, by contrast, can be called a postmodern philosopher, though here is not the place to try to explain or justify this distinction. I make a brief attempt to do so in "Postmodernism and the Aesthetic Turn," *Poetics Today* 10 (1989), 604–22.

14 Viewing ethics as a creative art suggests that the ethical agent has the same kind of freedom and power in life that the artist has in his art. One could well object that such is not the case for most members of society, notwithstanding the fact that even the poor have some options for stylization of life. For this reason, as I shall later argue, social (as well as aesthetic) reform is needed to make the ethical ideal of living life as art a more accessible and shared option.

15 Alisdair MacIntyre, *After Virtue* (London: Duckworth, 1982), 191.

16 See G. E. Moore, *Principia Ethica* (Cambridge: Cambridge University Press, repr. 1959), 188–9, henceforth abbreviated *PE*.

17 O. Wilde, *The Works of Oscar Wilde* (New York: Dutton, 1954), 934. Wilde's advocacy of the aesthetic life seems to combine aspects of all three genres I have distinguished. He variously urges (1) a life of the pleasures of aesthetic consumption (with the inspired momentary states of stasis and inactivity they afford); (2) the need for one's life to form an aesthetically pleasing whole; and (3) something approaching the Rortian-Faustian aesthetic life when he recommends that such unity be found in constant change. Indeed, Wilde already expounded Rorty's postmodern model of the ironist in the 1890s when he stated that the ideal aesthete "will realize himself in many forms, and by a thousand different ways, and will ever be curious of new sensations and fresh points of view. Through constant change, and through constant change alone, he will find his true unity" (987).

It should be noted that Pater also anticipated Rorty's Faustian aesthetic life in advocating a "quickened, multiplied consciousness," a thirst for the intense excitement of novelty, and a pragmatic experiential view of knowledge, not as providing any permanent truth (which is unattainable) but simply as "ideas," "points of view," or "instruments of criticism" (in Rorty's terms, "vocabularies") for enriching our experience and quickening its appreciation (see Walter Pater, *The Renaissance* (London: Macmillan, 1917), vii–xv, 233–9).

18 Michel Foucault, "On the Genealogy of Ethics: An Overview of Work in Progress," in Paul Rabinow (ed.), *The Foucault Reader* (New York: Pantheon, 1984), 341, 343. For elaboration of this idea, see Foucault, *The History of Sexuality* (New York: Random House, 1985, 1986), vols. 2 and 3.

19 Foucault, *Care of the Self* (*History of Sexuality*, vol. 3), 40, 65–6.

20 This interpretation of Nietzsche is attractively presented in Alexander Nehamas, *Nietzsche: Life as Literature* (Cambridge, Mass.: Harvard University Press, 1985). He writes: "The unity of the self, which therefore also constitutes its identity, is not something given but something achieved, not a beginning but a goal" (182). This goal "of the unified self is still compatible with continual change" and diverse experience (189). It allows a self, in Nietzsche's own words, "*all* the strong, seemingly contradictory desires – but in such a way that they go together under a yoke" (221), held fast, as are the

conflicting actions they may engender, in some coherent unity that may be very complex. My difficulty with Nietzsche and Nehamas is their attempt to ground this ideal of self-unity on more fundamental logical and ontological principles of unity. I discuss this problem in my "Nietzsche and Nehamas on Organic Unity," *Southern Journal of Philosophy* 26 (1988), 379–92.

21 It might be argued more generally that our culture's preoccupation with visibly standing out as a firmly determinate individual results from a male-dominated identification of self with phallus. Female sexuality, which lacks this protrusive visuality and singularity of the phallus but is rather constituted of overlapping, multiple folds, can suggest another model of self and society. See Luce Iriguray, *This Sex Which Is Not One* (Ithaca: Cornell University Press, 1985), 23–33.

22 Such pluralism is, in fact, more in tune with his advocacy of "an increasing willingness to live with plurality" and "an increasing sense of the radical diversity of private purposes." But Rorty too narrowly identifies this diversity with the ambitiously original self-creations of strong poets and ironists, "the radically poetic character of individual lives" (*CIS* 67). A more consistent pragmatic pluralism would recognize in the diversity of private purposes also the desire to be accepted as just one of the gang, a desire for similarity and belonging, free from the quest for radical distinction and individual originality.

23 See Pierre Bourdieu, "The Market of Symbolic Goods," *Poetics* 14 (1985), 13–44, and "The Production of Belief" in R. Collins et al., *Media, Culture, and Society: A Critical Reader* (London: Sage, 1986), 131–63.

24 See W. F. Haug, *Critique of Commodity Aesthetics: Appearance, Sexuality, and Advertising in Capitalist Society* (Minneapolis: University of Minnesota Press, 1986).

25 Fredric Jameson, *The Ideologies of Theory* (Minneapolis: University of Minnesota Press, 1988), vol. 2, 70.

26 For an illuminating critique of Fonda's aerobic videos in terms of their deficiencies and dangers for soma and selfhood, see Elizabeth Kagan and Margaret Morse, "The Body Electronic, Aerobic Exercise on Video: Women's Search for Empowerment and Self-Transformation," *The Drama Review* 32 (1988), 164–80. For a more wide-ranging feminist critique of our culture's preoccupation with transforming the body's external shape to fit socially privileged models, see Susan Bordo, " 'Material Girl': The Effacements of Postmodern Culture," *Michigan Quarterly Review*, 1990, 653–77.

27 William James, *Pragmatism and Other Essays* (New York: Simon and Schuster, 1963), 26.

Chapter 10   Somaesthetics: A Disciplinary Proposal

1 Michel de Montaigne, "Of Presumption," in *The Complete Essays of Montaigne* (Stanford: Stanford University Press, 1965), 484.

2 See Richard Shusterman, "Die Sorge um den Körper in der heutigen Kul-

tur," in Andreas Kuhlmann (ed.), *Philosophische Ansichte der Kultur der Moderne* (Frankfurt: Fischer, 1994), 241–77.

3   J. M. Guyau, *Les problèmes de l'esthétique contemporaine* (1884), 11th edn (Paris: Alcan, 1925), 20–1; cf. the book's English translation: *Problems of Contemporary Aesthetics* (Los Angeles: DeVorss, 1947), 23.

4   See Richard Shusterman, *Practicing Philosophy: Pragmatism and the Philosophical Life* (New York: Routledge, 1997), 127–9, 166–77, the first English text where I employ the term "somaesthetics." The term was introduced in *Vor der Interpretation* (Vienna: Passagen, 1996), 132, which is a revised German translation of my *Sous l'interprétation* (Paris: L'éclat, 1994). See also my "Somaesthetics and the Body/Media Issue," *Body and Society* 3 (1997): 33–49. The somatic was also central to the aesthetics I earlier developed in the first edition of *Pragmatist Aesthetics: Living Beauty, Rethinking Art* (Oxford: Blackwell, 1992), 6–7, 52–3, 258–61.

5   The definition forms the subtitle of James's book, *Pragmatism: A New Name for Some Old Ways of Thinking* (New York: Longmans, 1907), repr. in William James, *Pragmatism and Other Essays* (New York: Simon and Schuster, 1963).

6   Baumgarten first used the term in section 116 of his 1735 doctoral thesis, *Meditiationes philosophicae de nonnullis ad poema pertinentibus*. After giving a course of lectures on aesthetics in 1742 and 1749 at the University of Frankfurt-on-the-Oder, he published a long treatise (in Latin) entitled *Aesthetica* in 1750, complemented in 1758 by a shorter second part. My citations from Baumgarten are from the bilingual (Latin-German) abridged edition of this work, Alexander Baumgarten, *Theoretische Ästhetik: Die grundlengenden Abschnitte aus der "Aesthetica"* (1750/58), trans. H. R. Schweizer (Hamburg: Felix Meiner, 1988). The English translations are mine. Subsequent references to this work will be noted parenthetically in my text.

7   There exists, however, an English translation of Baumgarten's doctoral thesis and first book, cited above. Translated and edited by Karl Aschenbrenner and W. B. Hoelther, it bears the English title *Reflections on Poetry* (Berkeley: University of California Press, 1954).

8   "*Caro*" is often used in negative contrast to the soul, as in Seneca's famous remark: "In hoc obnoxio domicilio animus liber habitat. Numquam me caro ista compellet ad metum, numquam ad indignam bono simulationem" ("In this noxious dwelling, the soul lives free. Never shall my flesh drive me to feel fear, or to assume any pretence that is unworthy of a good man"), Seneca's *Epistles*, 65:22. "*Caro*" is also used in a conventional Latin phrase used to designate someone with contempt – "*caro putida*" (rotten or putrid flesh). See *Harper's Latin Dictionary* (New York: Harper, 1907), 294.

9   Baumgarten originally came from a Pietist background and was, of course, aware of the great risks that early Enlightenment philosophers still faced if they theorized in ways that conflicted with Church doctrine. His philosophical hero, Christian Wolff, was exiled from Halle (where Baumgarten studied and later taught), because his doctrines incensed the religious leaders there.

Texts by Spinoza and his followers, with their heterodox views on God and mind-body unity, were also frequently burned at that time. In short, the dominantly religious ideological context into which Baumgarten had to introduce aesthetics would have been very intolerant of philosophies that emphasized the body.

10 In the "Introduction" to *Practicing Philosophy*, I offer some tentative hypotheses concerning the historical reasons for philosophy's retreat from a full-bodied art of living into a mere academic discipline of theory. The explanations I offer build largely on the work of Pierre Hadot and Michel Foucault, but the bulk of my own efforts are devoted to exploring contemporary possibilities and models for practicing philosophy as an embodied art of living.

11 See Diogenes Laertius, *Lives of Eminent Philosophers* (Cambridge: Harvard University Press, 1991), vol. 1, 153, 163; Xenophon, *Conversations of Socrates* (London: Penguin, 1990), 172.

12 Of Diogenes the Cynic it is said: "He would adduce indisputable evidence to show how easily from gymnastic training we arrive at virtue." Even the pre-Socratic Cleobulus, a sage "distinguished for strength and beauty" and initiated in Egyptian philosophy, "advised people to practice bodily exercise" in their pursuit of wisdom. The citations in this paragraph come from Diogenes Laertius, *Lives of Eminent Philosophers* (Cambridge: Harvard University Press, 1991), vol. 1, 91, 95, 153, 221; vol. 2, 71, 215.

13 Yasuo Yuasa, *The Body: Toward an Eastern Mind-Body Theory* (Albany: SUNY Press, 1987), 25. In Yuasa's later book, *The Body, Self-Cultivation, and Ki-Energy* (Albany: SUNY Press, 1993), the term *shugyo* is translated as "self-cultivation." Derived from combining the two Chinese characters that respectively stand for "mastery" and "practice," *shugyo* literally means to "master a practice," but the idea that this requires self-cultivation and self-mastery is implicit and essential.

14 Having analyzed these practices in "Die Sorge um den Körper in der heutigen Kultur," I note here only a small sample of important primary sources. F. M. Alexander, *Constructive Conscious Control of the Individual* (New York: Dutton, 1924) and *The Use of the Self* (New York: Dutton, 1932); Moshe Feldenkrais, *Awareness Through Movement* (New York: HarperCollins, 1977) and *The Potent Self* (New York: HarperCollins, 1992); and Alexander Lowen, *Bioenergetics* (New York: Penguin, 1975).

15 Diogenes Laertius, *Lives of Eminent Philosophers*, vol. 1, 71; cf. vol. 1, 221; vol. 2, 119.

16 Pleasure, of course, does not exhaust the valuable feelings that somaesthetics, like aesthetics, should examine and achieve. But in challenging pleasure's monopoly of all value, we should not trivialize pleasure's worth and minimize its depth and range of varieties. For a debate on this issue, see Alexander Nehamas, "Richard Shusterman on Pleasure and Aesthetic Experience" (and my response), in *Journal of Aesthetics and Art Criticism* 56 (1998): 49–53. See

also a similar exchange with Wolfgang Welsch, "Rettung durch Halbierung? Zu Richard Shustermans Rehabilitierung ästhetischer Erfahrung," *Deutsche Zeitschrift für Philosophie* 47 (1999), 111–26; and my response, "Provaktion und Erinnerung: Zu Freude, Sinn, und Wert in ästhetischer Erfahrung," ibid., 127–37.

17　See, for example, Friedrich Nietzsche, *The Will to Power* (New York: Vintage, 1968); Maurice Merleau-Ponty, *The Phenomenology of Perception* (London: Routledge, 1962); and Owen Flanagan, *The Science of the Mind*, 2nd edn (Cambridge, Mass.: MIT Press, 1991).

18　While supervenience is a concept familiar to students of philosophy, that of supersets may require an explanation: "Supersets are two [or more body-building] exercises performed in a row without stopping." For more details, see Arnold Schwarzenegger, *Encyclopedia of Modern Bodybuilding* (New York: Simon and Schuster, 1985), 161.

19　See, for example, Michel Foucault, *Discipline and Punish* (New York: Vintage, 1979); *The History of Sexuality*, vol. 1, *An Introduction* (New York: Vintage, 1980); vol. 2, *The Use of Pleasure* (New York: Vintage, 1986); and vol. 3, *The Care of the Self* (New York: Vintage, 1988); and Pierre Bourdieu, *The Logic of Practice* (Stanford: Stanford University Press, 1990), and "La Connaissance par Corps," in *Meditations Pascaliennes* (Paris: Seuil, 1997).

20　I am not, of course, claiming that disciplines like yoga and *zazen* (or those of Feldenkrais and Alexander) are pursued entirely or primarily for their aesthetic experiences. But they do in fact underline their aesthetic dimensions and benefits. See, for example, the ancient *Hatha Yoga Pradipika* by Svatmarama Swami, trans. Pancham Sinh (Allabad, India: Lalit Mohan Basu, 1915), which speaks of how "a yogi's body becomes divine, glowing, healthy, and emits a divine smell," so that he or she "becomes next to the God of Love in beauty" (23, 57). See also Dogen's "Principles of Seated Meditation," in Carl Bielefeldt, *Dogen's Manuals of Zen Meditation* (Berkeley: University of California Press, 1988). For Feldenkrais and Alexander, see the references in note 14.

21　See Max Horkheimer and Theodor Adorno, *Dialectic of Enlightenment* (New York: Continuum, 1986), 232, 233.

22　Horkheimer and Adorno, *Dialectic of Enlightenment*, 233–4.

23　Ibid., 234.

24　Ibid., 235.

25　This is not to say that experiential somaesthetics can present no norms or ideals: the famed "runner's high," bodybuilder's "pump," and lover's orgasm could be seen as posing singular standards of experiential success that can sometimes wield an oppressive power.

26　For a helpful account of how classical Indian aesthetics emphasizes the body and its sensuous pleasures, see Rekha Jhanji, *The Sensuous in Art: Reflections on Indian Aesthetics* (Delhi: Motilal Banarsidass, 1989), a book that refutes the very transcendental-religious image of Indian aesthetics that has been so influential through the work of Ananda Coomaraswamy.

27　See David Hume, "Of the Standard of Taste," in E. F. Miller (ed.), *Essays Moral Political, and Literary* (Indianapolis: Liberty Classics, 1985), 236. The Nietzsche citation is from *The Will to Power* (New York: Vintage, 1968), section 820. Merleau-Ponty is another important philosopher who insists on the body's role in aesthetic perception and artistic creation. See his account of painting in "Eye and Mind," in Maurice Merleau-Ponty, *The Primacy of Perception* (Evanston: Northwestern University Press, 1964), 159–90.

28　Alexander Nehamas, in *The Art of Living* (Berkeley: University of California Press, 1998), offers an interesting study of philosophy's art of living in Socrates, Plato, Montaigne, Nietzsche, and Foucault. See also Wolfgang Welsch, *Undoing Aesthetics* (London: Sage, 1997), who advocates, through the concept of *aisthesis*, a very broad philosophical notion of aesthetics that is not primarily centered on art.

29　For further critique of the argument that philosophy cannot usefully treat somatic experiences because it is confined, by its disciplinary definition, to the linguistic realm, see *Practicing Philosophy*, ch. 6.

30　See Max Dessoir, who founded the German Society of Aesthetics and the *Zeitschrift für Ästhetik und allgemeine Kunstwissenchaft* and whose master work is translated as *Aesthetics and Theory of Art* (Detroit: Wayne State University Press, 1970); see also Thomas Munro, who later helped establish the American Society for Aesthetics and its official journal, *The Journal of Aesthetics and Art Criticism*. Munro's advocacy for aesthetics' independence can be found, for example, in "Aesthetics and Philosophy in American Colleges," *Journal of Aesthetics and Art Criticism* 4 (1946): 185–7; "Society and Solitude in Aesthetics," *Journal of Aesthetics and Art Criticism* 3 (1945): 33–42; and "Aesthetics as Science: Its Development in America," *Journal of Aesthetics and Art Criticism* 9 (1951): 161–207. For an account of Munro's strategies of borrowing from Dessoir (and others) in order to erect aesthetics as an independent field and to ensconce America as its prime locus, see Richard Shusterman, "Aesthetics Between Nationalism and Internationalism," *Journal of Aesthetics and Art Criticism* 51 (1993), 157–67.

31　For more details on Dewey's somatic theories and practices and his relationship to Alexander, see my *Practicing Philosophy*, ch. 1, 6.

32　Michel Foucault, *Foucault Live* (New York: Semiotext[e], 1996), 384; cf. 378.

33　See *Practicing Philosophy*, ch. 1, and also Richard Shusterman, "The Self As a Work of Art," *The Nation*, 30 June 1997, 25–8.

34　For more details on this theme in Emerson and Nietzsche, see Richard Shusterman, "Styles et styles de vie: originalité, authenticité, et dédoublement du moi," *Littérature* 105 (1997): 102–9.

35　Henry David Thoreau, *Walden*, in *The Portable Thoreau* (New York: Viking, 1969), 468.

Index

Abrahams, Roger, 321n6
academicism, 189
action, 266, 269
Adorno, T. W., xvii, 11, 20–1, 25–6, 42, 50–1,
  118, 142, 147–8, 178, 181–5, 192, 195, 198,
  213, 229–30, 273–4, 289nn24, 25, 290n34,
  295n23, 312n16, 316n23, 318n55, 319n61,
  320n63, 335nn21–24
advertising, 146, 205, 257, 273–4
aerobics, 272–4, 282
aesthetic, 48, 72, 154, 156, 171–2, 184, 197, 216,
  253; and cognitive, 8, 11, 13, 29, 48, 53, 118,
  143, 212–3, 215; and ethical, 48, 153–5, 162–7,
  212, 236–9, 245–61, 330n8; and political, xv,
  29, 173, 176, 215, 234; and practical, xv, 8–10,
  13, 29, 49–50, 53, 143, 193, 212–3; and social,
  xv, 53, 143, 147, 153, 156, 173–6, 213, 225–9;
  see also art
aesthetic attitude, 193, 198, 328n68
aesthetic education, 54, 153, 156, 163–7, 212–3
aesthetic effort, 182–5
aesthetic experience, xi, xiii, 15, 24–34, 46–58,
  63, 114, 118, 160, 195, 262, 293n16, 295n29;
  Dewey on, 7, 10–13, 15, 25–33, 53–6; explanatory limits of, 56–8; scope and value of, 10–
  13, 19–20, 26, 32–3, 46–55, 57, 295n29
aesthetic ideology, 139–40, 143–7, 195, 237; see
  also art, and ideology
aesthetic judgement, 8, 211–12, 245
aesthetic life, the, ix, 158, 238–9, 242, 245–61
aestheticism, 52, 155, 159–61, 165–6, 239, 251,
  259
aesthetics, x–xvii, 3–4, 6, 13–14, 63, 161, 194,
  215, 258, 262–7, 276–80, 282–83; analytic aesthetics, 3–22, 25, 27–30; pragmatist aesthetics,
  x–xvii, 3–33, 45, 62; as a discipline, 264–7
African-American culture, 173, 184, 186, 188,
  197, 209, 211, 218, 234, 316n26; and language,
  191, 202–3, 221–2, 316n26, 321n6, 322n7,
  323n19; and music, 184, 191, 197, 214, 228,
  234; see also blues; jazz; rap; rhythm and blues;
  rock music
agent (agency), 40–1, 43, 53–4, 60, 92, 240,
  307n36, 331n14

aisthesis, 264–9
Alexander, F. M., 268, 271–2, 280–1, 336n31
Alexander, Thomas, 286n5
ambiguity, 64, 218–23
American culture, 118, 169, 177, 191, 196–8,
  319n56
analytic philosophy, 3–6, 10–11, 14, 27–9, 62,
  64–5, 72, 77–9, 82, 84–5, 96, 127, 271
appropriation, 202–6, 221, 224
architecture, 189, 194
Aristippus, 268
aristocracy, 197–8; *see also* culture, aristocracy of
Aristotle, xiii, 36, 45, 52–4, 63, 73, 77, 119, 139,
  183, 206, 240–1, 249
Arnold, Matthew, 147
art, ix, xii–xiii, 28, 35, 94, 117–20, 148, 155, 167,
  172, 179, 186, 197, 211, 218, 236, 250–1,
  253–4, 317n33, 328n68; autonomy of, 9, 18,
  20–1, 42, 46, 139, 143, 165, 174, 192–5,
  211–14; and capitalism, 20, 23–4, 106, 146,
  256; and class, 20–1, 24, 49–51, 139–47, 157,
  170–1, 173, 195, 319n56; classification of the
  arts, 13, 15–17; compartmentalization of, 12–
  14, 19–24, 36, 46–55, 57, 140, 156, 160, 165–8;
  concept of, xv, 17–18, 22, 34, 37–8, 48–9; critique and justification of, 36, 139–47; definitions and theories of, 17, 25, 28–9, 34–59, 195;
  fine, 18–19, 26, 49–50, 153, 156, 160, 201, 265;
  functions of, 8–10, 52, 141–4, 186, 193–4,
  212–15, 228; high/low, high/popular, xi–xii,
  18–19, 20, 51, 141–8, 159–61, 167–200, 203,
  221, 314n4, 319n56, 326n51; and ideology,
  139–47, 168; and illusion, 36, 52, 139, 146–8,
  153, 219; industrial, commercial, or practical,
  49–50; institution of, 38–41, 49–51, 139–47;
  and life, xv, 9, 12–13, 19–22, 51–4, 140–7,
  154–7, 165–7, 193–5, 199; of living, xiii, 57,
  59, 154, 194–5, 254, 261, 263, 266–7, 333n10,
  335n28; and morality, 148, 153–6, 162–7; objects of, 25–6, 29–31, 36, 39, 53–4, 63, 76, 101;
  and originality or creativity, 50–1, 188–92,
  205–6, 231–2, 235, 253–4; and philosophy,
  36–7, 44–5, 52; political and economic influences on, 22–4, 46, 141–4, 172, 177, 192, 195,